W9-AMY-406

Responsibilities

Manuscript Materials

THE CORNELL YEATS

PLAYS

The Countess Cathleen, edited by Michael J. Sidnell and Wayne K. Chapman
The Land of Heart's Desire, edited by Jared Curtis
The Hour-Glass, edited by Catherine Phillips
The Words Upon the Window Pane, edited by Mary FitzGerald
The Herne's Egg, edited by Alison Armstrong
Purgatory, edited by Sandra F. Siegel
The Death of Cuchulain, edited by Phillip L. Marcus

POEMS

The Early Poetry, Volume I: "Mosada" and "The Island of Statues," edited by George Bornstein
The Early Poetry, Volume II: "The Wanderings of Oisin" and Other Early Poems to 1895, edited by George Bornstein
The Wind Among the Reeds, edited by Carolyn Holdsworth
"In the Seven Woods" and "The Green Helmet and Other Poems," edited by David Holdeman
Responsibilities, edited by William H. O'Donnell
The Wild Swans at Coole, edited by Stephen Parrish
Michael Robartes and the Dancer, edited by Thomas Parkinson, with Anne Brannen
The Winding Stair (1929), edited by David R. Clark
Words for Music, Perhaps, edited by David R. Clark
New Poems, edited by J. C. C. Mays and Stephen Parrish
Last Poems, edited by James Pethica

Responsibilities

Manuscript Materials

BY W. B. YEATS

EDITED BY

WILLIAM H. O'DONNELL

Cornell University Press

ITHACA AND LONDON

The preparation of this volume was made possible in part by grants
from the National Endowment for the Humanities, an independent federal agency.

First published 2003 by Cornell University Press
Printed in the United States of America

Library of Congress Cataloging-in-Publication Data

Yeats, W. B. (William Butler), 1865–1939.
Responsibilities : manuscript materials / by W. B. Yeats ; edited by William H. O'Donnell.
p. cm. — (The Cornell Yeats)
Includes bibliographical references.
ISBN 0-8014-4107-2 (cloth)
1. Yeats, W. B. (William Butler), 1865-1939. Responsibilities—Criticism, Textual. 2. Yeats, W. B. (William Butler), 1865-1939—Manuscripts—Facsimiles. I. O'Donnell, William H. 1940- II. Title.

PR5904.R3 2003
821'.8—dc21 2002041523

Cornell University strives to use environmentally responsible suppliers and materials to the fullest extent possible in the publishing of its books. Such materials include vegetable-based, low-VOC inks and acid-free papers that are recycled, totally chlorine-free, or partly composed of nonwood fibers. For further information, visit our website at www.cornellpress.cornell.edu.

1 3 5 7 9 cloth printing 10 8 6 4 2

THE CORNELL YEATS

The volumes in this series present all available manuscripts, revised typescripts, proof-sheets, and other materials that record the growth of Yeats's poems and plays from the earliest draftings through to the lifetime published texts. Most of the materials are from the archives of Senator Michael Yeats, now in the care of the National Library of Ireland, supplemented by materials held by the late Anne Yeats; the remainder are preserved in public collections and private hands in Ireland and around the world. The volumes of poems, with a few exceptions, follow the titles of Yeats's own collections; several volumes of plays in the series contain more than one play.

In all the volumes, manuscripts are reproduced in photographs accompanied by transcriptions, in order to illuminate Yeats's creative process—to show the poet at work. The remaining materials—such as clean typescripts and printed versions—are generally recorded in collated form in an apparatus hung below a finished text. Each volume contains an Introduction describing the significance of the materials it includes, tracing the relation of the various texts to one another. There is also a census of manuscripts, with full descriptive detail, and appendixes are frequently used to present related materials, some of them unpublished.

As the editions seek to present, comprehensively and accurately, the various versions behind Yeats's published poems and plays, including versions he left unpublished, they will be of use to readers who seek to understand how great writing can be made, and to scholars and editors who seek to establish and verify authoritative final texts.

The Yeats Editorial Board

Contents

Acknowledgments

The staffs of the many libraries at which I worked in preparing this volume were consistently helpful and I am pleased to acknowledge them: Boston College, Burns Library; British Library, Manuscript Students' Room; University of California Los Angeles, William Andrews Clark Memorial Library; University of Chicago, Special Collections; Emory University, Special Collections; Grinnell College; Harvard University, Houghton Library; National Library of Ireland Manuscript Room and newspaper collection; New York Public Library (Astor, Lenox, and Tilden Foundations), Henry W. and Albert A. Berg Collection and the Manuscripts and Archive Division; State University of New York at Stony Brook, Yeats Archive; University of Memphis; Oxford University, Bodleian Library; Princeton University, Special Collections; Stanford University Library, Special Collections; University of Texas at Austin, Harry Ransom Humanities Research Center; Trinity College, Dublin, Manuscript Room; Washington State University, Special Collections; and Yale University, Beinecke Rare Book and Manuscript Library.

The National Endowment for the Humanities has provided important support for this series and volume. My travel was assisted by a grant-in-aid from the American Philosophical Society, and by Faculty Research Grants and a sabbatical leave from the University of Memphis.

Michael Yeats was generous and helpful, as was the late Anne Yeats. I am grateful for the many who have assisted me in this work, among whom are Wayne K. Chapman, David R. Clark, Jared Curtis, Declan D. Kiely, Richard J. Finneran, David Garcia, Warwick Gould, Dymphna Halpin, George M. Harper, Philip and Ann Johnson, John Kelly, Phillip L. Marcus, J. C. C. Mays, John O'Donnell, Stephen Parrish, Ann Saddlemyer, Susan Scheckel, Ronald Schuchard, Michael J. Sidnell, Jon Stallworthy, and De-an Wu Swihart. The volume is dedicated to the memory of Mary Margaret FitzGerald, fellow student and scholar, and friend.

WILLIAM H. O'DONNELL

University of Memphis

Abbreviations

Chapman *YA6*	Additions and corrections to O'Shea (listed below) by Wayne K. Chapman, *Yeats Annual* 6 (1988): 234–245.
O'Shea	Edward O'Shea, *A Descriptive Catalog of W. B. Yeats's Library* (New York and London: Garland, 1985).
Nine Poems	*Nine Poems Chosen from the Works of William Butler Yeats* (New York: privately printed for John Quinn, April 1, 1914), twenty-five copies, not for sale; Wade 109 (Wade is listed below).
PWD	*Poems Written in Discouragement, By W. B. Yeats 1912–1913,* privately printed (Dundrum: Cuala Press, October 1913), fifty copies, not for sale; Wade 107.
Resp14	*Responsibilities: Poems and a Play* (Dundrum: Cuala Press, May 25, 1914), 400 copies; Wade 110.
Resp16	*Responsibilities and Other Poems* (London: Macmillan, October 10, 1916), 1,000 copies; Wade 115.
Resp16(NY)	*Responsibilities and Other Poems* (New York: Macmillan, November 1, 1916); Wade 116.
Resp17	*Responsibilities and Other Poems* (London: Macmillan, March 1917); Wade 115 (as a second impression).
SUNY-SB	Yeats archive at State University of New York at Stony Brook.
Tauchnitz	*A Selection from the Poetry of W. B. Yeats*, "Collection of British Authors: Tauchnitz Edition" series (Leipzig: Tauchnitz, 1913); Wade 103.
Wade	Allan Wade, *A Bibliography of the Writings of W. B. Yeats*, 3d ed., rev. by Russell K. Alspach (London: Rupert Hart-Davis, 1968).
VP	*The Variorum Edition of the Poems of W. B. Yeats*, ed. Peter Allt and Russell K. Alspach (New York: Macmillan, 1957).

Census of Manuscripts

In each of the following descriptions, unless otherwise stated, holographs are in black ink in Yeats's hand, pencil markings are in black, and typescripts are the ribbon original, double-spaced, ten characters per inch, and use a black ribbon or black carbon paper. Unless otherwise stated, each is a single page. For economy of reference, the following standardized notations are used in describing types of paper that are used in multiple manuscripts.

Paper types #1 through #5 are holograph manuscripts on three-hole loose-leaf notebook paper, with watermark WALKER'S / LOOSE / LEAF, rounded corners, and with no left or right margin rule. Four of these types are lined on recto and verso with a red horizontal double-rule at the top plus thirty-one blue (or pale blue) horizontal rules; the fifth type is unlined. Their dimensions and color of the ruled lines are as follows:

paper type #1	20.3 cm (h) by 12.7 cm (w), lined (pale blue)
paper type #2	20.3 cm by 16.5 cm, lined (pale blue)
paper type #3	20.3 cm by 16.5 cm, lined (blue)
paper type #4	20.3 cm by 16.5 cm, unlined
paper type #5	24.1 cm by 19.0 cm, lined (pale blue)

Yeats often inverted the leaves of lined loose-leaf paper, so that the ruled top margin becomes a bottom margin and the binder holes are at the right margin rather than the left. Those sheets are listed as "recto (inverted)" (i.e., ruled top margin at the bottom and ring binder holes at the right) or "verso (inverted)" (i.e., ruled top margin at the bottom and ring binder holes at the left).

Paper type #6, used for typescripts, is 26.1 cm by 20.1 cm, with watermark [gondola device] / VENEZIA / EXTRA STRONG and unruled.

Paper type #7 is for holograph manuscripts on leaves, 22.7 cm by 17.7 cm, torn from exercise book(s); all are ruled on recto and verso with 23 light blue rules and with chain lines, but no watermark.

Paper type #8 is for holograph manuscripts on leaves, 22.9 cm by 17.9 cm, torn from an adhesive pad at the top edge, with watermark MUDIE & SONS / 15 COVENTRY ST. W., unruled.

Paper types #9 and #10, used for typescripts, are respectively 26.7 cm by 20.3 cm and 26.1 cm by 20.1 cm, with watermark John McDonnel & Co Ltd / Swift Brook.

ABY Under this heading are listed printed volumes that carry revisions entered on the pages by Yeats, in pencil or ink, formerly in the possession of the late Anne Butler Yeats. Each volume is identified by the numbers assigned to it in Wade and in O'Shea, with additions and corrections to O'Shea in Chapman *YA6*.

ABY(1) *Later Poems* (London: Macmillan, 1922); Wade 134, O'Shea 2382c. Revisions to "[Pardon, old fathers]."

ABY(2) *Later Poems* (New York: Macmillan, 1924); Wade 135, O'Shea 2383. Revisions to "[Pardon, old fathers]" (with an inserted loose scrap of paper with a query probably by George Yeats) and "The Hour before Dawn."

ABY(3) *Responsibilities and Other Poems* (London, 1916); Wade 115, O'Shea 2412a, and Chapman *YA6*. Revisions to epigraph, "The Grey Rock," "The Hour before Dawn," "The Three Beggars," "To a Shade," "The Two Kings," and "The Well and the Tree."

ABY(4) *Later Poems* (London: Macmillan, 1922); Wade 134, O'Shea 2382. Revisions to "The Grey Rock," "The Hour before Dawn," and "The Two Kings."

ABY(5) *Responsibilities and Other Poems* (London, 1917); Wade 115 (second impression), O'Shea 2412c, and Chapman *YA6*. Revision to "The Two Kings," page 191, in ink in an unidentified hand.

ABY(6) *Selected Poems* (New York: Macmillan, 1921); Wade 128, O'Shea 2417. Revisions to "To a Shade."

ABY(7) *Responsibilities and Other Poems* (New York, 1916); Wade 116, O'Shea 2413, and Chapman *YA6*. Revisions to "An Appointment," "A Coat," and "The Grey Rock"; line numbering and "x"s in the left margin, and horizontal rules, but no revision of text in "The Hour before Dawn."

ABY(8) *Responsibilities and Other Poems* (London, 1916); Wade 115, O'Shea 2412, and Chapman *YA6*. Revisions to "To a Child Dancing in the Wind"; marking but no revisions to "The Grey Rock" and "The Two Kings."

Berg(1) ["The Grey Rock"] Holograph draft on fifteen sides of eight leaves of three-hole loose-leaf notebook paper of paper type #1, dated October 21, 1912. Removed from Lady Gregory's copy, presented to her by Yeats, of his *Collected Works* (1908), vol. 6, *Ideas of Good and Evil* (Wade 80). New York Public Library, Astor, Lenox, and Tilden Foundation (as for all "Berg" entries listed below).

Berg(2) ["The Grey Rock"] Five-page carbon typescript in purple, with ink corrections, on paper type #9 with a bayonet pin hole at the top left corner of each sheet. Signed in ink by Yeats.

Berg(3) "The Two Kings." Holograph with revisions on ten sheets of paper type #1, numbered [1]–10, signed and dated January 8, 1912. Originally kept in an envelope labeled, not in Yeats's hand, "W. B. Yeats / Original Manuscript / of / 'The Two Kings' / Signed"; ex-collection W. T. H. Howe and then W. Van R. Whitall.

Berg(4) "To a Wealthy Man who promised a Second Subscription to the Dublin Municipal Gallery if it were proved the People wanted Pictures." Typescript, pale blue ribbon, on paper type #10, with holograph revisions; revised title and additional revisions in blue pencil. Rust marks from a pin in left margin. The holograph notation "(1" at the top right matches a "(2" on Berg(8) (b) ("September 1913"); the order and titles correspond exactly to *Poems Written in Discouragement.*

Berg(5) "To a Wealthy Man who promised a Second Subscription to the Dublin Municipal Gallery if it were proved the People wanted Pictures." Typescript, blue-black ribbon, on paper type #10, with pencil correction of the title; lines 1–10 are indented and double-spaced; lines 11–36 are flush left and single-spaced. There is a large single hole and smaller pinholes in the upper-left corner of the typescript. In a five-page set with "Red Hanrahan's Song about Ireland," "The Song of Wandering Aengus," and "To Ireland in the Coming Times."

Berg(6) (a) Page proof, unmarked, of the eight-leaf pamphlet of *Poems Written in Discouragement*, on one uncut sheet, 29.7 cm by 25.5 cm, folded in quarters to 14.8 cm by 12.8 cm. This early proof has twelve lines per page, rather than the eighteen lines per page of the published pamphlet, which added "Paudeen" and "To a Shade" to the three poems in this early state: "To a Wealthy Man who promised a Second Subscription to the Dublin Municipal Gallery if it were proved the People wanted Pictures," "September 1913," and "To a Friend Whose Work has Come to Nothing." Cataloged and archived with the page proofs of *Resp14* that are described in Berg(14), below.

Berg(6) (b) Various page proofs of *Resp14* lightly marked. Revisions to "An Appointment," Notes, second part of ["To a Child Dancing in the Wind"], "The Peacock," "That the Night Come," "When Helen Lived," and "[While I, from that reed-throated whisperer]." Two holes have been punched in the left margin of these proofs, which are bound through the upper hole with white silk ribbon.

Berg(7) ["September 1913"] Two-page holograph, dated August 1913, on an uncut folded double sheet of stationery, 17.8 cm by 22.6 cm, folded to 17.8 cm by 11.3 cm, with letterhead printed in blue "18, Woburn Building, / Upper Woburn Place, / W.C."; chain and wire lines; pasted on the recto of blank fly leaf at the end of Lady Gregory's copy, presented to her by Yeats, of his *Collected Works* (1908), vol. 4, *The Hour-Glass. Cathleen ni Houlihan. The Golden Helmet. The Irish Dramatic Movement* (Wade 78).

Berg(8) (a), (b), (c) "September 1913." Typescript (a) and carbon copies (b) and (c), simultaneously typed, but variously corrected, in part by Yeats. The ribbon copy (a) has a holograph title, "New Ireland (written after reading certain newspaper correspondence about the Municipal Gallery of Modern Painting)," and is signed. The first carbon copy (b) is titled in ink in an unidentified hand, "September, 1913," and is unsigned. The second carbon copy (c) is untitled but is signed; (a), (b), and (c) are of paper type #6. The holograph notation "(2" at the top right of the first carbon copy (b) corresponds to its placement in *Poems Written in Discouragement*; see Berg(4) above.

Berg(9) "To a Friend Whose Work has Come to Nothing." Holograph fair copy on one page of an uncut, double sheet of light gray stationery, 17.6 cm by 22.0 cm, folded to 17.6 cm by 11.0 cm, with printed letterhead "Coole Park, / Gort, / Co. Galway"; watermark (left portion only) IMPERI[AL] / [device of intertwined letters A, C, N, S] / SILURI[AN]; pasted on recto of second blank fly leaf at the front of Lady Gregory's copy, presented to her by Yeats, of his *Collected Works* (1908), vol. 6, *Ideas of Good and Evil* (Wade 80).

Berg(10) ["The Three Hermits"] One-page uncorrected typescript, 32.8 cm by 20.2 cm, watermark as in paper types #9 and #10; probably typed by a commercial typist.

Berg(11) "The Hour before Dawn" Penciled correction, perhaps in Yeats's hand, on p. 216 of Lady Gregory's copy of *Later Poems* (London: Macmillan, 1922), (Wade 134), inscribed by Yeats with a date December 6, 1922; this is the only correction in the book, but Yeats later wrote holograph copies of two other poems on blank fly leaves of this volume in May 1925 and on August 5, 1929.

Berg(12) "The Peacock." Holograph letter, signed, to Lady Gregory, November 25 [postmark 1913], from Stone Cottage, Colman's Hatch, Sussex. Page 3 (of 4), on light gray stationery, 18.0 cm by 22.7 cm, folded to 18.0 cm by 11.3 cm.

Berg(13) "A Coat." Holograph inscription (lines 1–4 only) on the recto of the second blank fly leaf of a copy of *Cathleen ni Hoolihan: A Play in One Act and in Prose* (London: Bullen, 1902), (Wade 40), signed and dated December 1915.

Berg(14) Nearly complete set of marked early page proofs of *Resp14*, but its gathering (a) (front matter and "[Pardon, old fathers]") is partially uncut, is unmarked, and lacks the bayonet pin hole at top left corner of gatherings b, c, [extant portion of d], e, f (through the end of "A Coat," the last poem except for "[While I, from that reed-throated whisperer]"). There is a single page, without bayonet pin hole, with "[While I, from that reed-throated whisperer]" that could be associated with this early set of page proofs, if only because there is another loose page, but with straight pin holes that resemble, although do not match exactly, the straight pin holes of the proofs of the "Notes" pages, themselves on one single and one folded double sheet (all with printing only on one side of the paper). (For the contents and order of the poems, see p. xl below.)

Boston College ["The Witch"] Holograph in ink in the "Xmas 1908" vellum-bound notebook, fol. 88^{r}, dated May 29, [1912]. A pink vendor's label attached inside lower left corner of front cover, reads: CARTOLERIA / LEGATORIA / R. GRISPIGNI / ROMA / CAPO LE CASE 77. Front endpapers inscribed in black ink: "W B Yeats. / Abbey Theatre. Dublin. / and / 18 Woburn Buildings / Euston Road / London / Private." On rear endpaper: "W B Yeats / Xmas 1908" and at the lower part of the page, inverted: "c/o Lady ~~Gregory~~ ~~Laird~~ Layard / Ca' Capello / ~~S.~~ C San

Polo / Venice." The notebook has three strips of tan-colored leather in a triangular formation on the spine edge of the upper and lower covers. The covers are darkened by handling and age. The notebook measures 24.8 by 17.8 cm and is approximately 2.8 cm thick. The paper is handmade, laid paper, no watermark, with each page measuring approximately 24 by 16.5 cm. All edges are trimmed. Burns Library, W. B. Yeats papers, MS 94-01.

Bradford, *Writing of* The Player Queen "The Player Queen (Song from an Unfinished Play)." Three excerpts from two nearly identical typescripts, dated approximately 1916, recorded in a smooth text version by Curtis B. Bradford, *W. B. Yeats: The Writing of* The Player Queen, Manuscripts of W. B. Yeats series, ed. David R. Clark (DeKalb: Northern Illinois University Press, 1977), pages 378–379, 392, and 393.

Chicago(1) ["The Grey Rock"] Six-page typescript on paper type #6, signed and dated October 1912 by Yeats in ink, with corrections and title in ink perhaps in Yeats's hand, thick blue pencil compositor's marking, perhaps "1B," at top right corner of the first page, penciled line count at bottom right of each page, and a bayonet pin hole in the top left corner. Stamped in purple ink stamp in bottom margin of first and last pages "The Paget Literary Agency, / 569 FIFTH AVENUE, / NEW YORK." Separate front and back cover sheets of brown, thick poster paper, each with matching hole at top left from a bayonet pin; pasted on the front cover sheet is a label with the printed address "The Paget Literary Agency / 569 FIFTH AVENUE / NEW YORK [with device]" and typewritten title "AOIFE'S LOVER" / By / W. B. Yeats." Princeton(1) is the ribbon original, with different corrections. University of Chicago Library, *Poetry* Magazine Papers, 1912–1936, box 41, folder 9.

Chicago(2) "The Realists," "The Mountain Tomb," ["To a Child Dancing in the Wind"], "Fallen Majesty," ["A Memory of Youth"]. Three-page typescript with ink corrections and instructions in Yeats's hand and additional copyediting, labeling, and instructions in Ezra Pound's hand. Pages 1 and 2 are ribbon originals in blue; page 3 is a black carbon copy. Pages 1 and 3 are 25.9 cm by 20.2 cm with watermark STAG BRAND / J D & C; page 2 is 25.4 cm by 20.1 cm with watermark JOYNSON / EXTRA SUPERFINE. The five poems are titled "The Mountain Tomb" (p. 1 top), "To a Child Dancing upon the Shore" (p. 1 bottom), "Fallen Majesty" (p. 2 top), "Love and the Bird" [now "A Memory of Youth"] (p. 2 bottom), and "The Realists" (p. 3). They are in the same order in which they were published in *Poetry* (Chicago), December 1912. University of Chicago Library, *Poetry* Magazine Papers, 1912–1936, box 41, folder 10.

Chicago(3) ["The Mountain Tomb," "To a Child Dancing in the Wind," "Fallen Majesty"] Ezra Pound letter to Harriet Monroe, [November 4, 1912], with Yeats holograph signed postscript. University of Chicago Library, *Poetry* Magazine Papers, 1912–1936, box 37, folder 8.

Chicago(4) ["To a Child Dancing in the Wind"] Ezra Pound letter to Harriet Monroe, [postmark London, November 2, 1912]. University of Chicago Library, *Poetry* Magazine Papers, 1912–1936, box 37, folder 8.

Chicago(5) "[While I, from that reed-throated whisperer]" Typescript, 27.6 cm by 21.1 cm, with penciled notation, reportedly in Harriet Monroe's hand: "MS he left behind." (Yeats visited Chicago from February 23 to March 2, 1914; *Poetry* did not publish this poem.) University of

Chicago Library, *Poetry* Magazine Papers, 1912–1936, box 41, folder 10.

Emory(1) "To a Friend Whose Work has Come to Nothing." Holograph note on page 18 of Lady Gregory's copy of *Resp14*. Emory, PR5904 .R3.

Emory(2) "To a Shade," "The Hour before Dawn," "[While I, from that reed-throated whisperer]" Revisions in Yeats's copy of *Resp14*, used as copy for *Resp16*. Emory, PR5904 .R3, cop. 2.

Emory(3) ["To a Child Dancing in the Wind"] Holograph fair copy on Coole Park stationery. Emory, MS coll. no. 600 (W. B. Yeats), box 1, folder 24.

Emory(4) ["An Appointment"] Holograph, dated August 25, 1907, inscribed on the recto of the blank second fly sheet of Lady Gregory's copy of *Poems* (London: Unwin, 1901), (Wade 18). Lady Gregory added a four-line explanatory note in the top margin: "On the appointment of Count Plunkett to Curatorship of Dublin Museum & Geo. Russell & Birrell, Hugh Lane being a candidate." Emory, PR5900 .A3 1901, cop. 2.

Emory(5) "[While I, from that reed-throated whisperer]" Corrected page proof (same early printed state as Harvard[2] but with different corrections) of *Resp14*, with Ezra Pound's comments to the Cuala Press, watermark BALLYCLARE / CO ANTRIM. With a holograph note card, 22.5 cm by 13.5 cm, with printed in blue ink letterhead PRESIDENT'S HOUSE / AMHERST, MASSACHUSETTS, of revised lines that were used in *Resp14*. Emory, MS coll. no. 600 (W. B. Yeats), box 1, folder 31.

Foster-Murphy "To a Wealthy Man who promised a Second Subscription to the Dublin Municipal Gallery if it were proved the People wanted Pictures." Typescript, blue carbon, on paper variety #10. Dated January 15, 1913, in pencil by Lady Gregory. Corrections in black ink in Lady Gregory's hand, with some punctuation entered on the upper sheet that have come through on the carbon. Some corrections have been added only to compensate for the faintness of the carbon rather than typographic errors. Small pinholes in the upper-left corner of the typescript. Foster-Murphy Collection, box 14, folio 912, New York Public Library, Astor, Lenox, and Tilden Foundation.

Harvard(1) "To a Friend Whose Work has Come to Nothing," "To a Shade," "When Helen Lived," "The Three Beggars," "Beggar to Beggar Cried," "Running to Paradise," "The Hour before Dawn," "A Song from 'The Player Queen'," "The Realists," "The Witch," "The Peacock," ["To a Child Dancing in the Wind II. (Two Years Later)"], "A Memory of Youth," "The Magi," "The Dolls." Corrected page proofs (same early printed state as Emory[5] but with different corrections, probably by *Poetry* magazine) of *Resp14*, twelve loose sheets, 20.9 cm by 14.7 cm, watermark BALLYCLARE / CO ANTRIM. Pages 17–39, which became part of pages 18–40 in the published book, plus a trimmed typescript insert with text of "When Helen Lived" (purple ribbon copy, on stationery 12.6 cm by 13.7 cm, watermark PIONEER / FINE, fastened with a brass bayonet pin). Contents are "To a Wealthy Man who promised a Second Subscription to the Dublin Municipal Gallery if it were proved the People wanted Pictures" (ll. 23ff.) (p. 17; [*Resp14*, p. 16]) through "A Coat" (p. [40]; [*Resp14*, p. 40]). The earlier pages (to p. 16) of this set of page proofs are at Yale. These pages were furnished to *Poetry* (Chicago) as copy for the twelve poems published in its May 1914 issue (pp. 52–60) in the same order as in these proofs: "To a Friend whose Work has Come to Nothing," "Paudeen," "To a Shade," "When Helen Lived," "Beggar to Beggar Cried," "The Witch," "The Peacock," "Running to Paradise," "The Player Queen," "To a Child Dancing in the Wind," "The Magi," and "A Coat." The twelve other poems in these proof pages were not printed by *Poetry:* "To a Wealthy Man who promised a Second Subscription to the Dublin Municipal Gallery if it were proved the People wanted Pictures" (ll. 23ff.), "The Attack on 'The Playboy of the Western World' 1907," "The Three Beggars," "The Three Hermits," "The Realists," "The Mountain Tomb," "The Hour before Dawn," "A Memory of Youth," "Fallen Majesty," "Friends," "The Cold Heaven," and "The Dolls." This set of page proofs was made before "That the Night Come" and "An Appointment" were added to the book (Cuala, pp. [38–39]). In the top margin of page 17 is penciled the date January 27, 1914, presumably the date of receipt at *Poetry*. Yeats wrote in the bottom margin of page 17: "When done with these proofs / please send them to John Quinn / ? 58 Central Park West, New York / W B Yeats." In addition to the corrections that are listed in the apparatus for each poem, Harvard(1) has pencil copyediting by *Poetry* to convert the single quotation marks to double quotation marks. Houghton Library, *EC9.Y3455.914ra.

Harvard(2) "[While I, from that reed-throated whisperer]" Page proof of *Resp14* (same printed state as Emory[5] but with different corrections) with holograph title "Notoriety / (Suggested by a recent magazine article.)," signed, and with ink and pencil notations in other hands, 20.8 cm by 14.7 cm, watermark BALLYCLARE / CO ANTRIM, bayonet pin hole at top left. Faint impression in purple of *The New Statesman* date-time stamp, [?4] February 1914, where it was published February 7, 1914. Houghton Library, Autograph file *59MB156.

NLI 8760(18) ["The Grey Rock"] Holograph drafts of isolated passages of the poem, on four leaves (5^r–8^r) of a "Sapphire Series" exercise book, 20.5 cm by 16.4 cm, twenty lines per page ruled in light blue. This stapled exercise book has thirty-six pages, fourteen of which are post-production revisions to *Deirdre*. Yeats broke off from composition of the play here and then returned to the play following these pages. The exercise book also contains autobiographical notes dated June 8 and 9.

NLI 8763(2) ["To a Child Dancing in the Wind"] Holograph leaf of paper type #1. It is the fifteenth of sixteen leaves in a group of loose leaf pages of the play *The Hour Glass*, with a label probably by Curtis B. Bradford: "Pages of work toward the ending + miscellaneous pages. Originally scattered." Paper clip marks at top left.

NLI 8764(5) ["A Song from 'The Player Queen'"] Three holograph leaves of paper type #1, as folios $[27]^v$ (complete poem), $[28]^v$ (note), and $[11]^v$ (ll. 13–18 only; begins: "[?trumpet s] / P Queen / They are ~~more~~ [?coming] C It s the one [?~~that~~] too die dies") of a packet of manuscript of *The Player Queen*. SUNY-SB microfilm frames 2702750, 2702752, and 2702729. Draft 17 in Bradford, *Writing of* The Player Queen, pages 266 (commentary on fols. $[27]^v$) and 264 (smooth text of fol. $[11]^v$); dated approximately by Bradford as 1910.

NLI 8764(6) ["A Song from 'The Player Queen'" (ll. 5–20 only)] Holograph leaves of paper type #7, as folios 11 and 12 of a packet of manuscript of *The Player Queen*. SUNY-SB microfilm frames 2702817 and 2702818. Draft 21 in Bradford, *Writing of* The Player Queen, pages 315 (fol. 11) and 317 (fol. 12); dated approximately by Bradford as 1915.

NLI 8764(7) (a) ["A Song from 'The Player Queen'" (ll. 5–20 only)] Two typescript leaves of paper type #6, canceled in ink, folios 20 and 21 of a packet of typescript of *The Player Queen*. SUNY-SB microfilm frames 2702881 and 2702882. Closely related to drafts 20 and 21 in Bradford, *Writing of* The Player Queen, pages 314–317; dated approximately by Bradford as 1915.

NLI 8764(7) (b) ["A Song from 'The Player Queen'" (ll. 5–20 only)] Typescript leaf of paper type #6, with holograph ink corrections, folio 21 of a packet of typescript of *The Player Queen*. SUNY-SB microfilm frame 2702901. Closely related to drafts 20 and 21 in Bradford, *Writing of* The Player Queen, pages 314–317; dated approximately by Bradford as 1915.

NLI 8764(7) (c) ["A Song from 'The Player Queen'" (ll. 5–20 only)] Two typescript carbon leaves of paper type #6, with pencil corrections probably by the typist, folios [9] (begins: "brazen devil to the damination she deserves") and [10] (begins: "DECIMA. / I will never again be afraid of the kings on the wall.") of a packet of typescript of *The Player Queen*. SUNY-SB microfilm frames 2702956 and 2702957. Not transcribed in Bradford, *Writing of* The Player Queen.

NLI 8764(8) ["A Song from 'The Player Queen'"] Two holograph leaves on unlined paper, 25.3 cm by 20.1 cm, with no watermark, folios 8 and 10 of a packet of manuscript of *The Player Queen*. SUNY-SB microfilm frames 2702987, 2702989. Draft 27 in Bradford, *Writing of* The Player Queen, pages 352–354; dated approximately by Bradford as 1916.

NLI 8764(10) ["A Song from 'The Player Queen'" (ll. 5–8 only)] Three typescript leaves on thin, lightweight paper, 26.0 cm by 20.3 cm, with no watermark, carbon copy with handwritten red ink underscoring of character names and stage directions. Folios 19–21 of a packet of typescript of *The Player Queen* with typed label "THE / PLAYER QUEEN / (second carbon)" on a wine-colored paper cover with embossed address, "Ethel Christian, / TRANSLATIONS, TYPEWRITING & STENOGRAPHY, 56, SOUTHHAMPTON STREET. / STRAND, LONDON, W.C.2. / TEL. NO. GERRARD 604." SUNY-SB microfilm frames 2703113–2703115. Not transcribed in Bradford, *Writing of* The Player Queen.

NLI 8764(11) ["A Song from 'The Player Queen'" (ll. 5–20 only)] Two holograph leaves of paper type #3, folios [1]^{v} (inverted) (begins: "She pulled the thread & bit the thread") and [3]^{r} (begins: "she had. Her father was a drunken") of a packet of manuscript of *The Player Queen*. SUNY-SB microfilm frames 2703166 and 2703168. Draft 30 in Bradford, *Writing of* The Player Queen, pages 401–402; dated approximately by Bradford as 1916–1919.

NLI 8773(2) ["The Well and the Tree"] Holograph leaf near the end of this packet of manuscript of *At the Hawk's Well*.

NLI 13,586(1) "The Grey Rock." Fair copy holograph with one correction, on four leaves, on rectos only, numbered 1–4. Tan-colored paper, 25.8 cm by 20.1 cm, with twenty-four light gray ruled lines on versos only, no watermark, with traces of green at top edges, presumably from an adhesive used to attach the sheets in a pad. Paper clip rust marks at top left and each leaf has a horizontal crease across its middle.

NLI 13,586(2) (a) "The Two Kings." Ten-page typescript with Yeats's revision in ink. Paper type #6, with bayonet pin hole and paper clip rust marks at top left corner, with a horizontal crease at 13.0 cm from top.

NLI 13,586(2) (b) "The Two Kings." Ten leaves of holograph, numbered 1–9 and one unnumbered leaf with recto and verso. On paper type #1, folios 1–6 recto, folios 7–9 recto (inverted, with holes at right; red double rule at bottom). Paper clip marks at top left on folios 1–9 and on the unnumbered leaf when it is aligned with its verso up and inverted to match folios 7–9.

NLI 13,586(3) (a) ["To a Wealthy Man who promised a Second Subscription to the Dublin Municipal Gallery if it were proved the People wanted Pictures"] Seven leaves of holograph, dated December 24 and 25, 1912. Three leaves have text on the recto only, and four leaves have text on the recto and verso. On paper type #1, with paper clip rust marks at top left. The folio numbers refer to the arbitrary sequence in which the leaves are filed at NLI; the probable working order, which is used here, is [3], [2], [4], [5]^r (end of poem with dating December 24, 1912), [6], [1], [7]^r (end of poem with dating December 25, 1912).

NLI 13,586(3) (b) ["To a Wealthy Man who promised a Second Subscription to the Dublin Municipal Gallery if it were proved the People wanted Pictures"] Corrected typescript, carbon copy, on paper type #6 with a vertical crease at the middle and three horizontal creases in thirds, and then the bottom third folded again in half. Paper clip rust marks at top left and small tears at left and right end of the upper horizontal crease, and at right edge. TCD(2) is the ribbon copy.

NLI 13,586(4) ["Paudeen"] Holograph fair copy on a leaf of paper type #7, torn from an exercise book, with the torn edge at the left and creases from having been folded into quarters.

NLI 13,586(5) ["When Helen Lived"] Holograph fair copy on a leaf of paper type #7, torn from an exercise book, with the torn edge at left, a vertical crease from having been folded in half, and a hole near the top left corner, probably from a bayonet pin; the hole extends to the top left corner, as if this leaf had been pulled out of a pinned group.

NLI 13,586(6) ["The Three Beggars"] Three holograph leaves of paper type #1, with paper clip marks at the top left. In the NLI binder what should be the first leaf is filed out of sequence as the third one.

NLI 13,586(7) (a) ["The Three Beggars"] Two holograph leaves of paper type #1, each with paper clip marks at top left and and creases from having been folded into quarters.

NLI 13,586(7) (b) ["The Three Beggars"] Unnumbered holograph of paper type #4, with paper clip marks at top left and and creases from having been folded into quarters.

NLI 13,586(8) (a) ["The Hour before Dawn"] Six leaves of holograph, dated October 19, 1913, on paper type #7, torn from an exercise book and numbered 1–6, with paper clip marks at top left.

NLI 13,586(8) (b) ["The Hour before Dawn"] Three leaves of holograph instructions for revisions to be entered to the printed text of *Resp16* (Wade 115, 116). The revisions were adopted in *Later Poems* (London: Macmillan, 1922), (Wade 134). On unlined paper, 20.8 cm by 17.9 cm, numbered 1–3, with chain lines but no watermark. Paper clip marks at top left and a vertical crease from having been folded in half.

NLI 13,586(9) (a) ["A Song from 'The Player Queen'" (ll. 1–12 only)] Holograph leaf of light gray note paper with deckled edges, 17.7 (to 17.8) cm by 12.9 (to 13.3) cm, and watermark NEWTON / DECKLE EDGE. Paper clip marks at top left, extreme top left corner is folded down. Horizontal creases from having been folded into thirds. Folio [2]^{r} (begins: "My mother dandled me & sang"). SUNY-SB microfilm frame 2902371. Not transcribed in Bradford, *Writing of* The Player Queen.

NLI 13,586(9) (b) ["A Song from 'The Player Queen'" (ll. 13–20 only)] Holograph leaf of paper type #1, with paper clip marks at top left. Folio [1]^{r} (begins: "My mother could not help but braid"). SUNY-SB microfilm frame 2902370. Not transcribed in Bradford, *Writing of* The Player Queen.

NLI 13,586(10) (a) and **(b)** "The Realists" / "Realists." Two drafts on two leaves of holograph on paper type #1 with paper clip marks at top left when aligned as they were used: folio [2] recto (inverted) and folio [1] verso (inverted). Folio [1] has two crease marks, which when viewed from folio [1]^{r} (inverted), are at the upper right one-third and the lower left one-third, each at an angle of approximately forty-five degrees.

NLI 13,568(11) "The Witch." Holograph leaf of paper type #1.

NLI 13,586(12) (b), verso ["To a Child Dancing in the Wind"] Untitled holograph on a leaf of paper type #3, with paper clip marks at top left and top center, creases from having been folded into quarters, and the top left corner folded down onto the verso. The creases resemble those of NLI 13,586(13). On the recto is a holograph of ["The Mountain Tomb"], signed "Collevile" (for "Colleville") and below it a holograph, written with a wider pen nib, of ["The New Faces"].

NLI 13,586(13) ["To a Child Dancing in the Wind"] (recto, top half); "Fallen Majesty" (recto, bottom half); and ["A Memory of Youth" (ll. 10–11 only)] (verso) Holograph leaf of paper type #3, with creases from having been folded into quarters. The creases resemble those of NLI 13,586(12) (b). ["To a Child Dancing in the Wind"] is untitled, lightly revised, and is written with a narrower pen nib than "Fallen Majesty," which is a fair copy. On the verso, the holograph fragment of "A Memory of Youth" is written on an upward slant in the middle of the page. A penciled fragment of an unidentified work is written vertically in the bottom center of the recto.

NLI 13,586(14) ["To a Child Dancing in the Wind II. (Two Years Later)"] Holograph leaf of paper type #8. Dated December 3. Paper clip marks at top left and top right, vertical crease from having been folded in half and horizontal creases from having been folded roughly in quarters.

NLI 13,586(15) ["A Memory of Youth"] Holograph leaf of paper type #4.

NLI 13,586(17) [Note to] "The Dolls" [and "The Magi"] Holograph leaf of paper type #8 with a torn piece and paper clip mark at top left. In the upper margin is a penciled editorial notation, probably not in Yeats's hand: "Notes to Poems."

NLI 21,855 ["An Appointment"] Typescript, carbon copy with revisions in Yeats's hand in ink and pencil, with typewritten date August 25, 1907. On a leaf of plain paper, with the bottom portion torn off, 15.5 cm (at left edge, 16.0 cm at right edge) by 20.1 cm, watermark McDonnel & C° L^TD / [Sw]ift Brook.

NLI 21,873 ["September 1913"] Two-page typescript, purple ribbon copy, with corrections in ink probably by the inexpert typist and one correction in black pencil. On recto and verso of one leaf of lightweight paper, 26.0 cm by 20.2 cm, unlined and with no watermark. A triangular piece is missing from the blank right margin (recto) at the right edge of the center horizontal crease, 1.0 cm high at the right edge and 3.5 cm wide. Bayonet pin hole at bottom left (recto). The leaf was folded into eights, with one vertical crease and three horizontal creases. Typed period at the end of line 16 pierces the paper. The typing on the recto continues into the bottom margin, with vignetted typed words at the extreme bottom edge and extending all the way to the right edge, as though the typist tried to squeeze in one line (29) in the extreme bottom margin and then continued into the right margin with another line (30) before turning the paper over and typing the full final four lines (29–32).

NLI 30,009 Page proofs of *Selected Poems* (1929) (Wade 165), pages 49–128, marked in ink by Yeats. *Responsibilities* poems are on pages 107–128, where this incomplete set ends with "To a Child Dancing in the Wind II. (Two Years Later)." Those poems are in gathering "H" (pp. 97–112), date-stamped "R. &. R. Clark, Ltd. / 8 May 1929 / Edinburgh," and gathering "I" (pp. 113–128), date-stamped "R. &. R. Clark, Ltd. / 7 May 1929 / Edinburgh"; both of those gatherings are stamped "Second Proof" and labeled in ink "Revise." The sheets are 19.0 cm by 25.4 cm, folded to 19.0 cm by 12.8 cm, and are not watermarked.

NLI 30,044 [Front matter of *Resp16* (Wade 115, 116): Preliminary list of contents] One-page typescript on paper type #5, single-spaced, typed on recto and verso, with pencil markings, probably not in Yeats's hand, on the recto only. It presumably was a status list for use in assembling materials for submission to Macmillan.

NLI 30,096 [Front matter: Epigraph of *Responsibilities*] Holograph leaf of thin tan-colored paper, 25.9 cm by 20.1 cm, unruled on the recto but with twenty-six pale gray rules on the verso, and with no watermark. Paper clip mark at top left and crease marks from being folded in quarters. This item is undated and could be a draft of the epigraph for *Resp14*, but it might well be from the mid- or late-1930s, when the same type of paper was used for a list of contents for two volumes of plays, after 1934, presumably for the never-published Edition de Luxe (later, the "Coole Edition") of Macmillan, London, and/or for the never-published "Dublin Edition" of Charles Scribner's Sons, New York.

NLI 30,262 [Poems and notes] Marked page proofs of *Poems* in the never-published Edition de Luxe of Macmillan, London, stamped "Second Proof"; the *Responsibilities* poems are on pages [224]–[264], in gatherings P–S, date-stamped August 2, 1932; the *Responsibilities* notes are pp. 461–463, in gathering 2G, date-stamped October 4, 1932. Page 463 has a correction in Thomas Marks's hand; see p. xli below.

NLI 30,263 [Notes only] Marked galley proofs of *Poems* in the never-published Edition de Luxe of Macmillan, London, date-stamped September 12, 1931. The notes to the *Responsibilities* poems are on slips C27 and C28, stamped "FIRST PROOF" and labeled in ink "Marked Proof." The galley proofs for the *Responsibilities* poems are not extant.

NLI 30,286 ["A Song from 'The Player Queen'" (ll. 11–12 only)] One-page typescript with holograph ink revision, on paper 25.6 cm by 20.1 cm, no watermark, recto is unlined, verso has twenty-six pale gray rules, the left edge is stained and has some tears. There is no residue of binding glue. Folio 31; this single typescript leaf is in a packet of manuscript of *The Player Queen*. The original folder is labeled in blue pencil "Miscellanies" in an unknown hand. SUNY-SB microfilm frame 2100144. Not transcribed in Bradford, *Writing of* The Player Queen.

NLI 30,314 [Notes] "Poems written in Despondency." Five leaves of holograph on heavy-weight stationery paper, 22.9 cm by 17.9 cm, watermark MUDIE & SONS / 15 COVENTRY S^{T}. W., unruled, numbered [1], 2–5. Bayonet pin hole at top left.

NLI 30,358 The Maud Gonne Notebook. An octavo notebook of sixty-eight leaves, with chain lines and a partially visible watermark with a heraldic shield above elaborately ornamental lettering ending "Co[?]", measuring 19.2 cm by 12.5 cm with deckle edges on all three sides, and two endpapers, bound in brown leather, 20 cm by 14 cm, with leather ties. The notebook is inscribed by Maud Gonne on the first leaf, "from Maud Gonne / Xmas 1912 C," and was used by Yeats up to the end of 1915 as a diary and journal. It contains holograph drafts or portions of eight poems collected in this Cornell Yeats series volume: "The Magi" on folio 28^{v}, "The Dolls" on folios 28^{v}–29^{r}, "To a Friend Whose Work has Come to Nothing" on folio 29^{r}, "Running to Paradise" on folios 29^{v}–30^{r}, "When Helen Lived" on folio 30^{v}, "To a Shade" on folios 31^{r}–31^{v}, "The Witch" on folios 33^{r}–33^{v}, and "To a Child Dancing in the Wind" on folio 47^{v}.

NLI 30,364 (a) "[Pardon, old fathers]" Holograph, dated December 1913, on paper type #8 with stains, a small portion of the top left corner torn off, a paper clip mark at top left, and a horizontal crease from having been folded in half.

NLI 30,364 (b) "[Pardon, old fathers]" Holograph fair copy, dated January 1914, 25.9 cm by 20.1 cm, written on the verso, with twenty-six pale gray rules on the recto only; no watermark. Paper clip marks and tears at top left of verso; creases and tears at right edge of verso; vertical crease from having been folded in half.

NLI 30,514 (a), (b) "A Coat." Two holograph leaves, each a separate draft of the poem and each with paper clip marks at top left. Only leaf (b) is titled. They are accompanied by a printed label from the Trinity College, Dublin exhibition, "W. B. Yeats: Manuscripts and Printed Books," 1956, in which they were number 65.

NLI 30,515 ["To a Child Dancing in the Wind"] on recto and ["Friends"] on verso. Holograph leaf of paper type #1, with a diagonal crease and with paper clip marks at top right of verso.

NLI 30,517 ["The Three Beggars" and "The Two Kings"] Twenty-one leaves of holograph on paper type #1. Folio [1]v (inverted) is an unidentified verse fragment; folio [1]r (inverted) is "The Three Beggars"; folios [2]–[20] are nineteen leaves (six of which have writing on verso and recto); and folio [21]r is an unidentified tetrameter fragment. All leaves have paper clip marks at top left-center (when viewed as written upon, i.e., verso (inverted) for folios [1]–[20]; the last leaf, folio [21], which is the only one that is not inverted, shares the paper clip mark at top left-center (when viewed as written upon). Folio [1] has a vertical crease from having been folded in half; no other leaves are creased. Folio [21] is the only leaf that has a torn center ring binder hole.

NLI 30,528 "To a Child Dancing in the Wind." Holograph of instructions, which refer to page numbers in *Resp16,* for *Resp17,* for printing the poem as two numbered sections in *Resp17*, on the right half, 17.9 cm by 11.7 cm, of a folded sheet of pale blue stationery with watermark NEWTON MILL and printed letterhead (in bright blue, at top right) "18, Woburn Buildings, / W.C." Paper clip mark at top center.

NYPL "To a Shade." Corrected typescript, purple ribbon original, on light blue stationery, 22.3 cm by 17.7 cm, with watermark IMPERIAL SILURIAN and device of intertwined letters, perhaps "M," "A," and "&"; similar to Lady Gregory's stationery in Berg(9) but without the letterhead. With a forwarding letter from Lady Gregory to John Quinn, October 11, [1913], and an envelope postmarked October 12, 1913. New York Public Library, Astor, Lenox, and Tilden Foundation, Manuscripts and Archive Division, John Quinn Memorial Coll., box 15, section 1, folder 2.

Princeton(1) ["The Grey Rock"] Six-page typescript with one holograph correction in blue-black ink and copyediting, presumably by *The British Review,* in purple ink and pencil, on paper type #6, fastened with a brass bayonet pin at the top left. Stamped in purple ink, at top left "THE BRITISH REVIEW" and at top right "JAN 28 1913." Chicago(1) is a carbon copy of Princeton(1) with different corrections. Princeton University Library, J. Harlin O'Connell Collection, record no. 2164.

Princeton(2) "The Three Hermits." Two-page typescript carbon copy with holograph corrections and copyediting, presumably by *The Smart Set*, in pencil, on paper 26.0 cm by 20.0 cm, watermark "95 UNIQUE" NOTE / *PBM*, with a bayonet pin hole at top left. Stamped in purple ink at top right "THE SMART SET." Princeton University Library, General MSS. [MISC] Yeats, William Butler, folder 2.

Stanford "A Coat." Holograph fair copy, inscribed to James Healy, signed and dated 1938, on a blank fly leaf of an uncut copy of *Resp14*. Stanford University Library, 71 02030.

TCD(1) ["To a Wealthy Man who promised a Second Subscription to the Dublin Municipal Gallery if it were proved the People wanted Pictures"] Corrected typescript on paper type #6, originally enclosed with TCD(2). NLI 13,586(3) (b) is a carbon copy of TCD(1). Trinity College, Dublin, MS 7001/1728/2. [Joseph Hone, *W. B. Yeats*, p. 265, slightly misquotes this typescript.]

TCD(2) ["To a Wealthy Man who promised a Second Subscription to the Dublin Municipal Gallery if it were proved the People wanted Pictures"] Holograph letter, signed, to Hugh Lane,

January [?2 *or* 1], [1913], to which TCD(1) is an enclosure. Trinity College, Dublin, MS 7001/1728/1.

TCD(3) "To a Shade." Typescript, signed and dated September 1913, with a correction probably by Yeats, on paper type #9. Trinity College, Dublin, MS 7001/1729/1.

Texas(1) "To a Wealthy Man who promised a Second Subscription to the Dublin Municipal Gallery if it were proved the People wanted Pictures." Holograph, signed, on two sheets of paper type #1 (though these sheets lack the watermark). University of Texas at Austin, Harry Ransom Humanities Research Center, MS file (Yeats, WB) Works.

Texas(2) "To a Wealthy Man who promised a Second Subscription to the Dublin Municipal Gallery if it were proved the People wanted Pictures." Typescript, double-spaced title, single-spaced text, twelve characters per inch, with pencil corrections and editorial notations, on paper 28.0 cm by 21.8 cm, watermark (left half only) WORONOCO / STRATHMORE / U.S.A. University of Texas at Austin, Harry Ransom Humanities Research Center, MS file (Yeats, WB) Works.

Texas(3) "To a Wealthy Man who promised a Second Subscription to the Dublin Municipal Gallery if it were proved the People wanted Pictures." Typescript, title double-spaced, text single-spaced, ten characters per inch, with ink corrections, on paper type #6. University of Texas at Austin, Harry Ransom Humanities Research Center, folder 12.7, Alice Corbin Henderson correspondence, Yeatses, 1911–1923 + N.D.

WashStU "The Well and the Tree." Holograph revisions to delete this poem in marked copy of *Resp17*, pages v and 49. Washington State University, Library Archives, PR5904 .R3 1917.

Yale "[Pardon, old fathers]," "The Grey Rock," "The Two Kings." Corrected page proofs (same early printed state as Emory(5) but with different corrections) of *Resp14,* on seven double sheets, 20.9 cm by 29.3 cm, folded to 20.9 cm by 14.7 cm, and two half sheets 20.9 cm by 14.7 cm, watermark BALLYCLARE / CO ANTRIM. These sheets contain the front matter through page 16 (p. 15 in *Resp14*); "To a Wealthy Man who promised a Second Subscription to the Dublin Municipal Gallery if it were proved the People wanted Pictures," which connects exactly with Harvard(1); stray pages 37–38 (l. 13 of "Friends" through l. 8 of "An Appointment") with a query in Ezra Pound's hand that led to a correction (p. 15 in *Resp14*); and the Notes section. All sheets except the half-sheet with pages 37–38 have holes at top left (when folded) from having formerly been fastened with a straight pin. Yale University, Beinecke Rare Book and Manuscript Library, YCAL MSS 43, Ezra Pound Papers, box 137, folder 5590.

Introduction

I

This volume in the Cornell Yeats series contains twenty-eight poems that were included in *Responsibilities: Poems and a Play,* published May 25, 1914 (colophon: "Finished on May Eve, 1914") by the Cuala Press, and one poem that was added for the publication, on October 10, 1916, of the Macmillan (London) *Responsibilities and Other Poems*. That additional poem, "The Well and the Tree," was from the then still unpublished play *At the Hawk's Well*, and after that play was published, in March 1917, the poem was not subsequently published separately from the play. Four other poems, all of which had been added to the second edition of *The Green Helmet and Other Poems*, published in London (Macmillan, 1912) and then were republished in the 1914 Cuala Press *Responsibilities: Poems and a Play*, are found in *The Green Helmet* volume of this series: "On Those that Hated 'The Playboy of the Western World,' 1907," "Friends," "The Cold Heaven," and "That the Night Come."[1]

All but two of the twenty-nine poems in this volume were written in the two and one-half years prior to their publication in the Cuala Press volume on May 25, 1914. One of the two exceptions is "The Well and the Tree," which was first published October 10, 1916 in *Responsibilities and Other Poems* from Macmillan (London), prior to the first publication of the play in which it appears, *At the Hawk's Well*. The play was published six months later, in March, 1917, and the poem was never again published separately from the play. The other exception is "An Appointment," which is dated August 25, 1907 and was first published in *The English Review* in February 1909, but was not included in the Cuala Press volume *The Green Helmet and Other Poems*, finished September 30, 1910 and published in December, 1910. "An Appointment" is an occasional poem, as Lady Gregory recorded in a note she wrote in the margin of her copy: "On the appointment of Count Plunkett to Curatorship of Dublin Museum & Geo. Russell & Birrell,

[1]Those poems had not been printed in the Cuala Press edition of *The Green Helmet and Other Poems* (December 1910 [Wade 84] and New York, January 1911 [Wade 85]). The London edition of *The Green Helmet and Other Poems*, published in October 1912 (Wade 101) added six poems, four of which were reprinted in *Responsibilities*. These four appear in *"In the Seven Woods" and "The Green Helmet and Other Poems,"* ed. David Holdeman, Cornell Yeats series (Ithaca: Cornell University Press, 2002).

Hugh Lane being a candidate."[2] The few occasional poems in *The Green Helmet and Other Poems* are less directly political than is "An Appointment," which might explain its exclusion from that 1910 volume. But *Responsibilities*, with its several bluntly occasional poems, provided a congenial home for that earlier poem.

As was his habit, Yeats paid careful attention to the arrangement of the poems in book form. The volume is framed by its opening and closing poems, both of which are untitled and are printed in red in *Responsibilities: Poems and a Play* (1914). They were written after the other poems. The prefatory poem, as it is called in Yeats's notes to *Responsibilities: Poems and a Play* (1914), is explicitly a dedication for this book and is addressed to his ancestors. It was composed January 2 or 3, 1914 (Yeats to Lady Gregory, postmarked January 3, 1914). The closing poem, written in early 1914 and first published February 7, 1914, as "Notoriety / Suggested by a recent magazine article," is a response to excerpts from George Moore's *Vale* that were unflattering to Yeats and Lady Gregory, published in the *English Review* in January and February 1914.

After the prefatory poem, the volume opens with two longer poems with ancient Irish settings, "The Grey Rock" (written October 1912) and "The Two Kings" (written January 1912). That pair is followed by a group of seven poems with bitter rhetoric aimed at the Dublin opponents of the Hugh Lane gallery controversy and the earlier attacks on Parnell and Synge. Of these seven poems, two are dated September 16, 1913 ("To a Friend Whose Work has Come to Nothing" and "Paudeen"), and three others were written during that same month, while visiting Lady Gregory at Coole Park ("September 1913," "To a Shade," and "When Helen Lived"). The seven topical poems are:

"To A Wealthy Man who promised a Second Subscription to the Dublin Municipal Gallery if it were proved the People wanted Pictures" (written December 24, 1912; dated January 8, 1913 in its first printing in *The Irish Times*, January 11, 1913)
"September 1913" (written August 1913; dated September 1913 in its first printing in *The Irish Times*, September 8, 1913)
"To a Friend Whose Work has Come to Nothing" (written September 16, 1913)
"Paudeen" (written September 16, 1913)
"To a Shade" (written September 29, 1913)
"When Helen Lived" (written between September 20 and 29, 1913)
"On Those that Hated 'The Playboy of the Western World, 1907'" (written April 5, 1910) [reprinted from *The Green Helmet and Other Poems*].

Yeats placed later in the volume an eighth poem with a similar topic, "An Appointment." It

[2]Census of Manuscripts, Emory(4), above. Count George Noble Plunkett was appointed Curator of the National Museum of Ireland in 1907. Augustine Birrell (1850–1937), who was appointed Chief Secretary for Ireland (1907–1916), was a Dublin Castle supporter of the Abbey Theatre. One contribution to Yeats's and Lady Gregory's antagonism toward Count Plunkett may have been from their assumption that he authored a pseudonymous attack in the Dublin press in 1904 against the J. Staats-Forbes Collection exhibition organized by Hugh Lane. The author ("Viator") may well have been Lt. Col. George Tindall Plunkett (1842–1922), who, after his retirement from the army in 1894, was Director of the Science and Art Institutions (National Museum of Ireland) from 1895 until 1907. He was notoriously unfriendly to modern art and to Hugh Lane, and, in 1905, had mounted a public attack against the legitimacy of a Corot painting purchased from the Staats-Forbes Collection by the Prince of Wales for donation to Hugh Lane's Municipal Collection; see *Collected Letters of W. B. Yeats,* vol. 3, 685, n. 4, and Thomas Bodkin, *Hugh Lane and his Pictures*, (1932; 2d ed., Dublin: Browne and Nolan, 1934), pp. 16–17.

had been written in 1907 or 1908, long before this group of seven poems and four years earlier than any other poem in the collection, including the six poems that had been published in the 1910 volume *The Green Helmet and Other Poems*. He placed "An Appointment" in a group of four poems from *The Green Helmet and Other Poems*, near the end of the collection, possibly because he might have judged "An Appointment" to be a less accomplished poem than the seven in this section.

Next in *Responsibilities: Poems and a Play* (1914) is a group of five poems about beggars. For *Responsibilities and Other Poems*, editions of 1916 and 1917 only, Yeats inserted into this group "The Well and the Tree," a lyric that tonally resembles the beggar poems, from the as yet unpublished play *At the Hawk's Well*. Those poems are:

"The Three Beggars" (published November 15, 1913)
"The Three Hermits" (March 5, 1913)
"Beggar to Beggar Cried" (March 5, 1913)
[1916 and 1917 only: "The Well and the Tree" (published October 10, 1916)]
"Running to Paradise" (written September 20, 1913)
"The Hour before Dawn" (written October 19, 1913).

The remaining sixteen poems are arranged according to their subject matter and style rather than the chronology of composition, although the groupings are more mixed than in the first half of the book. That had also been the case in Yeats's previous collection *The Green Helmet and Other Poems,*[3] which in its Cuala Press version provided a section title "Raymond Lully and his wife Pernella" for the first eight poems, followed by a catch-all section title of "Momentary Thoughts" for the remaining eleven poems. Three of the four poems from *The Green Helmet and Other Poems* that were reprinted in *Responsibilities* are placed together among these sixteen poems: "Friends," "The Cold Heaven," and "That the Night Come." Also, among these sixteen poems are three sets of paired poems, though the pairings were not stable. In the first two of the pairs the first poem was written separately from the second poem in the pair. "The Witch" and "The Peacock" were written in May 1912 and November 1913, respectively. They were first published without the I/II notation, both in a journal and in *Responsibilities: Poems and a Play* (1914), where they are not even consecutive.

The second such pair, "To a Child Dancing in the Wind" and "Two Years Later," were written in November 1912 and December 1912 or 1913, respectively; they were first published separately, in December 1912 and May 1914, respectively. On the first printing of "To a Child Dancing in the Wind" it was titled "To a Child Dancing upon the Shore." And on the first printing of "Two Years Later" it used the title that later was adopted for the first of the pair or as an overall title, "To a Child Dancing in the Wind."

The third pair, "The Magi" and "The Dolls," was written on the same date (or at least were given the same date by Yeats), September 20, 1913, but "The Magi" was printed in two periodicals prior to the first publication of "The Dolls," in *Responsibilities: Poems and a Play* (1914). Their I/II notation was dropped in 1923.

---

[3]Cuala 1910 (Wade 84) and New York, January 1911 (Wade 85); the section titles were dropped for the next edition, London: Macmillan, October 1912 (Wade 101), with six poems added, four of which were later included in *Responsibilities*.

To sum up, the sixteen poems in *Responsibilities* (1914) are:

"A Song from 'The Player Queen'" (published May 1914)
"The Realists" (published December 1912)
"The Witch" (written May 24, 1912)
"The Peacock" (written November 25, 1913)
"The Mountain Tomb" (written August 1912)
"To a Child Dancing in the Wind" (written November 1912) and "Two Years Later" (December 3, 1912 or 1913)
"A Memory of Youth" (written ?August 13, 1912, published December 1912)
"Fallen Majesty" (published December 1912)
"Friends" (written January 1912; published 1912 in *The Green Helmet and Other Poems*)
"The Cold Heaven" (published 1912 in *The Green Helmet and Other Poems*)
"That the Night Come" (published 1912 in *The Green Helmet and Other Poems*)
"An Appointment" (written 1907, published February 1909)
"The Magi" (written September 20, 1913)
"The Dolls" (written September 20, 1913)
"A Coat" (written 1912).

Following the sixteen poems comes the play *The Hour-Glass*, in the mixed verse and prose version that Yeats had written 1910–1912 and which had been printed in Edward Gordon Craig's periodical, *The Mask*, in April 1913 and then again in a small edition of fifty copies, marked "Privately Printed," from the Cuala Press in January 1914. By contrast, the Cuala Press published *Responsibilities: Poems and a Play* in an edition of 400 copies in May 1914. The inclusion of *The Hour-Glass*, which fills thirty-five pages in that Cuala Press edition, results in a respectably sized volume, with its colophon on page [83], followed by only five blank pages—in sharp contrast with the Cuala Press's *The Green Helmet and Other Poems*, which has its colophon on page [33], followed by fifteen blank pages.

After the play, *Responsibilities: Poems and a Play* returns to poetry, closing with the second of the two framing poems, again untitled and printed in red. At the back of the volume are Yeats's three notes to the poems and one note to the play, all written in 1914.

II

The *Responsibilities* poems illustrate the wide spectrum of Yeats's interests in those years. From immediately contemporary issues, especially the public debate over the proposed Hugh Lane Gallery of Modern Art, the settings range all the way back to Irish prehistory with "The Two Kings," which Yeats sometimes referred to as the "Tara poem." In late 1907, the Dublin Corporation voted to acquire Clonmell House, 17 Harcourt Street, as a temporary art gallery, and Hugh Lane, a nephew of Lady Gregory, brought his collection of modern pictures and statues from London and installed them in Clonmell House, which officially opened as the Dublin Municipal Gallery of Modern Art on January 20, 1908. Lane undertook responsibility for its operating expenses when the Dublin Corporation discovered that a special act of Parliament would be necessary to give it the authority to spend money on a municipal gallery; that arrangement continued until the act was passed in 1911. Lane received the Freedom of the City of Dublin in February 1908 and was knighted in January 1909. He continued to flourish as a private art dealer in London, while making frequent visits to Dublin, and continued to pressure the Dublin Corporation on the necessity of building a permanent gallery, which was a condition necessary before he would formally transfer his thirty-nine continental pictures. In 1912 Lane commissioned Edwin Lutyens to design a gallery, and on November 5, 1912, Lane made that condition formal and included a proviso that the thirty-nine pictures "will be removed from Dublin at the end of January 1913, if the building of a new and suitable gallery is not decided upon." The Lord Mayor of Dublin supported a public meeting that was held at Mansion House on November 29, 1912, to form a committee to raise money for the project. With the clock ticking down to Lane's deadline of the end of January 1913, the Dublin Corporation pledged to provide £22,000, but only if the committee gave at least £3,000 and, importantly, the site for the gallery.[4] Some of the several sites considered earlier had been as costly as £50,000,[5] hence the importance of a free site such as the controversial bridge across the Liffey, which Lane strongly supported. But the bridge site had an estimated cost of £45,000, so the committee would need to raise £23,000, a task it never accomplished. Hugh Lane was elected Director of the National Gallery of Ireland on February 26, 1914, while continuing his association with the Municipal Gallery. His death when the *Lusitania* was torpedoed on May 7, 1915 and the long-continuing controversy over the unwitnessed codicil to his will are subsequent to the period of *Responsibilities*.

Yeats's first poem on the Municipal Gallery controversy was "To a Wealthy Man who promised a Second Subscription to the Dublin Municipal Gallery if it were proved the People wanted Pictures." That twenty-two-word title, perhaps the longest in the whole history of literature, was originally even longer, at thirty-one words: "To a friend who promises a bigger subscription than his first to the Dublin Municipal Gallery if the amount collected proves that there is a considerable 'popular demand' for the pictures." But *The Irish Times*, when it published the poem on January 11, 1913, added a much simpler title headline, "The Gift," and relegated Yeats's lengthy title to a head note within square brackets. This poem, which in a draft (NLI 13,586[3] [a]) is dated December 25, 1912, and is printed in *Responsibilities: Poems and a Play* (1914) with the date "December, 1912," carried a different date in *The Irish Times*: "January 8th, 1913." That date presumably was supplied editorially by *The Irish Times*, and might well simply have been the date of Yeats's letter of transmittal, which is not extant.

The poem's publication in the staunchly Unionist and pro-aristocracy *Irish Times* was deliberately chosen, as we know from Yeats's letter accompanying the copy of the poem that he sent to Hugh Lane on January 1 or 2, 1913. Yeats told him, "I will try & see Hone & see if fitting publication & comment could be made in the Irish Times" (see p. 207 below). Those plans were fully realized, for the poem was complemented (and also complimented) by editorial commentary titled "Art and Aristocracy," on the facing page of *The Irish Times:*

> Mr. Yeats's new poem, which we publish in another column, will help on those who are engaged in this interesting occupation. Without necessarily agreeing with his view, they will perceive its intellectual sincerity. It is a reproach to a friend who waits to see whether there is a "considerable popular demand" for the pictures before he will

[4]Quoted in Thomas Bodkin, *Hugh Lane and His Pictures*, pp. 33, 35.

[5]Lady Gregory, *Hugh Lane's Life and Achievement, with Some Account of the Dublin Galleries* (London: Murray, 1921); rpt. in Lady Gregory, *Sir Hugh Lane: His Life and Legacy*, Coole Edition of the Works of Lady Gregory, vol. 10 (Gerrards Cross: Smythe, 1973), p. 88.

> send a larger subscription than his first. The point is clear enough. There is no use in being angry with "the people." We are asked to clear our minds of democratic cant. Mr. Yeats's poem lifts the discussion out of the region of sentimentality.[6]

The article then approvingly admires the courage of Yeats, as a Nationalist, in publicly seeking to persuade the Unionist aristocracy to ignore democratic public opinion, and continues in a manner perfectly attuned to Yeats's opinions, only slightly adapted for the Unionist readers:

> But note the craft of Mr. Yeats, which one must admire even more than his courage. He reminds our aristocracies of birth and wealth, not of their duties, but of their privileges. This reproach to a friend is really the most subtle of compliments. It is among the friend's privileges to—
>
> "Look up in the sun's eye and give
> What the exultant heart calls good."
>
> Ercole d'Este, Duke Guidobaldo, Cosimo de Medici, the greatest patrons of the liberal arts the world has known, were more than patrons of the liberal arts. They illustrate for all time an attitude which must be that of aristocracy if the word has any meaning. Deprived temporarily of his political power, Cosimo did not grow embittered, or forget that it was still his prerogative to patronise Michelozzo. Who can say that Mr. Yeats's analogy is impertinent to Ireland to-day?
>
> Irish Unionism, at least south of the Boyne, derives its main strength from the upper classes. Our upper classes have lost a part of their former reputation for taste in learning and books and a delight in the arts, and who knows but that Unionism has suffered thereby? Without forgetting the modern achievement of Trinity College, which is mainly Unionist, we find it impossible to doubt that Anglo-Irish gentlemen have, in these respects, fallen from the high estate of their ancestors in the eighteenth century.

Immediately below the poem was an article titled "Municipal Art Gallery. / Further Subscriptions." reporting the meeting on January 9, 1913, of the Municipal Art Gallery Building Fund Committee, and listing the names and amounts of new subscriptions. The political context of *The Irish Times* is evident from the articles on either side of the poem. On the left was a report of an election speech by a Unionist candidate in a Londonderry election, and on the right was a glowing account of a Unionist women's meeting on January 10, 1913, under the headline "Against Home Rule. / Women's Demonstration in Dublin. / Enthusiastic Proceedings. / Speeches by Lady Powerscourt. . . ." The reporter admired a scroll inscribed "We will not have Home Rule," which was "prominently displayed on the platform, which was effectively draped with Union Jacks, while a profusion of flowers and evergreens made an artistic setting to the scene." The remainder of the newspaper column has a letter signed "Guarantor," strongly supporting the gallery: "Every public-spirited citizen who is not ground down by poverty should gladly subscribe."

---

[6]Page 6, columns g–h; for attribution of the unsigned editorial to John Hone, see Roy F. Foster, *W. B. Yeats: A Life*, vol. 1: *The Apprentice Mage, 1865–1914* (Oxford and New York: Oxford University Press, 1997), p. 479. Foster's plate 17 (p. 480) reproduces the upper half of page 7 of *The Irish Times*, January 11, 1913, columns e–g, which includes Yeats's poem.

The Monday, January 13, 1913, issue of *The Irish Times* had four letters dated January 11, 1913, under the headline "The Modern Art Gallery," three of which are pointed responses to the archly imperious, autocratic tone of Yeats's poem. In the first of those an anonymous Dublin wit displayed considerable satirical skill in concocting a lengthy letter purportedly from an American millionaire, Montagu Macnaughten, who was visiting Dublin and read Yeats's poem in the Saturday morning paper. The American millionaire rails against the influence of art galleries and Greek lyric poetry, which threatens to degenerate America "into a nation of false and effeminate loungers":

> Art galleries in America are proving almost as useful as the study of Greek and Latin poetry in the production of effeminate and lascivious men from whom our Republic has everything to fear and nothing to hope. Many of us are now so absolutely convinced of this fact that we are forming an association to secure the compulsory closure of all public galleries of painting and sculpture, and we intend to follow this up by a thorough reform in the teaching of Greek and Latin classics.

Then he makes an offer that is extravagantly generous, though admittedly drastic:

> I cannot give a better proof of the sincerity and confidence of my opinion on this subject than the proposal which I now make. I offer to subscribe the sum of £100,000 (one hundred thousand pounds) to the funds of any British and Irish association formed for the purpose of securing the closure of all public art galleries in these islands by means of State legislation, the association also undertaking to secure such a reform in the teaching of Greek and Latin classics as will put the scientific thinking of these ancients in its proper place, and relegate their poets to a very subordinate position.

Even the otherwise supportive *Irish Times* editorial staff joined in the sport of this attack on Yeats's insistence that Ireland should have a supply of Italian Renaissance princes, offering only a wry disclaimer: "This letter came to us under the Kingstown post mark. We have never heard of a Mr. Montagu Macnaughten. The name does not appear in the 1912–1913 Edition of 'Who's Who in America.'"[7]

That letter is followed by one signed "Val d'Arno" in which Yeats is taken to task for thinking that Dublin has any connection with Renaissance Florence. He invites Yeats to recognize that Dublin in 1913 is "a society which no longer rests on the minute pivot of aristocracy, but firmly turns on the broader base of popular will and choice. To the Grecian mind, and for mediæval Italy, the world existed for the leisure class; to-day its fuller purpose is to broaden the life and thought of the entire people. Paudeen and Biddy count now as never before, and their 'pennies and half-pennies' are a better security for any worthy cause than the support of the few superior people whose generosity marks rather their egoistic sense of exclusive gifts than any real sympathy with the beautiful and the true." The writer next invokes the necessity of attention to social priorities, even for a Cosimo d'Medici prancing on horseback through Florence: "If Cosimo saw everyday, as he caracoled on the streets of his native city, the nakedness and hungry want that stare at us in our daily round of visits to our poor, I doubt much that he would have

---

[7]"Montagu Macnaughten" (pseudonym), letter to the editor, *The Irish Times*, Monday, January 13, 1913, p. 6, col. e.

put the plans for the Library of San Marco in the first place of his scheme for the uplifting of his people." Ruskin's opinion that the collecting of contemporary art should be the business of private individuals rather than governments supports the writer's conclusion that "Dublin is quite within her rights as a modern and progressive city if she leave the Lane collection of modern painting to the cultured care of those who can afford the private possession of canvases whose merits, however real, have not yet matured by age into that steady fame which alone justifies a formal act of civic recognition." The letter then, with deliberately sharp irony, quotes the poem in a call for the aristocracy to pay for the project themselves — without a penny from the government or the common citizens.

The last of the four letters takes the opposite tack but the writer is equally upset at "the hopeless atavism" of the poem's message. The letter announces that "the modern proletarian looks with suspicion on the good things provided for him by a benevolent plutocracy." Its writer, who signs himself "Paudeen," concludes, "I do wish you would start a shilling fund. Biddy also would subscribe."

The Irish Times published no more letters on this topic until Saturday, January 18, when it gave prominent notice to a retaliatory letter, dated January 17, 1913, from Yeats's enemy William M. Murphy,[8] objecting to the diversion of any Dublin Corporation funds for "fads or luxuries" such as the art gallery and specifically attacking the second line of the poem: "If 'Paudeen's pennies,' so contemptuously poetised a few days ago in the Press by Mr. W. B. Yeats, are to be abstracted from 'Paudeen's' pocket, at least give him an opportunity of saying whether he approves of the process or not." Murphy concludes his letter: "Hitherto only one side of the case has been presented to the public. I greatly admire the public spirit of the subscribers to this Gallery project, and would be rejoiced if the promoters could accomplish their object — through private benefactions; but I would ask them to keep their hands out of the pockets of the ratepayers. Speaking for myself, I admire good pictures, and I think I can appreciate them, but as a choice between the two, I would rather see in the City of Dublin one block of sanitary houses at low rents replacing a reeking slum than all the pictures Corot and Degas ever painted."

Yeats would dismiss Murphy's reaction as uncultivated and Philistine, and, far from being dissuaded from writing further topical, public poems, he went on to take his revenge in "September 1913," which was similarly published in *The Irish Times,* September 8, 1913, under the title of "Romance in Ireland."

III

The two and a half years when Yeats was writing the poems in *Responsibilities* include an important association with Ezra Pound. A survey of Pound's two reviews of *Responsibilities: Poems and a Play*, 1914 and 1916, can be useful as background before we turn to an examination of the two poets' collaborative revision of "The Two Kings" as recorded on the Yale page proofs. Pound's earlier review of *Responsibilities: Poems and a Play* (1914) for *Poetry* (Chicago) is much more substantial.[9] And as can often happen with reviews, it gives at least as many insights on Pound as it does on Yeats's poems. Pound opens by establishing his own modernist credentials:

---

[8]Page 8, column e, elaborately headed " 'MODERN ART GALLERY.' / [HALF RULE] / Is it Wanted? / Letter From Mr. W. M. Murphy. / TO THE EDITOR OF THE IRISH TIMES" and with its opening paragraph printed in a larger type.

[9]Ezra Pound, [review of *Resp14*] "The Later Yeats," *Poetry* (Chicago), 4, 2 (May 1914): 64–69, quoted here; it has been collected in *Literary Essays of Ezra Pound*, ed. T. S. Eliot (Norfolk, Conn.: New Directions, 1954), pp. 378–381.

> I live, so far as possible, among that more intelligently active segment of the race which is concerned with today and tomorrow; and, in consequence of this, whenever I mention Mr. Yeats I am apt to be assailed with questions: "Will Mr. Yeats do anything more?", "Is Yeats in the movement?", "How *can* the chap go on writing this sort of thing?" And to these inquiries I can only say that Mr. Yeats' vitality is quite unimpaired, and that I dare say he'll do a good deal; and that up to date no one has shown any disposition to supersede him as the best poet in England, or any likelihood of doing so for some time.

Pound then defends Yeats's stature as the "best poet in England" and, while acknowledging that although Yeats is a symbolist and does not qualify as an *Imagiste,* "he has written *des Images* as have many good poets before him." And he admires that Yeats earlier "has driven out the inversion" and has learned to write "with prose directness" so that four years earlier, in poems such as "No Second Troy" in *The Green Helmet and Other Poems*, there gradually emerged a "new note." He praises *Responsibilities: Poems and a Play* (1914) for the developments since *The Green Helmet and Other Poems:* "And since that time one has felt his work becoming gaunter, seeking greater hardness of outline." Pound of course strongly admires this "hardness," which he finds especially in "The Magi," but also in "September 1913," and "To a Child Dancing in the Wind" (although not in its companion poem, "Two Years Later").

Pound is less happy with such poems as "When Helen Lived" and "The Realists," while admitting that they can "serve at least to show that the tongue has not lost its cunning." Somewhat surprisingly, because Pound's own poetry would soon engage in biting criticism of immediately contemporary cultural, political, and economic issues, here he all but ignores the *engagé* poems in *Responsibilities: Poems and a Play* (1914). They receive only one mention, in a single sentence buried in the review's last paragraph: "In the poems on the Irish gallery we find this author certainly at *prise* with things as they are and no longer romantically Celtic, so that a lot of his admirers will be rather displeased with the book." That prediction proved to be correct, as many readers and reviewers came to the volume hoping for a return to the Celtic Twilight mood. But Pound approvingly observes, "That is always a gain for a poet, for his admirers nearly always want him to 'stay put,' and they resent any signs of stirring, of new curiosity or of intellectual uneasiness." Pound singled out two poems with which he is specifically not happy, "The Two Kings" and "The Grey Rock," both of which are narratives set in ancient Ireland: "On the other hand, it is impossible to take any interest in a poem like *The Two Kings*—one might as well read the *Idyls* [*sic*] of another"—the damnably (for Pound) old-fashioned *Idylls of the King* (1859–1885) of Tennyson. Pound is somewhat gentler in his dispraise of the other poem: "*The Grey Rock* is, I admit, obscure, but it outweighs this by a curious nobility, a nobility which is, to me at least, the very core of Mr. Yeats' production, the constant element of his writing." Then in an afterthought that closes the review, Pound revisits his reservations about the obscurity of "The Grey Rock," ostensibly to soften his dislike, but then likens it to Robert Browning's notoriously obscure *Sordello* (1840): "I have said the [*sic*] *Grey Rock* was obscure; perhaps I should not have said so, but I think it demands unusually close attention. It is as obscure, at least, as *Sordello*, but I can not close without registering my admiration for it all the same."

Neither here nor elsewhere did Pound revise his dislike of "The Two Kings," even though he, along with Sturge Moore, had had a considerable hand in its revisions, as Yeats's correspondence of the time and the ten-page Yale page proofs show, making them among the most interesting documents in this volume (pp. 180–205 below). Pound's part in this collaborative revision with

Yeats of that long poem during the winter of 1913 at Stone Cottage, Sussex, is somewhat akin to his more extensive marking, nearly a decade later, of T. S. Eliot's *The Waste Land*. The opening lines of "The Two Kings" can illustrate the evolution of the poem, beginning with extended struggling in the first two holograph manuscripts, NLI 30,517 and NLI 13,586(2), which read, respectively:

> Eoha the Chief King of Ireland came,
> After long absence warring in the west

and

> Eocha Chief King of Ireland came at length
> Worn out after a dozen months of war

Those are followed by a third holograph, marked "Final" that was finished on January 8, 1912:

> We ride but slowly though so near our home
> King Eocha said and he that bore his shield

That reading was repeated, with the addition of punctuation, in a corrected typescript NLI 13,586(2) (a) and was published October 1913 in *Poetry* (Chicago) and *The British Review:*

> 'We ride but slowly though so near our home,'
> King Eochaid said, and he that bore his shield

Two letters Yeats wrote to Lady Gregory in early January 1913 suggest the collaborative roles played by Pound and Sturge Moore and praise their suggestions, specifically mentioning "The Two Kings." On the first of the month, he wrote that "on Monday night I got Sturge Moore in and last night Ezra Pound and we went at it line by line and now I know what is wrong and am in good spirits again. I am starting the poem about the King of Tara and his wife again, to get rid of Miltonic generalization." In a second letter, dated January 3, he wrote more expansively,

> My digestion has got rather queer again — a result I think of sitting up late with Ezra and Sturge Moore and some light wine while the talk ran. However the criticism I have got from them has given me new life and I have made that Tara poem a new thing and am writing with a new confidence having got Milton off my back. Ezra is the best critic of the two. He is full of the middle ages and helps me to get back to the definite and the concrete away from modern abstractions. To talk over a poem with him is like getting you to put a sentence into dialect. All becomes clear and natural.[10]

The collaborative revision with Pound and Moore, entered by Yeats and Pound on the Yale page

---

[10]Both letters are in the Henry W. and Albert A. Berg Collection of English and American Literature, New York Public Library, Astor, Lenox, and Tilden Foundation.

proofs that must date before January 27, 1914 (that date is penciled on Harvard[1], which is the second half of this set of proofs) transformed the proof version,

> "We crawl like snails athough [*sic*] so near our home["],
> King Eochaid said, and he that bore his shield

to the more direct phrasing given in Pound's hand in ink in the bottom margin and accepted by Yeats:

> King Eochaid came at sundown to a wood
> Westward of Tara. Hurrying to his queen

The sequence of revisions on the Yale proofs, from evidence on its page 15, has Pound and Yeats working in alternation:

(1) Pound's suggestions in pencil,
(2) Yeats's revision in ink,
(3) Pound's suggestions in ink using a broad-nibbed pen,
(4) Yeats's revision in ink using a narrow-nibbed pen.[11]

Pound began by tightening the opening passage as not sufficiently direct. He first revised in pencil by marking lines 10–11 for probable deletion:

> Having no thought but for his queen Edain,
> Outrode his troop that after twelve months' war

He inserted "Eochaid" in line 13: "And Eochaid came" and suggested replacing

> Where in the middle wood
> A clump of beech trees made an empty space
> He thought to have given his horse the spur, but saw
> Between the pale green light of the beech leaves
> And the ground ivy's bluer light, a stag
> Whiter than curds, its eyes the tint of the sea. (ll. 14–19)

with

> he saw a stag
> Whiter than curds, its eyes had the tint of the sea.

Pound's marking of these lines was presumably meant only as a suggestion for Yeats to pursue in revision. Then Pound went to work on the passage in ink, providing the ink version in the

---

[11]This is shown by the pencil revision canceled in narrow-nibbed pen ink, and then at the bottom margin, the series of three ink passages, one under the other, the first narrow nib and canceled in broad nib, then below that passage Pound wrote a passage in broad nib, and then below both of those Yeats wrote a third passage in narrow nib.

bottom margin and continuing it in the right margin:

> King Eochaid came at sundown to a wood
> Westward of Tara. Hurrying to his queen
> He had out ridden his war-wasted men
> Who with empounded cattle trod the mire.
> Where certain beeches made an empty space
> And where the pale green boughs had mixed their light
> With the ground ivy's blue he saw a stag
> Whiter than curds, its eyes had the tint of the sea.

Pound's second review of *Responsibilities*, for the 1916 London edition, is content with a brief defense of Yeats against readers who wanted him to continue in the manner of the 1890s Celtic Twilight. Reviewing for *Poetry* (Chicago) in December 1916, Pound asserts that the book shows "the simple fact that Mr. Yeats has not 'gone off'. He is the only poet of his decade who has not gradually faded into mediocrity, who has not resigned himself to gradually weaker echoes of an earlier outburst." He continues, "There is a new robustness; there is the tooth of satire which is, in Mr. Yeats' case, too good a tooth to keep hidden. *The Coat*, the wild wolf-dog that will not praise his fleas, *The Scholars*, are all the sort of poem that we would gladly read more of. There are a lot of fools to be killed and Mr. Yeats is an excellent slaughter-master, when he will but turn from ladies with excessive chevelure appearing in pearl-pale nuances."[12]

IV

"The Two Kings" is a rare instance of documentary evidence of extensive, substantive collaborative revision with Ezra Pound,[13] but the manuscript materials for several of the poems show punctuation and title changes that were made by persons other than Yeats. In one of those instances Yeats's explicit invitation for revision of the punctuation is extant. His signed instruction to *Poetry*, for the first publication of "The Realists," in the December 1912 issue of that Chicago periodical states: "I have had to correct & punctuate in a great hurry to catch the first post. I would be much obliged if you would revise the punctuation[.]" (Chicago[2], 3; see p. 329 below.) Even without such instructions *Poetry* did not hesitate to change Yeats's punctuation, as in "The Grey Rock," published there in April 1913. *Poetry* added a comma after "spoke" in line 95 that is not present in the typescript sent to them or to *The British Review*, where it was published in the same month. The comma added by *Poetry* has been retained in all subsequent printings of the poem (*VP* 275).

Two other poems that have unusually complex textual histories invite attention here. The investigation of the textual history of "A Song from 'The Player Queen'" relies on Curtis B. Bradford's posthumous volume *The Writing of* The Player Queen, as listed in the Census of Manuscripts above. Bradford describes the draft that he labels number 17 of the play, in which

---

[12]E[zra] P[ound], [review of *Resp16*] "Mr. Yeats' New Book," *Poetry* (Chicago), 9:3 (Dec. 1916), 150–151; "hair" (chevelure) and "pearl-pale" occur prominently in the poems of *The Wind among the Reeds* (1899).

[13]Humphrey Carpenter, in *A Serious Character: The Life of Ezra Pound* (Boston: Houghton Mifflin, 1988), suggests that Ezra Pound, on the typescript Chicago(2), made the ink revisions of wording in "The Mountain Tomb," l. 7; "To a Child Dancing in the Wind," l. 9; and "Fallen Majesty," l. 8 (p. 191).

the song first appears: "Draft 17 was written on loose sheets of notebook paper which are in complete disorder, and the writing is very difficult to read. After many days of work trying to arrange the sheets in some sort of order, I am still not certain of my arrangements; many passages I have been unable to read. In short, I am not able to recover a coherent version of Draft 17 full enough to print, so I have had to be content to present it in summary and quotation" (pp. 257–258). Those difficulties are compounded by the extremely large quantity and relatively chaotic state of the manuscript materials of *The Player Queen* at the National Library of Ireland, and also by Bradford's otherwise useful policy of giving a very smooth reading text, so that it can sometimes be difficult to identify which particular manuscript or typescript is associated with a particular portion of his reading text. The three excerpts given here are from two nearly identical typescripts, dated approximately 1916, recorded in a smooth text version by Bradford (pp. 378–379, 392, and 393). Bradford also gives the smooth text of three additional instances of unrevised excerpts from the song in a late typescript version of *The Player Queen* that I have not located.[14]

The other poem with a complex history is the two-part "To a Child Dancing in the Wind" and "Two Years Later." However, its manuscript materials are much simpler than those of "A Song from 'The Player Queen'" and a patient reader should be able to trace the composition fairly easily. It might be helpful to remind the reader that the only undivided printing of the two parts of the poem was in *Poetry* (Chicago), December 1912, and that the poem was first printed with the I and II division in 1914 in the Cuala Press *Responsibilities: Poems and a Play* (1914). A complete record of the evidence for the title changes of this poem requires mentioning that in addition to the holograph instructions in NLI 30,528 for printing the poem as two numbered sections in *Responsibilities: Poems and a Play* (1914), a set of corrected page proofs, Harvard(1), for the second half of *Responsibilities: Poems and a Play* (1914) has very faint, penciled instruction in the copy editor's hand, with an arrow to the printed title "TO A CHILD DANCING UPON THE SHORE" above part I: "Print this poem after above title."

A brief mention should be made of the pre-publication changes to the selection and arrangement of these poems in the two Cuala Press volumes *Poems Written in Discouragement, 1912–1913* and *Responsibilities: Poems and a Play* (1914) and in the three issues of the Macmillan *Responsibilities and Other Poems*.

The eight-page, stitched booklet *Poems Written in Discouragement, 1912–1913* was privately printed by Cuala Press in October 1913, in a run of only fifty copies, not for sale (Wade 107). At first it was to contain only three poems: "To a Wealthy Man, who promised a Second Subscription if it were proved the People wanted Pictures," "September, 1913," and "To a Friend Whose Work has Come to Nothing." Typescripts of the first and second of those poems (Berg[4] and [8] [b]) are marked respectively "(1" and "(2". An early page proof (Berg[6] [a]), with the eight pages on a single, uncut sheet, has just those three poems and is printed with only twelve lines per page to fill as much space as possible on the eight pages. Soon afterward, a fourth and fifth

[14]*W. B. Yeats: The Writing of* The Player Queen, Manuscripts of W. B. Yeats series, ed. David R. Clark (DeKalb: Northern Illinois University Press, 1977). The late version of the song appears in Bradford's "Draft 29" (two nearly identical typescripts, dated approximately by Bradford as 1916); see note to p. 379: (a.) [*stanza 1; similar to NLI 8764(8) (b)*] *Writing of* The Player Queen, pp. 378–379: *"Decima (putting on dress, sings).* / My mother dandled me and sang / How young it is, how young / And made a golden cradle / That on a willow swung."; (b.) [*ll. 9–10*] p. 392: *"Decima (singing).* / She pulled the thread, and bit the thread / And made a golden gown."; and (c.) [*ll. 11–12*] p. 393: *"Decima (singing).* / She wept because she dreamt that I / Was born to wear a crown."

poem were added, "Paudeen" and "To a Shade," so that a later page proof (Berg[7]) has all five poems printed with eighteen lines per page, rather than the earlier twelve lines per page.

Early proofs (Berg[14]) of the Cuala Press *Responsibilities: Poems and a Play* (1914), prior to the addition of the play *The Hour-Glass,* are titled " 'Responsibilities' by W. B. Yeats" (rather than "Responsibilities: Poems and a Play by William Butler Yeats") and have a variant selection and ordering of the poems after "Beggar to Beggar Cried": "The Realists," "I The Witch," "II The Peacock," "The Mountain Tomb," "Running to Paradise," "The Hour before Dawn," "The Player Queen," "To a Child Dancing in the Wind," "A Memory of Youth," "Fallen Majesty," "Friends," "The Cold Heaven," [omits "That the Night Come" and "An Appointment"], "The Magii" [*sic*], "The Dolls," and "A Coat."

Finally, a brief mention should be made of the variants among the three issues of the Macmillan volume: *Responsibilities and Other Poems* published in London on October 10, 1916, *Responsibilities and Other Poems* published in New York on November 1, 1916, and *Responsibilities and Other Poems* published in London in March, 1917 (Wade 115, as a "second impression"). The New York *Responsibilities and Other Poems* (1916) was typeset from a set of page proofs sent from Macmillan (London) and has different spacing of letters throughout, adds hyphenation at two line endings, in "[Pardon, old fathers]," page 1, line 8 ("hux- / ter's") and "Paudeen," page 35, line 8 ("crys- / taline"), and has differences of page division in "Reconciliation," pages 92–93, and in the notes, pages 183–188. The New York *Responsibilities and Other Poems* (1916), page 29, omits a period at the end of the title of "To a Wealthy Man . . . wanted Pictures." and at page 38 mistakenly dates "To a Shade" as "September 29th, 1914." rather than "September 29th, 1913."; *Responsibilities and Other Poems* (New York, 1916), page 1, line 8.[15]

V

For *Responsibilities: Poems and a Play* (1914), Yeats wrote one short note and two long notes to the poems. His drafting of the two longer notes is recorded in holograph manuscripts of five pages and one page, respectively (NLI 30,314, 1^r–5^r, and 13,586[17]). In *Responsibilities: Poems and a Play* (1914) the two longer notes are titled "Poems beginning with that 'To a Wealthy Man' and ending with that 'To a Shade'" and "The Dolls." Those extensive drafts are of high interest because they show the alternative wordings that Yeats considered as he composed these notes for *Responsibilities: Poems and a Play* (1914); Roy Foster quoted from them in his biography of Yeats.[16] In the appendix below I have provided a transcription of their manuscript drafts in a simplified format that, for economy and clarity, ignores line divisions and a few canceled false starts of partial words. The Census of Manuscripts includes a description of their manuscript materials.

The manuscript title "Poems written in Despondency" for the first note is written in a slightly different color of black ink and is very near the top edge of the paper, presumably indicating that it was added sometime after that page had been written (NLI 30,314, 1^r). That preliminary title corresponded to that of the October 1913 pamphlet, whose contents were the same five poems as are in that section of *Responsibilities: Poems and a Play* (1914). The other long note, which

[15]For a detailed description of a marked-up copy of *Responsibilities and Other Poems* (1917) see Wayne K. Chapman, "The Annotated *Responsibilities:* Errors in the *Variorum Edition* and a New Reading of the Genesis of Two Poems, 'On Those That Hated "The Playboy of the Western World", 1907' and 'The New Faces,'" *Yeats Annual* 6 (1988): 108–133.

[16]Roy F. Foster, *W. B. Yeats: A Life*, vol. 1, p. 501.

refers to both "The Dolls" and "The Magi," was originally titled "The Magi & The Dolls" in its manuscript, but Yeats then canceled the first three words, leaving simply "The Dolls" (NLI 13,586[17]).

No manuscript is extant for Yeats's third note in *Responsibilities: Poems and a Play* (1914), on the term "free of the ten and four" (*VP* 817–818). For Yeats's note on *The Hour-Glass* in *Responsibilities: Poems and a Play* (1914), see that play's volume in this series, where Catherine Phillips provides photographs and full transcriptions of a one-page holograph.[17] It is on the same type of paper as the five-page holograph of notes "Poems written in Despondency" (NLI 30,314).

There is an early set of page proofs (Yale) in which the notes were set in a much smaller font so that they occupy only three pages rather than the five pages in the later version (Berg[6][b]) and in *Responsibilities: Poems and a Play* (1914).

In 1931–1932, for Macmillan's never-published Edition de Luxe of Yeats's collected works, the Macmillan editor Thomas Mark made minor corrections to these notes, pointing out to Yeats that Samuel Butler's reference to Montreal having hidden the Discobolus in a "cellar" should be changed to a "lumber-room" or an "attic" (it was corrected to "lumber-room") and deleting "the" in the quoted phrase "free of the ten and four" of line 3 of "[Pardon, old fathers]" to match the poem.[18] He also added two commas. The notes are found in the marked galley proofs date-stamped "12 September 1931" (NLI 30,263) and in page proofs date-stamped "2 August 1932" (NLI 30,262, pp. 461–462).

---

[17]Catherine Phillips, ed., *The Hour-Glass: Manuscript Materials*, by W. B. Yeats, Cornell Yeats series (Ithaca: Cornell University Press, 1994), pp. 360–361; the manuscript transcribed is from NLI 8763(2).

[18]Thomas Mark was matching it to the poem's text in all printings except *The Collected Poems of W. B. Yeats* (London and New York, 1933 and 1950) (Wade 171–172, 211–211A), their many reprintings, and the scholarly editions based on them, like *The Poems,* revised edition, ed. Richard J. Finneran, *The Collected Works of W. B. Yeats*, vol. 1 (New York: Macmillan, 1989; London: Macmillan, 1991) and *Yeats's Poems,* ed. A. Norman Jeffares (London: Macmillan, 1989).

Transcription Principles and Procedures

This volume presents the record of the growth of its twenty-nine poems from their earliest extant drafts, through their early publication in periodicals or in little collections or anthologies, as was the case for all but four of the poems, and finally to their form in the 1914 Cuala Press *Responsibilities: Poems and a Play* (Wade 110) or, as explained above, the 1916 Macmillan *Responsibilities and Other Poems*. From there on, and with an overlap at the juncture, the record can be traced in the Allt and Alspach variorum edition of the poems. The variorum's four errors in the *Responsibilities* poems are limited to spelling and punctuation.[1] All the early printed readings are presented here, along with transcriptions of the earliest and most interesting manuscripts. Manuscripts that are exceptionally complex or that reflect a unique state of a poem are also presented in full transcription, usually with facing photographs. Simpler manuscripts, along with most typescripts, are reduced to entries in an *apparatus criticus* of variant readings.

Beneath the first transcription of each poem—normally the earliest complete draft—are given two kinds of information. (1) Under *found in* are listed the manuscripts in the Census in which each poem appears. (2) Under *published in* are listed the periodical or separate publications of each poem up to and including the 1916 printing. Beneath the last transcription—normally the one closest to the final version—appears an *apparatus* showing variants (from the revised form of the text above) that appear in all manuscripts or typescripts not transcribed and in marked proof sheets and printed texts up through *Responsibilities and Other Poems* (1916). The listing of variants for "The Hour before Dawn" is divided into two listings for simplicity in presenting an important set of extensive holograph revisions for a later version, including an unadopted reading.

Yeats's manuscript revisions entered on the pages of later printed editions, as described in the Census of Manuscripts under the "ABY" entries, are also included in the *found in* listings and the *apparatus*. Proof sheets are listed in the *apparatus* only where revisions are entered on them.

[1]Corrections to *The Variorum Edition of the Poems of W. B. Yeats*, ed. Peter Allt and Russell K. Alspach (New York: Macmillan, 1957):

"The Grey Rock" *VP* 275, line 112: *Poetry* (Chicago) "faithfulest" *not* "faithfullest",

"The Two Kings" *VP* 281, line 111: *Poetry* (Chicago) "you" *not* "you",

"To a Wealthy Man . . . wanted Pictures" *VP* 287, title: *Resp16* [but not *Resp16(NY)*] and *Resp17* have a period at the end of the title,

"September 1913" *VP* 289, title: *PWD* "September, 1913" *not* "September 1913".

The prepublication printed sources are abbreviated as follows:

BR	*The British Review*
ER	*The English Review*
HW	*Harper's Weekly* (New York)
IT	*The Irish Times*
NS	*The New Statesman*
P	*Poetry* (Chicago)
SS	*The Smart Set* (New York)

Omitted from the *apparatus* record are variants involving the exchange of "and" for "&" and variants of type style, spacing, underlining, and nonsubstantive punctuation in titles. In the *apparatus*, the following abbreviations are used:

del	deleted or deletion
rev	revised or revision

To transcribe Yeats's manuscripts with absolute fidelity is impossible. A glance at the photographs in this volume will show how difficult his hand is to read, especially when he is writing for his eye alone and with a carelessness reflecting the excitement of literary creation. He left the endings of many words unfinished or represented by a vague line, formed letters carelessly and inconsistently, was a poor and erratic speller, and punctuated unsystematically.

The photographs will enable the interested reader to see what Yeats wrote. The task of an editor is to present a transcript in which the often obscure or illegible texts are read, and this inevitably requires a certain amount of interpretative translation. The principles in accordance with which this process has been carried out, and the conventions used in presenting the resultant reading, are listed below.

1. Where there is no reasonable doubt what word Yeats intended, even though letters may seem to be missing or run together at the end of it, that word is generally transcribed in full. The alternative would be to resort to "my*tolg*s" rather than "mythologies" in the transcription of line 3 of the earliest version of "A Coat." The frequent instances of "to" written as what looks like "t" are uniformly recorded here as "to." Yeats's actual spelling is sometimes difficult or impossible to determine absolutely, and in most such cases the standard spelling is given. On the other hand, Yeats's spelling is preserved when it is clearly legible, even if it is incorrect. He tended to favor "prey" over "pray," and frequently wrote "scholours," "lonliness," "sleap," and so on.

2. Yeats frequently broke words at unusual points, or broke words not normally divided. Such words are joined in the transcriptions unless the width of the break approximates the spacing Yeats normally left between words, indicating that he considered the word in question to be actually two words or one needing hyphenation (though he himself rarely inserted hyphens). Where Yeats left space for an apostrophe but failed to insert it, the space is shown here, as in, for example, "there ll" and the like. The facsimiles of course provide the reader the opportunity to check such distinctions.

3. Symbols for illegible words and editorial conjectures:

[?and]	a conjectural reading
[?and word]	two consecutive words that are conjectural readings
[?]	an unintelligible word
[? ? ?]	several unintelligible words (approximately one "?" per word)
[~~?~~]	a canceled unintelligible word

4. Overwritings are indicated thus: ha$\left\{\begin{array}{l}\text{s}\\ \text{ve}\end{array}\right.$ for "have" converted to "has."

5. There are throughout the drafts certain obscure marks or blots, which may have been made accidentally. In cases where their significance has not been determined, they are silently omitted.

6. Cancelation of single lines or of words within a line is indicated by a horizontal cancelation line or, for cancelation of only a punctuation mark, a slanted cancelation line. The cancelation line is straight even where Yeats's was wavy. Where Yeats intended to cancel an entire word but only struck through part of it, the cancelation line in the transcription extends through the entire word. However, even when it seems likely that Yeats meant to cancel an entire phrase or line, no word that he did not at least partially cancel is canceled in the transcriptions.

7. Cancelation of an entire passage is indicated by a vertical bracket in the left margin.

8. Yeats's "stet" marks are preserved, as are his underscorings to indicate italics. Caret symbols that Yeats placed just below the line are raised to line level.

9. In the transcriptions of typescript material, minor and obvious typing errors such as strike-overs may not be recorded, but all holograph corrections of typescript are indicated.

10. Spacing and relative position of words and lines approximate the originals insofar as printed type can reproduce handwritten and typescript material.

11. The following typographical conventions have been adopted to represent the various physical features of the texts:

roman type	ink
italic type	pencil
boldface type	typescript or print

Responsibilities

Transcriptions

[NLI 30,364 (a)]

See Yeats to Lady Gregory, postmark January 3, 1914: "I enclose a poem which I wrote today, inspired by Moore's article. I propose to put it in italics at the beginning of my book. Tell me if you like it. (Free of six and four is a certain exemption from excise which certain merchants had under the Irish parliament, one of my ancestors had it). The poem is very carefully accurate and as my old grandfather is the most prominent in it I think it turns the tables on the enemy" (Henry W. and Albert A. Berg Collection of English and American Literature, New York Public Library, Astor, Lenox, and Tilden Foundation). The "enclose[d] . . . poem" is untraced.

[PARDON, OLD FATHERS]

[NLI 30,364 (a)]

Pardon old fathers if you still remain
if
~~Old fathers of mine — if you should linger near~~
~~In ear shot still~~ somewhere in earshot for
~~Where you once lived to learn~~ the stories end
^the
Old Dublin ~~me~~ merchants, free of six [?] & four
into
Or trading out of Galway ~~out~~ of Spain
Robert
Old county scolors — ~~You that were~~ Emmets friend
A hundred year old memory to the poor
or that has left me
Merchant~~, [?scholar]~~, soldier — that [?~~leave~~] the blood
That has not passed through any huxsters loin
who
Pardon, [~~?~~] you did not count the cost
Old Butlers when^ you took to horse & stood
Beside the Brackesh waters of the Boyne
Till you bad master [?blenched] & all was lost
~~Old~~ You merchant skipper that leaped over board
[?]
But ~~After~~ an old hat in Biskay Bay
You most of all silent & fierce old man
~~Because it was the spectacle of your~~
Because you were the spectacle that stired
My fancy & set my boyish lips to say
[~~?~~] Only the wasteful [?virtues] earn the sun
Pardon that for a barren passions sake
[?Although] I have come close on forty nine
I [?have] no child I have nothing but a book
Nothing but that to prove your blood & mine
[?~~Jan~~] WB Yeats
Dec 1913

---

found in NLI 30,364 (a) *transcribed above*
NLI 30,364 (b) *transcribed below (printed here as the last item)*
Yale
Berg(6) (b)
ABY(1), pp. 174–175 *transcribed below*
ABY(2)
NLI 30,009, p. 109 *transcribed below*
NLI 30,262
published in *Resp14*

[ABY(1), 174]

[ABY(1), 174]

that
Merchant & scholar ~~who~~
~~Scholar & merchant that~~ have
^
Soldiers that gave whatever die was cast,
~~And~~ ~~and old~~ ~~and~~ old ~~Armstrong~~
~~An Armstrong or a Butler that withstood~~
A Butler and Armstrong that withstood
Beside the brackish waters of the Boyne
James & his Irish when the Dutchman crossed;

1 The bracketed ll. 2–5 have an arrow on the facing page (p. 175) to between ll. 9 and 10 of that page.

Pardon, old fathers, if you still remain
Somewhere in ear-shot for the story's end,
Old Dublin merchant "free of ten and four"
Or trading out of Galway into Spain;
And country scholar, Robert Emmet's friend,
A hundred-year-old memory to the poor;
Traders or soldiers who have left me blood
That has not passed through any huxter's loin;
Pardon, and you that did not weigh the cost,
Old Butlers when you took to horse and stood
Beside the brackish waters of the Boyne
Till your bad master blenched and all was lost;
You merchant skipper that leaped overboard
After a ragged hat in Biscay Bay,
You most of all, silent and fierce old man
Because you were the spectacle that stirred
My fancy, and set my boyish lips to say
"Only the wasteful virtues earn the sun";
Pardon that for a barren passion's sake,
Although I have come close on forty-nine
I have no child, I have nothing but a book,
Nothing but that to prove your blood and mine.

January 1914.

175

[ABY(1), 175]

~~An Armstrong or a Butler~~
~~that withstood~~

PARDON, old fathers, if you still remain
Somewhere in ear–shot for the story's end,
Old Dublin merchant "free of ten and four"
Or trading out of Galway into Spain;
Old/ **~~And~~ country scholar, Robert Emmet's friend,** [?]
A hundred–year–old memory to the poor;
~~Traders or soldiers who have~~ left me blood
That has not passed through any huxter's loin;
Pardon, and you that did not weigh the cost,
Old Butlers when you took to horse and stood
Beside the brackish waters of the Boyne
Till your bad master blenched and all was lost;
~~A~~/ **~~You~~ merchant skipper that leaped overboard**
After a ragged hat in Biscay Bay,
Old [?] **~~You~~ most of all, silent and fierce old man** stet
~~Because you were the~~ spectacle that stirred a ~~daily~~/
My fancy, and set my boyish lips to say
"Only the wasteful virtues earn the sun";
Pardon that for a barren passion's sake,
Although I have come close on forty–nine
I have no child, I have nothing but a book,
Nothing but that to prove your blood and mine.

January 1914.

~~the daily~~
Being the daily

Printed text in red and italic.

[NLI 30,009, p. 109]

Pardon, old fathers, if you still remain
Somewhere in ear–shot for the story's end,
Old Dublin merchant "free of ten and four"
Or trading out of Galway into Spain;
Old/ ~~And~~ country scholar, Robert Emmet's friend,
A hundred–year–old memory to the poor;
Merchant and scholar/ ~~Traders or soldiers~~ who have left me blood
That has not passed through any ~~huxter's~~ loin, huckster's ~~?~~
~~Pardon, and you that did not weigh the cost,~~
~~Old Butlers when you took to horse and stood~~ '/ ?
~~Beside the brackish waters of the Boyne~~
~~Till your bad master blenched and all was lost;~~
Old/ ~~You~~ merchant skipper that leaped overboard
After a ragged hat in Biscay Bay,
You most of all, silent and fierce old man
Because ~~you were~~ the ^ spectacle that stirred daily/
My fancy, and set my boyish lips to say
"Only the wasteful virtues earn the sun";
Pardon that for a barren passion's sake,
Although I have come close on forty–nine/ ,/?
I have no child, I have nothing but a book,
Nothing but that to prove your blood and mine.

January 1914.

/Soldiers that gave, whatever die was cast:
A Butler or an Armstrong that withstood
Beside the brackish waters of the Boyne
James & his Irish when the Dutchman crossed;

5, 7, 13, 16, 23–26 All the handwriting in the left and bottom margins is by Yeats; in the right margin he canceled the copyeditor's question mark at l. 8 and wrote the insertion at l. 16.

[NLI 30,364 (b)]

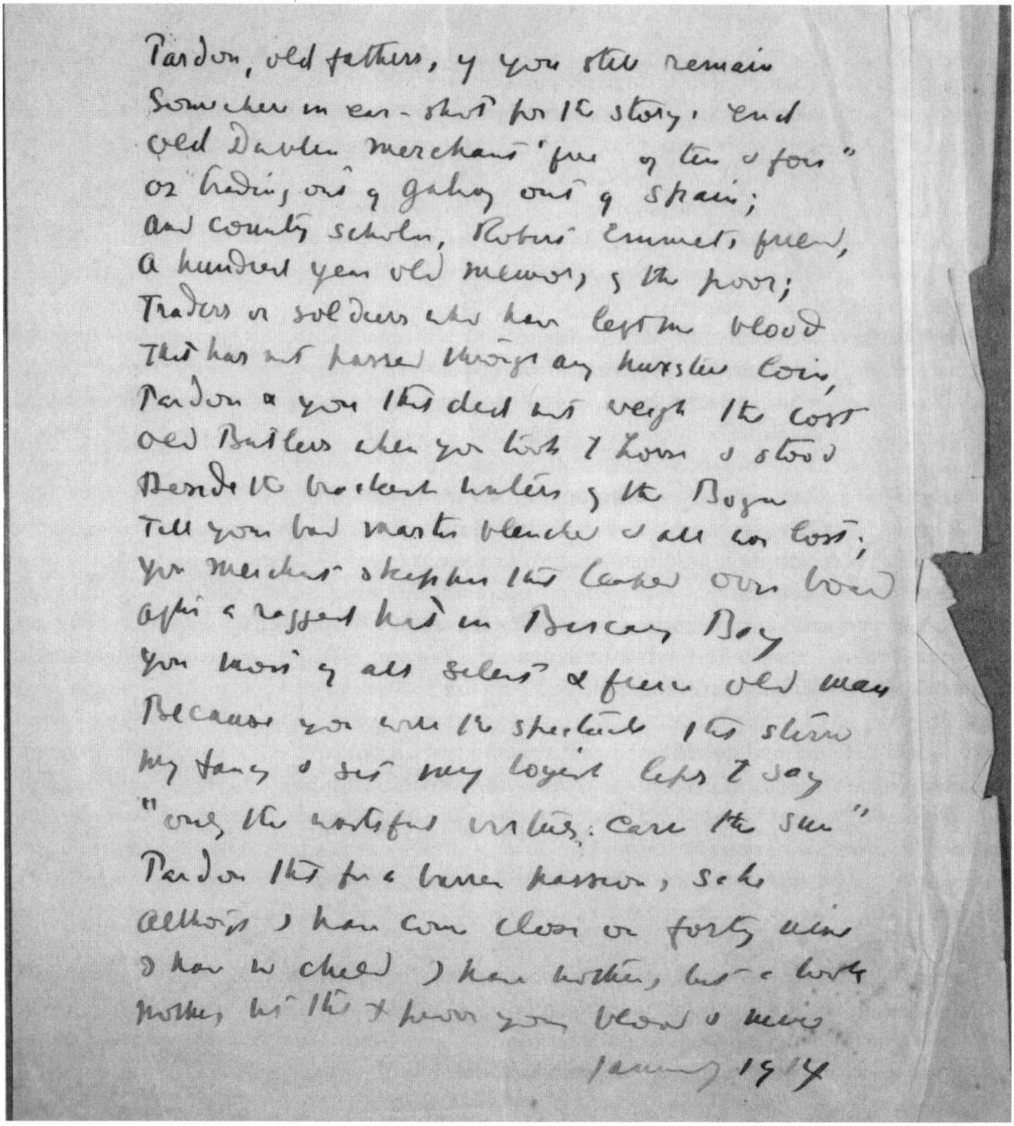

2 story's *Yale, Berg(6), Resp14* end, *Yale, Berg(6), Resp14*
3 free *rev to* 'free *Yale* ten *rev to* six *Berg(6)* four"] four *rev to* four' *Yale*
4 out of] into *Yale, Berg(6), Resp14*
5 And *rev to* Old *ABY(2)* Emmet's *Yale, Berg(6), Resp14*
6 hundred-year-old *Yale, Berg(6), Resp14* of] *rev to* to *Yale* to *Berg(6), Resp14*
7 Traders or soldiers] Merchant and scholar *Yale, Berg(6)* Traders or soldiers *rev to* merchant and scholour *ABY(2)*
8 huxsters] huxter's *Berg(6), Resp14* huckster's *Yale*
9 Pardon [?]] Soldiers Pardon, and *Berg(6), Resp14* cost, *Berg(6), Resp14*
9–12 *read* Soldiers that gave, whatever die was cast:
A Butler or an Armstrong that withstood
Beside the brackish waters of the Boyne
James and his Irish when the Dutchman crossed; *Yale*

[NLI 30,364 (b)]

Pardon, old fathers, if you still remain
Somewhere in ear–shot for the storys end
Old Dublin merchant ‘free of ten & four”
Or trading out of Galway out of Spain;
And county scholar, Robert Emmets friend,
A hundred year old memory of the poor;
Traders or soldiers who have left me blood
That has not passed through any huxsters loin,
Pardon [~~?~~] you that did not weigh the cost
Old Butlers when you took to horse & stood
Beside the brackish waters of the Boyne
Till your bad master blenched & all was lost;
You merchant skipper that leaped over board
After a ragged hat in Biscay Bay
You most of all silent & fierce old man
Because you were the spectacle that stirred
My fancy & set my boyish lips to say
“Only the wasteful virtues earn the sun”
Pardon that for a barren passions sake
Although I have come close on forty nine
I have no child I have nothing but a book
Nothing but that to prove your blood & mine
January 1914

9–12 *rev to* Soldiers that gave whatever die was cast —
A Butler or an Armstrong that withstood,
Beside the brackish waters of the Boyne
James and his Irish when the Dutchman crossed; *ABY(2)*
13 You] Old *Yale* And *Berg(6), Resp14* You *rev to* Old *ABY(2)* over board] overboard *Berg(6), Resp14*
14 Bay, *Berg(6), Resp14* Bay, *rev to* Bay; *NLI 30,262*
15 all, *Yale, Berg(6), Resp14*
16 you were the spectacle] the spectacle *Yale* you were the spectacle *rev to* of the daily spectacle *ABY(2)*
17 fancy, *Yale, Berg(6), Resp14*
18 sun, *rev to* sun’; *Yale* sun;’ *Berg(6), Resp14*
19 passion’s sake, *Yale, Berg(6), Resp14*
20 forty-nine *Yale, Berg(6), Resp14*
21 child, *Yale, Berg(6), Resp14* book, *Yale, Berg(6), Resp14*
22 mine. *Yale, Berg(6), Resp14*
22/ *date added in ink probably in Yeats’s hand Yale* January, 1914. *Berg(6), Resp14*

ABY(2) has an undated and unsigned query, written, probably by George Yeats, in black ink on a scrap of paper torn from the back of an envelope and now loosely inserted at pp. 240–241 (“In Memory of Major Robert Gregory”). The query refers to “[Pardon, old fathers],” ll. 9–12, where Yeats made an autograph revision. The query reads: “Do you make out that Butler has changed his allegiance in the last version of the poem on Ancestors. It is not quite clear.”

18 In the Yale marked proofs the printed comma at the end of the line is obscured by the ink revision mark and might be a period.

[NLI 13,586(1), 1]

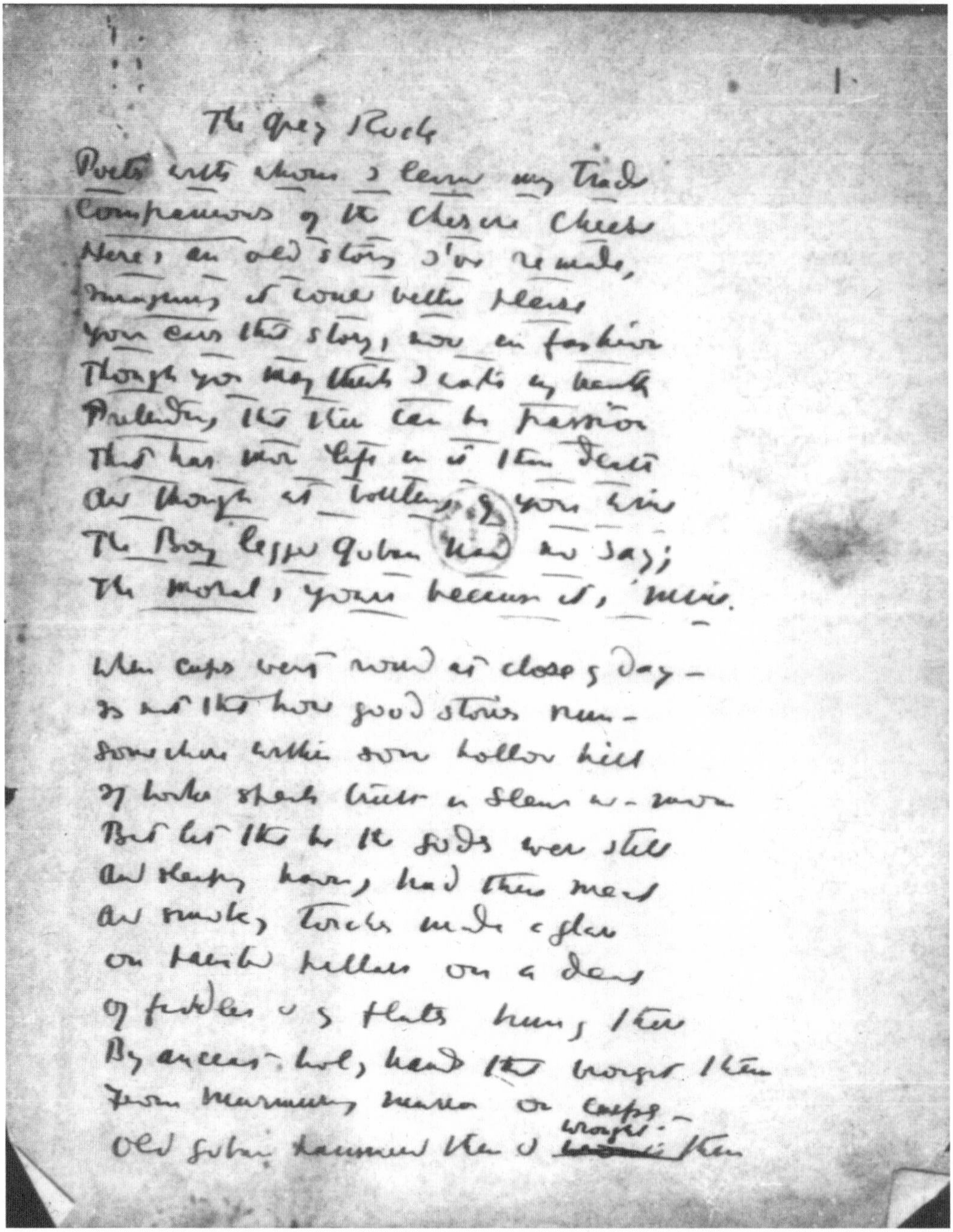

THE GREY ROCK

[NLI 13,586(1), 1]

1.

The Grey Rock

Poets with whom I learned my trade
Companions of the Cheshire Cheese
Here s an old story I've remade,
Imagining it would better please
Your ears that story s now in fashion
Though you may think I waste my breath
Pretending that there can be passion
That has more life in it than death
And though at bottling of your wine
The Bow legged Goban had no say;
The moral s yours because it s mine.

When cups went round at close of day —
Is not that how good stories run —
Somewhere within some hollow hill
If books speak truth in Slieve na–mon
But let that be the gods were still
And sleepy having had their meal
And smoky torches make a glare
On painted pillars on a deal
Of fiddles & of fl utes hung there
By the ancient holy hands that brought them
From murmuring Murias on cups —
wrought
~~wrou~~
Old Goban hammered them & { gilt them

---

found in NLI 13,586(1) *transcribed above and below*
NLI 8760(18) *transcribed below*
Berg(1) *transcribed below*
Berg(2) *transcribed below*
Princeton(1)
Chicago(1)
Yale
ABY(7)
ABY(3)
ABY(4)
NLI 30,009
NLI 30,262
published in *The British Review* (London), April 1913
Poetry (Chicago), April 1913
Resp14

[NLI 13,586(1), 2]

[NLI 13,586(1), 2]

2.

And put his pattern round their tops
To hold the wine they buy of him
But from the juice that made them wise
All those had lifted up the dim
Imaginations of their eyes
For one that was like woman made
Before their sleepy eye–lids ran
And trembling with her passion said
'Come out & dig for a dead man
Who's burrowing somewhere in the ground
And mock him to his face & then
Hollo him on with horse & hound
For he is the worst of all dead men.

We should be dazed & terror struck
If we but saw in dreams that room
Those wine drenched eyes & curse our luck
That emptied all our days to come.
I knew a woman none could please
Because she dreamed when but a child
Of men & women made like these
And after when her blood ran wild
Had ravelled her own story out
And said "In two or in three years

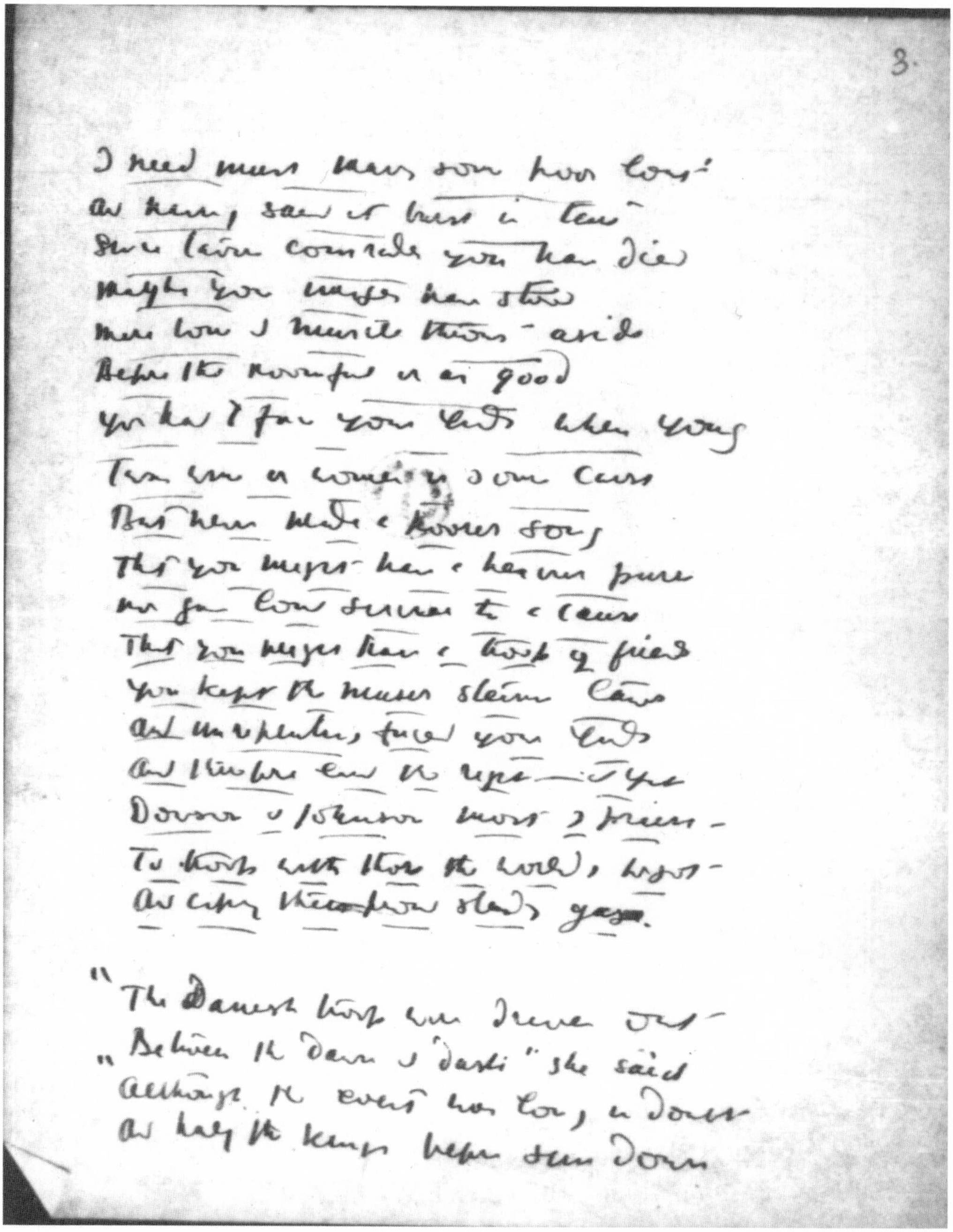

[NLI 13,586(1), 3]

3.

I need must marry some poor lout'
And having said it burst in tears
Since tavern comrades you have died
Maybe your images have stood
Mere bone & muscle thrown aside
Before that roomful or as good
You had to face your ends when young
Twas wine or women or some curse
But never made a poorer song
That you might have a heavier purse
Nor gave loud service to a cause
That you might have a troop of friends
You kept the Muses sterner laws
And unrepenting faced your ends
And therefore earned the right — & yet
Dowson & Johnson most I praise —
To troop with those the world s forgot
And copy their proud steady gase.

"The {D danish troop was driven out
Between the dawn & dusk" she said
"Although the event was long in doubt
Although the Kings before sun down

51 The mark following "thrown" on the manuscript is very probably a stray mark or part of the underscoring of l. 50.

[NLI 13,586(1), 4]

[NLI 13,586(1), 4]

4

All was accomplished”
                    “When this day
Murrough, the King of Irelands son
Foot after foot was giving way

[NLI 8760(18), 5r]

[NLI 8760(18), 5r]

Down by the sea the Irish men
[?Have] fought a great battle [?with] [?the] [?dane]
& the kite
[?Even] [?had [?the [?raven [?all] cry out
Along the edge of the sea. The [?] [?]
[?] [?] [?in [?the] middle of the battle
[?] [?] [?] [?] [?giving] [?way [?where]
[?Murragh] the King of Ireland [?son] [?led] [?that]
When he saw the Danes falling under the
blows of a [?hand] [?he] could [?not] see. & [?then] fell [?back]
He cried out who are you that fight
[?] [?of] [?magic] [?art]. The voice of that
hidden man [?replied] [?of] [?air] your
friend [?come] to fight at your side
~~[?from] [?the] side of my [?] [?] [?] [?]~~
[?Murragh] the King of Ireland son replied
'[?will] [?but] [?] [?of] [?for] [?my] [?friend] [?] [?it] [?is]
[?Again] [?on] [?] to [?find] [?invisible]'

[NLI 8760(18), 5^{v}]

[NLI 8760(18), 5^{v}]

[?the] [?Gael] [?&] [?Gael] has [?met] [?] fight
Even [?now] [?raven] & [?kite]
are [?bearing] [?the] dead – at first
M the King of Ireland son was [?] [?]
~~Wounded~~ & bled [?from] his wound when
suddenly he saw the danes [?falling] below him
~~& above [?the] [?blow~~]
& [?heart] one cry out his battle cry
Soon he [?stood] [?alone] & said
I heard the cry of [?Develan] that was
once my friend, & [?but] [?had] not [?seen] [?him]
[?Then] [?Develan] before him stood & said
I will have no [?safety] [?that] of kings son
[?] [?] [?], & [?] I [?] [?my] [?] [?]
[?] [?] – that Aoife gave me
who I left the great rock & her [?love]
Two hundred she has promised me
That I might fight beside [?].
Then [?Murragh] answered.

[NLI 8760(18), 6[r]]

[NLI 8760(18), 6^{r}]

Then [?Murragh] answered
For dreams come [?] You or I
[?] [?] [?] – & in that fight they died
[?]
There was [?] he had [?] [?if] hour [?] [?] [?]
[?rock] for all of [?] – I [?who]
had gone to him [?of] [?dream] [?body] –
happier men beyond [?] in the middle
of the Sacred Hill but to [?] left [?is] & that
[?] [?] [?] [?] [?] [?above] [?] [?ghost].
[?and] all [?her] body shook [?with] sobs – [?~~but~~]
~~the more holy ones [?] [?up] &~~
& she cast herself upon the ground,
Then [?] one arose, [?] one says
'ever do men betray the godsí & cast
upon her the wine out of the cups – [?]
The [?] [?load] of the holy wine [?she] [?ran]
[?] [?] [?forgot] [?all].

[NLI 8760(18), 6^v]

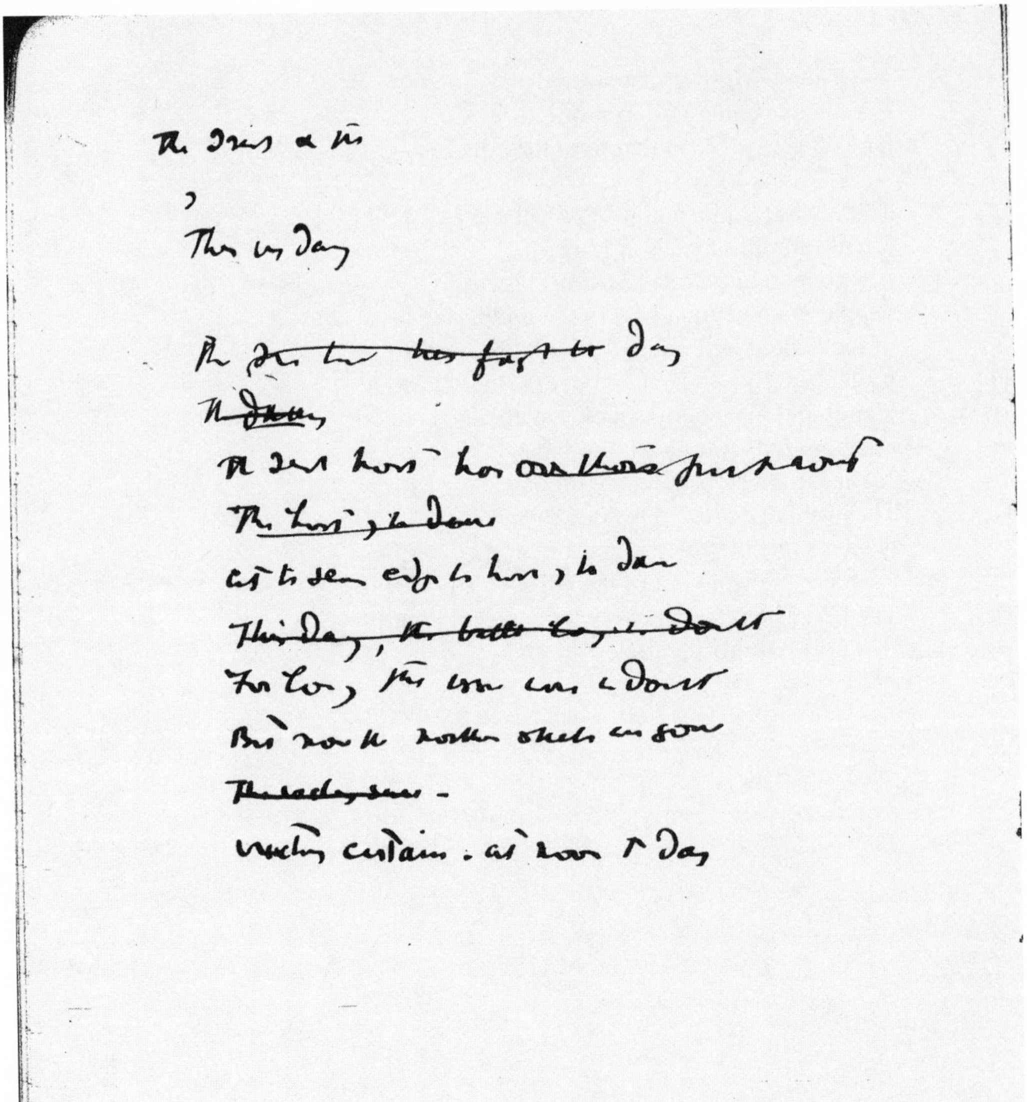

[NLI 8760(18), 6^{v}]

The Irish & the
I
This very day

The ~~Irish [?host] has fought [?the]~~ day
~~[?The] [?Danes]~~
The Irish host has ~~over [?thrown]~~ [?]
~~The host of the Danes~~
At [?the] [?seas] edge the [?host] of the [?danes]
~~This day, the battle [?lay] in doubt~~
For long the issue was in doubt
But now the [?northern] [?] [?are] gone
~~The [?] [?sure]~~ –
Victory certain at [?noon] today

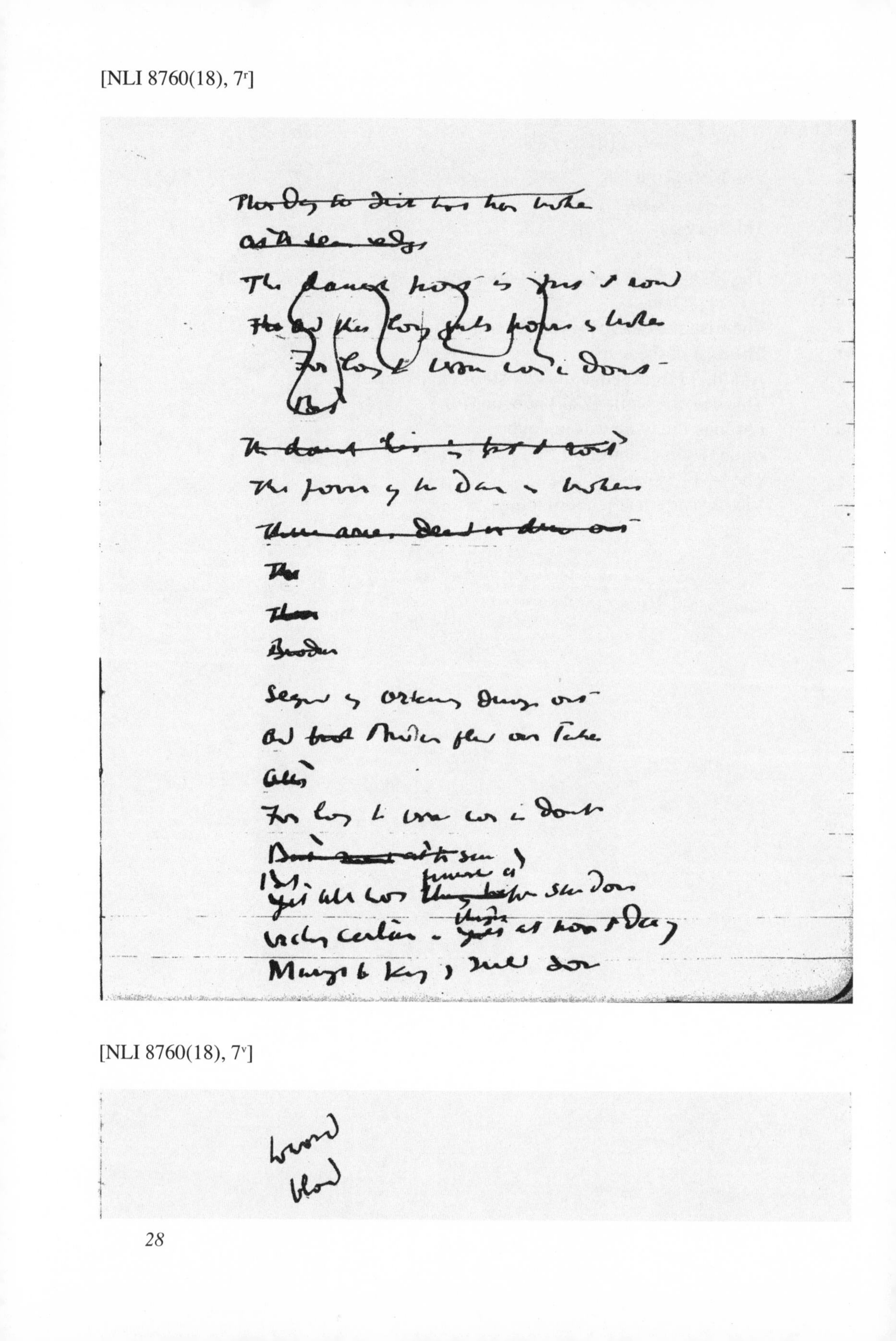

[NLI 8760(18), 7r]

[NLI 8760(18), 7v]

[NLI 8760(18), 7r]

1 ~~This day the Irish host has [?broken]~~
2 ~~At the seas edge~~
3 The danish host is put to rout
4 The and [?their] long [?] power [?is] [?broken]
5 For long the issue was in doubt
6 But
7 ~~The [?danish] [?host] is put to rout~~
8 ~~The power of the Danes is broken~~
9 [?There] [?], dead [?or] [?driven] out
10 ~~The~~
11 [~~?There~~]
12 [~~?Broken~~]
13 [?] of [?Orkney] [?driving] out
14 And [~~?~~] [?] fl ed [?our] [?]
15 ~~Altho~~
16 For long the issue was in doubt
17 ~~But [?now] at the~~ sun
But finished at
18 ~~Yet~~ all was ~~through before~~ sun down
though
19 Victory certain – ~~yet~~ at [?noon] [?today]
20 [?Murragh] the King of Ireland son

[NLI 8760(18), 7v]

1 [?]
2 blood

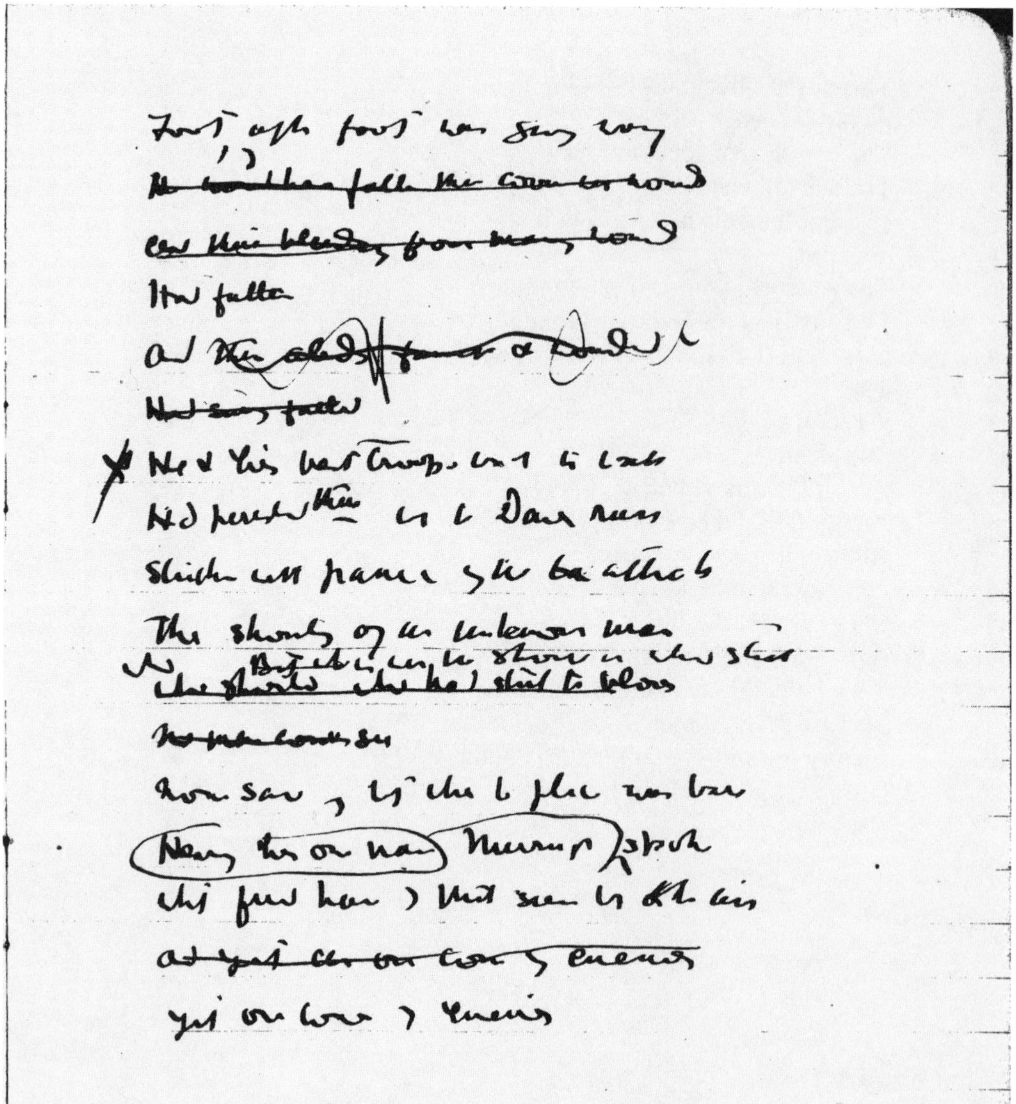

[NLI 8760(18), 8r]

Foot after foot was giving way
[?]
~~He [?would] [?have] fallen [?then] [?cover] [?] [?wounds]~~
~~And [?then] bleeding from many wounds~~
Had ~~fallen~~
And ~~then [?] [?] & wounded~~ [?]
~~Had [?surely] [?failed]~~
~~X~~ He & his best troops, [?] [?] [?]
there
[?Had] perished – but [?the] Danes ran
Stricken with panic by [?the] [?ba] attack
The shouting of an unknown man
[?Who] ~~But [?who]~~ [?it] was [?had] shouted [?] who [?struck]
~~Who shouted who had [?struck [?the] blows~~
~~No man could~~ see
None saw [?] but [?when] [?the] place was bare
(Hearing his own [?name]) [?Murragh] spoke
What friend have I that seems [?of] ~~& [?to]~~ air
~~And yet can over come my enemies~~
Yet over come my enemies

[Berg(1), 1r (not inverted)]

Poets with whom I learned my trade
Companions of the Cheshire Cheese
Here's an old story I've remade
Imagining 'twould better please
Your ears than stories now in fashion.
Though you may think I waste my breath
Pretending that there can be passion
That has more life in it than death
Though at the bottling of your wine
The bow-legged Goban had to say
The moral's yours because it's mine.

When cups went round at close of day
~~[illegible]~~
Is that not how good stories run
Somewhere within some hollow hill
If books speak truth in
Slieve na mon
But let that be
The gods were still
And sleeping
having had their meal
And smoky
torches made a glare
On peaceful pillows
on a deal

[Berg(1), 1r (not inverted)]

Poets with whom I learned my trade
Companions of the Cheshire Cheese
Heres an old story I have remade
Imagining it would better please
Your ears than stories now in fashion
Though you may think I waste my breath
Pretending that there can be passion
That has more life in it than death
And though at bottling of your wine
The bow legged Goban had no say
The morals yours because its mine.
When cups went round at close of day
~~When wine [?] [?was]~~
Is that not how good stories run
Some where within some hollow hill
If books speak truth in Slieve na mon
But let that be The gods were still
And sleepy having had their meal
And [~~?~~] smoky torches made a glare
On painted pillars [?and] [?a] deal

Only this first sheet and the last one are are not inverted. All of the sheets, as written upon, have the binder holes at the left, but only the first and the last sheet have the printed top margin red double-rule at the top of the page as written upon.

[Berg (1), 2r (inverted)]

[Berg (1), 2^{r} (inverted)]

[?~~of~~]
of old stringed instruments hung there
~~Since~~
~~By holy fingers that~~
the
By∧ancient holy holy hands that brought them
From murmuring, [~~?G~~] Murias, on cups —
It was old hammer
The [?crafty] bow legged Goban∧wrought them
And put pattern round the tops
To hold the wine they buy of him.

Suddenly these gods raised their eyes
With memory & forknowledge dim
From the strong juice that makes them wise
For one that was like woman made
But from the juice that made them wise
For one that was like woman made
Before their sleepy eyelids ran
And trembling with her passion said
‘ Come out & dig for a dead man
Who's burrowing somewhere in the ground
And mock him to his face & then
Hollow him on with horse & hound
For he is the worst of all dead men'
We should be dazed & terror struck

we but saw in dreams
If ~~dreams could show to~~ us that room
And those fierce eyes & curse our luck
That emptied all our days to come

Because of this manuscript's complexity, the line numbering here is page-by-page rather than continuous.

5 On the facing page, 1^{v} (inverted), Yeats wrote the replacement for this canceled passage, with a bracket and insertion arrow to here:

Old Goban hammered , ~~them [?&]~~ [?wro]
them & wrought them
And put his pattern round their tops

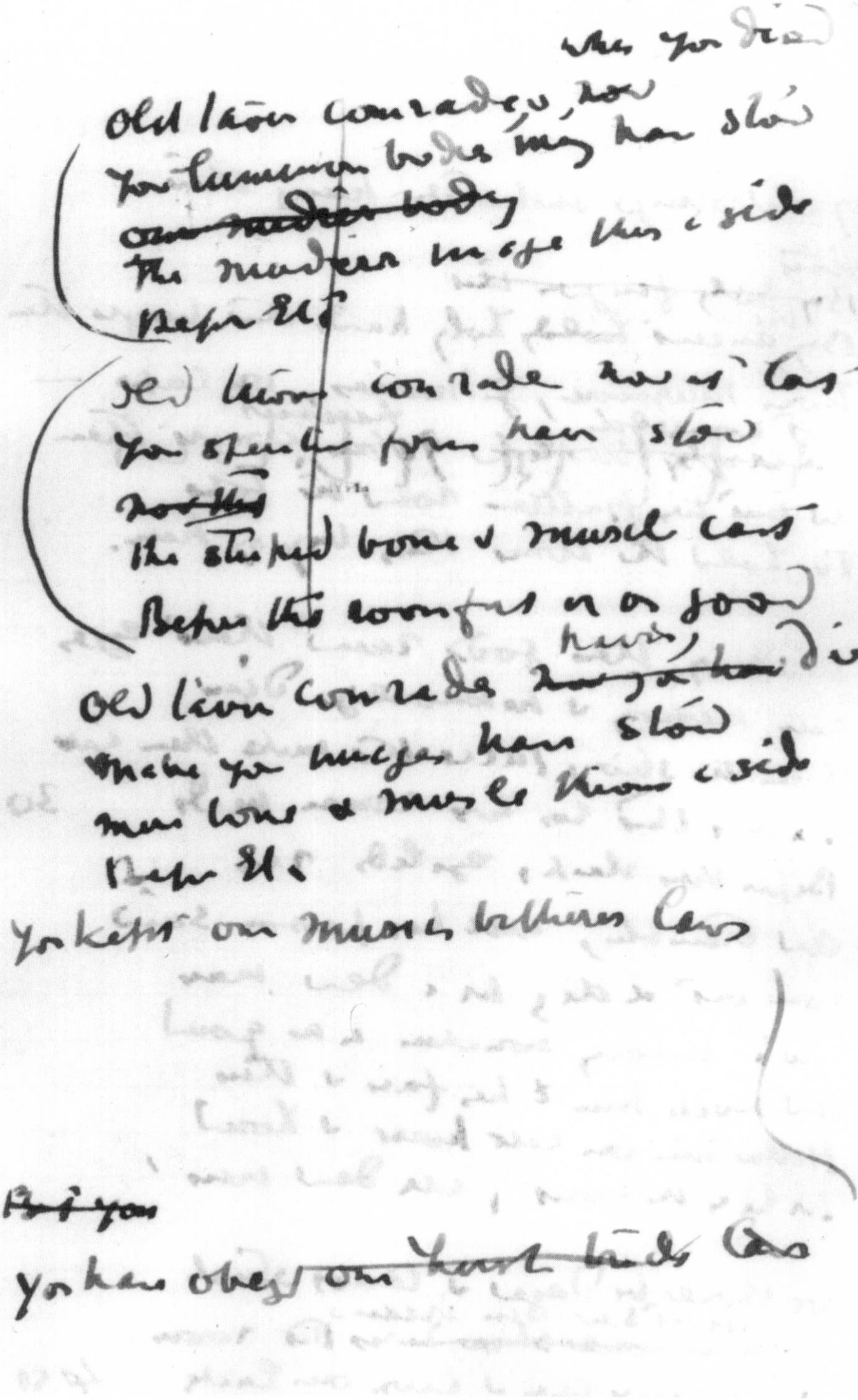

[Berg (1), 2v (inverted)]

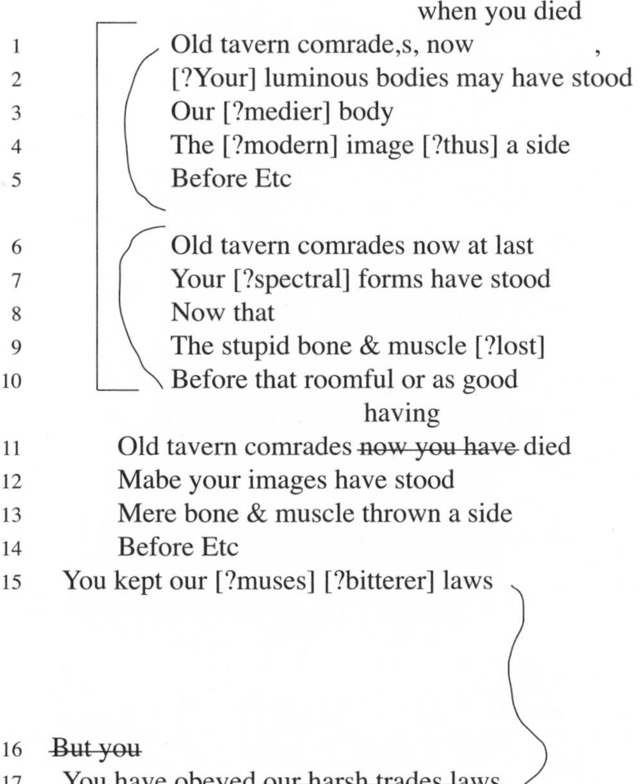

when you died
Old tavern comrade,s, now ,
[?Your] luminous bodies may have stood
Our [?medier] body
The [?modern] image [?thus] a side
Before Etc

Old tavern comrades now at last
Your [?spectral] forms have stood
Now that
The stupid bone & muscle [?lost]
Before that roomful or as good
having
Old tavern comrades ~~now you have~~ died
Mabe your images have stood
Mere bone & muscle thrown a side
Before Etc
You kept our [?muses] [?bitterer] laws

~~But you~~
You have obeyed ~~our harsh trades laws~~

Inserts for its facing page, 3r (inverted), ll. 16–18.
Because of this manuscript's complexity, the line numbering here is page-by-page rather than continuous.

[Berg (1), 3r (inverted)]

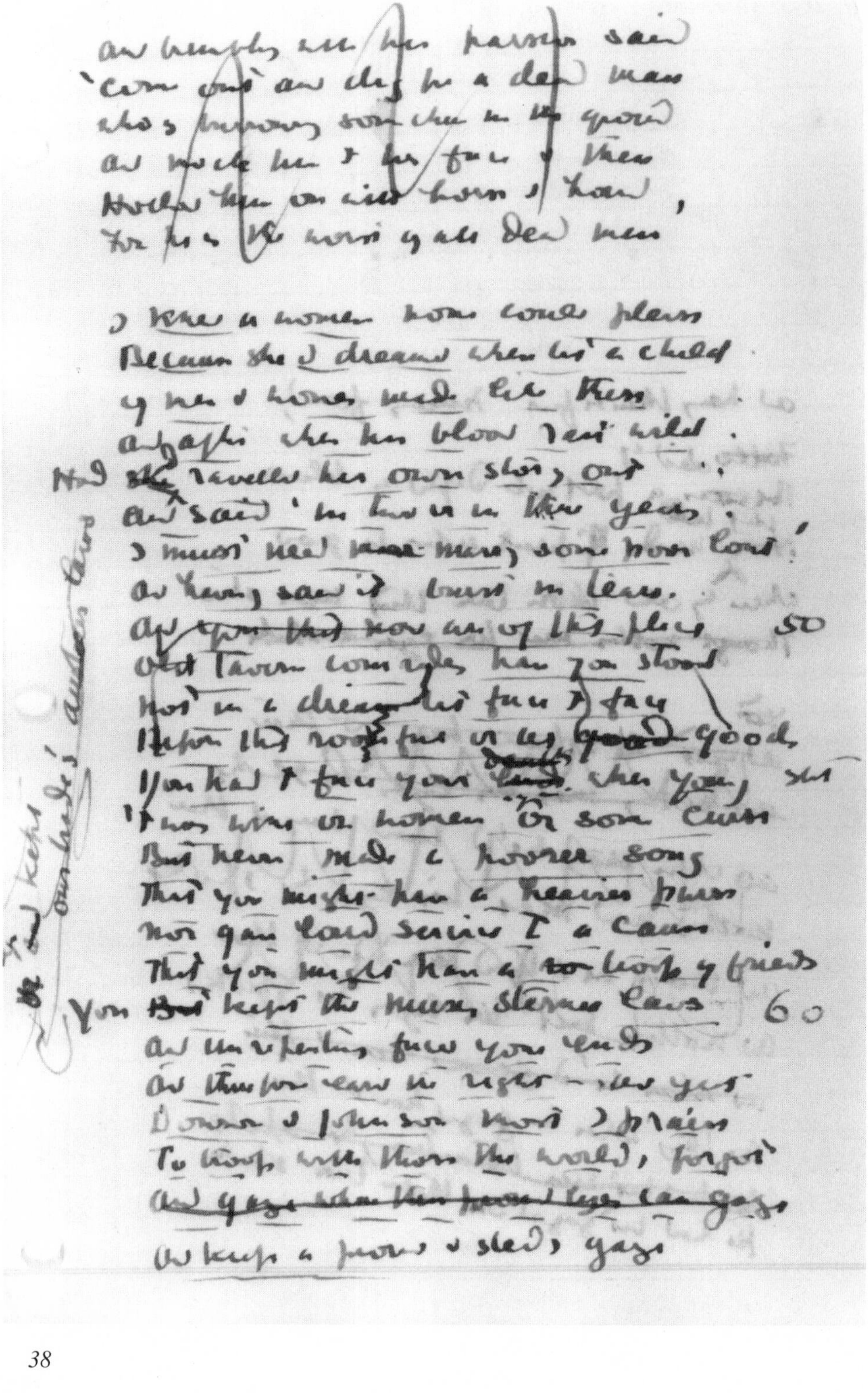

[Berg (1), 3r (inverted)]

And trembling with her passion said
‘ Come out and dig for a dead man
Who s burrowing some where in the ground
And mock him to his face & them
Hollow him on with horse & horn
For he is the worst of all dead men’

I knew a woman none could please
Because she dreamed when but a child
Of men & women made like these
And after when her blood ran wild
Had ~~She~~ ravelled her own story out
And said ‘In two or in three years
I must need [?] marry some poor lout’
And having said it burst in tears.
And you that now are of that place
Old tavern comrades have you stood
Not in a dream but face to face
Before that roomful or as ~~good~~ good
[~~?deaths~~]
You had to face your ends when young stet
‘ Twas wine or women or some curse
But never made a poorer song
That you might have a heavier purse
Nor gave loud service to a cause
That you might have a ~~ro~~ troop of friends
You ~~But~~ kept the muses sterner laws
And unrepenting faced your ends
And therefore earned the right — and yet
Dowson and Johnson most I praise
To troop with those the world s forgot,
And gaze where their proud eyes can gaze
And keep a proud & stedy gaze

[?Y] or And kept our trade’s austerer laws

Because of this manuscript’s complexity, the line numbering here is page-by-page rather than continuous.

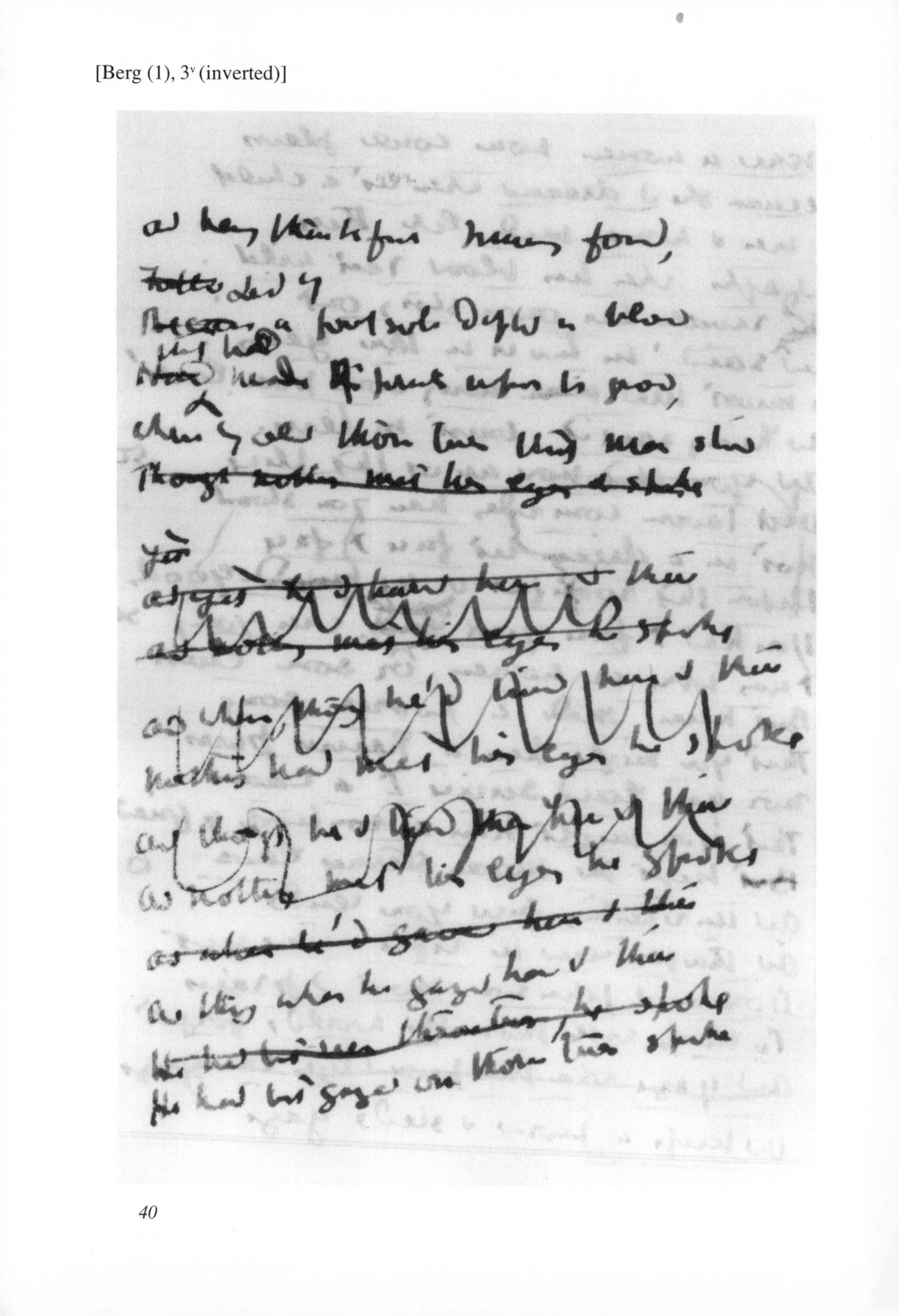

[Berg (1), 3v (inverted)]

[Berg (1), 3^{v} (inverted)]

And being thankful Murrough found,
[~~?~~] Led by
~~Because~~ a footsole dipped in blood
That ^had
~~Had~~ made ~~its~~ prints upon the ground,
Where by old thorn trees that man stood
~~Though nothing met his eyes & spake~~

~~Yet~~
And yet he [?] turned here & there
as nothing met his eyes he spake
And when, though he'd turned here & there
Nothing had met his eyes he spoke
And though he d turned then here [?&] there
As nothing met his eyes he spoke
And when he'd [?gased] here & there
And though when he gazed here & there
~~He had but seen thorn trees, he spoke~~
He had but gazed on thorn trees spoke

Inserts for its facing page, 4^{r} (inverted), ll. 16–20.
Because of this manuscript's complexity, the line numbering here is page-by-page rather than continuous.

[Berg (1), 4ʳ (inverted)]

[Berg (1), 4r (inverted)]

~~From Clontarf strand this day she said~~
~~The Danish host was driven out~~
~~Though the even was long"~~
troop
' The Danish ~~host~~ was driven out
Between the dawn & dusk
~~From Clontarf strand this day~~' she said
' [?Altho] the event was long in doubt
[?Altho] the king of Irelands dead
before
And half his [?kings], ~~at the~~ sundown
All was accomplished — When this day
Murrough the king of Irelands son
Foot after foot was giving way
He & his best troops back to back
Had perished there but the Danes ran
~~was being slacked~~
When the fight slacked
The [?charge] being finished
Stricken with panic from the attack
The shouting of an unseen man.
When they had left [?him] Murrough found
When by old thorn trees that man stood
He [?] followed prints upon the ground
Made by a foot sole dipped in blood
But though he turned him here & there
He [?saw] no footsole [?therefore] spoke
' Who is the friend that seems but air
And yet could give so fine a stroke'

Because of this manuscript's complexity, the line numbering here is page-by-page rather than continuous.

[Berg (1), 4v (inverted)]

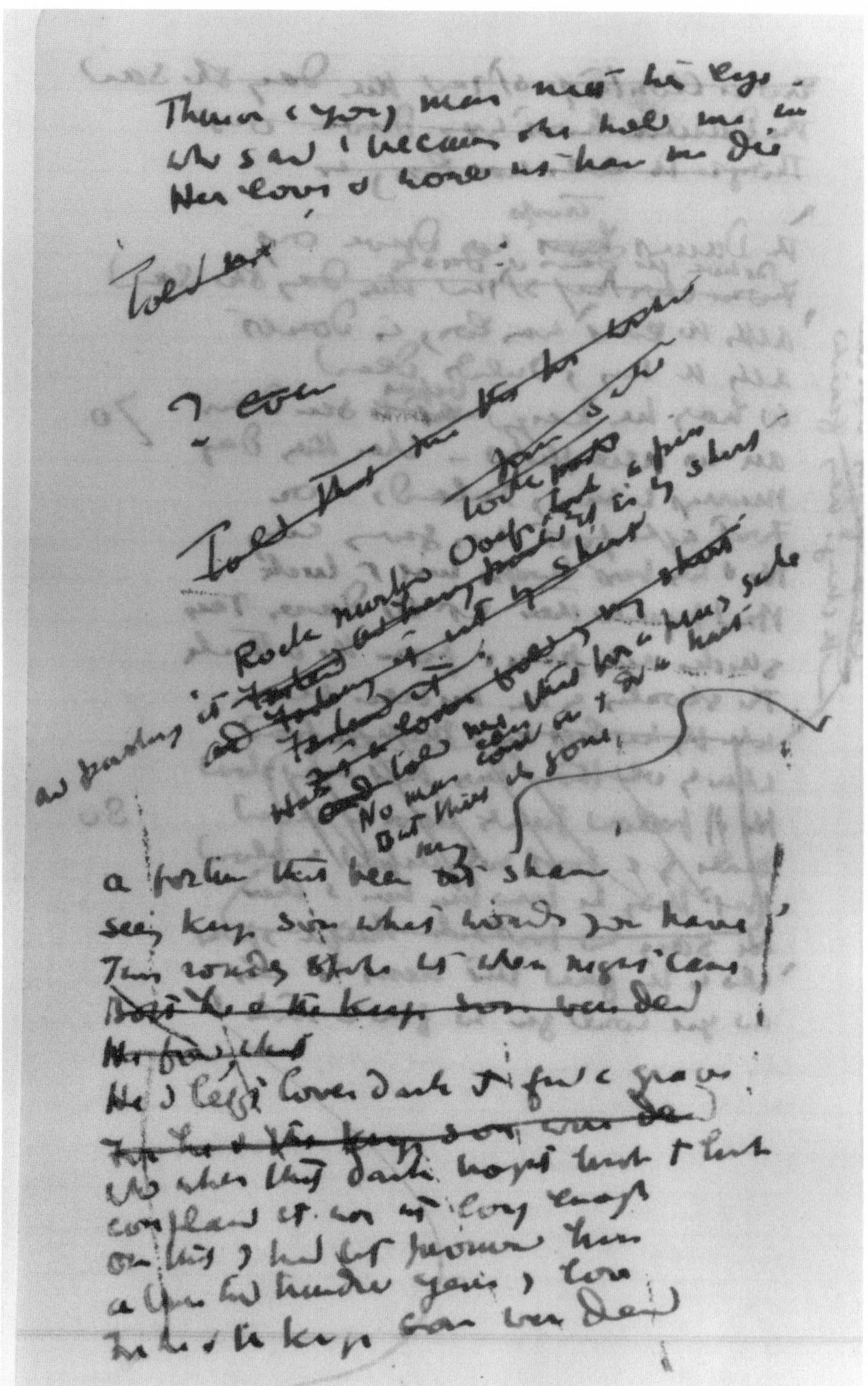

[Berg (1), 4ᵛ (inverted)]

Thereon a young man met his eye
Who said 'because she hold me in
Her love & would not have me die

'~~Told me~~'

? ~~even~~

~~Told that [?] that [?] [?]~~

~~from [?]~~
took [?~~pin~~]
Rock nurtured Ooefe ~~took~~ a pin
And pushing it ~~Fastened And having pushed~~ it in my shirt
~~And Fastening it into my shirt~~
~~Fastened it~~
~~Into a lower fold of my shirt~~
Has ~~And~~ told me that for a pin s sake
can
No man ~~could~~ see to do me hurt
But there its gone

my
A fortune that had been ~~but~~ shame
Seeing Kings son what wounds you have'
[?This] roundly spoke but when night came
~~Both he & the Kings son were dead~~
~~He found [?what]~~
He d left [?lower] dark to find a grave
~~For he & the Kings son were dead~~
Who when that dark [?brought] back [?at] [?last]
Complained it was not long enough
[?Oh] that I had [?but] [?power] [?here]
A [?twice] two hundred years of love
For he & the Kings son were dead

Inserts for its facing page, 5ʳ (inverted), ll. 14–25, together with ll. 7–13.
Because of this manuscript's complexity, the line numbering here is page-by-page rather than continuous.

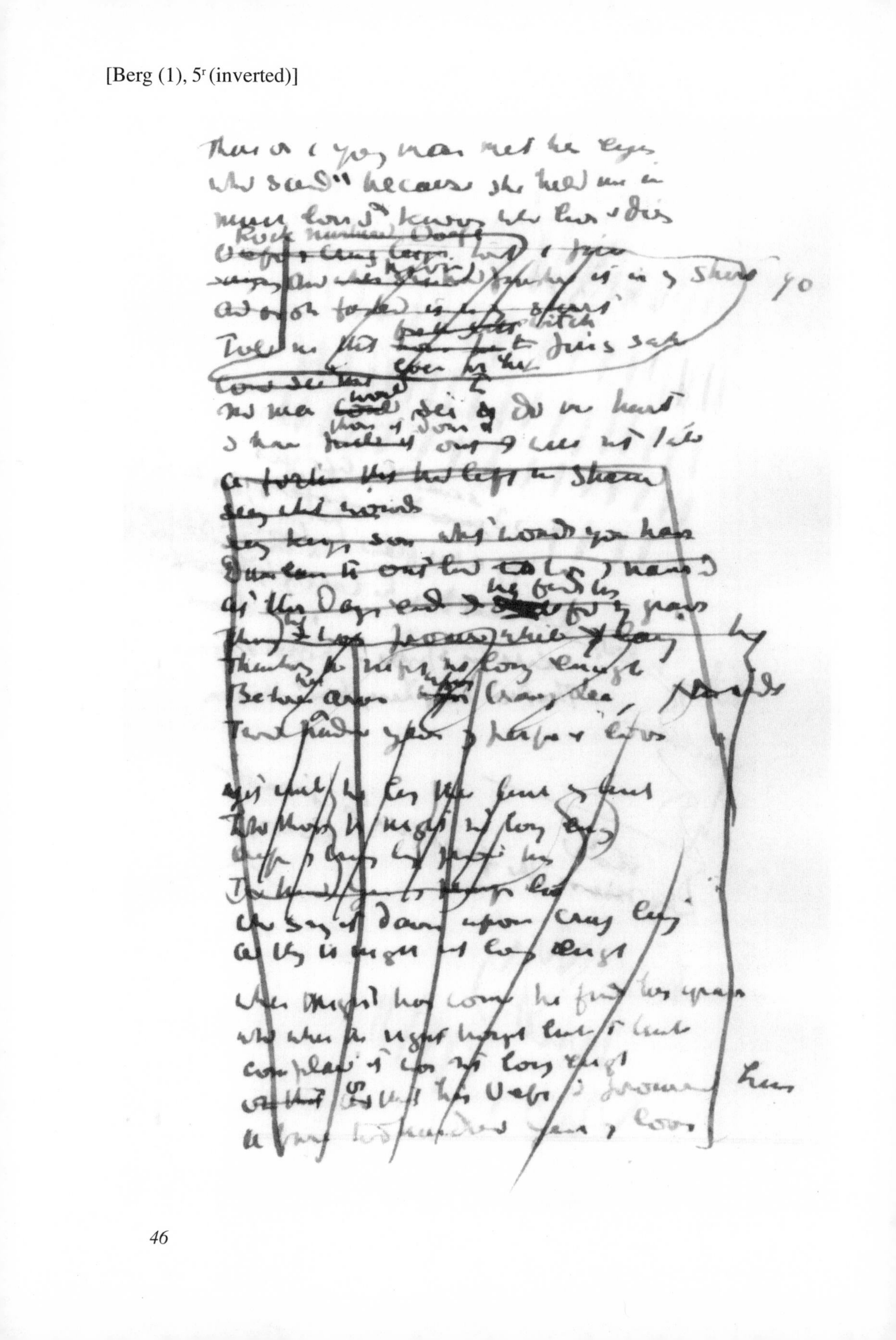

[Berg (1), 5^r (inverted)]

[Berg (1), 5r (inverted)]

There on a young man met his eyes
Who said "because she held me in
Much love [?&] [~~?~~] knows who lives & dies
    Rock nurtured Ooefe
~~Oefe [?   ?   ?]~~ took a pin
                having
~~Saying~~ And ~~when she had~~ pushed it in my shirt
~~And [?so]~~ [?she] ~~[?folded] it in my shirt~~
~~for the [?] witch~~
Told me that ~~now for the~~ pin's sake
            ever for her
~~Could see me~~
        would   to
No man ~~could~~ see [~~?me~~] do me hurt
        [?thrown] it down &
I have ~~picked it out~~ I will not take
A fortune that had left me shame
Seeing what wounds
Seeing Kings son what wounds you have
[?Develan] the outlaw [?that] [?was] [?] [?name]'
                he find his
At this days end ~~I [?shall]~~ find my grave
    [?he]
[?Thus] ~~I~~ [?] [?Powers] [?while] I [?lay]
Thinking [?the] [?night] [?not] long enough
        [?her] [?]
[?Believes]‸[?] [~~?~~] [?Crag] [?Lea], [?in] [?side]
Two hundred years of perfect love

Yet while he [?   ?   ?   ?   ?]
Who [?thought] the night not long enough
Ooefe [?] [?crying] [?long] [? ?]
[?   ?   ?   ?   ?   ?]
Who say at dawn upon [?Crag] [?]
And [?they] [?that] night not long [?enough]
When [?] [?has] come he [?find] [?   ?]
Who when the night [?brought] [?last] [?to] [?]
Complained it was not long enough
            Or
~~[?Oh] that And~~ that his Oefe [?] [?promised] [?him]
A [?] two hundred years of love

Because of this manuscript's complexity, the line numbering here is page-by-page rather than continuous.

[Berg (1), 5^{v} (inverted)]

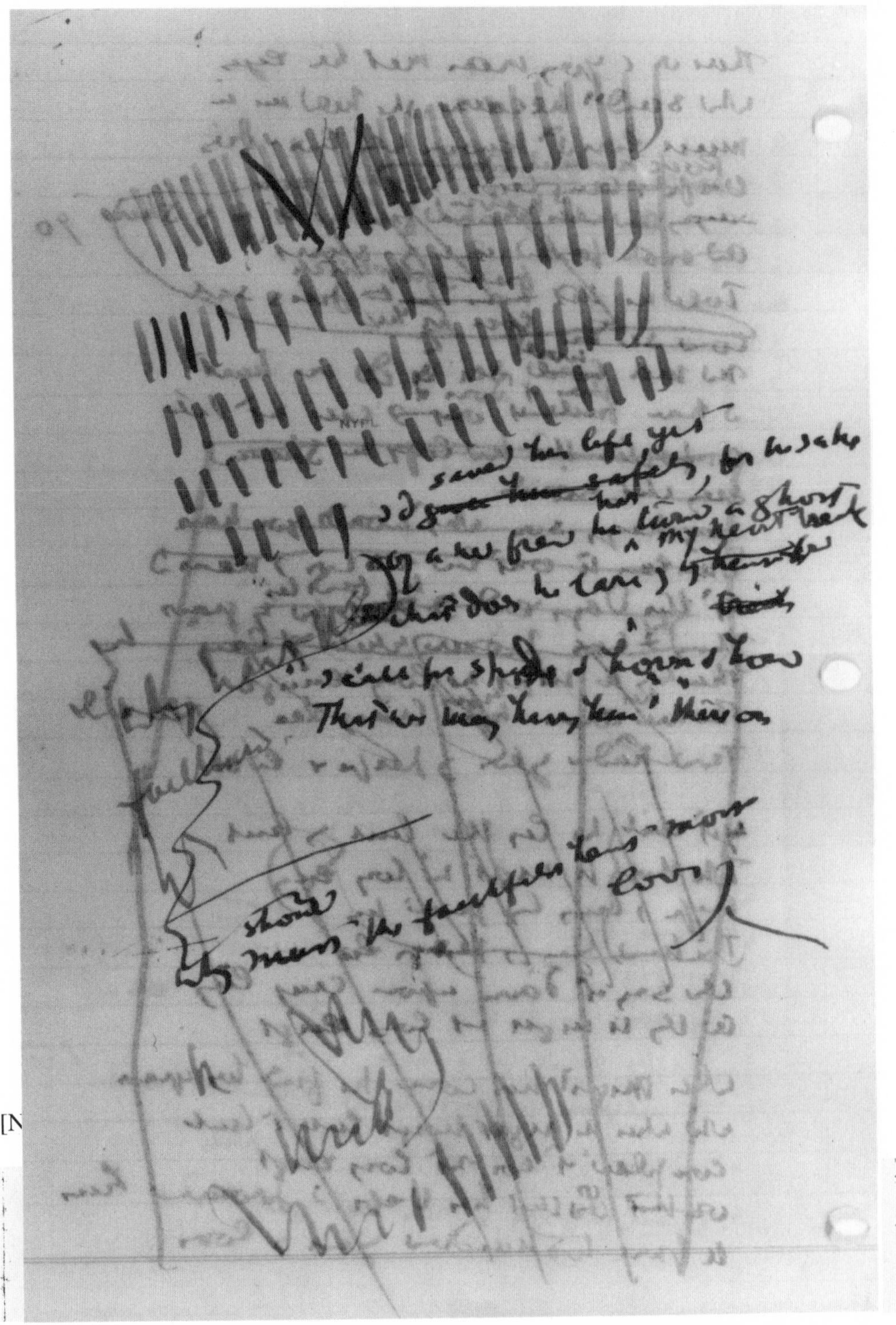

[N

[Berg (1), 5^v (inverted)]

saved his life yet
I d ~~gave~~ him safety, for the sake
has
of a new friend he ^ turned a ghost
my heart break
What does he care [?if] ~~[?my] [?heart] [?br]~~
[~~?break~~]
I call for spade & horse & hound
That we may harry him' There on

should
Why ~~must~~ the faithfulest heart most
love

~~Why [?have] this~~
[?] [?]
[?] [?]
h [?]
[?]
[?]

Inserts for its facing page, 6^r (inverted), ll. 8–13.

Because of this manuscript's complexity, the line numbering here is page-by-page rather than continuous.

1–6 The canceled passage, designated here as ll. 1–6 was written with a poorly inked pen nib, in the lower left portion of the page, but earlier than ll. 7–13.

11/12 The sloping horizontal rule separates ll. 7–11 from ll. 12–13.

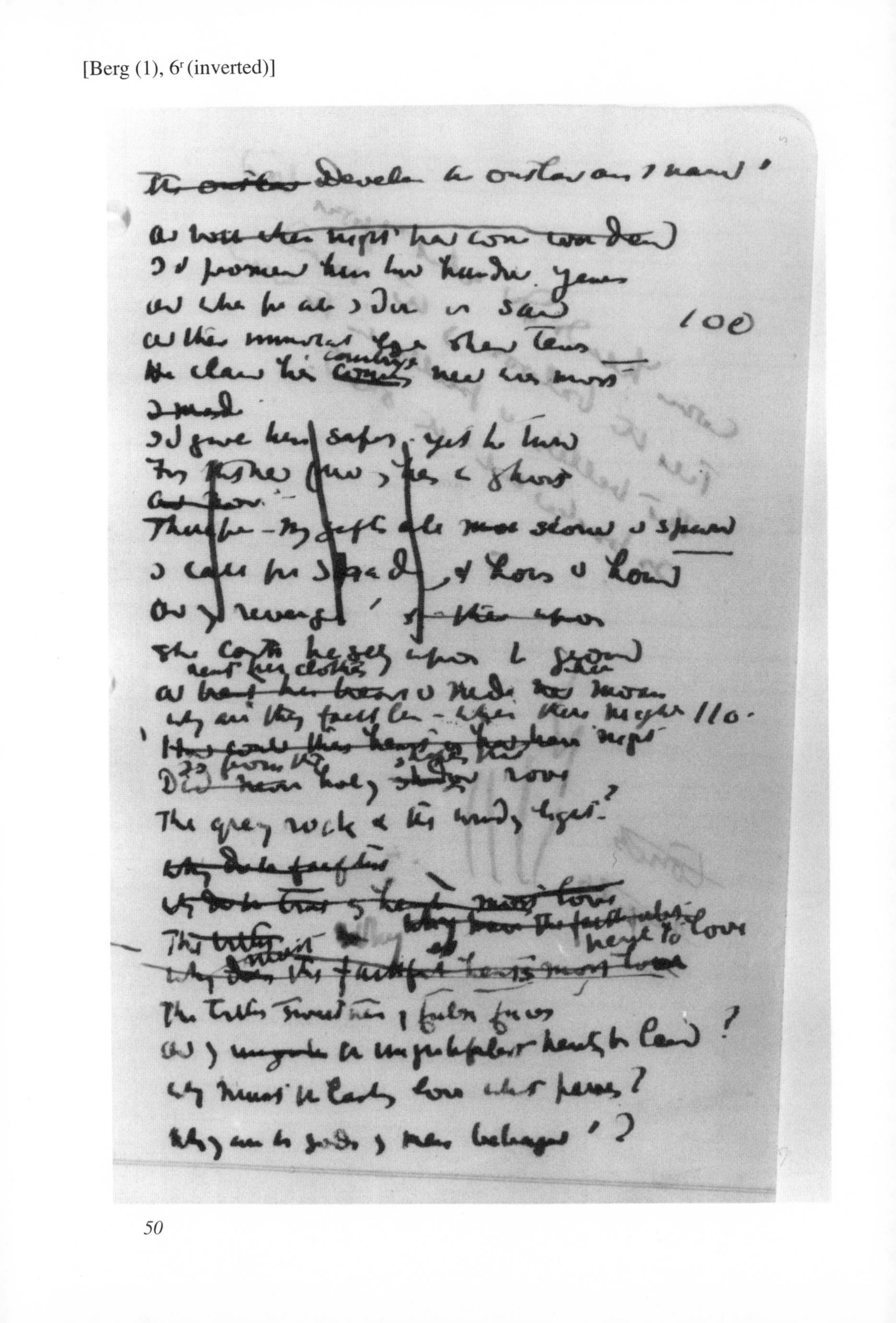

[Berg (1), 6r (inverted)]

[Berg (1), 6r (inverted)]

1 ~~The outlaw~~ [?Develan] the outlaw am I named'
2 And ~~both when night had come wondered~~
3 I'd promised him two hundred years
4 And when for all I done or said
5 And these immortal eyes shed tears —
countrys
6 He claimed his ~~counry~~ need was most
7 I ~~made~~
8 I d gave him safety yet he turned
9 [?From] that new friend[?,] hes [?a] ghost
10 ~~And now~~ —
11 Therefore — my gifts all [?] scorned & spurned
12 I call for [?Spade], & hourse & hound
13 And my revenge' [?&] ~~there upon~~
14 She [?casts] herself upon the ground
rent her clothes her
15 And ~~beat her breat~~ and made [~~?new~~] moan
Why are they faithless — when their might
16 '~~How could this heart [?or] [?had] [?have]~~ [?might]
Is from that shades that
17 ~~Did [?never]~~ holy ~~shadow~~ rove
18 The grey rock & the windy light?
19 ~~Why do the [?]~~
20 ~~Why do the true of heart most love~~
21 ~~The [?truly]~~ [~~?~~] Why ~~Why have the faithfulest~~
heart to love
~~must~~
22 ~~Why [?does] the faithful hearts most love~~
23 The bitter sweetness of false faces
24 And if [~~?~~] the ungratefulest [?hearts] be laid?
25 Why must the lasting love what passes?
26 Why are the gods by men betrayed'?

Because of this manuscript's complexity, the line numbering here is page-by-page rather than continuous.

9 "friend[?,] hes" could perhaps be "friend [?of] hes [*for* his]".

13 The revision from ll. 7–11 of the facing page, 5v (inverted), goes here.

22 This line has underscoring as though Yeats intended to write "stet" in the margin, but instead he then wrote out the insertion line on the facing page, 5v (inverted), with an insertion arrow to here.

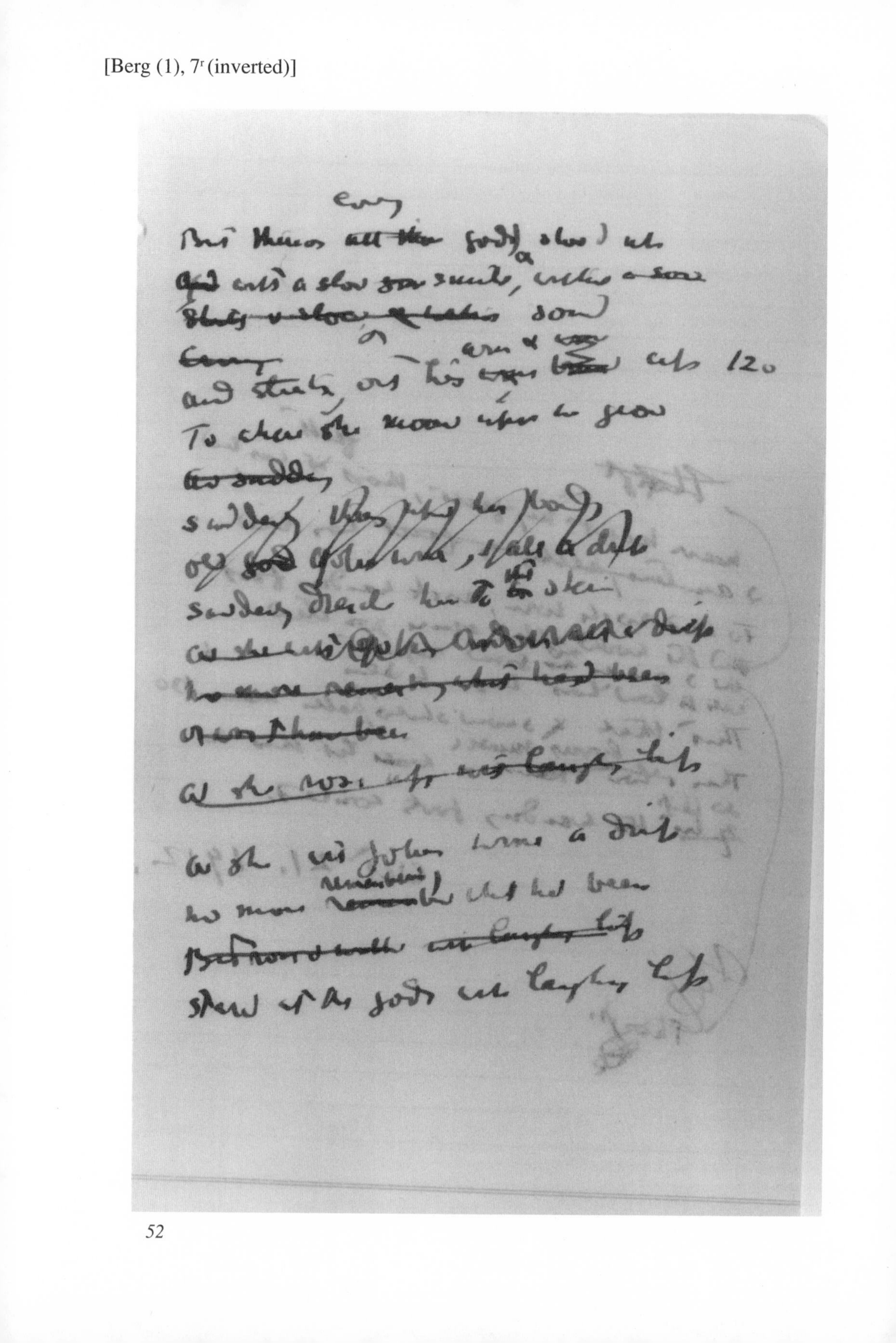

[Berg (1), 7r (inverted)]

[Berg (1), 7r (inverted)]

every
1 But thereon ~~all [?]~~ gods stood up
&
2 And with a slow [?] smile, without a [?sound]
3 ~~[?Stately] & slow~~, sound
[?or]
4 ~~[?Every]~~
arm & wine
5 And stretching out his ~~wine [?brimmed]~~ cup
6 To where she moaned upon the ground
7 ~~And [?suddenly]~~
8 Suddenly [?there] [?upon] her body
9 Old god Gobans wine, [?&] all a drip
that
10 Suddenly drenched her to ~~the~~ skin
11 ~~And she with [?Gobans] [?] all a drip~~
{d
12 ~~No more remembering what ha{s been~~
13 ~~Or was to have been~~
14 ~~And she rose up with laughing lip~~
15 And she with Gobans wine a drip
rememberring
16 No more ~~remembered~~ what had been
17 ~~But rose & [?] with laughing lip~~
18 Stared at the gods with laughing lip

Because of this manuscript's complexity, the line numbering here is page-by-page rather than continuous.
The facing page, 6v (inverted), has a draft of "The Balloon of the Mind"; transcribed in *The Wild Swans at Coole: Manuscript Materials*, ed. Stephen Parrish, Cornell Yeats series (Ithaca: Cornell University Press, 1994), p. 213.

[Berg (1), 7^v (inverted)]

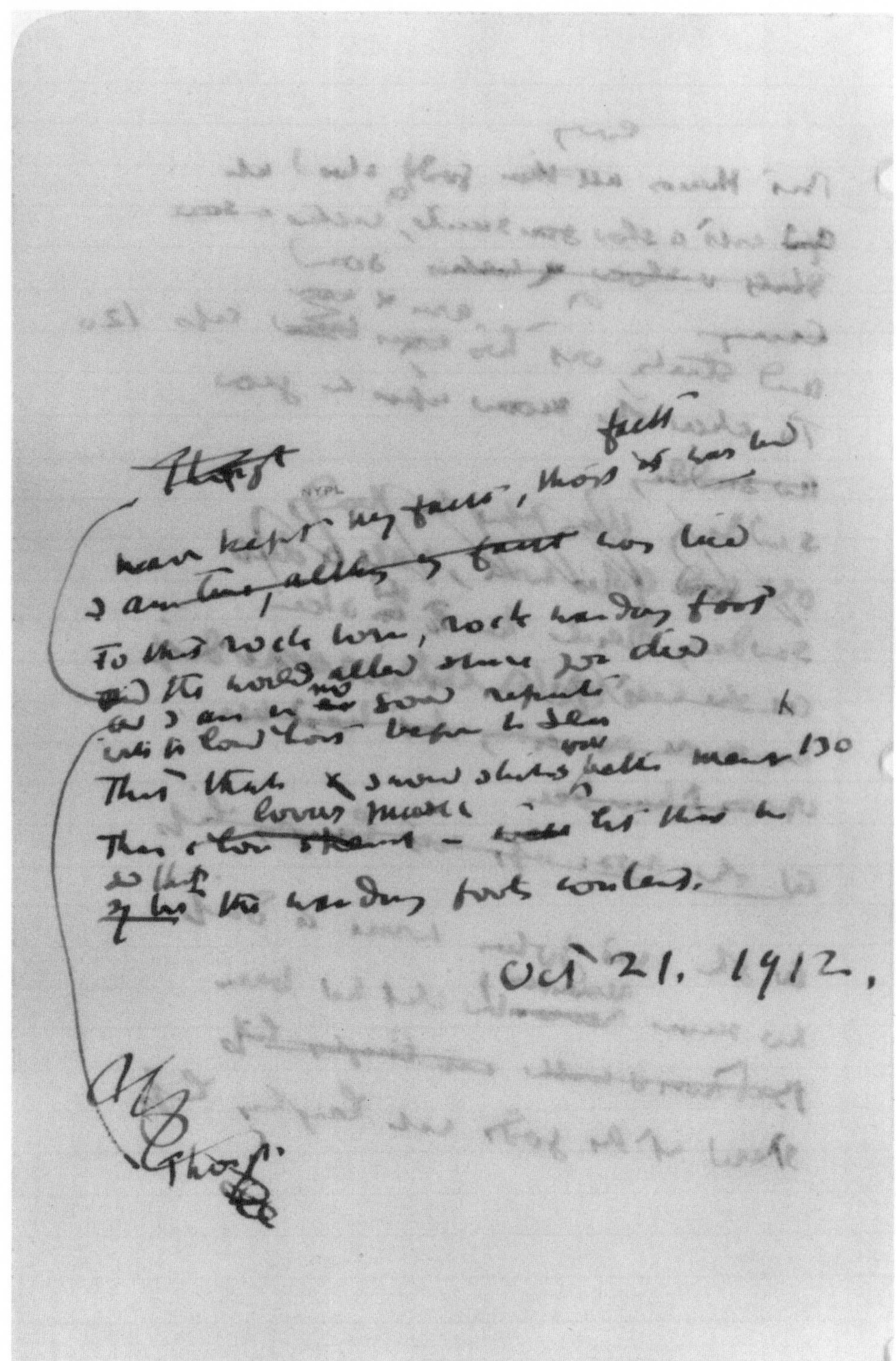

[Berg (1), 7v (inverted)]

1 ~~Though~~

faith

have kept my faith, though ~~it~~ was tried

2 I ~~am true, although my faith~~ was tried

3 To that rock born, rock wandering foot

4 And the worlds altered since you died

no

5 And I am in [~~?~~] good repute

6 With the loud host before the sea

s [?were]

7 That think a sword stroke{ ^better meant 130

lovers music

8 Than ~~a love [?]~~ — ~~well~~ let that be

So that

9 ~~If but~~ the wandering foots content.

Oct 21, 1912.

10 ~~Though~~

Two replacement passages for the canceled facing page, 8r.

Because of this manuscript's complexity, the line numbering here is page-by-page rather than continuous.

1 "~~Though~~" is a rejected replacement of "And" in l. 4.

10 "~~Though~~" is a rejected replacement of "And" in l. 5.

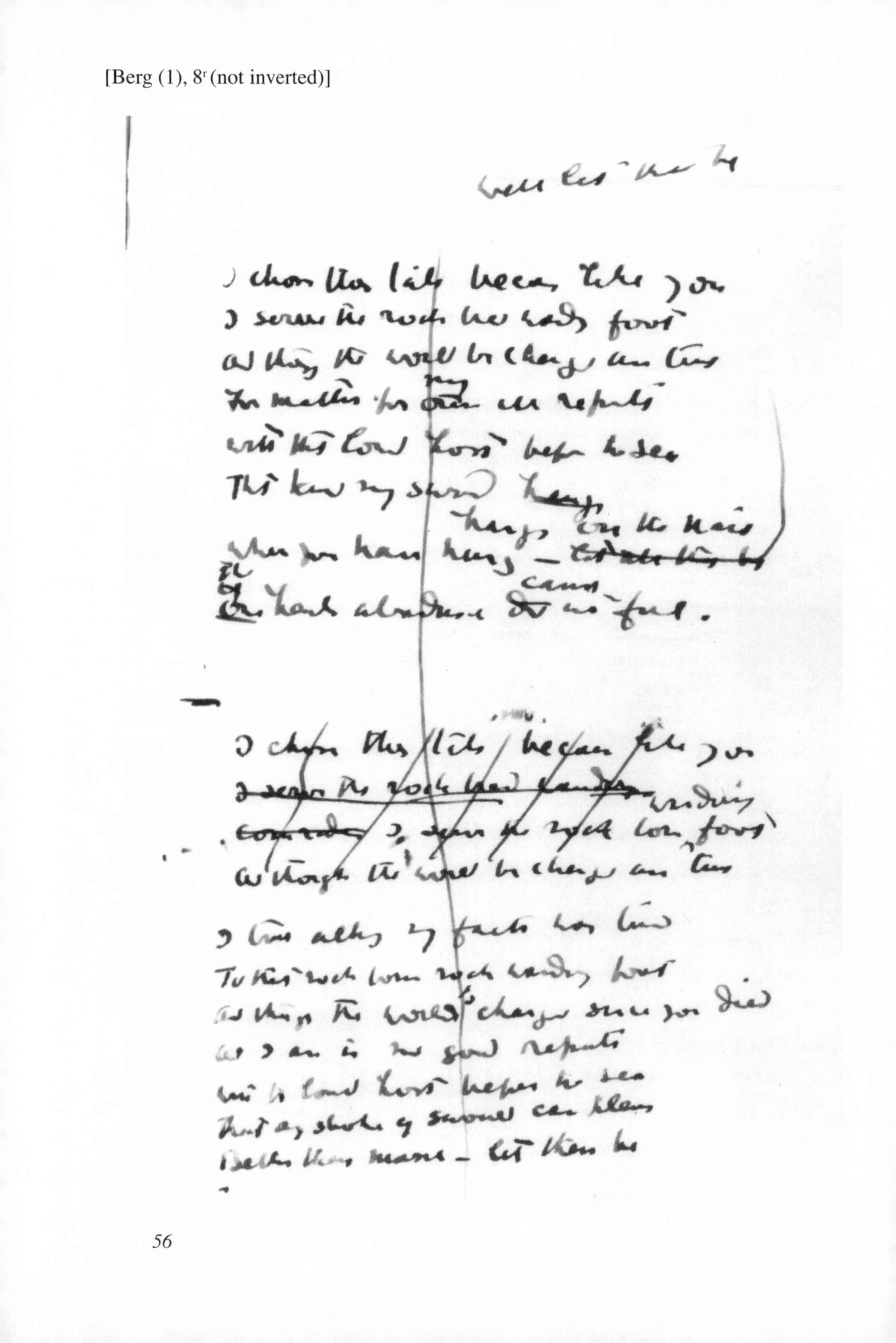

[Berg (1), 8r (not inverted)]

[Berg (1), 8[r] (not inverted)]

1 Well let that be

2 I chose this tale because like you
3 I serve the rock [?] [?wandering] foot
4 And though the world be changed [?untrue]
my
5 For matter for ~~our~~ [?all] [?repute]
6 With that loud host before the sea
7 That [?knew] my sword ~~hangs~~
hangs on the nail
8 Where you have hung — ~~let all that be~~
[?The]
[?If] [?cann]
9 ~~One~~ [?hearts] [?abundance] [~~?did~~][?not] fill.

—

10 ~~I chose this tale because like you~~
11 ~~I serve the rock bred [?wandering]~~
~~wandering~~
12 ~~Comrades I serve the rock [?worn] ^ foot~~
13 ~~And though the world be changed [?an] [?]~~
14 I [?true] [?although] [?my] [?faith] was tried
15 To that rock born rock wandering foot
's
16 And though the world changed since you died
17 And I am in no good repute
18 With the loud host before the sea
19 That [?any] stroke of sword can please
20 [?Better] [?than] [?] — let them be

---

1 The upper half of the curved line that leads down the right margin from "Well let that be" to the canceled "let all that be" at l. 8 is uninked, but is visible on the manuscript.

9 "[~~?did~~]" could perhaps be "[~~?do~~]".

12 "[?worn]" could perhaps be "[?torn]".

14 "I" could perhaps be "&".

19 "[?any]" could perhaps be "[?my]".

20 "[?]" could perhaps be "[?many]" or "[?mine]".

[Berg (2), 1, 2]

[1]

Poets with whom I learned my trade
Companions of the Cheshire Cheese
Here's an old story I've remade
Imagining 'twould better please
Your ears than stories now in fashion
Though you may think I waste my breath
Pretending that there can be passion
That has more life in it than death
And though at bottling of your wine
The bow–legged Goban had no say
The moral's yours because it's mine

When cups went round at close of day
Is not that how good stories run?
Somewhere within some hol{l} ow hill
If books speak truth, in Sl{ie/i}venaman
But let that be, the gods were still
And sleepy, having had their meal
And smoky torches make a glare
On painted pillars, on a deal

---

title Aoife's Lover *Princeton (in pencil, overwritten in purple ink)* Aoife's Lover. *Chicago (black ink, perhaps in Yeats's hand)* The Grey Rock *Yale, BR, P, Resp14*

1–11 *marked to be set in italics Princeton, Chicago set in italics Yale, BR, P, Resp14*

1 trade, *Yale, BR, P, Resp14*

2 Cheese, *Yale, BR, P, Resp14*

3 remade, *Yale, BR, P, Resp14*

5 fashion, *Princeton, Chicago, Yale, BR, Resp14* fashion. *P*

8 death, *Princeton, Chicago, Yale, BR, P, Resp14*

10 say; *Princeton, Chicago, Yale, BR, P, Resp14*

11 mine. *Princeton, Chicago, Yale, BR, P, Resp14*

12 day — *Princeton, Chicago, Yale, BR, P, Resp14*

13 run? — *Princeton, Chicago, Yale, BR, P, Resp14*

14 hill, *BR, P*

15 Slievenaman] Slievenamon *Princeton, Chicago* Slievenamon, *Yale, Resp14* Slievenamon; *BR* Slievenamon— *P* In their great house at Slievenamon, *rev to* In their great house at Slievenamon. *ABY(4)*

16 And sang a drowsy song, or snored, *rev to* They sang a drowsy song, or snored, *ABY(4)*

17 sleepy *Princeton, Chicago* meal] meal, *Princeton, Chicago, Yale, BR, Resp14* meal: *P* meal *rev to* meat *ABY(3)* For all were full of wine and meat; *rev to* For all were full of wine and meat. *ABY(4)*

18 And smoky torches made a glare *rev to* The smoky torches made a glare *ABY(4)*

19 On painted pillars, on a deal] On painted pillars, on a deal *rev to* On metal Goban had hammered out at, *ABY(3)*

---

14 In "hollow" the second "l" is a correction written in black ink where the typescript has one blank space. This and all the other corrections in ink probably were by the typist; the only change made in pencil (l. 81) is perhaps in Yeats's hand.

{O
{of fiddles and of flutes hung there**

{i
By the anc{oent holy hands that brought them
From Murias murmuring Murias in cups
Old Goban hammered them and wrought them
And put his pattern round their tops
{m.
To hold the wine they buy of hi{

Suddenly these gods raised their eyes
{e
With memory and foreknowl{rdge dim

[Berg(2), 2]

From the juice that made them wise
For one that was like woman made
Before their sleepy eyelids ran
{r
And t{eembling with her passion said

---

20 Of fiddles and of flutes hung there] Of fiddles and of flutes, hung there *BR* Of old stringed instruments, hung there *Chicago, Princeton, P* Of fiddles and of flutes hung there *rev to* On old deep silver rolling there *ABY(3)*

21 By the ancient holy hands that brought them *rev to* Or on some still unemptied [?] cup *ABY(3)*

22 Murias, on cups — *Princeton, Chicago, Yale, BR, P, Resp14* From murmuring Murias, on cups — *rev to* That he, when frenzy stirred his thewes *ABY(3)* That he, when frenzy stirred his thewes, *rev to* That he, when frenzy stirred his thews, *NLI 30,009*

23 them, *Yale, BR, P, Resp14* Old Goban hammered them and wrought them, *rev to* Had hammered out on mountain top *ABY(3)*

24 And put his pattern round their tops *rev to* To hold the sacred stuff he brews *ABY(3)*

25 To hold the wine they buy of him. *rev to* That only gods may buy of him. *ABY(3)*

26 Suddenly these gods raised their eyes] But [*rev to* Now *ABY(3)*] from the [*rev to* that *ABY(3)*] juice that made them wise *Princeton, Chicago, Yale, BR, P, Resp14, ABY(3)*

27 With memory and foreknowledge dim] All those had lighted up the dim *rev to* All those had lifted up the dim *Princeton (purple ink), Chicago (black ink; perhaps in Yeats's hand)* All those had lifted up the dim *Yale, BR, P, Resp14*

[Berg(2), 2]

28 From] But from *Princeton, Yale, BR, P, Resp14*

28/ [*2 lines inserted here:*]
All those had lighted up the dim *rev to* All those had lifted up the dim
Imaginations of their eyes *Princeton (purple ink)*
All those had lighted up the dim *rev to* All those had lifted up the dim
Imaginations of their eyes *rev to* Imaginations of their eyes; *Chicago (black ink; perhaps in Yeats's hand)*
All those had lifted up the dim
Imaginations of their eyes, *Yale, BR, Resp14* (eyes; *P*)

30 sleepy eyelids ran] sleepy lids had ran, *rev to* sleepy eye-lids ran, *Princeton (purple ink), Chicago (black ink; perhaps in Yeats's hand)* sleepy eyelids ran, *P*

31 said, *Yale, BR, Resp14* said: *P* said *rev to* said, *NLI 30,009*

[Berg (2), 2, 3]

‘Come out and dig for a dead man
{’s
Who{ burrowing somewhere in the ground
And mock him to his face and then
Hollo him on with horse and hound
For he is the worst of all dead men.’

{l
We shou{dd be dazed and terror struck
{f
I{[?] we but saw in dreams that room
And those fierce eyes and curse our luck
That emptied all our days to come
I knew a woman none could please
Because she dreamed when but a child
Of men and women made like these
And after when her blood ran wild
Had ravelled her own story out
And said ‘In two or in three years
I need must marry some poor lout ’
And having said it burst in tears.
Old tavern comrades now you have died
Maybe your images have stood
Mere bone and muscle thrown aside
{t
Before tha{n roomful or as good

---

32 man, *Princeton, Chicago, Yale, BR, P, Resp14*
33 ground, *Princeton, Chicago, Yale* ground; *P*
35 hound, *Yale, BR, P, Resp14*
37–51 *marked to be set in italics Princeton, Chicago set in italics Yale, BR, P, Resp14*
37 struck, *Yale, BR, Resp14* terror struck, *rev to* terror-struck *NLI 30,009 (with a query)*
38 If, *Princeton, Chicago* room *rev to* room, *Yale (pencil)* room, *BR, Resp14*
39 And those fierce eyes] And those fierce eyes, *Chicago, P* And those fierce eyes *rev to* those wine-drenched eyes, *Princeton (blue-black ink, in Yeats's hand)* Those wine-drenched eyes, *Yale, BR, Resp14*
40 come, *Princeton, Chicago* come. *Yale, BR, P, Resp14*
41 please, *Yale, BR, Resp14*
43 these; *Yale, BR, P, Resp14*
44 after, *Princeton, Chicago, BR, P, Resp14* wild, *Princeton, Chicago, Yale, BR, P, Resp14*
45 out, *Yale, BR, P, Resp14*
46 said, *Yale, BR, P, Resp14*
47 need *rev to* needs *NLI 30,009, NLI 30,262* lout,’ *Yale, BR, P, Resp14*
48 said it *rev to* said, it *NLI 30,262*
49 Old] Since *Princeton, Chicago, BR* Since *rev to* Since, *Yale (pencil)* Since, *Resp14* comrades *rev to* comrades, *Yale (pencil)* comrades, *Resp14, P* died, *Yale, BR, P, Resp14*
50 stood, *Princeton, Chicago, Yale, BR, P, Resp14*
51 aside, *Princeton, Chicago, Yale, BR, P, Resp14*
52 good. *Princeton, Chicago, Yale, BR, P, Resp14*

You had to face your ends when young
Twas wine or women or some curse
But never made a poorer song

[Berg(2), 3]

That you might have a heavier purse
Nor gave loud service to a cause
That you might have a troop of friends
You kept the Muses sterner laws
And unrepenting faced your ends
And therefore earned the right — and yet
Dowson and Johnson most I praise
To troop with those the world's forgot
e
And keep a proud and stady gaze.

' **The Danish troop was driven out**
Between the dawn and dusk ' **she said**
' **Although the event was long in doubt**
Although the King of Ireland's dead
{A
{**and half the kings before sundown**
{m
All was acco{[?]**plised**

---

53 young — *Princeton, Chicago, Yale, BR, P, Resp14*
54 You *rev to* "You *Princeton (pencil)* women, *Yale, BR, Resp14* curse — *Princeton, Chicago, Yale, BR, P, Resp14*

[Berg(2), 3]
56–64 *marked to be set in italics Princeton, Chicago set in italics Yale, BR, P, Resp14*
56 purse, *Yale, BR, Resp14* purse; *P*
58 friends *rev to* friends. *Chicago* friends. *Yale, BR, P, Resp14*
59 Muses' *Yale, BR, P, Resp14* laws, *Yale, BR, Resp14*
60 ends, *Yale, BR, Resp14* ends; *P*
61 right — ond *rev to* right — and *Princeton (purple ink), Chicago (black ink, perhaps in Yeats's hand)*
62 praise — *Princeton, Chicago, Yale, BR, P, Resp14*
63 forgot, *Yale, BR, P, Resp14*
64 And keep a proud and steady] And copy their proud steady *Princeton, Chicago, Yale, BR, P, Resp14* gaze. *rev to* gaze." *Princeton (pencil)*
66 dusk,' *Yale, BR, P, Resp14* said; *Yale, BR, P, Resp14*
67 doubt, *Princeton, Chicago, Yale, BR, P, Resp14*
68 dead, *Yale (printed comma circled in pencil), BR, Resp14*
69 kings, *Princeton, Chicago, BR, P, Resp14* kings *rev to* kings, *Yale (pencil)* sundown, *Yale (printed comma circled in pencil), BR*
70a accomplished. *Princeton, Chicago, P* accomplished.' *Yale, BR, Resp14* accomplished." *rev to* accomplished. *ABY(4)*

[Berg (2), 3, 4]

{h
W{en this day
71 **Murrough the King of Ireland's son**
72 **Foot after foot was giving way**
{h
73 **He and {gis best troops back to back**
74 **Had perished there, but the Danes ran**
{c
75 **Stricken with pani{ s from the attack**
76 **The shouting of an unseen man.**
77 **And being thankful Murrough found**
{L
78 **{led by a footsole dipped in blood**
79 **That had made prints upon the ground**
80 **Where by old thorn trees that man stood**
though
81 **And ~~oh~~ ^ when he gazed here and there**

[Berg(2), 4]

82 **He had but gazed on thorn trees spoke**
83 **Who is the friend that seems but air**
84 **And yet could give so fine a stroke**
85 **Thereon a young man met his eye**
86 **Who said ' Because she held me in**

70b 'When *Yale, BR, P, Resp14* "When this day *rev to* When this day *ABY(4)*
71 Murrough, *Yale, BR, Resp14* son, *Yale, BR, Resp14*
72 way, *Princeton, Chicago, Yale, BR, P, Resp14*
74 ran, *Yale, BR, Resp14*
75 attack, *Yale (with a penciled query of the printed comma), BR, P, Resp14*
76 man; *Princeton, Chicago, Yale, BR, P, Resp14*
77 found, *Princeton, Chicago, Yale, BR, P, Resp14*
79 ground, *Princeton, Chicago, Yale, BR, P, Resp14*
80 thorn trees *rev to* thorn-trees *NLI 30,262* stood; *Princeton, Chicago, Yale, BR, P, Resp14*
80/81 *penciled horizontal rule ABY(7)*
81 there, *Yale, BR, Resp14*

[Berg(2), 4]
82 thorn trees *rev to* thorn-trees *NLI 30,262* trees, *Princeton, Chicago, BR, P, Resp14* spoke] spoke, *Yale, BR, Resp14* spoke: *P*
83 'Who *Princeton, Chicago, Yale, BR, P, Resp14*
84 stroke' *Princeton, Chicago* stroke?' *Yale, BR, P, Resp14*
85 eye, *Yale, BR, Resp14*
86 said, *Yale, BR, P, Resp14*

---

81 This change, which is the only one in pencil, is perhaps in Yeats's hand.

m
Her love and would not have{ne die
f
Rock–nurtured Aoi{[?]e took a pin
And pushing it into my shirt
f
Promised that {[?]or a pin's sake
No man should see to do me hurt
I
But there it's gone ~~and~~ will not take
The fortune that had been my shame
Seeing King's son what wounds you have .'
Twas roundly spoke but when night came
r
He had betr {[?]ayed me to his grave
For he and the King's son were dead.
I'd promised him two hundred years
o
And when for all I'd d{ne or said
And these immortal eys shed tears
He claimed his country's need was most
I'd saved his life yet for the sake
Of a new friend he has turned a ghost
What does he care if my heart break
I call for spade and horse and hound

---

87 love, *Yale, BR, P, Resp14* die, *Yale, BR, P, Resp14*
88 pin, *Yale, BR, Resp14*
89 shirt, *Yale, BR, Resp14*
90 Promised] She promised me *rev to* promised *Princeton (purple ink), Chicago (black ink)* sake, *Yale, BR, Resp14*
91 hurt; *Princeton, Chicago, Yale, BR, P, Resp14*
92 gone; *Princeton, Chicago, Yale, BR, Resp14* gone, *P*
94 Seeing, *Princeton, Chicago, Yale, BR, P, Resp14* son, *Princeton, Chicago, Yale, BR, P, Resp14* have.' *rev to* have." *Princeton (purple ink), Chicago (black ink)*
95 'Twas *Princeton, Chicago, BR, P, Resp14* spoke, *Yale, BR, P, Resp14*
96 betrrayed] betrayed *Princeton, Chicago, Yale, BR, P, Resp14* grave, *Yale, BR, P, Resp14*
98 years, *Yale, BR, P, Resp14*
99 said — *Princeton, Chicago, Yale, BR, P, Resp14*
100 tears — *Princeton, Chicago, Yale, BR, P, Resp14*
101 most, *Princeton, Chicago, Yale, Resp14* most. *BR, P*
102 life, *Princeton, Chicago, Yale, BR, P, Resp14*
103 ghost. *Princeton, Chicago, Yale, BR, P, Resp14*
104 break? *Princeton, Chicago, Yale, BR, P, Resp14*

---

92 The cancel of "and" and the correction to "I" here and one other instance below (l. 129) are the only instances of corrections that are carbon impressions of corrections from the ribbon original rather than being made directly in ink.

[Berg (2), 4, 5]

106 **That we may harry him thereon .'**
{el
107 **She cast hers {lef upon the ground**
108 **And rent her clothes and made her moan**
109 **Why are they faithless when their might**

[Berg(2), 5]

110 **Is from the holy shades that rove**
111 **The grey rock and the windy light**
112 **Why should the faithless heart most love**
113 **The bitter sweetness of false faces**
114 **Why must the lasting love what passes**
115 **Why are the gods by men betrayed '.**

116 **But thereon every god stood up**
117 **With a slow smile and without sound**
118 **And stretching out his arm and cup**
119 **To where she moaned upon the ground**
120 **Suddenly drenched her to the skin**
121 **And she with Goban's wine adrip**
122 **No momore remembering what had been**
{s
123 **Stared at the god{ with laughing lip.**
124 **I have kept my faith though faith was tried**

---

106 him thereon.'] him. Thereon *Princeton* him. Thereon *rev to* him.' Thereon *Chicago (black ink)* him.' Thereon *Yale, P, Resp14* him." / *stanza division* / Thereon *BR*

108 moan, *BR* moan, *rev to* moan: *Yale* moan: *P, Resp14*

109 'Why *Princeton, Chicago, Yale, BR, P, Resp14*

[Berg(2), 5]

111 cindy *rev to* windy *Princeton (purple ink), Chicago (black ink)* light? *Princeton, Chicago, Yale, BR, P, Resp14*

112 faithless] faithfulest *Princeton, Chicago, P* faithfullest *Yale, BR, Resp14*

113 faces? *Princeton, Chicago, Yale, BR, P, Resp14*

114 passes, *Yale, BR, Resp14* passes? *P*

115 betrayed!' *Princeton, Chicago, Yale, BR, P, Resp14*

117 sound, *Yale, BR, P, Resp14*

119 ground, *Yale, BR, P, Resp14*

120 skin; *Princeton, Chicago, Yale, BR, P, Resp14*

121 adrip, *Princeton, Chicago, Yale, BR, P, Resp14*

122 been, *Princeton, Chicago, Yale, BR, P, Resp14*

124–131 *marked to be set in italics Princeton, Chicago set in italics Yale, BR, P, Resp14*

124 faith *rev to* faith, *Yale (pencil)* faith, *P* tried *rev to* tried, *Yale (pencil)* tried, *P, Resp14*

---

115 The single quote and period added here in ink became an exclamation point in later versions, perhaps by misreading.

To that rock–born, rock–wandering foot

And the world's altered since you died
{o
And I am in n{ good repute
With the loud host before the sea
That think sore st sword strokes were better meant
Than lover's music — let that be
So that the wandering foot's content

W B Yeats

---

125 foot, *Yale, BR, Resp14* foot; *P*

126 died, *Yale, BR, P, Resp14*

128 sea, *BR, P, Resp14*

129 sword strokes *rev to* sword-strokes *NLI 30,262*

130 lovers *Princeton, Chicago* lovers' *BR* be, *BR, P, Resp14*

131 content. *BR, P, Resp14*

131/ W. B. Yeats] W. B. Yeats *Princeton (added in purple ink, not in Yeats's hand)* W B Yeats *Chicago (added in black ink, perhaps in Yeats's hand)* W. B. Yeats. *BR (small caps)* William Butler Yeats *P (italics) no signature Yale, Resp14*

131/ Oct. 1912 *Princeton (added in purple ink, not in Yeats's hand)* Oct 1912 *Chicago (added in black ink, perhaps in Yeats's hand)*

---

129 The correction is a carbon impression of a correction from the ribbon original.

131/ Signature is in Yeats's hand.

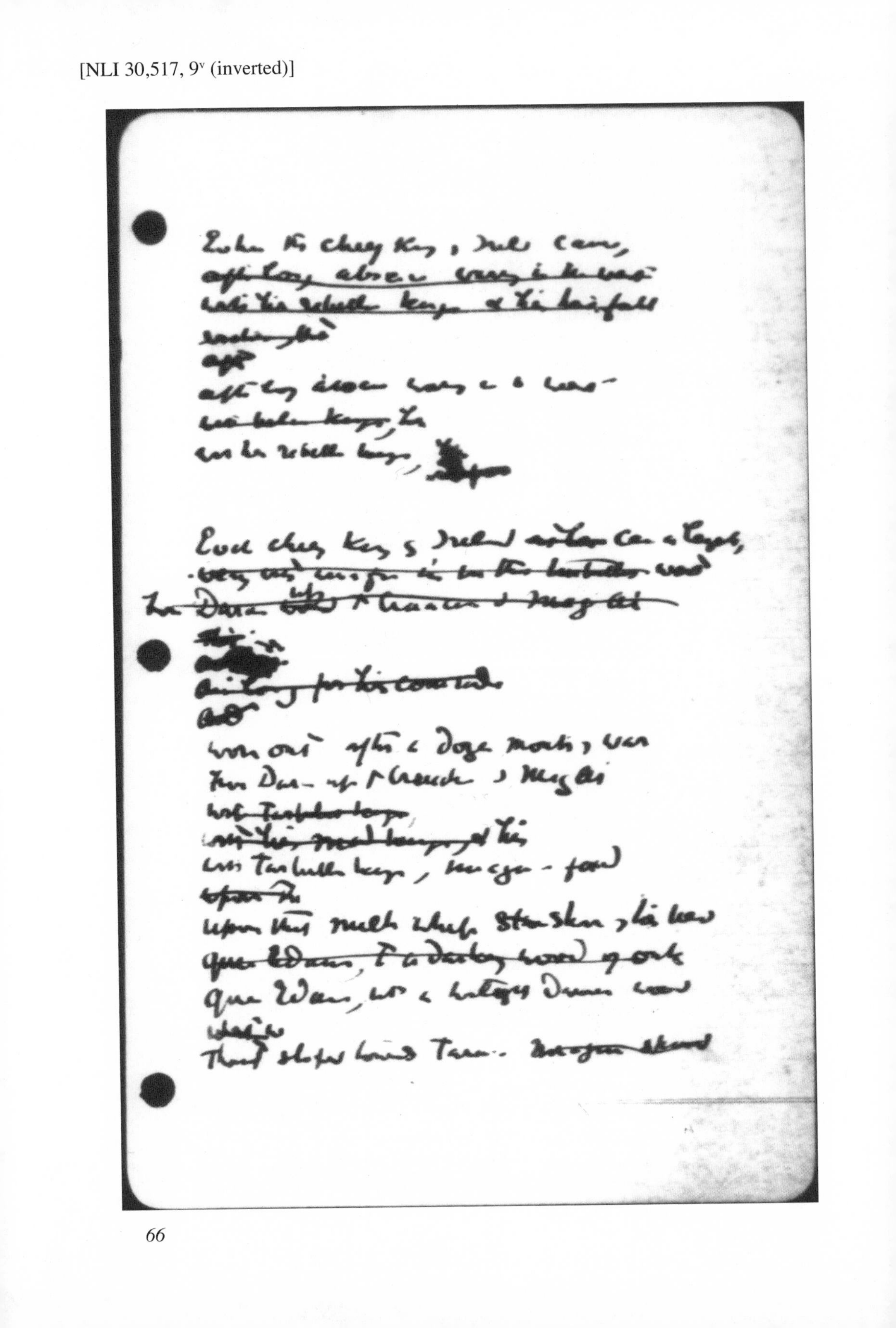

[NLI 30,517, 9v (inverted)]

THE TWO KINGS

[NLI 30,517, 9v (inverted)]

Eoha the Chief King of Ireland came,
~~After long absence warring in the west~~
~~With his rebellious kings & his [?hat] [?fall]~~
[~~?~~], [?~~the~~]
~~After~~
After long absence warring in the west
~~With [?] [?kings~~, he
[With] his [?rebellious] kings, [~~?~~]
[~~?~~]

Eoch Chief King of Ireland ~~as [?he]~~ came a length,
~~Very [? ?] from [?in] [?] the turbulent~~ west
~~up~~
From ~~[?Durus] [?] to [?Cruachan] & Mag Ai~~
[~~? ?~~]
[~~?~~]
~~[?] long from his comrade~~
~~[?And]~~
Worn out after a dozen months of war
From [?Duras] up to Cruachan & Mag Ai
~~With turbulent kings~~,
~~With his [?mad] kings, &~~ his
With turbullent kings, [?imagination] [?fixed]
~~Upon the~~
Upon that milk white [~~?~~] [?sharer] of his bed
~~Queen Edain, to a darkening wood of oak~~
Queen Edain, [?into] a [? ?] wood
~~What [?]~~
That sloped towards Tara. [~~? ?~~]

---

found in NLI 30,517 *transcribed above and below*
NLI 13,586(2) (b) *transcribed below*
Berg(3) *transcribed below*
NLI 13,586(2) (a) *transcribed below*
Yale *transcribed below*
ABY(3)
ABY(5)
ABY(4)
NLI 30,262
published in *The British Review*, October 1913
Poetry (Chicago), October 1913
Resp14

[NLI 30,517, 12v (inverted)]

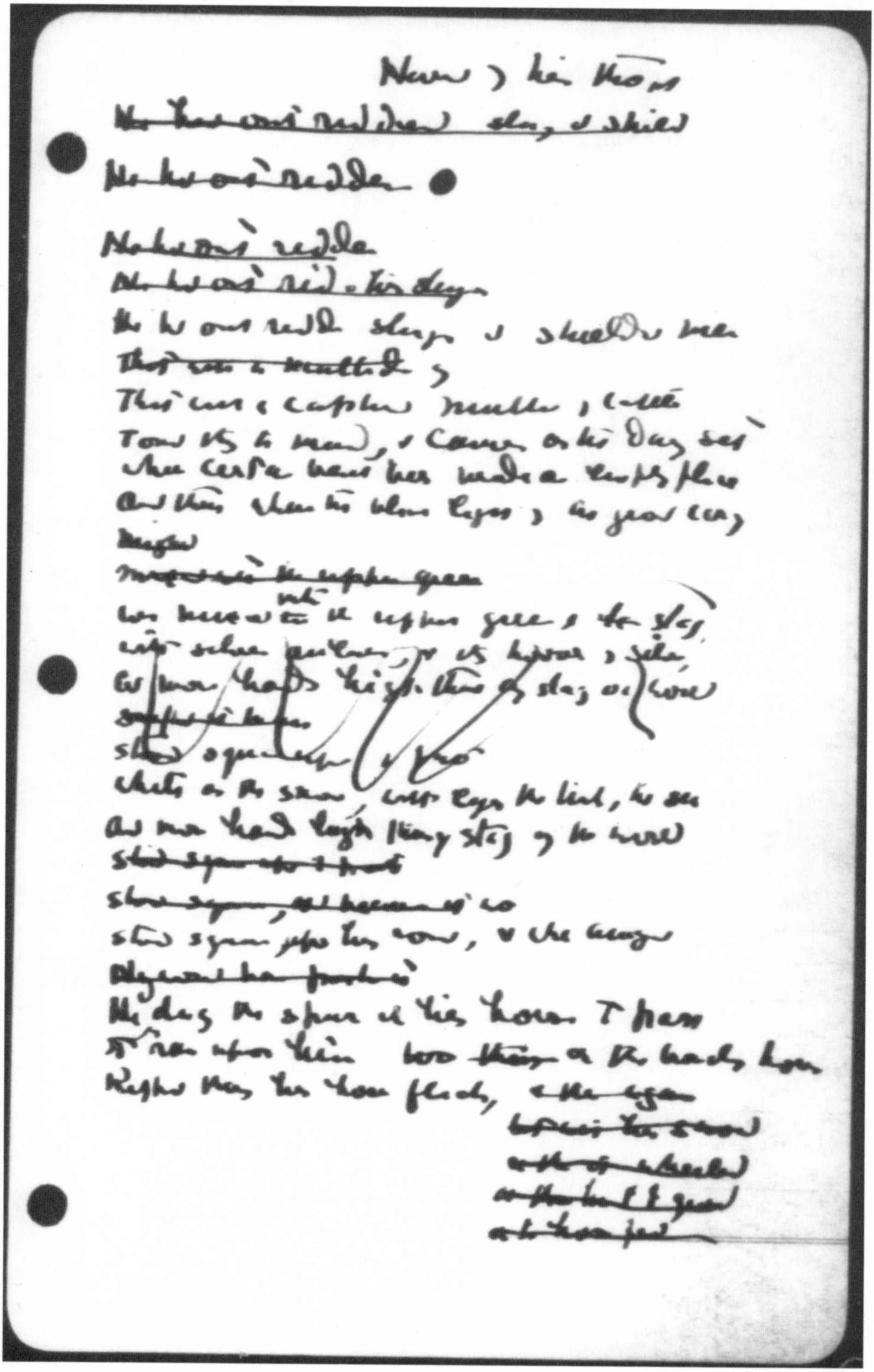

[NLI 30,517, 12^{v} (inverted)]

[?Haven] of his thought
~~He had out [?ridden] stag & [?shield]~~
~~He had out ridden~~

~~He had out ridden~~
~~He had out rid [?his] [?]~~
He had out ridden stags & [?shielded] men
~~That [?were] a multitude~~ of
That with a captured multitude of cattle
Toiled through the mud, & came on the day set
Where certain beech trees made an empty place
And there where the blue light of the [?ground] ivy
~~[?Mingled~~]
~~[?Mingled] with the upper green~~
into
Was mixed ~~to~~ the upper green, [~~?~~] stag,
With silver [?antlers], & its hooves of silver,
And more hands high than any stag or hound
~~[?] [?it] [?from]~~
Stood squarely [?in] front
White as the snow, with eyes the tint of the sea
And more hands high than [?any] stag of the world
~~Stood square upon [?the] [?path]~~
~~Stood square, [?] [?because] it~~ [?]
Stood square upon his road, & [?then] [?amazed]
~~[?] [?would] have push it~~
He dug the spur into his horse to pass
It ran upon him ~~[?from] [?those]~~ [and] the branching horns
Ripped through his horses flank, ~~& then again~~
~~but with his sword~~
~~& [?then] [?it] wheeled~~
~~& [?then] [? ?] [?ground]~~
~~& [? ? ?]~~

[NLI 30,517, 13[v] (inverted)]

[NLI 30,517, 13[v] (inverted)]

~~Right through his horses shoulder, while~~ sword

~~Right through his horses [?] flank~~
~~Right through his horses flank shoulder — all but [?through]~~
Right through his horses flank. [?Before] his sword
~~shoulder~~, & half through
~~His~~
~~His sword blade~~
~~His [?answering] sword stroke [?missed]~~ & the ~~stag wheeled~~.
For ~~certain moments they [?] fought~~
but
flank & all ^ through
He missed his answering stroke & the stag wheeled.
~~For certain moments then they fought, & [?once]~~
For certain moments then they fought, & always
His sword was caught upon [?one] [?bough] of horn
And the horn sounded as though it had been ~~silver~~ metal
A silver bell in a kings house, or maybe
~~sounding pillar of silver but at last~~
A sounding pole of silver but at last
~~He [?leaped] upon the [?ground]~~
He [?lept] upon the ground & with his [?hands]
& once
His sword was caught upn a [?branch] of horn
And the horn sounded as though it had been metal
A silver bell in [?a] kings house [?in] [? ?]
A sounding pole of silver, & once [?] house
[?Wondered] [?] [?though]

[NLI 30,517, 11v (inverted)]

[NLI 30,517, 11v (inverted)]

1 ~~To the [? ? ?] [?second] days [?they] fought~~
[? ? ? ?]
2 ~~For certain moments they fought [?] and [?always]~~ [?thrice]
3 His sword was caught upon a branch of horn
4 And the horn sounded as though it had been metal
5 A silver bell in a kings house [? ? ? ?]
6 A sounding pole of ~~silver, [?until] the horse~~
7 ~~[?but] the horse~~
8 silver, ~~and [?thrice]~~
9 ~~and [?three]~~ [?times]
10 ~~The horse [? ?] blood~~ but at last
11 His horse, the entrails showing through its skin fell dead
[?And] [?]
12 And [?] [?~~throwing~~] away his sword King Eocha closed
13 And he caught the magical horn in those strong hands
14 And [?stared in the] sea green eye, & so
15 Hither & thither, to & fro [?they] trod
16 Till all the place was ~~beaten into mire~~
beaten into [?mire]
thigh [?]
17 The strong [?~~feet~~] & the agile ~~feet~~ were [?met]
18 The hands that gathered up the might of the world
19 ~~With horn & hoof that~~
20 ~~With [?tangled] horn & hoof [? ? ? ?]~~
elaborate wilderness of the [?air]
21 Amid the ~~[?wilderness] of the~~ [?that]
22 Through bush they plunged, & over ivied roots,
23 ~~And where the [?flint] caught fire, [?]~~
24 And where [?] stone struck fire and over head
25 The squirrels whinned, & [~~?~~] [?] screamed.
26 ~~But now, forcing that snow white~~
upon tree
27 But [?now] forcing ~~against~~ the great bole of ~~a [?beech]~~
28 ~~The snow white~~ [?]
29 The snow white [?flank] [?] [?threw down the] beast

---

2 The facing page, 13r (inverted), has the following revision of l. 2, with an insertion arrow leading here:
[~~?~~] certain ~~[?that] [?]~~
They fought for [~~?~~] moments [?there] [~~?~~] ^ [~~?~~]
[?]

19 The facing page, 13r (inverted), has the following revision, with an insertion arrow leading toward the canceled ll. 19–20:
[?with] hoof & horn that had sucked in [?their] speed

[NLI 30,517, 10v (inverted)]

[NLI 30,517, 10ᵛ (inverted)]

And [?kneeled] upon [?with] drawn knife — On the instant
~~It vanished [?under] [?under]~~
It vanished like a shadow in a dream
And he had thought but a dream or a shadow
~~But for the trodden ground [?&] the dead horse~~
~~And his [?exhausted] body~~
But for the trodden ground, the screaming birds
And his dead horse
                                        and
It vanished like a ~~d a~~ shadow ~~in a dream~~ a cry
~~And a loud cry,~~
                                        cry
So mournful that it seemed the∧~~by~~ of one
Who [?] [?lost] [?some] [?unimaginable] [?]
[~~?Blue~~] P
                        blue and the green ~~light~~ leaf
[?] believes the ~~blue light [?of] the~~ [?ground]
                [~~?~~]
~~And [?perished] [?into] [?to] [?say], & [?he] [?that] had~~ [?thought]
~~And [?perished] [?in] [?the] air, & he had thought~~
                    [?into]   air   crumbling
And [?climbed]∧that [~~?~~] [?&] [~~?~~] away
~~And he had thought it all a dream or a~~ shadow
~~But for the troddn ground, the screaming birds~~
~~And the dead horse.~~
And all had seemed a shadow or a vision
But for the trodden ground, the screaming birds
And the dead horse. Eoha gazed about him
~~And [?then] [?the] [?secret] [?of]~~
An then, as terror stricken as a child
Who has seen a garden [?image] or twisted tree
        half   to
In the∧light, & run ~~[?upon] its [?way]~~ its own house
                                        at every ~~[?footstep]~~ footfall
[?Its] terror, growing wilder ~~with the [?spread]~~
He ran [?towards] the house [?his] father had built
On peopled [?~~tara~~] Tara. Presently he came
Before the many coloured wall, the posts
Of polished yew circled about with [?silver]
Of the great doors ~~& the wide [?or] high roof of~~

Insertions for an unlocated draft associated with NLI 13,586(2) (b), 2–3 (pp. 116–119 below).

[NLI 30,517, 10r (inverted)]

[NLI 30,517, 10^{r} (inverted)]

[?] gra[?] [?] [?way]

wound
Nor on the ancient beaten path that
From well side, or from plough land was there noise

And yet nor mouth nor slipper
made a noise
Nor on the ancient beaten paths that
wound
[?or]
From well side ~~nor~~ from
plough land was there noise.

Nor was there sound of life but [?that] far off
[?Though nearer than] before the [?cattle] lowed

1 Ink blots obscure the text in the first half of the line: "[*two blots*] gra[*blot*]".

[NLI 30,517, 11r (inverted)]

[NLI 30,517, 11^{r} (inverted)]

Before the [?unshuttered] windows & the posts
Of polished yew circled about with silver
Of [?the] great door & door & window shone
[?Lighted] by the [?many hanging] lamps within

Insertions for an unlocated draft associated with NLI 13,586(2) (b), 3 (pp. 118–119, below).

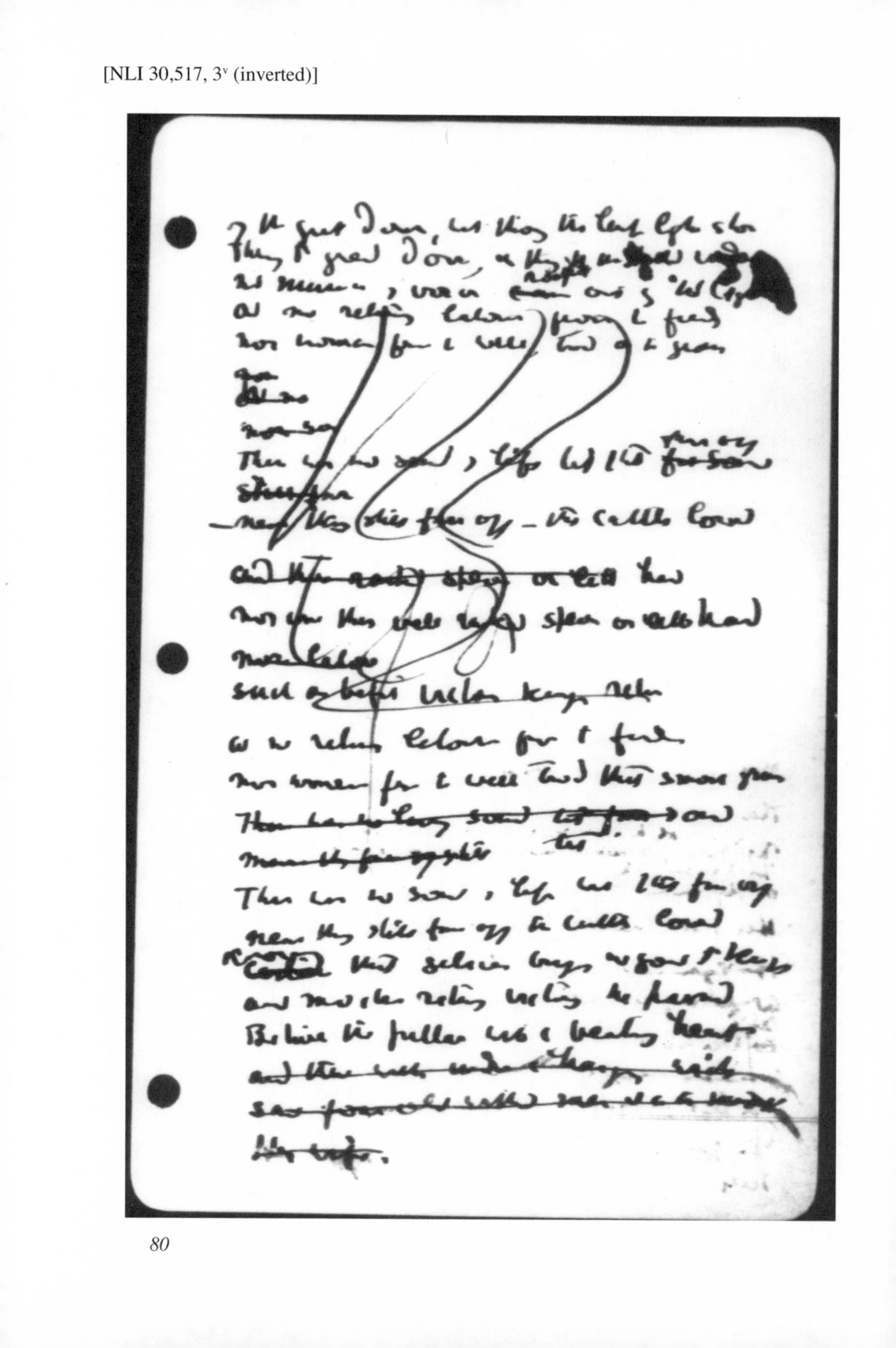

[NLI 30,517, 3v (inverted)]

[NLI 30,517, 3v (inverted)]

of the great door, but though the lamp light shone
Through the great door, & [?through] [~~?~~] the [?shuttered windows]
[?]
No murmur of voices ~~came~~ out of the [?light]
And no returning labourers from the fields
Nor women from the well, trod on the [?grass]
~~Nor~~
~~[?] No~~
~~Nor [?was]~~
far off
There was no sound of life but that ~~far sound~~
~~Still far~~
— Near though still far off — the cattle lowed
~~And [?there] ranked spears on [?either]~~ hand
Nor [?on] this [?wall] ranked spears on either hand
~~Nor [?labors]~~
Such as befit [?victorious] kings return
And no returning labourers from the fields
Nor women from the well trod that smooth [?grass]
~~There was no living sound but [?] sound~~
~~More [?than] far off still but~~
There was no sound of life but that far off
Near though still far off the cattle lowed
Knowing
~~Certain~~ that silence brings no good to kings
And mocks returning victory he passed
Between the pillars with a beating heart
~~And [?there] [?] under a [?hanging wick]~~
~~Saw four old withered men & a [? ?]~~
~~His wife.~~

[NLI 30,517, 3r (inverted)]

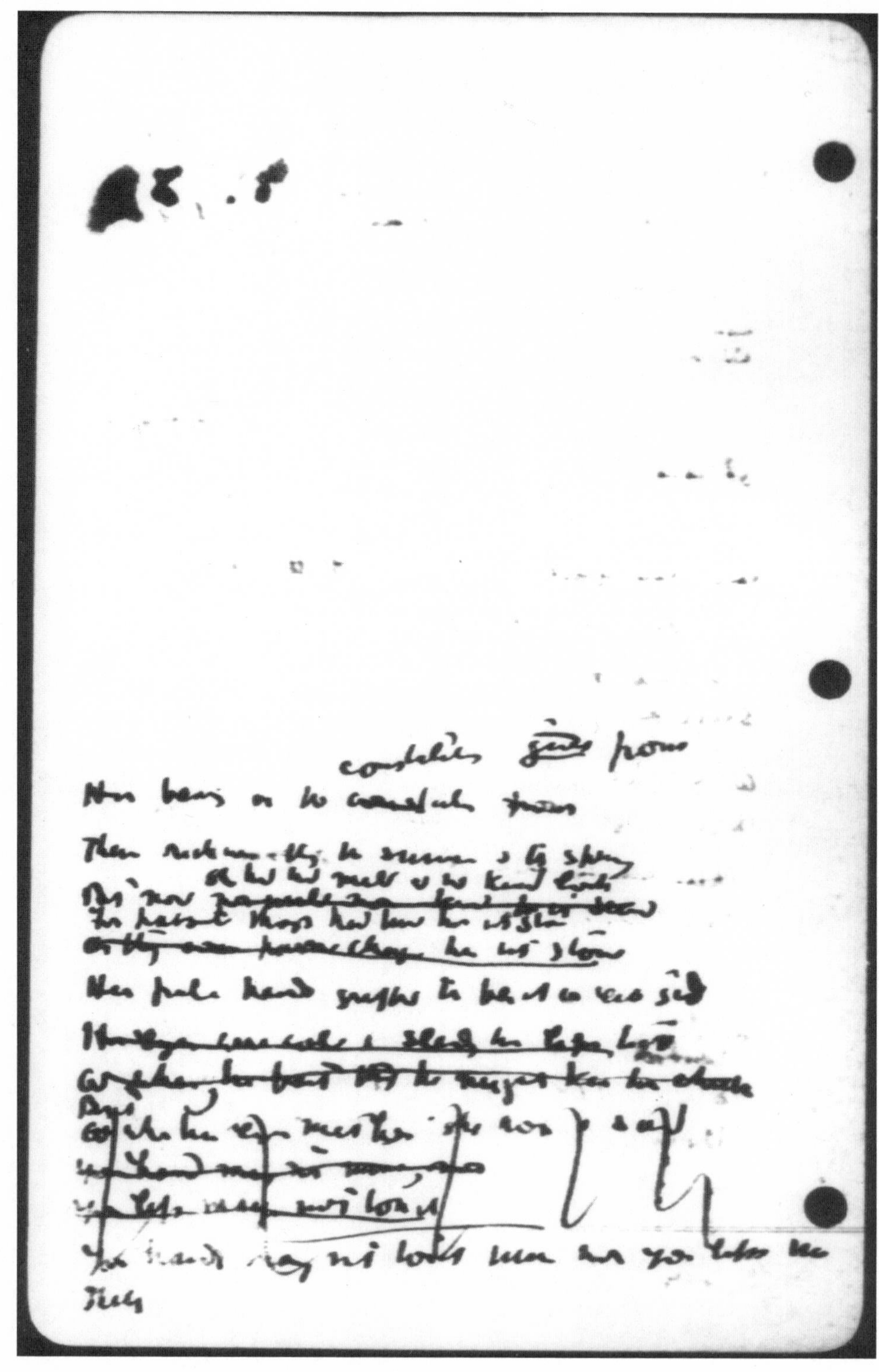

[NLI 30,517, 3[r] (inverted)]

[?constellations] ~~give~~ pour
1 Her beauty [?as] the ~~const~~ ation ~~pour~~
2 Their richness [?through] the summer & the spring
she had no mild & no kind look
3 But now ~~[?nor] sweet nor kind for it seemed~~
For [?passionate] thought had turned into stone
4 ~~[?As though] some passion changed her into stone~~
5 Her pale hands gripped the bench on either side
6 ~~Her eyes were cold & steady her lips~~ tight
7 ~~And when he bent that he might kiss her cheek~~
But
8 ~~And~~ when his eyes met hers she rose & said
9 ~~Your hand may not mine, [?nor]~~
10 ~~Your lips may not touch~~
11 Your hands may not touch mine nor your lips [?no]
12 [?]

Insertions for an unlocated draft associated with NLI 13,586(2) (b), 3–4 (pp. 118–121 below).

[NLI 30,517, 14v (inverted)]

[NLI 30,517, 14[v] (inverted)]

And then waits, ~~alone [?]~~ under a [?hanging wick]
Pale faced [? ?]
[?Saw] where
~~And [?saw where] [?~~ ?] ~~[?the hanging]~~ [?wick]
~~Pale faced~~ , alone
And saw where in the midst of the great hall
~~Alone~~ Pale faced, alone [?] upon [?a] bench, his wife
[?]
Sat upright with a sword between her feet.
~~And when he [?would have take] her in his arms~~
~~She [?]~~
A kind mild woman had she been, who gave
~~Who gave her beauty, [?as] his gods rain~~
~~Who had given her beauty as gods give the~~ rain
~~To the parched field~~
~~Beauty, as~~
[?~~the~~]
~~Her beauty, as [?her] god [?her] gods to the [?parched]~~ field
~~as gods [gave] to the parched~~ field
[~~?~~]
~~[?The] clouds [? ?] [?rain]~~
~~as the~~ [?that]
~~Her [?beauty]~~ ^ ~~the [?gods pour out] [?]~~ [?water]
On ~~the [?parched] world,~~
[?the]
Her beauty as the heavens pour [?out] ^ [?waters]
[?]
On the parched field, but [~~? ? ?~~ ?]
[?~~soft~~]
[?Mild] [? ? ?]
Her hands on either side [?had gripped] the bench
Her eyes were cold & steady her lips tight

[NLI 30,517, 14r (inverted)]

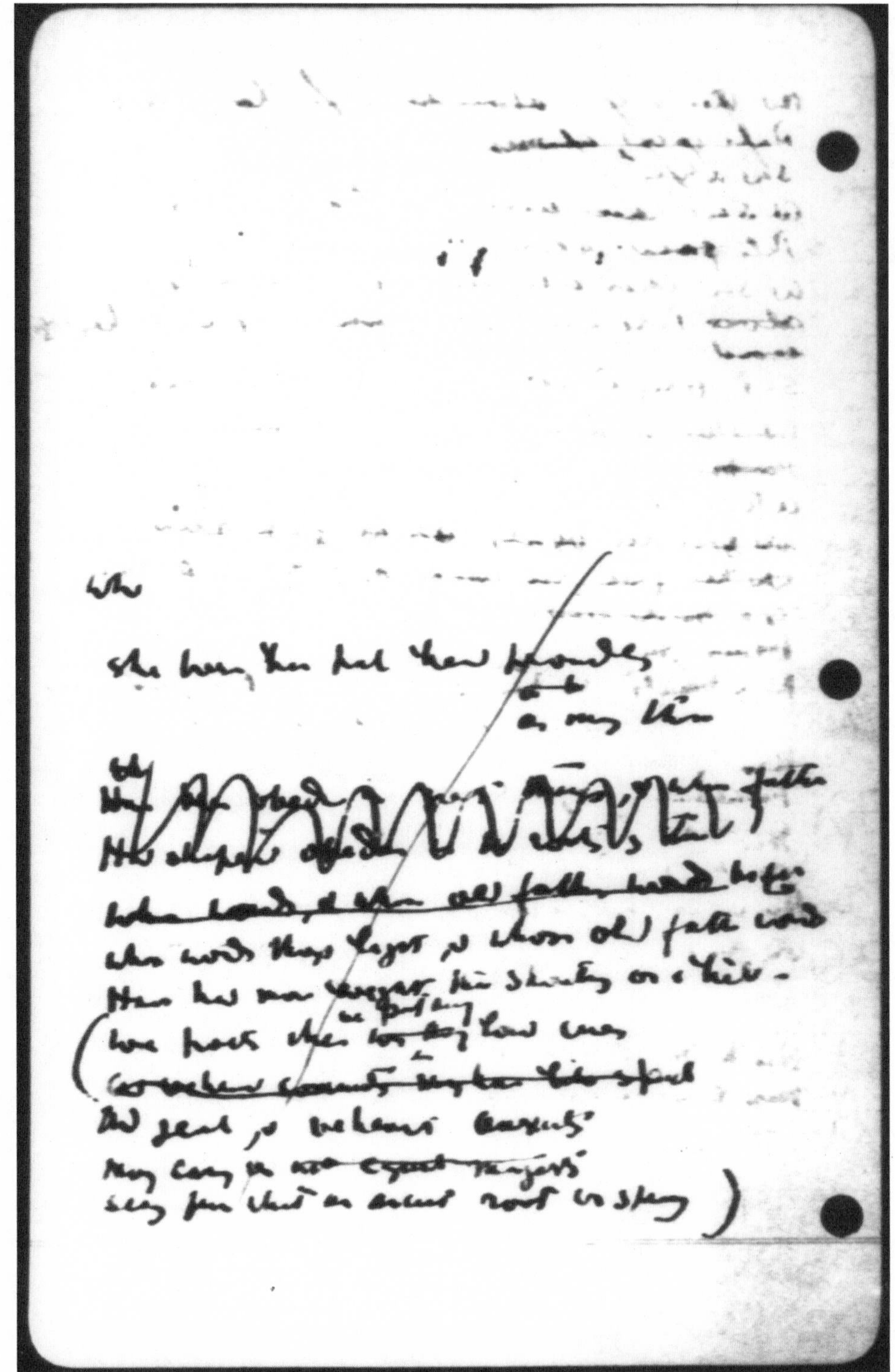

[NLI 30,517, 14[r] (inverted)]

[?]

She [?bore] her pale head proudly
~~as [?]~~
as may those
[~~?~~]
[?Have] been obedient in great things, & when [?father]
Had shaped obedience in the roots of [?time]
~~Whose words, & whose old fathers words before~~
Whose words though light, & whose old fathers words
Have had more weight than shouting on a hill —
we [?put] [?any]
(We poets when ~~we [?any]~~ loved ones
~~[?And] vehement [?comments[may have like [?]~~
[?] [?geal], & vehement anxiety
May carry [?the] ~~[?] equal [?majesty]~~
Seeing from what an ancient root we spring)

[NLI 30,517, 15ᵛ (inverted)]

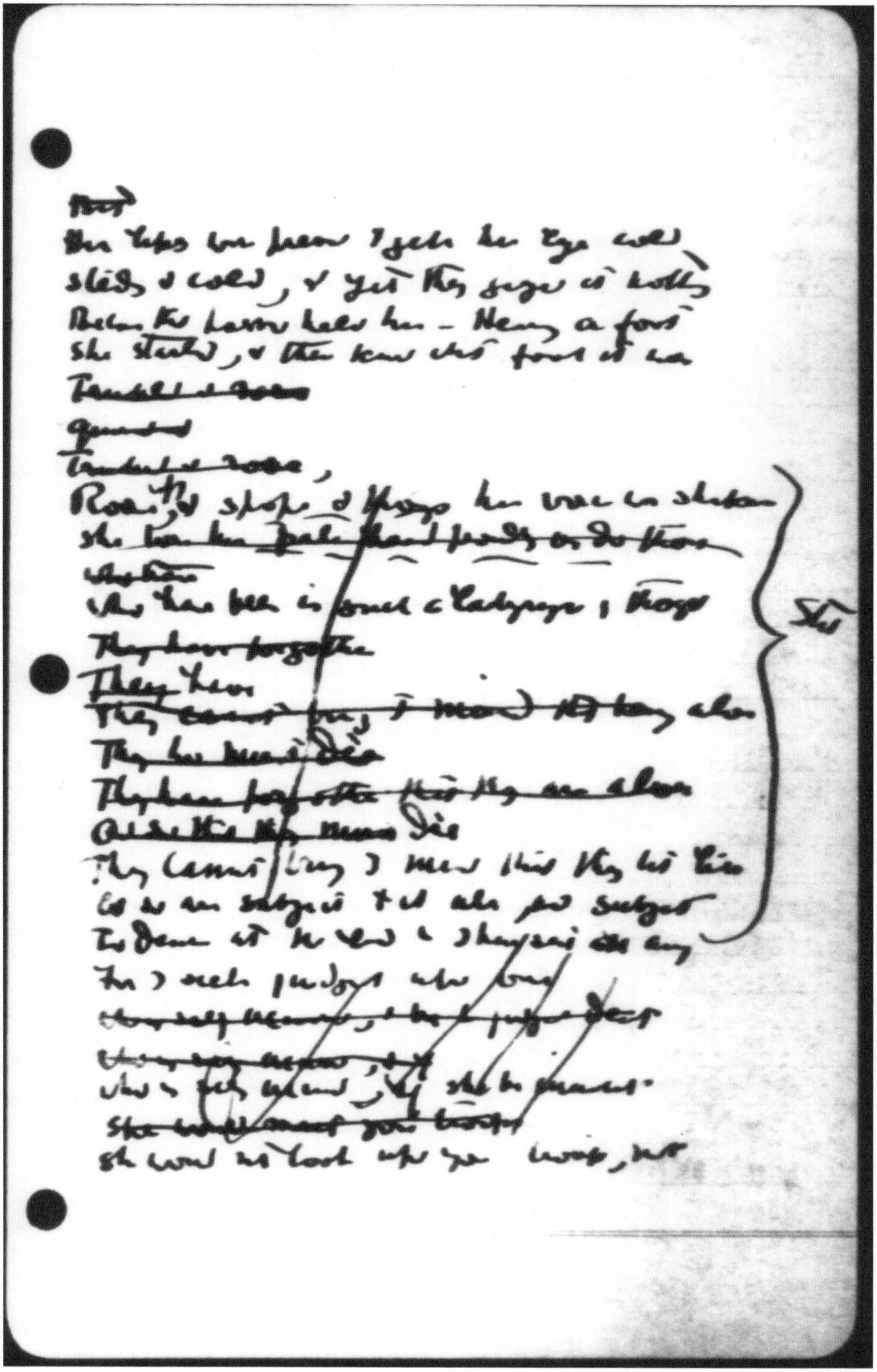

[NLI 30,517, 15ᵛ (inverted)]

~~But~~
Her lips were pressed together her eyes cold
Steady & cold, & yet they gazed at nothing
Because the passion held her — Hearing a foot
She started, & then knew what foot it was
~~Troubled & rose~~
[~~?~~]
~~Troubled & rose~~,
up
Rose , & spoke & though her voice was shaken
~~She bore her pale head proudly as do those~~
~~Who have~~
Who have been in such a labyrinth of thought Stet
~~They have forgotten~~
~~They~~ have
~~They cannot bring to mind that being~~ [?alive]
~~They [?] must die~~
~~They have forg [?] that they are [?alive]~~
~~And [?] that they [?must]~~ die
They cannot bring to mind that they [?but] [?live]
And [?so] [?are] subject to it all, so subject
To death at the end ‘I have sent [?all] away
For I seek judgment upon one
~~Who is self accused, & be [?the] judge [?]~~
~~[?Who] is self accused, & [?if]~~
Who is self acused, if she be innocent
~~She would meet [?your] [?troops]~~
She would not look upon your troops, [?not]

[NLI 30,517, 8v (inverted)]

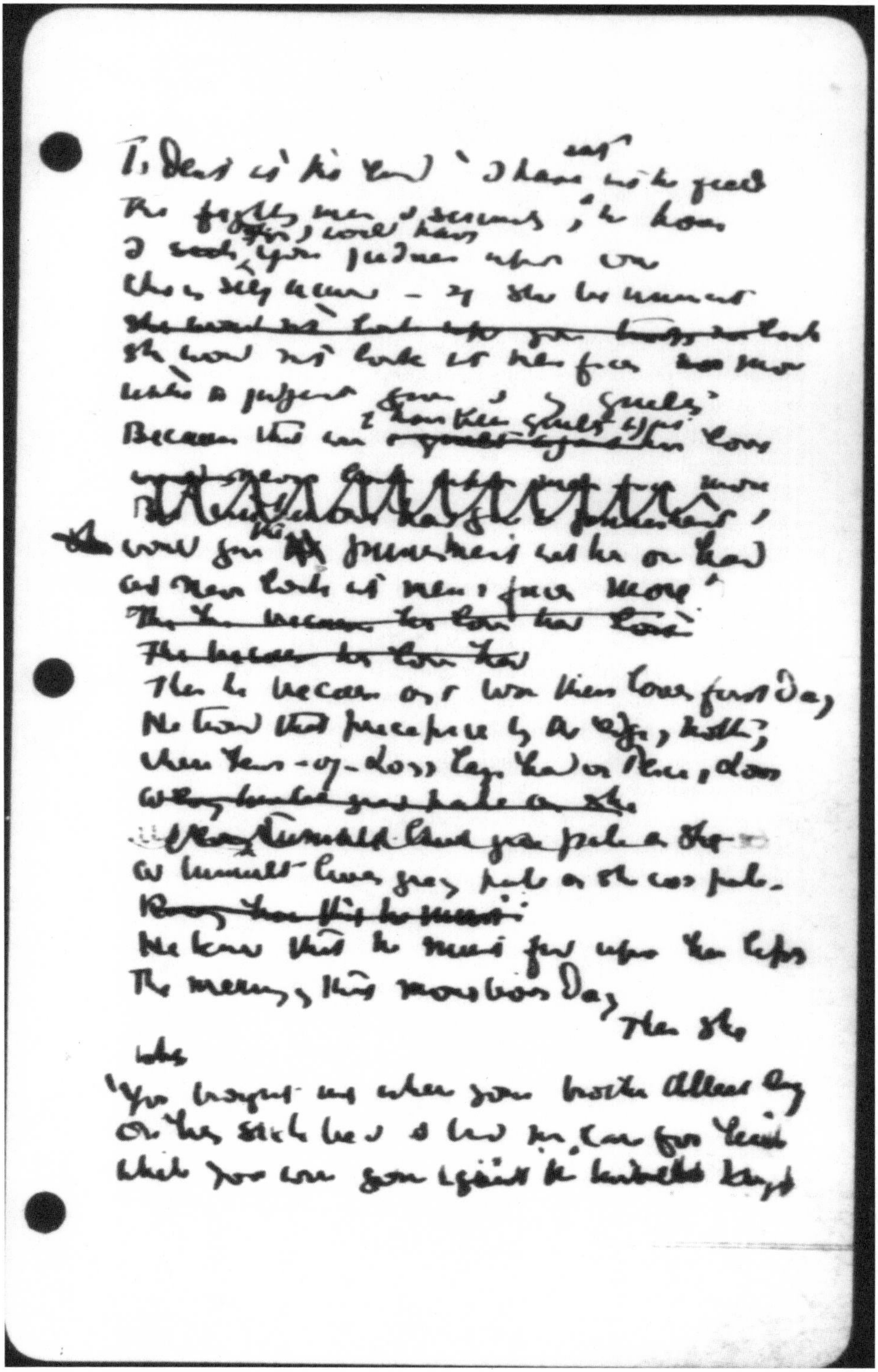

[NLI 30,517, 8[v] (inverted)]

[?sent]
[?To death at that hand] 'I have ^ into [?the] fields
The fighting men & servants of ^ the house
For I would have
I ~~seek~~ ^ your judgment upon one
Who is self accused — If she be innocent
~~She would not look upon your troops nor look~~
She would not look in mens faces [~~?~~] more
Until the judgment given & if guilty
to have been guilty against?
Because that were ~~a guilt against her~~ love
would never look upon mens face more
But with her own hand give the punishment'
the
~~She~~ Would give [?~~her~~] punishment with her own hand
And never look into men's faces more.'
~~Then he because [?his] love had lost~~
~~Then because [?his] had~~
Then he [?became] as [?] was their loves first day
He [?trod] that precipice by the edge of nothing
Where [?Fear]–of–[?Loss] lays hand on Peace of Love
~~[?] [?lay long] [?] grew pale as she~~
~~[? ?] [?turn all] [?] grew pale as she~~
And tumult [?lives grey] pale as she was pale.
~~[?Rembering] [?] that he must~~
He knew that he must find upon her lips
The meaning of that monstrous day
Then she
[~~?~~]
'You brought me where your brother [?Alleel] lay
On his sick bed & bid me care him
While you were gone [? ? ?] [~~?~~]

---

9 "would" perhaps is double-canceled.

[NLI 30,517, 16v (inverted)]

[NLI 30,517, 16ᵛ (inverted)]

And should he die to heap his burial mound
And raise his pillar stone'.
                                        Eocha said
~~Living or dead I love~~
' ~~Living or dead [?her]~~ l
                                whole
                              [~~?~~]
If he is living still, the ^ worlds mine.
~~If dead~~
But if not living half of it is gone'

~~She [but] [? ?]~~
' I bid them bring his bed in [?this] house
And daily gave him food with my own hands

' I bid them make his bed under this roof
And daily gave him food with my own hands
And many weeks past by, & when I said
' What is this trouble' he would answer nothing
Though always at my words his trouble grew'
~~Yet a [?few] [?]~~
[?Yet] I , being certain that his end was near
    Till I [?had] lit upon that root &
~~unless I found that root &~~ [?stubb] it out
But asked the more, until at he said
Weary of many questions — There are things
~~That may not though they may be~~ read in the eyes
~~[?Be spoken]','~~
~~That [?may] [?], [?though] the eyes discover them~~
~~[?Be] s~~

[NLI 30,517, 16r (inverted)]

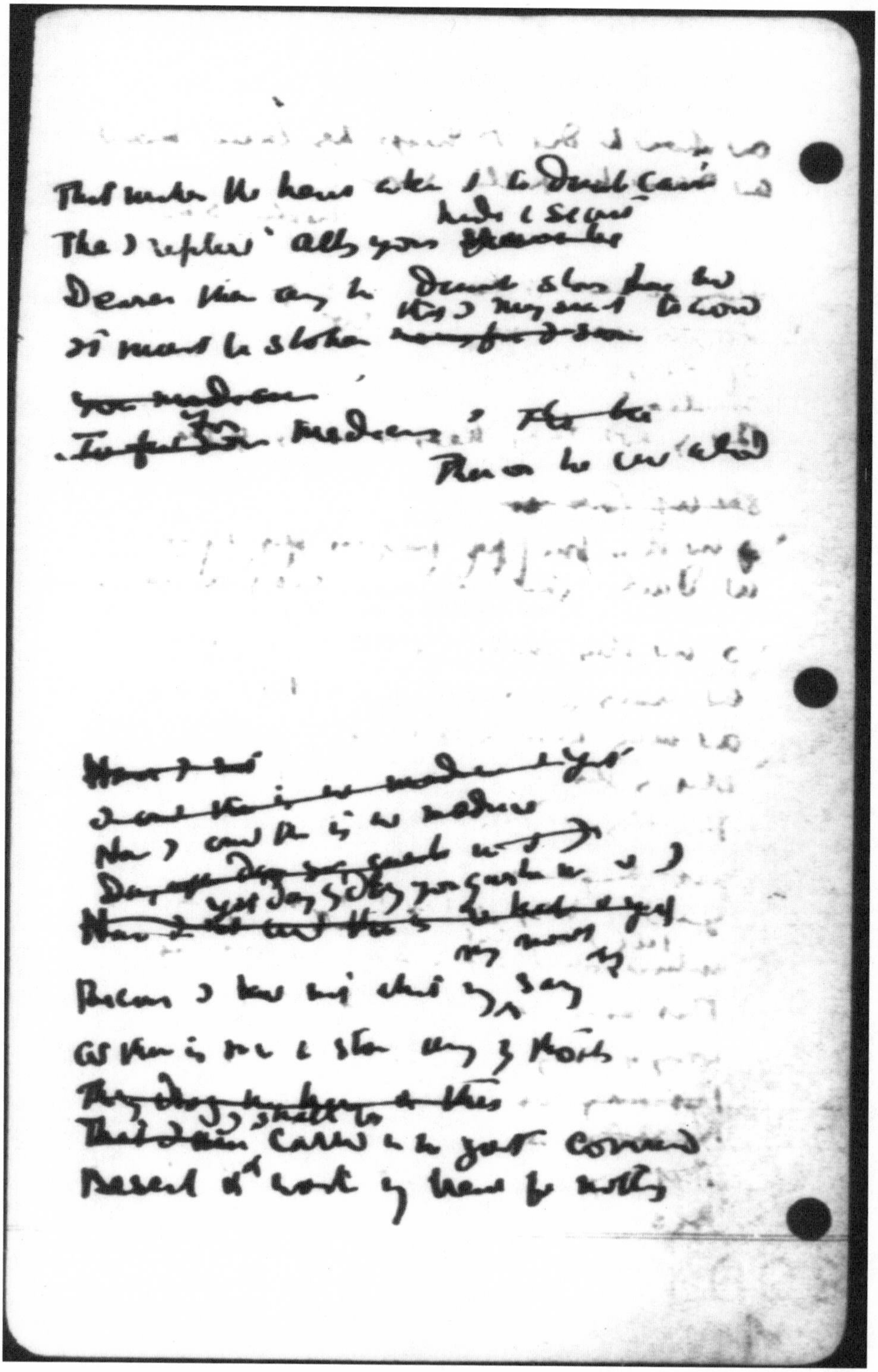

[NLI 30,517, 16r (inverted)]

1 That make the heart akin to the dumb [?cairn]
hide a secret
2 Then I replied 'Although you ~~[?] be~~
3 Dearer than any the dumb stone [?has] [?hid]
that I may search the world
4 It must be spoken ~~[?now] for I [?give]~~
5 ~~You [?ready] [?ears]~~'
For
6 ~~To find [?some]~~ medicine' ~~Then he~~
7 Thereon he cried aloud

8 ~~[?Have] I [?not]~~
9 ~~I [?own] there is no medicine~~ yet
10 Now I cried this is the medicine
11 ~~Day after day you question me & I~~
Yet day by day you question me & I
12 ~~Have I not [?told this] [? ? ?] & yet~~
my mouth [~~?~~]
13 Because I know not what [?my] ^ say'
14 And there is such a storm among my thoughts
15 ~~They drag me here & there~~
I shall be
16 ~~That I am~~ ^ carried in the gust command
17 Beseech & waste my breath for nothing

These two passages are probably insertions for an unlocated draft associated with NLI 13,586(2) (b), 5 (pp. 122–123 below).

[NLI 30,517, 17^{v} (inverted)]

[NLI 30,517, 17v (inverted)]

That may not though the eyes have made them known
Be spoken by the lips' But I replied
Although it be your hearts most secret thing
It must be spoken now that I may know
~~[?Where] to turn, that we may~~
[?] to go for help' Whereon he cried
Why do you question me day after day
~~[?Knowing] my thoughts are~~ dizzy ~~& my~~
~~Knowing my mind is dizzy, & my thought~~
~~Knowing my mind is such it stops my thought~~
[?Hardly] [? ?] comrades [? ?]
~~Knowing my mind is such & stops my thought~~
I as that I
~~[?] [?] the master of my words~~
~~And there is such a storm [?among] thoughts~~
I am no longer master of my word
~~That you must~~
~~[?That]~~ And there is such a storm [?among] my thoughts
I know not where they carry me' Then I

[?Have] I not said there is no help & yet
question me and I
Day after day ~~you come [? ?] [?question]~~
[? ?]
Because I [?] master of my words
And there is such a storm among my thoughts
I ~~know [?not] where they [?carry] me,~~ I
I know where the d carried me, command
Beseech, [?all] the while but [?waste my] breath
That

[NLI 30,517, 20^{v} (inverted)]

[NLI 30,517, 20[v] (inverted)]

Then I '[~~?~~]
Although [?that] thing you hide [?were] evil.
The speaking of it could be no great wrong
And evil must it be if it [?is] worse
That from [?heaped] stones that keep all [?virtues down]
And loosen upon us dreams that waste our life
And shows & shadows that but [?turn] the brain'
But finding him still silent I stooped down
~~And whispering that the women might not hear~~
And whispering, that no [~~?~~] ear but his might know
Said 'If a woman has put this on you
~~[?]~~
My men shall bring her though it by sail
For ~~Long~~Loclan, or from [~~?~~]
long lost [?Sarrico]
That she may look her handy work
~~And quench~~
And quench the rick she has fired' Then he
[?Being caused] by his thoughts [?when his thoughts]
And speaking what ~~they wo~~ he would not & [?they] would
~~Because of bodily weakness,~~
Through bodily weakness, murmured in my ear
' ~~You only of all women can cure me~~'
You — even you yourself — could work the cure'
I rose up at the bedside & went out
~~Between despair [? ?] & anger, & nine days~~
In anger, despair, & for nine days
~~By [?thoughts] [? ? ? ? ?], & yet~~
He had his food from other hands, ~~[&?] [?said]~~

13–14 The bracket is Yeats's.

[NLI 30,517, 19v (inverted)]

[NLI 30,517, 19ᵛ (inverted)]

the nine
~~And these nine days my mind [? ?] the~~
[?my many times]
~~went [?whirling] round [?in] the [?same] zodiac~~
~~And [?   ?] day my thoughts went to~~ & fro
[~~?~~]
[?~~But~~]
And for nine days I [~~?~~] stayed [? ?] [?thought]
[?]
That the only thing that^[? ?],
Beyond our question, beyond our pity even
~~[?   ?] old [?],~~
~~Is the heaped burying mound~~,
Is the [?heaped burying] mound & the grey stone

And for nine days my mind, went chasing round
[?This one] [?] zodiac, & always
~~It came~~
~~[?It found] that thought~~
one
It came to where it started — [?that] [^~~?~~] thing,
~~Alone~~
~~But one beyond all medicine~~
all
One thing alone [?] beyond ~~our~~ medicine
Beyond our [?questions], beyond our pity even
[?The] heaped up [?   ?] & the grey stone
So when the nine days gone, I stood again
Before his chair, & [~~?~~] once more whispered
[?Bend head] [?] hope put vigour in his [?]
Tonight'
my head
Before his [~~?~~] chair, & bending down [?my]   [?]/
That none might hear, [?   ~~?~~   ?   ?   ~~?~~   ?   ?]
[~~?   ?   ?   ?~~] [?]
[?When his] household [?was] asleep, to go
[?For] hope [?would] put the vigour [?in] limbs

28 The slash after the undeciphered word at the right margin perhaps indicates that the word is an addition to l. 29.

[NLI 30,517, 7^{v} (inverted)]

[NLI 30,517, 7ᵛ (inverted)]

To that old empty woodmans house [?hid hides]
[?Within] the [?border] of the little wood
Westward of [?Tara] [?] [?~~&~~] [?there to wait a friend]
That could — as he had told her work [?his] cure
And would be no harsh friend', ~~& then again~~
                    ~~who? to [?night might]~~ [?can came]
                    When had [?night c] [?]
I
~~I groped my way [?round]~~ the
                    boughs
I groped my way through bows & over roots
~~And found him, in [?] by the light~~
~~And found~~ him
~~To the old house, & found him~~
And found, a [~~?~~] torch that sputtered in the socket
~~And in its light, your brother~~
~~And on a heap of [?skins] [?upon] I [?found]~~
And stretched out sleeping on a pile of skins
Your brother — though I called him by his name
~~And [?took] his hand~~
And took [?his] hand in [?mine he did] not [?wake]
~~I waited till the dawn began to [?] [?break]~~
I waited till the dawn began to glimmer
~~Then fearing to~~ be
~~Then fearing that some labourer on his~~ way
~~To~~ [?]
~~To pasture, or to plough land might~~
~~Then fearing to be found by [?labourers]~~
Then fearing that some labourers on his way
To pasture land or plough land might see me
Went out, ~~& [?   ?] [?to light my way]~~

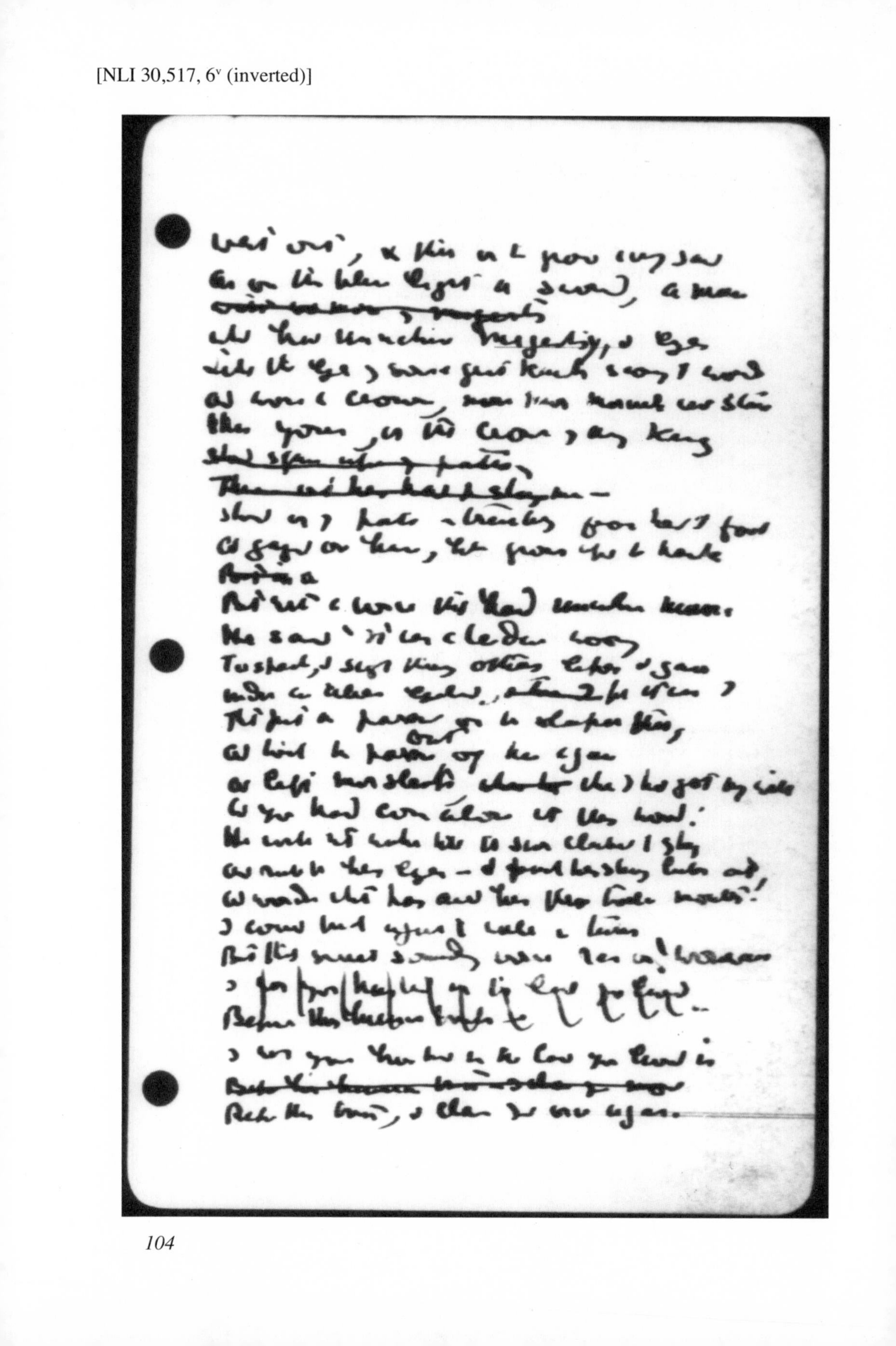

[NLI 30,517, 6ᵛ (inverted)]

[NLI 30,517, 6v (inverted)]

Went out, & [?there] on the ground ivy saw
As on the blue light a sword, a man
~~With [?no] more of majestry~~
Who had [?unnatural] majesty, & eyes
Like the eyes of some great [?kite] scouring the woods
And wore a crown, ~~more~~ [?more marvelous] with stone
Than yours, or the crown of any king
~~Stood square upon my path~~
~~Then out his hand [?to] stay~~ me —
Stood in my path — trembling from hand to foot
And gazed on him, like grouse upon a hawk
~~But in~~ a
But with a voice that had unnatural music
He said 'It was a tedious wooing
To [?speak], & sigh through others lips & gase
Under an alien eyelid, ~~[? ?] I~~ for it was I
That put a passion in the sleeper there,
                                        out
And took the passion ^ of [?him] again
And left mere sleep, ~~[?when] he~~ when I had got my will
[?And] you had come alone [?into] this wood.'
He will not wake till the sun climbs [?the] sky
And rub [?] his eyes — & push his strong limbs out
And wonder what has ailed him these twelve months.'
I cowered back against the wall in terror
But that sweet sounding voice ran on 'Woman
I was your husband in the land you lived
Before this human [?] —
I was your husband in the land you lived in
~~Before [?his human birth] — [?&]~~ when you [?]
Before this [?birth], [?&] claim you once again.

[NLI 30,517, 18^{v} (inverted)]

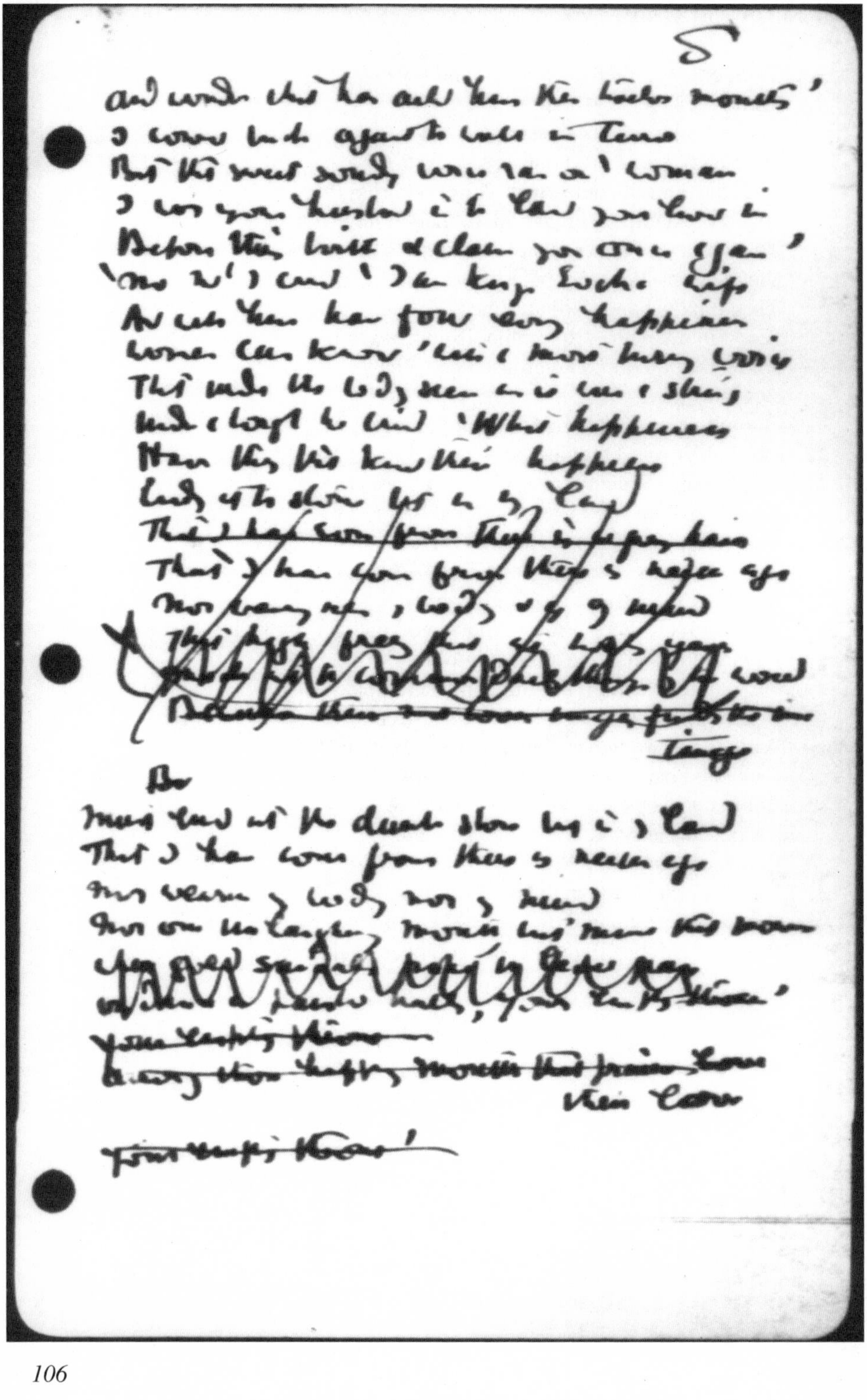

[NLI 30,517, 18[v] (inverted)]

8

And wonder what has ailed him these twelve months'
I cowered back against the wall in terror
But that sweet sounding voice ran on 'Woman
I was your husband in the land you lived in
Before this birth & claim you once again'
' No No' I cried 'I am King Eocha wife
And with him have found every happiness
Women can know' with a most burning voice
That made the body seem as it were a string
Under a bough he cried 'What happiness
Have they that know their happiness
Ends [?at] the stone but in my land
~~That I have come from there is no grey hair~~
That I have come from these is neither age
Nor [?wearyness] of body and [?of] of mind
That [?high feeling] that [?at twenty] years
[?] [?with common daily things of the world]
[?Because there no lovers image finds the true]
~~image~~
[~~?~~]
Must end at the dumb stone but in my land
That I have come from there is neither age
Nor [?weariness] of body nor of mind
Nor one unlaughing mouth, but mine that mourns
When [?gold] sandals [?] in [? ?]
[?Or dance in] painted [?halls], your empty throne'
~~Your empty throne~~
~~Among those happy mouths that [?praise] love~~
their love
~~Your empty throne'~~

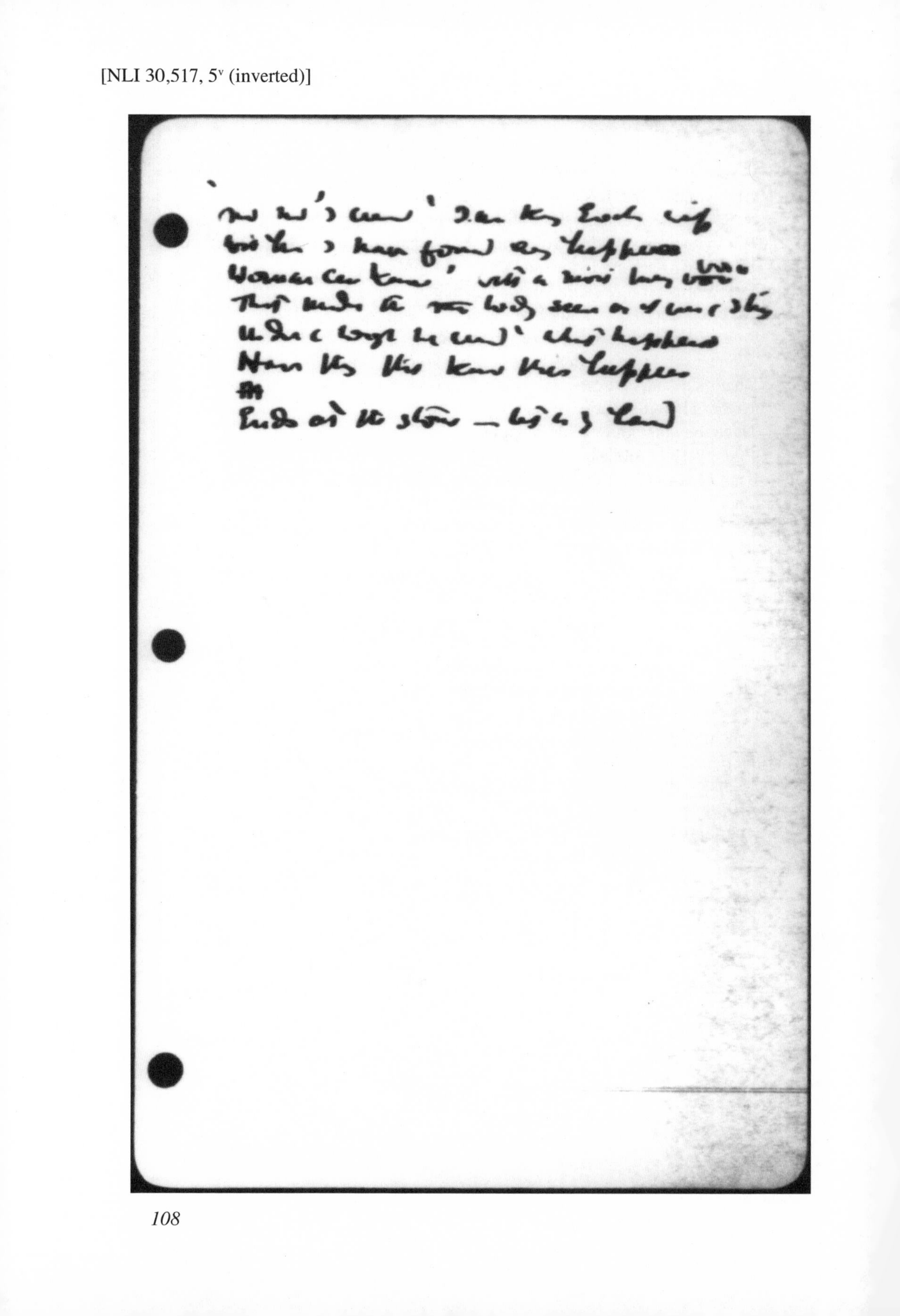

[NLI 30,517, 5v (inverted)]

[NLI 30,517, 5v (inverted)]

‘ No no’ I cried ‘I am King Eochas wife
With him have found every happiness
voice
Woman can know’ with a most burning [~~?~~]
That made the [~~?~~] body seem as it were a string
Under a bough he cried ‘What happiness
Have they that know their happiness
~~M~~
Ends at the stone — but if of land

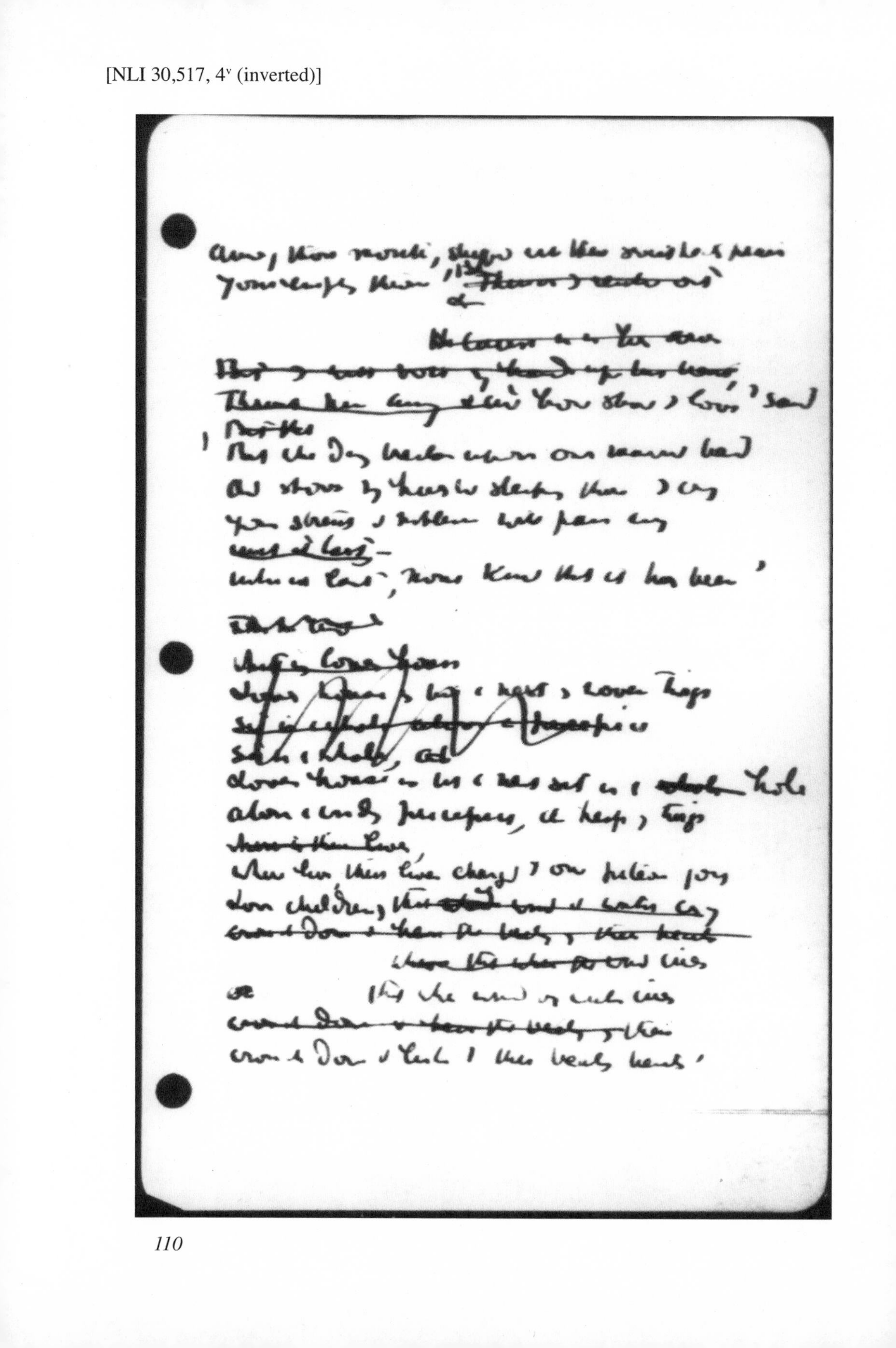

[NLI 30,517, 4v (inverted)]

[NLI 30,517, 4[v] (inverted)]

Among those mouths, [?stuffed] with their sweethearts praise
[?]
Your empty throne" ~~Thereon I reached out~~
~~&~~
~~He [?carressed] [?her] in his arms~~
~~But I will [?touch] my hands upon his heart,~~
~~Thrust his away & [?cried]~~ 'How should I love' said
~~But [?the]~~
But the day breaks upon our married bed
And shows my husband sleeping there I cry
Your strength & nobleness will pass away
~~[?will] at last~~ —
When [?at] last, none [?know] that it has been'

~~Then he [?cried] '~~
~~What is loves house~~
Loves house is but a nest of woven twigs
~~Set in a whole above a precipice~~
Set in a whole, ~~ab~~
Loves house is but a nest set in a ~~whole~~ hole
Above a windy precipice, [?the a] heap of twigs
~~[?Wherein] there lives,~~
Where live their lives changed to one priceless joy
[?~~if~~]
Loves children, ~~that above wind & water cry~~
~~Crouch down & hear the beating of their hearts~~
~~[?When that] when the wind~~ cries
~~Cr~~ that when wind or water cries
~~Crouch down & hear the beating of~~ their
Crouch down & listen to their beating hearts'

6 The closing quotation mark after "love" might possibly be a question mark.

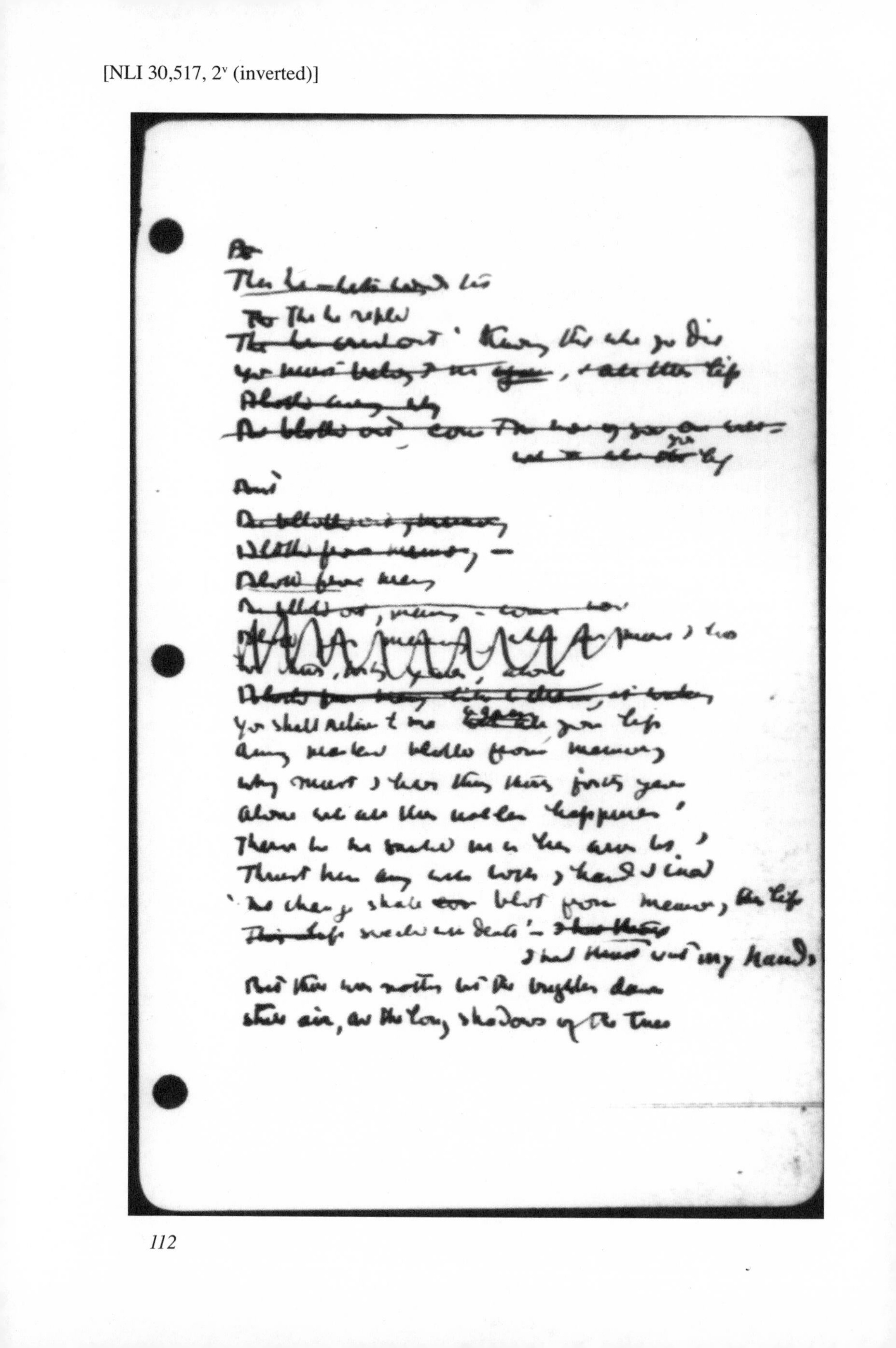

[NLI 30,517, 2^v (inverted)]

[NLI 30,517, 2ᵛ (inverted)]

~~A~~
~~Then he — with [?words~~ let]
~~The~~ Then he replied
~~Then he cried out~~ 'Knowing that when you die
~~You must belong to me again~~, ~~& all this life~~
~~Blotted away why~~
~~[?Be] blotted out, come to me now of your our will —~~
your
~~will & all the life~~
~~But~~
~~Be blotted out of memory~~
~~Blotted from memory~~ —
~~Blotted from~~ memory
~~Be blotted out of memory — come now~~
Blotted from memory, [?when you] must I live
For thirty, forty years, alone
~~Blotted from memory like [?a] [?dream], at waking~~
[?again]
You shall return to me ~~[?with] all~~, your life
Among mankind blotted from memory
Why must I [?live through] thirty forty years
Alone with all this nobler happiness'
Thereon he [?had fastened] me in his arms but I
Thrust him away with both my hands & cried
' No change shall ~~ever~~ blot from memory this life
~~This life~~ sweetened with death' — ~~I had [?thrust]~~
I had thrust out my hands
But there was nothing but the brighter dawn
Still air, and the long shadows of the trees

The Two Kings.

[NLI 13,586(2) (b), 1]

The Two Kings. (1

at length
Eocha Chief King of Ireland came ~~[?in] length~~
Worn out after a dozen months of war
From Duras up to [?Cruachan] & [~~?~~] Magh Ai
With turbulent kings, imagination fixed
upon that milk white sharer of his bed
Queen Edane, to a darkening little wood
That slopped towards Tara — [?Hurried by] love
He had out ridden that war broken troop
[?Victorious], [?nearly] escaped from death
That with a captured multitude of cattle
Toiled [?through] the mud, & came on the day set
Where certain beach trees made an [?empty] place
And there where the blue light of the ground ivy
Was mixed with the [?upper] green, a stag
white as a curd &
~~Whiter than snow with eyes~~ the [?tint] of the sea
[?amazed]
Stood square upon his road, & [?then] [~~?~~]
He dug his spur into his horse flank [?to pass]
It ran upon him. & the [?branching] horns
[?through]
Ripped through his horse flank & all but [~~?~~]
He missed his answering stroke & the stag wheeled
They fought for certain moments [?thin] & [?thick]
His sword was caught upon a branch of horn
silver
And the horn sounded as it had been ~~metal~~
~~A [?silver] bell in a kings house as is~~ maybe
~~[?A] [?sounding pole of] silver [?] but at last~~
The sounding pillar in the assembly house
That s [?stricken] by the hammer of a king
[?Commanding] all to silence but at last
[?This] horse the entrails showing [~~?~~] through its skin
fell dead

9 "[?Victorious]" could be "[?Victories]"; "[?nearly]" could be "[?newly]".

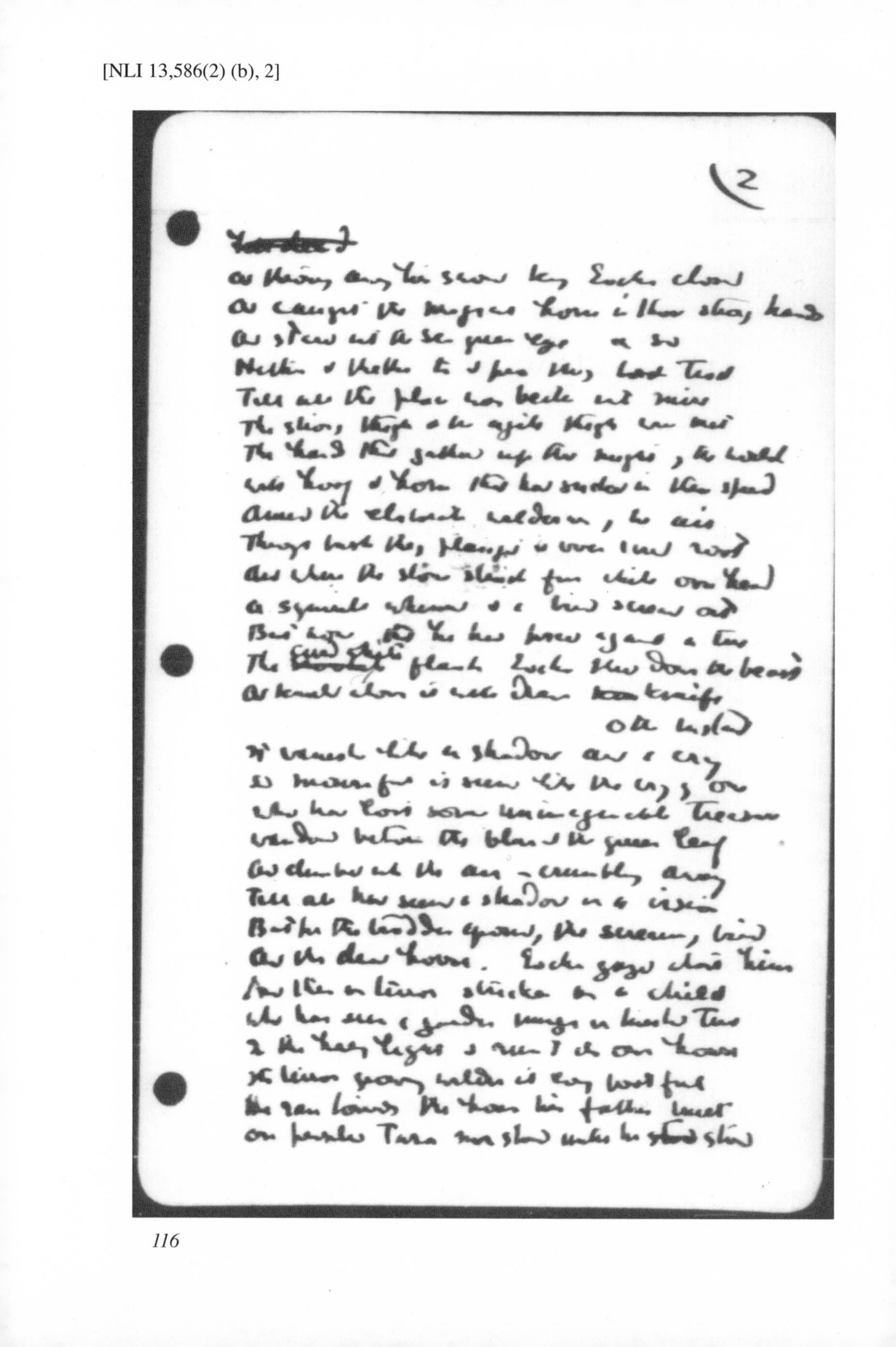

[NLI 13,586(2) (b), 2]

[NLI 13,586(2) (b), 2]

2

~~Fell dead~~
30 And throwing away his sword King Eocha closed
31 And caught the magical horn in those strong hands
32 And stared into the sea green eye & so
33 Hither & thither to & fro they [?~~tord~~] trod
34 Till all the place was beaten into mire
35 The strong thigh & the agile thigh were met
36 The hands that gathered up the might of the world
37 With hoof & horn that had sucked in their speed
38 Amid the elaborate wilderness of the air
39 Through bush they plunged & over ivied root
40 And where the stone struck fire while over head
41 A squirrell whinned & a bird screamed out
42 But now that he had forced against a [?tree]
curd white
43 The ~~[?sno] white~~ flank Eocha threw down the beast
44 And kneeled above it with drawn [~~?~~] knife
O the instant
44 It [?vanished] like a shadow and a cry
45 So mournful it seemed like the cry of one
46 Who has lost some unimaginable treasure
47 Wandered between the blue & the green leaf
48 And climbed into the air — crumbling away
49 Till all had seemed a shadow or a vision
50 But for the trodden ground, the screaming bird
51 And the dead horse. Eocha gazed about him
52 And then as terror stricken as a child
53 Who has seen a garden image or twisted tree
54 In the half light & run to its own house
55 Its terror growing wilder at every foot fall
56 He ran towards the house his fathers built
57 On peopled Tara nor slowed until he [?~~stood~~] stood

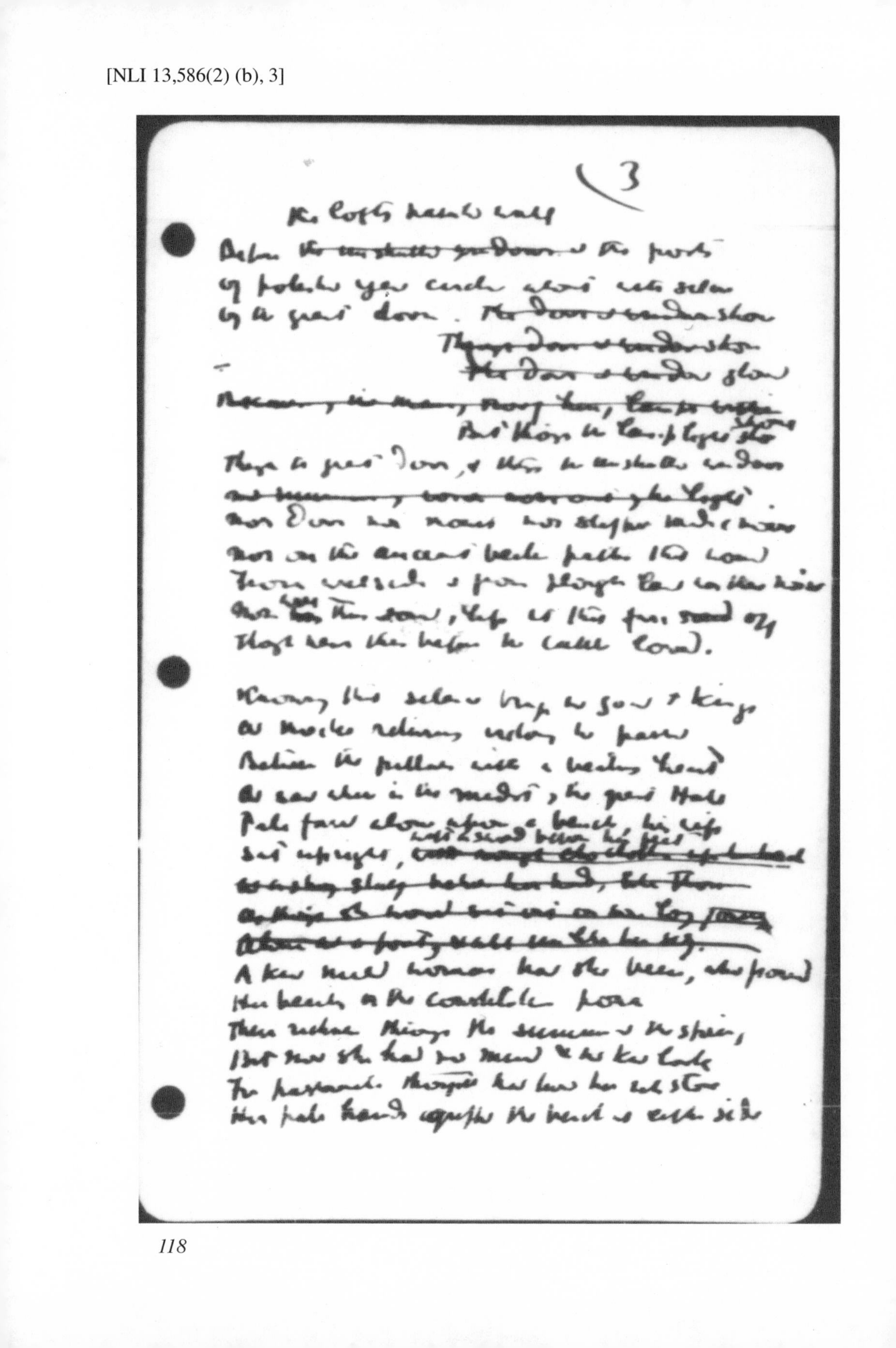

[NLI 13,586(2) (b), 3]

[NLI 13,586(2) (b), 3]

3

the lofty painted [?wall]
58 Before ~~the [?unshuttered] windows &~~ the posts
59 Of polished yew circled about with silver
60 Of the great door. ~~The door & windows~~ [?shone]
~~[?Through] door & window [?shone]~~
~~The door & window~~ glowed
~~Because the many roof hung lamps [?within]~~
shone
61 But though the lamp light ~~sho~~
62 [?Through] the great door, & [?through] the [?unshuttered] windows
63 ~~No murmur of voices [?most] out of the light~~.
64 Nor door nor [?mouth] nor slipper made a noise
65 Nor on the ancient beaten paths that wound
66 From welside & from plough land was there noise
were
67 Nor [?~~was~~] there sound of life but that farr ~~sound~~ off
68 Though [?nearer than] before the cattle lowed.

69 Knowing that silence brings no good to kings
70 And mocks returning victory he passed
71 Between the pillars with a beating heart
72 And saw where in the midst of the great Hall
73 Pale faced alone upon a bench, his wife
with a sword before her feet
74 Sat upright, ~~with rough clo clothes up [?her] back~~
75 ~~As a [? ? ?] her hands, like those~~
76 ~~As though she [?would] set out on some long journey~~
77 ~~Alone [?] a [?] front, & all unlike her self~~.
78 A kind mild woman had she been, who [?poured]
79 Her beauty [?as] the constelations pour
80 Their richness through the summer & the spring
81 But now she had no mild & no [?kind] look
82 For passionate thought had turned her into stone
83 Her pale hands gripped the bench at either side

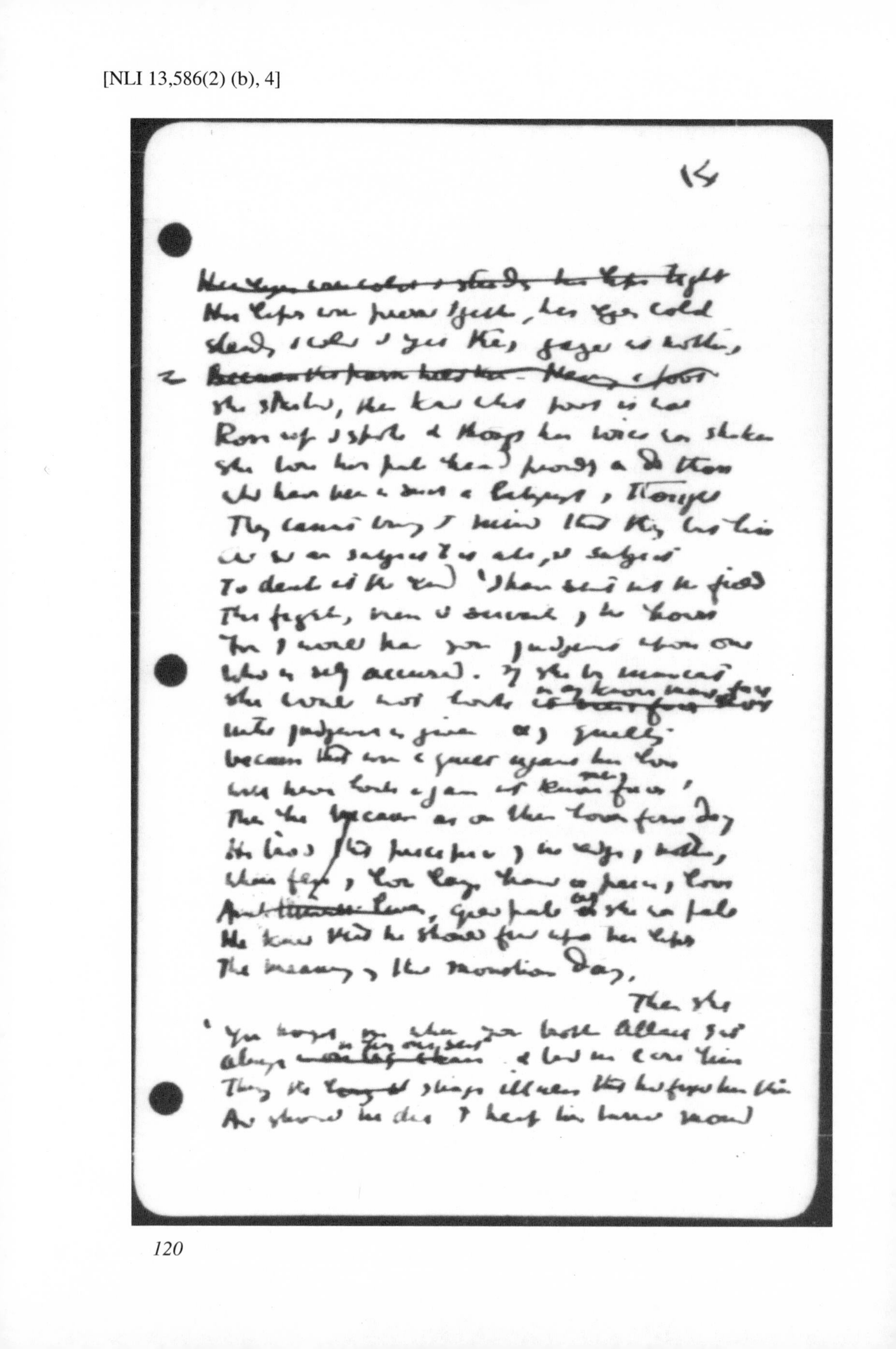

[NLI 13,586(2) (b), 4]

[NLI 13,586(2) (b), 4]

\4

~~Her eyes were cold & steady her lips tight~~
Her lips were pressed together, her eyes cold
Steady & cold & yet they gazed at nothing
~~Because that passion held her — Hearing a foot~~
She started, then knew what foot it was
Ran up & spoke & though her voice was shaken
She bore her pale head proudly as do those
Who have been in such a labyrinth of thought
They cannot bring to mind that they [?but] [?live]
And [?so] as subject to it all, [?if] subject
To death at the end 'I have sent [?into] the field
The fighting men & servants of the house
For I would have your judgement upon one
Who is self accused. If she be innocent
in any known mans face
She would not look ~~[?at] mens faces [?]~~
Until judgement is given & if guilty
because that were a guilt against her love
mens
Will never look again at known faces'
Then he [?became] as on their loves first day
He trod that precipice of the edge of nothing
Wheere fear of loss lays hand on peace of love
as
~~And tumult lives,~~ grew pale [?~~or~~] she was pale
He knew that he should find upon her lips
The meaning of that monstrous day.
Then she
' You [?brought] me where your brother [?Alleel] sat
in his one seat
Always ~~in one big chair~~ & bid me care him
[?Through] the ~~long il~~ strange illness that had fixed him there
And should he die to heap his burial mound

102–104 The vertical stroke probably is a cancel.

[NLI 13,586(2) (b), 5]

[NLI 13,586(2) (b), 5]

[~~?~~]5

And raise his pillar stone'
Eocha said
If he be living still the whole worlds mine
'But if not living I have but half the world'

' I bid them make his bed under this roof
And daily made him food with my own hands
And many weeks pased by, & when I said
' What is the trouble' he would answer nothing
Though always at my words his trouble grew'
And ~~But~~ I to kind the root & [?stubb] [?it] out
But asked the more, until he spoke these words
Weary of many questions There are things
dumb
That make the heart akin to the ~~grey~~ stone
Then I replied Although you hide a secret
[?Dearer] than any that the dumb stone hides
It must be spoken that I may search the world
For medicine. Thereon he cried aloud
Day after day you question me and I
Because I knew not what my mouth may say
And there is such a storm among my thoughts
I shall be caried in the gust, command
Beseech [?and] waste my breath for nothing'
Then I 'Although that thing you hide were evil
The speaking of it could be great wrong
And evil must it be if it were worse
That dumb stone that keeps all virtue down
And loosens on us dreams that waste our life
Shadows & shows that can but turn the brain'
But finding him still silent I stooped down
And whispering that no ear but his might [?know]
Said 'If a woman has put this on you

[NLI 13,586(2) (b), 6]

[NLI 13,586(2) (b), 6]

[?6]

142 My men shall bring her whether it be by horse
143 From that well guarded Cruachan, or by sail
144 From Loch lan, or from long lost [?Sairaco]
145 That she may look upon her handy work
146 And quench the rick she fired' Then he
Being
147 [?~~Beyond~~] [?cared] by his thought beyond [?his] thought
148 And speaking what he would not though he would
149 ~~Through bodily [?weakness], murmured [?in] my ear~~
150 ' You even you yourself could work [?the] cure'
151 But at those words, I rose & went out
And for nine days he fed from other hands
152 ~~In anger and despair and [?for] nine days~~
153 ~~He had his food from other hands than~~ mine
154 And for nine days my mind went wheeling round
155 In the one desolate zodiac and always
156 It came to where it started that one thought
157 One thing alone [?and] beyond all [?medicine]
158 Beyond our questioning, our pity even
[?] [?dumb]
159 The ~~[?heaped up [?barrel]~~ mound & to ~~grey~~ [?stone]
160 So when the ninth day [?d] gone I stood again
161 Before his chair & bending down my head
162 Told him that when Orian rose & all
163 The women of his household were asleep
164 To go — for hope would give his limbs the power —
165 To that old empty wood mans house thats [?hidden]
166 [?within] the border of the little wood
167 Westward of Tarra — There to await a friend
168 That could — as he had told her — work a cure
169 And would be no harsh friend'
When night had come

[NLI 13,586(2) (b), 7]

[NLI 13,586(2) (b), 7]

7

170 I groped my way
through boughs & over roots
171 And found a torch that sputtered in the socket
172 And stretched out [?sleeping] on a pile of skins
but
173 Aleel ~~& those~~ though I called him [?by] his name
174 ~~And to~~ And [?touched] him on [?his] face he would not wake
175 I watched until the Dawn began to glimmer
176 Then fearing that some labourer on his way
177 To pasture land or plough land would have seen me
178 Went out, among the rocks & the ground ivy
179 As on the blue light of a sword a man
180 Who had unnatural majesty & eyes
181 Like the eyes of some great kite scouring the
woods
more
182 And wore a crown [~~?~~] marvellous with [?stones]
183 Than that they claim [?for these] Byzantium king
184 Stood on my path — Trembling from head to foot
{I
185 {[?A] gazed on him like grouse upon a hawk
186 But with a voice that had unnatural music
187 He said 'It [?was] a long & weary wooing
188 To speak & sigh through others lips & gaze
189 Under an alian eyelid for it was I
in
190 That put a passion ~~on~~ the sleeper there
191 And took the passion out of him again
192 And left mere sleep when I had got my will
193 And you had come alone [?into] this wood [?]
194 ~~He will not wake till the sun climbs the sky~~
195 ~~He will not wake till the sun [?climb] [?]~~
196 When the sun s climbed the ladder he will wake
197 And rub his eyes & [?push] his strong limbs out

[NLI 13,586(2) (b), 8]

8

And wonder what has ailed him these twelve months'
I could but cry again in terror
But that sweet sound, ran on 'Woman
I was your husband in the land you lived in
Before this life & claim you once again
'No one' I cried 'I am King Eochaid's wife
And with him have found every happiness
Women can know' 'with a most burning love
That made the body seem as it were a string
Under a bow he cried ' What happiness
Have they that know their happiness
Must end at the dream stone but in my land
There is not weariness, nor ~~or body~~ not body's lod?
~~nor ebbing loves delight nor age~~
nor ebbing of loves pleasure nor old age
Nor any unlaughing morals but mine this moment
Among those miracles crammed with the sweetest pain
Your empty throne'
How should I love I said
~~But that day breaking on our marriage bed~~
~~But this when day is breaking on my bed~~
But that when day breaks on our marriage bed
And shows my husband sleeping there I say
"Your strength a while ago will pass away"
Love? Honour is but a nest set in a hole
above a windy precipice, a heap of twigs
where love, there but change / or present joy
Love's children shelter [illegible] lies

[NLI 13,586(2) (b), 8]

8

And wonder what has ailed him these twelve months'
I cowered back against the wall in terror
But that sweet sounding voice ran on 'Woman
I was your husband in the land you lived in
Before this birth & claim you once again.
' No no' I cried 'I am King Eocha's wife
And with him have found every happiness
Women can know' with a most burning voice
That made the body seem as it were a string
Under a bow he cried 'What happiness
Have they that know their happiness
Must end at the dumb stone but in my land
nor
There is no weariness of mind ~~or body~~ body
~~Nor ebb of loves delight nor age~~
Nor ebbing of loves pleasure nor old age
Nor [?one] unlaughing mouth but mine that mourns
Among those mouths crammed with their sweet hearts praise
Your empty throne'
How should I love' I said
~~But that day breaking on our marriage bed~~
~~But that when day is breaking on my bed~~
But that when day breaks on our marriage bed
And shows my husband sleeping there' I cry
"Your strength & nobleness will pass away"
Loves house is but a nest set in a hole
Above a windy precipice, a heap of twigs
Where live, their lives changed, our piteous joy
Loves children that when wind or [?water] [?cries]

[NLI 13,586(2) (b), 9]

9

Crowd down to look at their beating hearts'
Then he replied 'Knowing this the deeds come
You shall return to me again, your life
Among mankind blotted from memory
Why must I have been thirty, forty years
Alone with all this useless happenings'
Thereon he seized me in his arms but I
Thrust him away with both my hands & cried
No change shall blot from memory the life
[illegible] until death'
I have thrust out my hands
But there was nothing but the brightening dawn
Still air & the long shadows, the trees"
etc
She had no more to say, & from her eyes
Upon King Eochaid's face, & shortly love
He touched her hand with his lips & said
'I thank you for your kindness to my brother
And for your love this has been doubly tested
For this your promise & for that refusal'

Thereon the bellowing of those captive herds
Sounded about the walls & through the door
Jostled & shouted those that were wasted men
And in their midst King Eochaid's brother stood.
He had heard the din between the land & the clouds
And ridden out to welcome them and now
Gives his hand to this man and to that
Praising their great victory and gave them joy
Of their return to the ancestral house

Dec. 1912

[NLI 13,586(2) (b), 9]

~~Cr~~ 9

Crouch down & listen to their beating hearts'
Then he replied 'Knowing that when death come
You shall return to me again, your life
Among mankind blotted from memory
Why must I live then thirty, forty years
Alone with all this use less happiness'
Thereon he seized me in his arms but I
Thrust him away with both [?my] hands & cried
No change shall blot from memory this life
Sweetened with death'
I had thrust out my hands
But there was nothing but the brightening dawn
Still air & a long shadow of the trees"
[?~~She~~]
She had no more to say & fixed her eyes
till
Upon King Eocha's face, ~~and~~ [?showing] love
He touched her forhead with his lips & said
' I thank you for your kindness to my brother
And for your love that has been double tested
For that you promised & for that refused'

Thereon the bellowing of those captive birds
Sounded about the walls & through the door
~~Broke shouting those~~
Jostled & shouted those war [~~?~~] wasted men
And in their midst King Eocha brother stood.
He had heard that din between the land & [?the] clouds
And ridden out to welcome them and now
Praised their great victories and gave them joy
Of their return to the ancestral house
Dec 1912

[NLI 13,586(2) (b), 10[v] (inverted)]

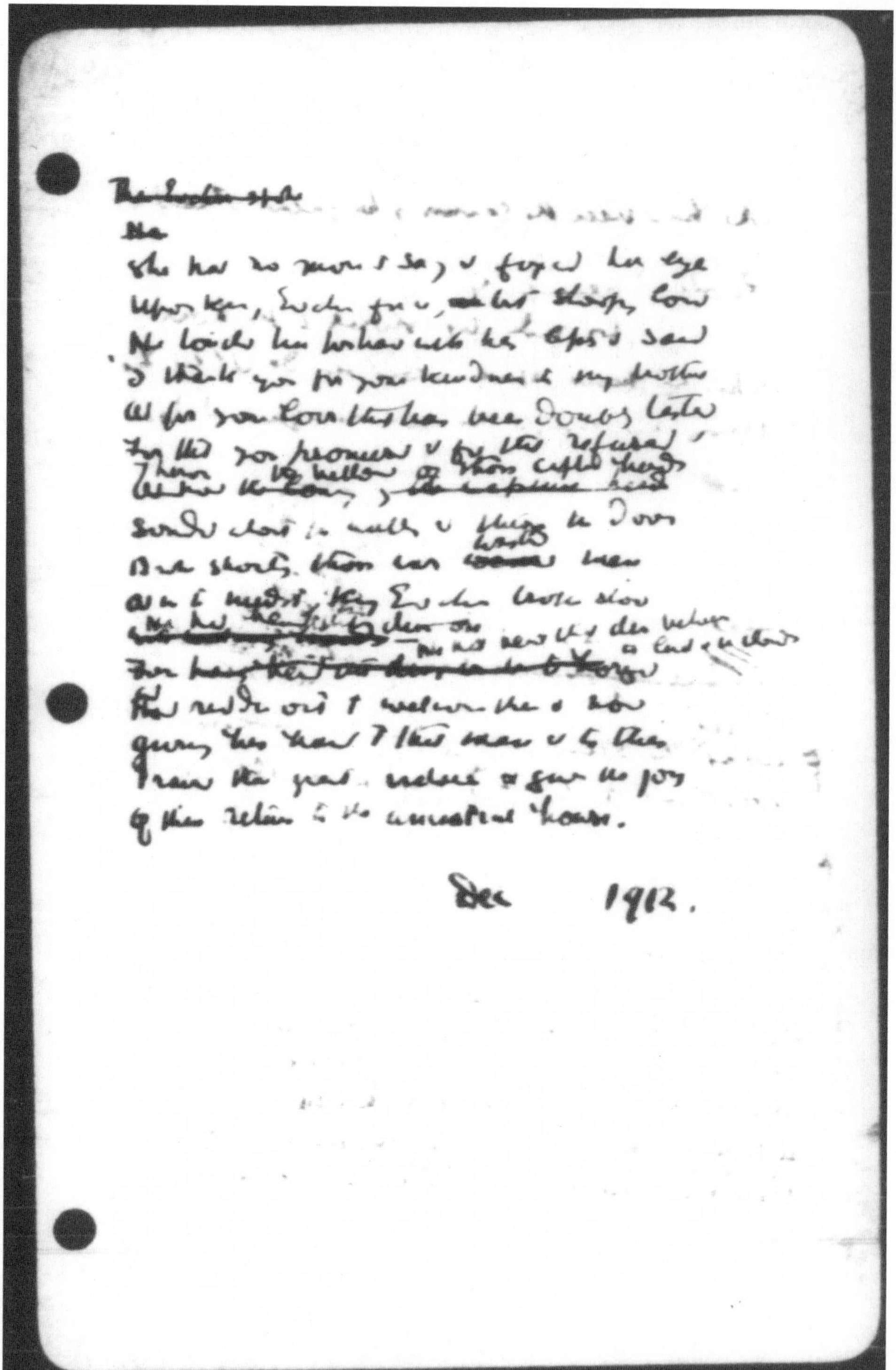

She had no more to say & fixed her eyes
Upon [illegible], [illegible]
He touched his forehead with his lips & said
I thank you for your kindness & my brother
All for your love that has been doubly tested
By that your promise & by that refusal
[illegible]
Sounded about the walls & through the doors
But shortly there was [illegible]
[illegible]
[illegible]
[illegible]
[illegible] reached out to welcome them & [illegible]
[illegible]
[illegible]
Of their return to the ancestral house.

Dec 1912.

[NLI 13,586(2) (b), 10v (inverted)]

~~Then Eocha spoke~~
~~He~~
She had no more to say & fixed her eye
Upon King Eocha face, [~~?~~] but stooping low
He touched her forhead with his lips & said
' I thank you for your kindness to my brother
And for your love that has been doubly tested
For that you promised & for that refused'
Thereon the bellow of those captive herds
~~And now the lowing~~ of ~~the captive herd~~
Sounded about the walls & through the door
wasted
Broke shortly those war ~~wearied~~ men
And in the midst, King Eocha brother stod
He had heard [?din]
~~With [? ?]~~ hands —
He had heard that din between
the land & the clouds
For ~~having heard that din on [? ?] [?horizon]~~
And
~~Had~~ ridden out to welcome them & now
Giving his hand to that man & to this
Praised their great victories & gave them joy
Of their return to the ancestral house.

Dec 1912.

Close variant of the final fifteen lines of the poem (compare pp. 130–131 above); the other side of the sheet (pp. 134–135 below) has drafts of the opening of the next version.

[NLI 13,586(2) (b), 10r (inverted)]

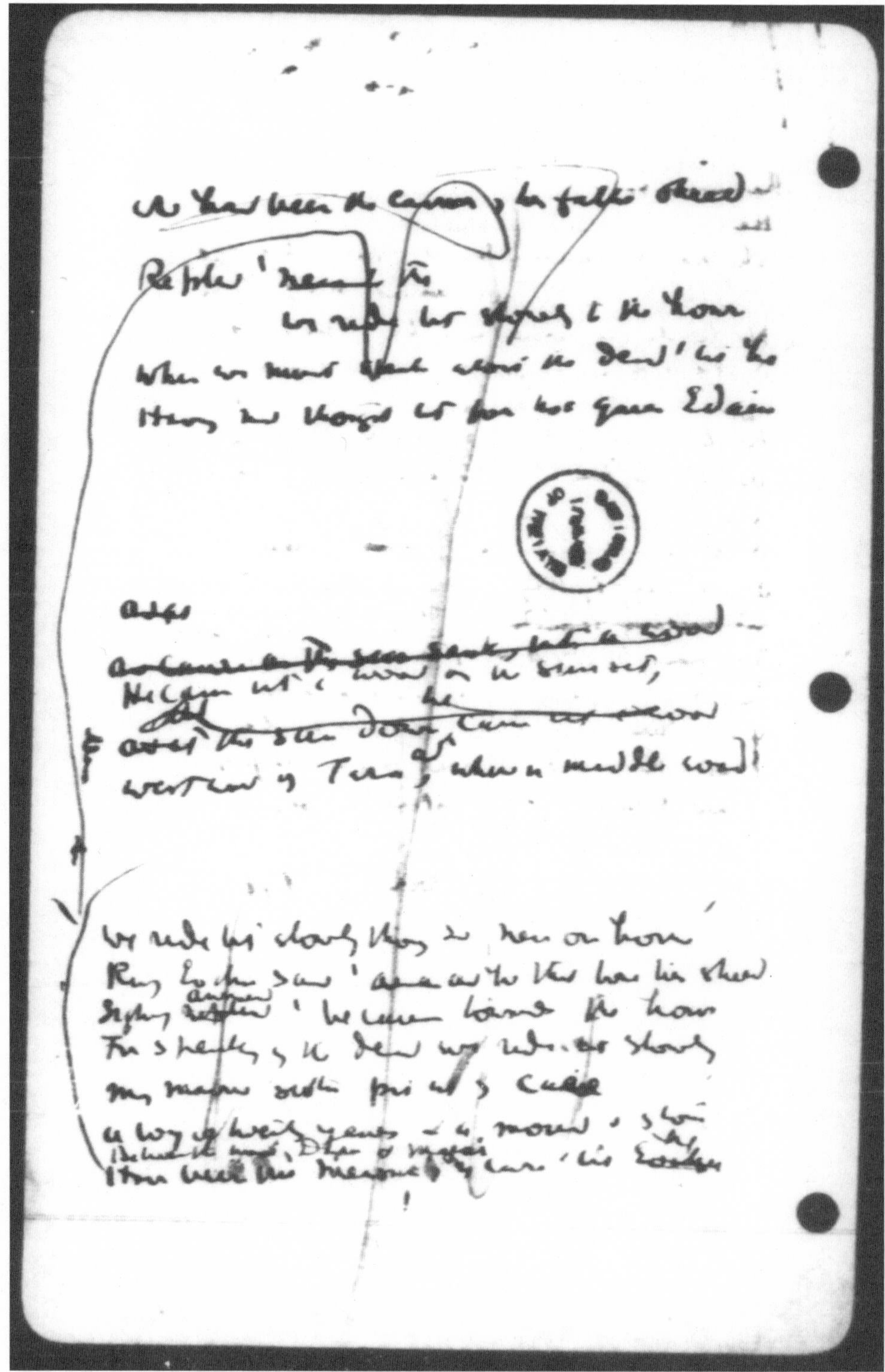

[NLI 13,586(2) (b), 10r (inverted)]

who had been the carrier of her father' shield

Replied ~~'[? ?]~~ the
We ride but slowly to the hour
When we must speak about the dead' but he
Having [?no] thought but for his Queen Edain

~~And [?]~~
~~And came as the sun sank, into a wood~~
He came into a wood as the sun set,
[?~~At~~] ~~he~~
[?] ~~And at the sun down came into [?a] wood~~
[?and]
Westward of Tara, where in middle wood

' We ride but slowly though so near our home'
King [?Eocha] said '~~And [?as]~~ And he that bore his shield
answered
Sighing ~~replied~~ 'because towards the hour
For speaking of the dead we ride but slowly
My married sister [?put in my care]
A boy of twenty years — a mound & stone
Between the wood of [?Duras] & Magai he
Have been the measure [?of my] care' but ~~Eochu~~

Draft of the opening of the next version, on 1r of Berg(3), pp. 136–137 below.

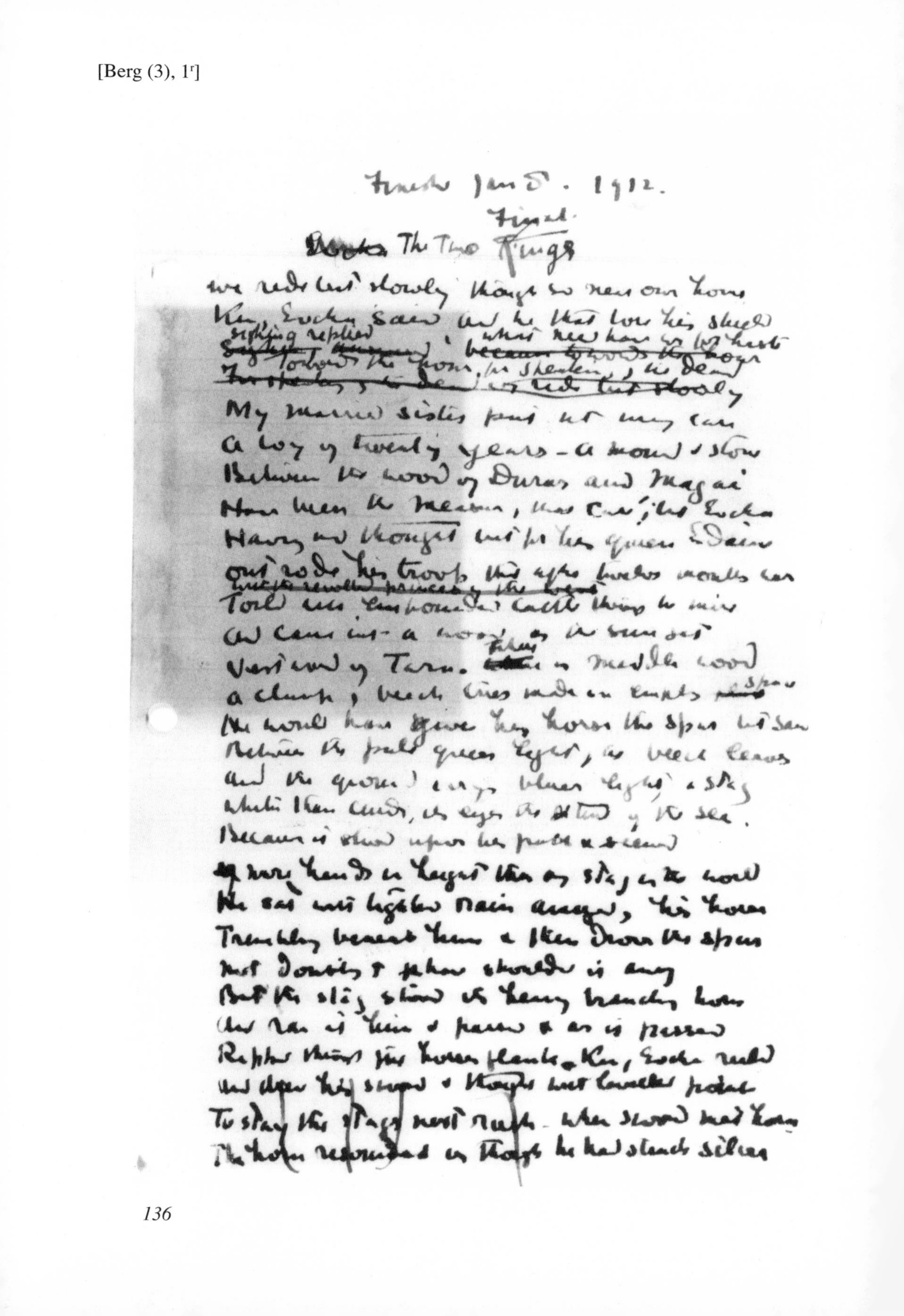

[Berg (3), 1r]

[Berg(3), 1r]

Finished Jan 8. 1912.
<u>Final</u>.
~~Eocha~~ The Two Kings
We ride but slowly though so near our home
King Eocha said and he that bore his shield
Sighing replied what need have we for haste
~~Sighing answered~~ '~~because towards the hour~~
Towards the hour for speaking of the dead
~~For speaking of the dead we ride but slowly~~
My married sister put into my care
A boy of twenty years — a mound and stone
Between the wood of Duras and Magai
Have been the measure of that care', but Eocha
Having no thought but for his queen Edain
Out rode his troop that after twelve months war
~~With the revolted princes of the west~~
Toiled with empounded cattle through the mire
And came into a wood as the sun set
There
Westward of Tara. ~~Where~~ in middle wood
space
A clump of beech trees made an empty ~~place~~
g
He would have [?]iven his horse the spur but saw
Between the pale green light of the beech leaves
And the ground ivys bluer light, a stag
Whiter than curds, its eyes the [~~?~~] tint of the sea.
Because it stood upon his path & seemed
[~~?~~] More hands in height than any stag in the world
He sat with tightened rain angered, his horse
Trembling beneath him & then drove the spur
Not doubting to ~~p~~ have shouldered it away
But the stag stood its heavy branching horns
And ran at him & passed & as it passed
Ripped through the horses flank [?/] King Eocha reeled
And drew his sword & thought with levelled point
To stay the stags next rush — when sword met horn
The horn resounded as though he had struck silver

2

But drew his sword & thought with levelled point
To stay the stag's next rush. When sword met horn
The horn resounded as though it had been silver.
Horn locked in sword, they tugged & struggled there
As though a stag & unicorn were met
In Africa on mountain of the moon,
Until at last it drew the unlocked horn
Through the entrails of the horse. Dropping his sword
Eochaid seized both horns in his strong hand
And stared into the sea green eye & so
Hither & thither to & fro they trod
Till all the place was beaten into mire
The strong thigh and the agile thigh were met
The hands that gather up the might of the world
And hoof & horn that had sucked in their speed
Among the elaborate wilderness of the air
Through bush they plunged, & over ivied root
And when the stone struck fire & in the leaves
A squirrel whinnied & a bird screamed out
But when at last he forced those sinewy flanks
Against a beech bole & threw down the beast
And knelt above it with drawn knife. On the instant
It vanished like a shadow, & a cry
So mournful that it seemed the cry of one
Who had lost some unimaginable treasure
Wandered between the blue & the green leaf
And climbed into the air crumbling away
Till all had seemed a shadow or a vision
But for the trodden mire, the pool of blood,
The disembowelled horse. King Eochaid gazed

[Berg(3), 2^{r}]

{ 2
{ [?]
But drew his sword & thought with levelled point
To stay the stags next rush. When sword met horn
The horn resounded as though it had been silver.
they
Horn locked in sword, ~~they~~ tugged & struggled there
As though a stag & unicorn were met
In Africa on mountain of the moon,
Until at last it drove the unlocked horn
Through the entrails of the horse. Dropping his sword
the
Eocha seized both ^ horns in his strong hands
And stared into the sea green eye & so
Hither & thither to & fro they trod
Till all the place was beaten into mire
The strong thigh and the agile thigh were met
The hands that gathered up the might of the world
And hoof & horn that had [?sucked] in their speed
Among the elaborate wilderness of the air
Through bush they plunged, & over ivied root
And [?~~though~~] where the stone struck fire & in the leaves
A squirrel whinnied & a bird screamed out
sinewey
But when at last he ~~had~~ forced those ~~sinewy~~ flanks
Against
~~Eocha a Tree~~ a beech [?bole] & threw down the beast
And knelt above it with drawn knife. On the instant
It vanished like a shadow, & a cry
So mournful that it seemed the cry of one
Who had lost some unimaginable treasure
Wandered between the blue & the green leaf
And climbed into the air crumbling away
Till all had seemed a shadow or a vision
But for the trodden mire, the pool of blood,
The disembowelled horse. King Eocha

---

33 The other side of this sheet, 2^{v} (inverted), has a canceled fragment:
~~Horn locked in sword~~

44 "[?sucked]" could be "[?struck]".

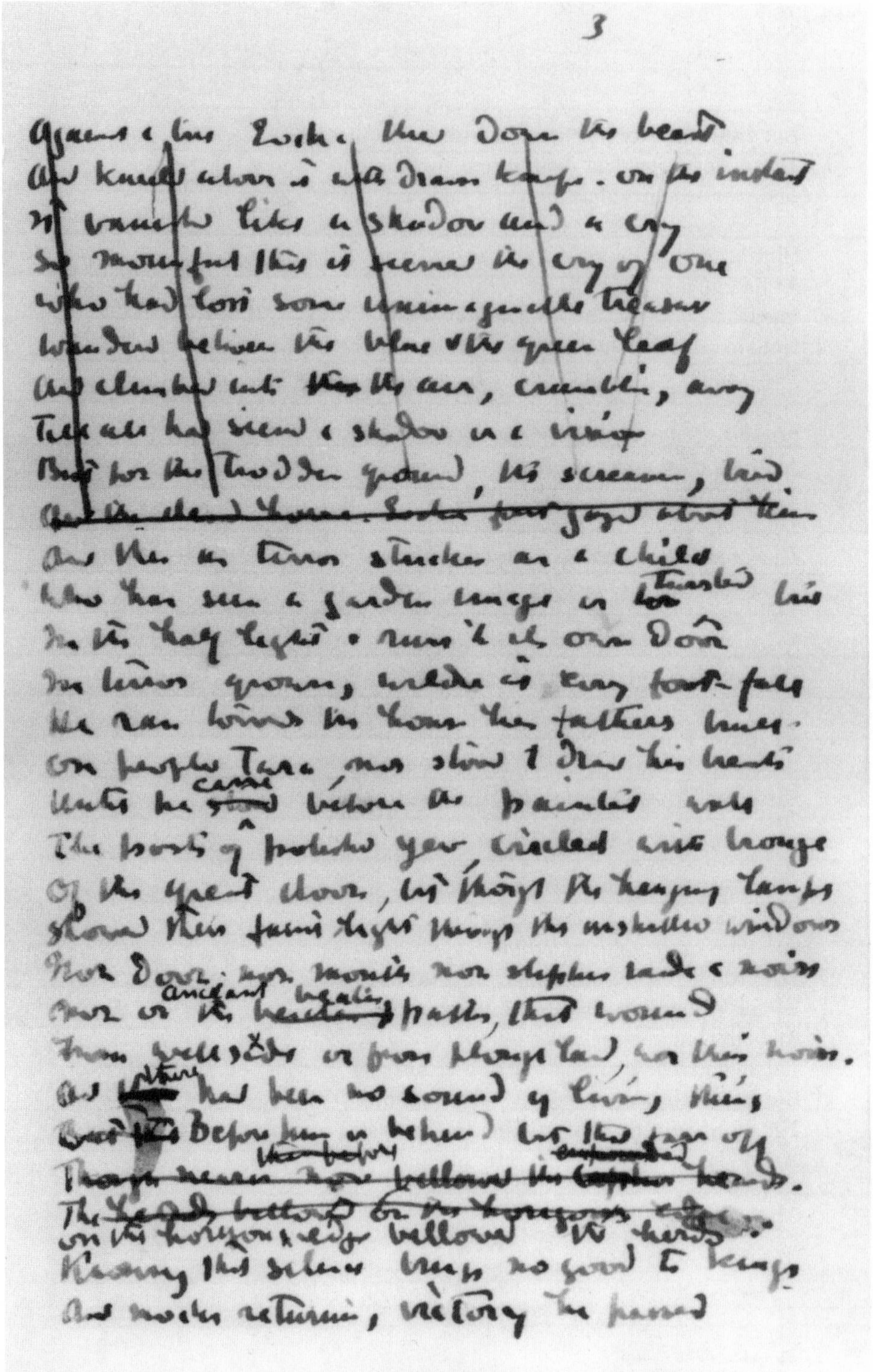
3
Against a [illegible] Eochai[illegible] [illegible] down the beast
And knelt above it with drawn knife. On the instant
It vanished like a shadow and a cry
So mournful that it seemed the cry of one
Who had lost some unimaginable treasure
Wandered between the blue & the green leaf
And climbed into ~~the~~ the air, crumbling away
Till all had seemed a shadow or a vision
But for the trodden ground, the scream, and
~~[illegible]~~
And then as terror stricken as a child
Who has seen a garden image in ~~[illegible]~~ twilight his
In the half light & runs to [illegible] door
[illegible] ground, [illegible] footfalls
He ran towards his home his fathers [illegible]
On [illegible] & drew his breath
Until he ~~stood~~ came before the painted wall
The posts of polished yew circled with bronze
Of the great door, but though the hanging lamps
Showed their faint light through the unshuttered windows
Nor door, nor mouth, nor slipper made a noise
Nor on the ancient ~~[illegible]~~ paths, that wound
From well side or from [illegible], nor this room.
And ~~[illegible]~~ there had been no sound of living thing
~~[illegible]~~ Before him or behind but that far off
~~[illegible]~~
The ~~[illegible]~~ on the horizon edge bellowed the herds.
Knowing that silence brings no good to kings
And mocks returning victory, he passed

[Berg(3), 3ᵛ (inverted)]

3

Against a tree Eocha threw down the beast.
And knelled above it with drawn knife. On the instant
It vanished like a shadow and a cry
So mournful that it seemed the cry of one
Who had lost some unimaginable treasure
Wandered between the blue & the green leaf
And climbed into [~~?~~] the air, crumbling away
Till all had seemed a shadow or a vision
But for the trodden ground, the screaming bird
And the dead horse. Eocha first gazed about him
And then as terror stricken as a child
twisted
Who has seen a garden image or [~~?~~]^ tree
In the half light & runs to its own door
Its terror growing wilder at every foot–fall
He ran towards the house his fathers built
On peopled Tara, nor stood to draw his breath
came
Until he ~~stood~~^ before the painted wall
The posts of polished yew, circled with bronze
Of the great doors, but though the hanging lamps
Showed their faint light through the unshuttered windows
Nor door nor mouth nor slipper made a noise
ancient beaten
Nor on the^ ~~beaten p~~ paths, that wound
From wellside or from plough land, was there noise.
there
And [~~?~~] had been no sound of living thing
~~But [?that]~~ Before him or behind but that far off
~~than before~~ ~~empounded~~
~~Though nearer now bellowed the captive heards.~~
The ~~herds bellowed on the horizons edge.~~
On the horizon, edge bellowed the herds
Knowing that silence brings no good to kings
And mocks returning victory he passed

81 The caret below the line may be an "X" instead.

4

Below the gallery with a beaten head
And saw where in the middle of the great hall
Pale faced alone upon a bench his wife
Sat upright with a sword before her feet
A kind mild woman had she been, who poured
Her beauty as the constellations pour
Their richness through the summer & the spring
But now she had no mild & no kind look
Her hands on either side had grasped the bench
Her eyes were cold & steady, her lips tight
Some passion had made her stone. Hearing a foot
She started & then knew whose foot it was

[illegible]

'I have sent out into the fields & woods
The fighting men & servants, & the house
For I have heard your judgement upon one
Who is self accused. If she be innocent
She would not look in any known man's face
Till judgement has been given, & if guilty
Because that were a quarrel against her kings
Would never look again on known man's face'
And at these words he paled as she had paled
Knowing that he should find upon her lips
The meaning of that monstrous day.' Then she

And when he thought to take her in his arms
She motioned him afar & rose & spoke

[illegible]

[Berg(3), 4v]

4

Between the pillars with a beating heart
And saw where in the midst of the great hall
Pale faced alone upon a bench his wife
Sat upright with a sword before her feet
A kind mild woman had she been, who poured
Her beauty as the constellations pour
Their richness through the summer & the spring
But now she had no mild & no kind look
Her hands on either side had gripped the bench
Her eyes were cold & steady her lips tight
Some passion had made her stone. Hearing a foot
She started & then knew [?what] foot it was

The other side of this sheet is blank except for a note "See back" (4r, inverted).

4

Before the pillar with a battered head
And saw there in the middle of the great hall
Pale faced alone upon a bench his wife
Sat upright with a sword before her feet
A kind mild woman had she been, who poured
Her beauty as the constellations pour
Their richness through the summers & the springs
But now she had no mild & no kind look
Her hands on either side had grasped the bench
Her eyes were cold & steady, her lips tight
Some passion had made her stone. Hearing a foot
She started & then knew whose foot it was
[illegible]
'I have sent out into the fields & woods
The fighting men & servants of the house
For I would have your judgement upon one
Who is self accused. If she be innocent
She would not look in any known man's face
Till judgment has been given & if guilty
Because that was a quarrel against the King
Would never look again on known man's face'
And at these words he paled as she had paled
Knowing that he should find upon her lips
The meaning of this monstrous day.'
Then she
And when he thought to take her in his arms
She motioned him afar & rose & spoke
[illegible]

[Berg(3), 4v, continued]

face was pale
102 [?Rose] up & spoke, [?&] though his [~~? ? ?~~] ~~her~~
She [? ? ? ? ? ?] though [?remember],
103 ~~She bore her pale head proudly as may those~~
104 ~~Stet~~ ~~[?Whose] [?words] [?though] light & [?] old [?] [?words]~~
[? ?] & [?] [?forefathers words] though light
105 [? ?], [? ?] [?forefathers words] though light
~~carried~~
106 Stet ~~Have had more weight than shouting on a hill~~
into
107 ‘ I have sent out [~~?~~] the fields & woods
108 The fighting men & servants of this house,
109 For I would have your judgement upon one
110 Who is self accused. If she be innocent
111 She would not look in any known mans face
Till has been
112 [~~?~~] judgment ~~is~~ given & if guilty
113 Because that were a guilt against her [~~?~~] king
114 Will never look again on known mans face’ ’
115 ~~But~~ And at these words he paled as she had paled
Knowing
116 ~~He knew~~ that he should find upon her lips
117 The meaning of that monstrous day’
Then she
[~~?~~] And take
118 ~~And~~ when he thought to ~~have taken~~ her in his arms
119 She motioned him afar & rose & spoke
120 And though [?her wine was] [?] [?making] , [?her] cheek pale
121 She [? ? ? ?] [?calm], as may those
122 Whose words & whose old fathers [?words] though light

110–111 Probably only a stray mark after “innocent” (l. 110) and above “face” (l. 111).
118–119 Marked to replace canceled ll. 102–105.

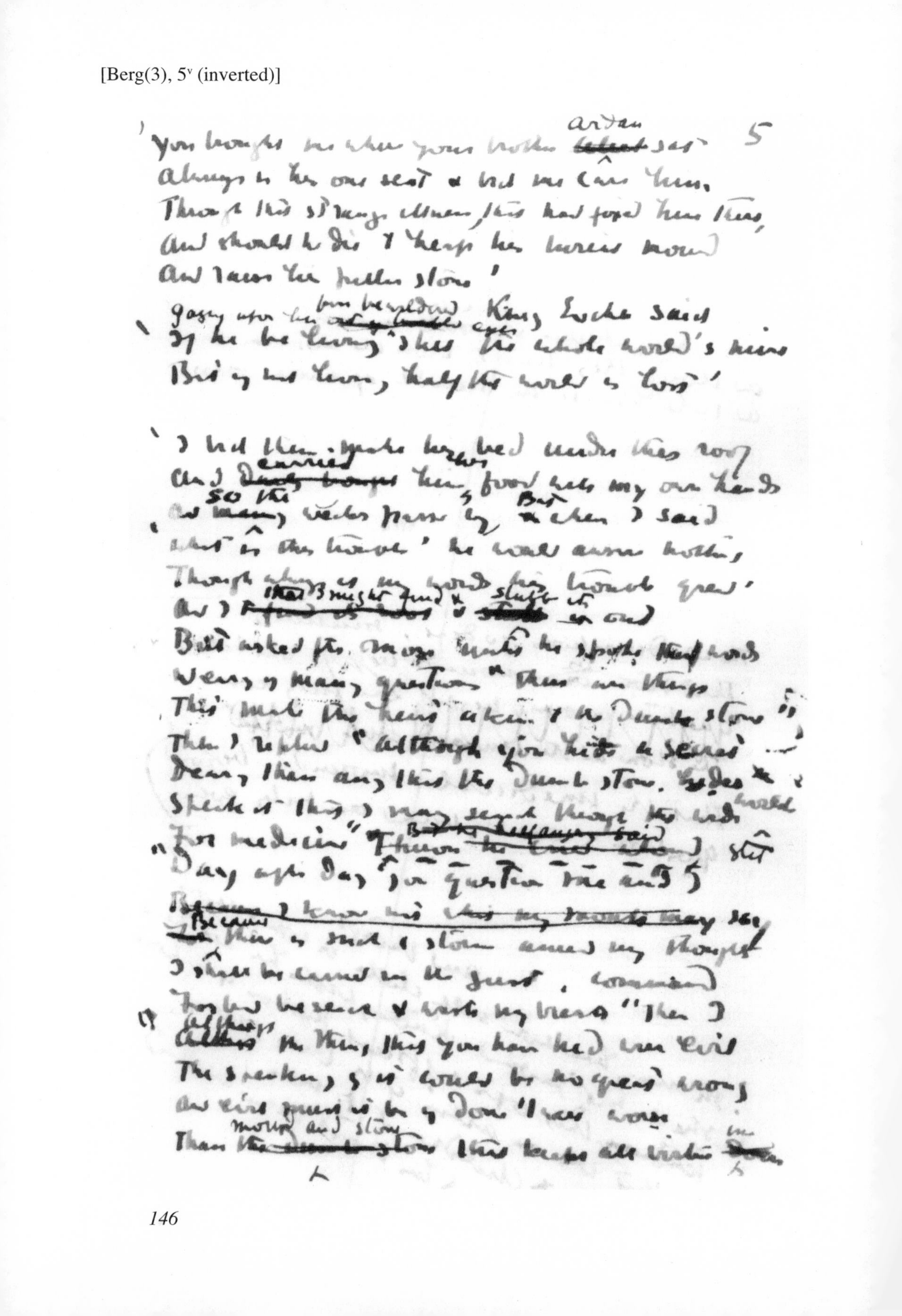

[Berg(3), 5v (inverted)]

[Berg(3), 5ᵛ (inverted)]

Ardan 5

123 ' You brought me where your brother [?~~Aleel~~] sat
124 Always in his one seat & bid me care him ^
125 Through that strange illness, that had fixed him there,
126 And should he die to heap his burial mound
127 And raise his pillar stone'
King Eocha said
from bewildered
Gazing upon her ~~out of [?troubled]~~ ^ eyes
128 ' If he be living still the whole world's mine
129 But if not living half the world is lost'

130 ' I bid them make his bed under this roof
carried his
131 And [?~~daily~~] ~~brought~~ him ^ food with my own hands
so the But
132 And ~~many~~ ^ weeks passed by, ~~&~~ when I said
133 ' What is this trouble' he would answer nothing
134 Though always at my words his trouble grew'
that I might find & stubb it
135 And I ~~to find its root~~ & ~~[?stub] it~~ ^ out
136 But asked the more until he spoke these words
137 Weary of many questions "There are things
138 That make the heart akin to the dumb stone".
139 Then I replied "Although you hide a secret
140 [?Dearer] than any that the dumb stone. ~~he~~ does [?]
world
141 Speak it that I may search through the wide ^
~~But he half angry said~~
142 For medicine" ~~Thereon he cried aloud~~ stet
143 "Day after day you question me and I
144 ~~Because I know not what my mouth may~~ say
Because
145 ~~For~~ ^ there is such a storm amid my thoughts
146 I shall be carried in the gust, command
147 Forbid beseech & waste my breath" Then I
Although
148 " [?~~Although~~] the thing that you have hid were evil
149 The speaking of it could be no great wrong
150 And evil must it be if done 'twere worse
mound and stone in
151 Than ~~the dumb stone~~ ^ that keeps all virtue ~~down~~ ^

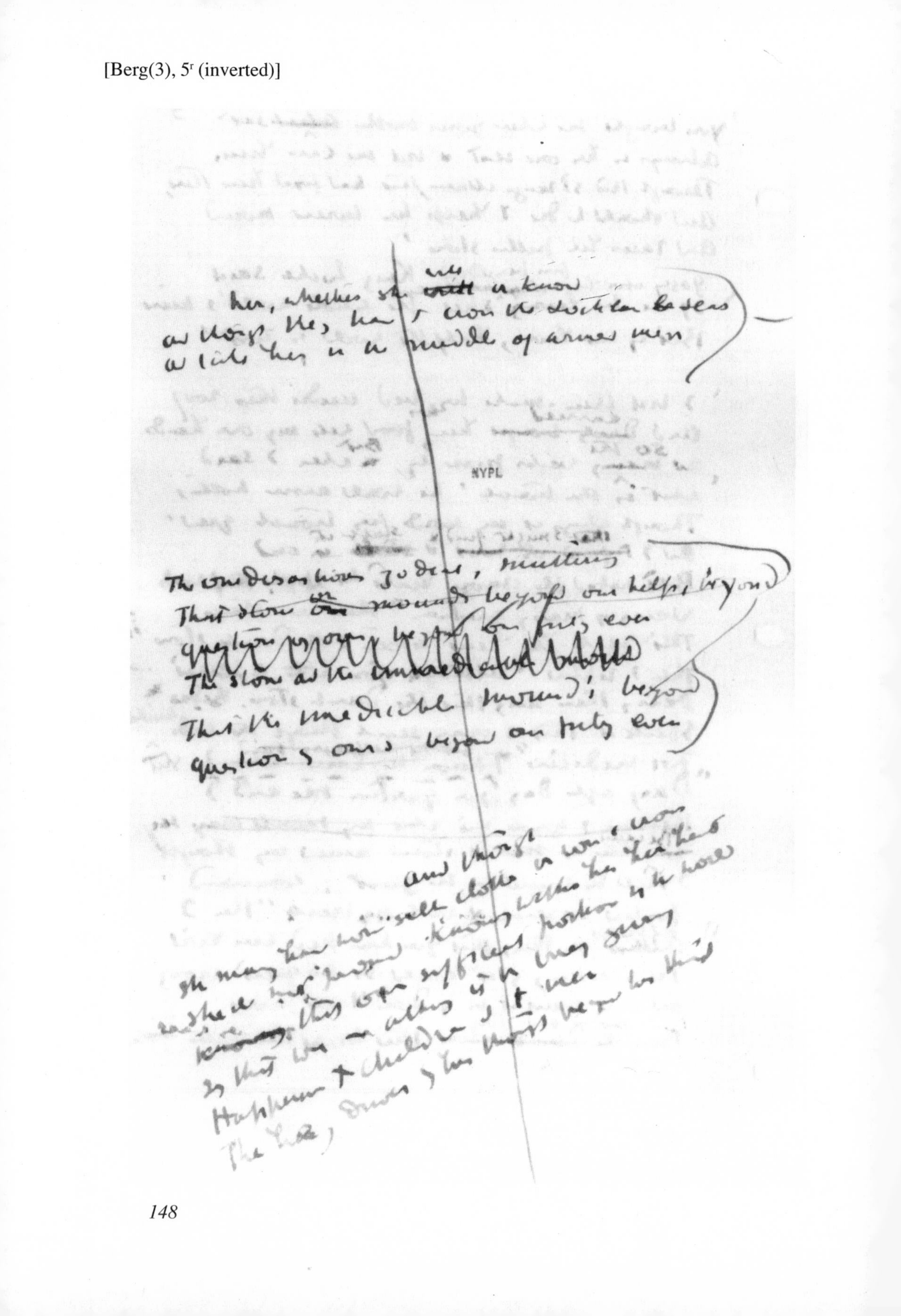

[Berg(3), 5r (inverted)]

[Berg(3), 5[r] (inverted)]

will
her, whether she ~~will~~ or know
And though they have to cross the [?Lochlan] [~~?~~] seas
And take her in the middle of armed men

The one disastrous zodiac, muttering
~~or~~
~~That stone [?or] mounds beyond our help, beyond~~
~~Question of our, beyond our pity even~~
~~The stone and the [?immedicable] mound~~
That the [?imedicable] mound's beyond
Question of ours beyond our pity even

And though
She may have worn silk clothes or worn a crown
She d not found knowing within her [?her] heart
~~Knowing~~ that our sufficient portion of the world
Is that we [?— although] it be brief giving
Happiness to children & to men
[?Then] he, driven by her thought beyond his [?thought]

The three canceled passages on this page are revisions to an unlocated facing page that was replaced by Berg(3), 6[r] (pp. 150–151 below), in which ll. 10–16 are incorporated at ll. 162–167.

6

and loosens on us dreams that waste our life
Shadows & shows that can but turn the brain"
But finding him still silent I stooped down
And whispering, that none but he should hear
Said "If a woman has put this on you
My men ~~shall bring her~~ whether ~~she will or no~~ it pleases her or displeases
And though she have to cross the loughs and seas
And take her in the middle of armed men
~~That she may~~ shall make her look upon her handy work
~~And quench~~ That she may quench the rick she has fired; & though
She may have worn silk clothes or worn a crown
She'll not be proud knowing within her heart
That our sufficient portion of the world
Is that we give, although it be brief giving,
Happiness to children and to men."
Then he, driven by his thought beyond his thought
And speaking what he would not though he would,
Cried 'You, even you your self could work the cure,'
And at those words I rose & I went out
And for nine days he had food from other hands
And for nine days my mind went whirling round
The one disastrous zodiac, muttering
That the immedicable mound's beyond
Question of ours beyond our pity even
But when nine days had gone I stood again
Before his chair & bending down my head
Told him that when Orion rose & all
The women of his household were asleep,
To go — for hope would give his limbs the power
To an old empty woodman's house that's hidden
close to a clump of beech trees in the wood

[Berg(3), 6[r]]

6

152 And loosens on us dreams that waste our life
153 Shadows & shows that can but turn the brain"
154 But finding him still silent I stooped down
155 And whispering that none but he should hear
156 Said "If a woman has put this on you
it please her or displease,
157 My men ~~shall bring her~~ whether ~~she will or no~~
158 And though they have to cross the Loughlan seas
159 And take her in the middle of armed men,
Shall make her
160 ~~That she may~~ ^ look upon her handy work
That she may quench
161 ~~And quench~~ ^ the rick she has fired, & though
162 She may have worn silk clothes or worn a crown
163 Shell be not proud knowing within her heart
164 That our sufficient portion of the world
165 Is that we give, although it be brief giving
166 Happiness to children and to men."
167 Then he, driven by his thought beyond his thought
168 And speaking what he would not though he would,
169 Cried 'You, even your self could work the cure,
170 And at these words I rose & I went out
{ h
171 And for nine days he { dad food from other hands
172 And for nine days my mind went whirling round
173 The one disastrous zodiac, muttering
174 That the immedicable mounds beyond
175 Question of ours beyond our pity even
176 But when nine days had gone I stood again
177 Before his chair & bending down my head
178 Told him that when Orian rose & all
179 The woman of his household were asleep,
180 To go — for hope would give his limbs the power
181 To that old empty woodmans house thats hidden
182 Close to a clump of beech trees in the wood

This page replaced an unlocated earlier one; see note to Berg(3), 5[r] (inverted) (pp. 148–149 above).

Westward of Tara, there to await a friend
That could, as he had told her, work her cure
And would be no harsh friend"
When night had deepened
I groped my way through boughs & over roots
Till oak & hazel ceased & birch began
And found the house, a spluttering torch within
And stretched out sleeping on a pile of skins
Aedan, & though I called to him & tried
To shake him out of sleep I could not rouse him
I waited till the night was on the turn
Then fearing that some labourer on his way
To plough or pasture land might see me there
Went out.
Among the ivy covered rocks
As on the blue light of a sword a man
Who had unmeasured majesty & eyes
Like the eyes of some great kite scouring the woods
Stood on my path. Trembling from head to foot
I gazed at him like grouse upon a kite
But with a voice that had unmeasured music
"A weary wooing and a long" he said
"Speaking of love through other lips & looking
Under an alien eye lid but it is not my craft
That put a passion in the sleeper there
And when I had got my will & drawn you here
Where I may speak to you alone, my craft
Sucked up the passion out of him again
And left mere sleep. He'll wake when the sun wakes
Push out his vigorous limbs & rub his eyes

[Berg(3), 7r]

7

Westward of Tara, there to await a friend
That could, as he had told her, work his cure
And would be no harsh friend"
                    When night had deepened
                    boughs
I groped my way through ~~bows~~ & over roots
Till oak & hazel ceased & beech began
      { f
And { hound the house, a sputtering torch within
And stretched out sleeping on a pile of skins
Ardan, & though I called to him & tried
To shake him out of sleep I could not rouse him
I waited till the night was on the turn
Then fearing that some labourer on his way
To plough or pasture land might see me there
Went out.
          Among the ~~ir~~ ivy covered rocks
As on the blue light of a sword a man
Who had unnatural majesty & ~~eyes~~ eyes
Like the eyes of some great kite scouring the woods
Stood on my path. Trembling from hand to foot
I gazed at him like grouse upon a kite
But with a voice that had unnatural music
"A weary wooing and a long" he said
"Speaking of love through other lips & looking
Under an alien eyelid for it was my craft
That put a passion in the sleeper there
And when I had got my will & drawn you here
Where I may speak to you alone, my craft
Sucked up the passion out of him again
And left mere sleep. He ll wake when the sun wakes
Push out his vigorous limbs & rub his eyes

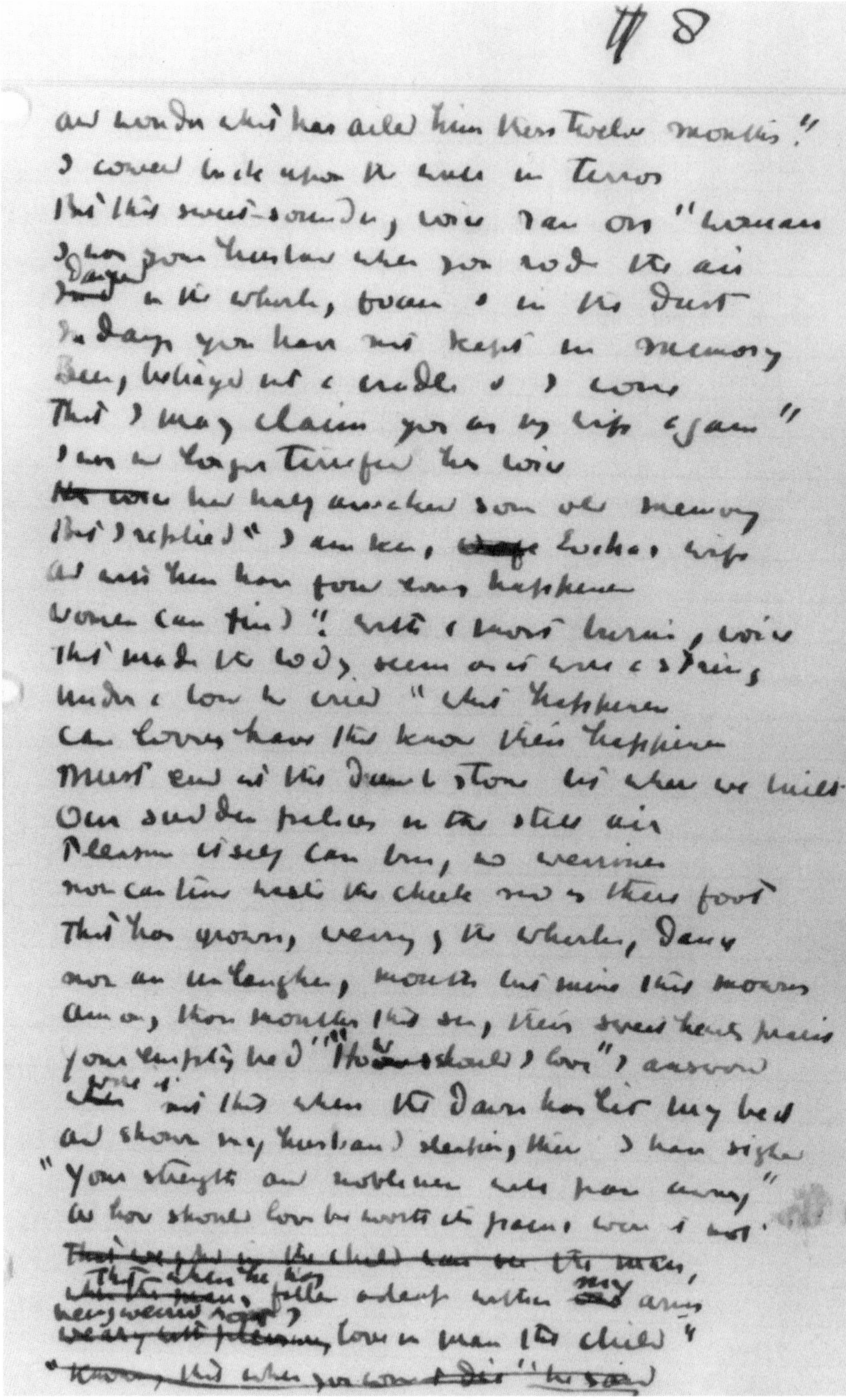

8

and wonder what has ailed him these twelve months."
I cowered back upon the wall in terror
But this sweet-sounding voice ran on "Woman
I was your husband when you rode the air
~~[illegible]~~ Danced in the whirling, foam & in the dust
In days you have not kept in memory
Being betrayed into a cradle & I come
That I may claim you as my wife again"
I was no longer terrified his voice
~~His voice~~ had half awakened some old memory
But I replied "I am King ~~[illegible]~~ Eochaid's wife
And with him have found every happiness
Women can find"! With a most masterful voice
That made the body seem as it were a string
Under a bow he cried "What happiness
Can lovers have that know their happiness
Must end at the dumb stone but where we build
Our sudden palaces in the still air
Pleasure itself can bring no weariness
Nor can time waste the cheek nor is there foot
That has grown weary of the whirling dance
Nor an unlaughing mouth but mine that mourns
Among those mouths that sing their sweethearts' praise
Your empty bed" "How should I love" I answered
"Were it not that when the dawn has lit my bed
And shown my husband sleeping, there I have sighed
"Your strength and nobleness will pass away"
Or how should love be worth its pains were it not
~~That [illegible] the child [illegible] the man,~~
That when he has fallen asleep within my arms
~~Being wearied out~~
~~Weary with pleasure~~ I love in man the child"
~~"Knowing that when you would die" he said~~

[Berg(3), 8ʳ]

~~7~~ 8

181 And wonder what has ailed him these twelve months."
182 I cowered back upon the wall in terror
183 But that sweet–sounding voice ran on "Woman
184 I was your husband when you rode the air
Danced
185 ~~In d~~ in the whirling foam & in the dust
186 In days you have not kept in memory
187 Being betrayed into a cradle & I come
188 That I may claim you as my wife again"
189 I was no longer terrified his voice
190 ~~His voice~~ had half awakened some old memory
191 But I replied "I am King [?~~Oefe~~] Eochas wife
192 And with him have found every happiness
193 Women can find". With a most burning voice
194 That made the body seem as it were a string
195 Under a bow he cried "What happiness
196 Can lovers have that know their happiness
197 Must end at the dumb stone but where we built
198 Our sudden palaces in the still air
199 Pleasure itself can bring no weariness
200 Nor can time waste the cheek [?nor] is there foot
201 That has grown weary of the whirling dance
202 Nor an unlaughing mouth but mine that mourns
203 Among those mouths that sing their sweethearts praise
w
204 Your empty bed" "Ho[?w] should I love" I answered
Were it
205 ~~When~~ not that when the dawn has lit my bed
206 And shown my husband sleeping there I have sighed
207 " Your strength and nobleness will pass away"
208 [?And] how should love be worth its pains were it not
209 ~~That we who in the child can see the man~~,
That when he has my
210 ~~When the mans~~ fallen asleep within ~~our~~ arms
being wearied^out I
211 ~~Weary with pleasure,~~ love in man the child"
212 ~~"Knowing that when you come to die" he said~~

9

~~Oh what can the midges~~, know of love
What can they know of love that do not know
She ~~builds~~ builds her nest upon a narrow ledge
Above a windy precipice" Then he
"~~Seeing~~ Seeing that when you come to the death bed
You must return whether you would or no,
This human life blotted from memory,
Why must I live some thirty, forty years
Alone with all this useless happiness"
Thereon he seized me in his arms, but I
Thrust him away with both my hands & cried
Never will I believe there is any change
Can blot out of my memory this life
Sweetened by death but if I could believe
That were a double hunger in my lips
For what is doubly brief"
~~Thereon~~ But now the shape
My hands were pressed to vanished suddenly
I staggered but a beech tree stayed my fall
And clinging to it I could hear ~~far off~~ the cocks
~~Crow at Tara~~
~~Crowing of cocks on Tara~~
Crow upon Tara" ~~She~~.
She had fixed her eyes
upon King Eochaid's face who lowered his face
And touched her forehead with his lips & said
"I thank you for your kindness to my brother
And for the love that you have shown your king
For that you promised & for that refused'

Thereon the bellowing of the empounded herds
Rose round the walls & through the bronze ring door

[Berg(3), 9r]

9

213 ~~Oh what can the undying know of love~~
214 What can they know of love that do not know
215 She [?~~bilds~~] builds her nest upon a narrow ledge
216 Above a windy precipice" Then he
217 "[?~~Seeing~~] Seeing that when you come to the death bed
218 You must return, whether you would or no,
219 This human life blotted from memory,
220 Why must I live some thirty, forty years
221 Alone with all this useless happiness"
222 Thereon he seized me in his arms, but I
223 Thrust him away with both my hands & cried
224 "Never will I believe theres any change
225 Can blot out of my memory this life
226 Sweetened by death but if I could believe
227 That were a double hunger in my lips
228 For what is doubly brief"
~~Thereon~~ But now the shape
229 My hands were pressed to vanished suddenly
230 I staggered but a beech tree stayed my fall
~~the~~ the cocks
231 And clinging to it I could hear ~~far off~~
Crow ~~upon Tara~~
232 ~~Crowing of cocks on Tara"~~
233 Crow upon Tara." ~~She~~
She had fixed her eyes
234 Upon King Eochas face who [?lowered] his face
235 And touched her forhead with his lips & said
236 "I thank you for your kindness to my brother
237 And for the love that you have shown your king
238 For that you promised & for that refused'

239 Thereon the bellowing of the empounded herds
240 Rose round the walls & through the bronze ringed [?door]

[Berg(3), 10^{v} inverted)]

10

[walled & shouted those were wasted men
and in the midst King Eochaid brother slow
he had heard that din on the horizon. Eiffe
and ridden out to welcome them & now
giving his hand to this man & to this
praised their great victories & gave them joy
of their return to this ancestral house.

W B Yeats
Maud

[Berg(3), 10v inverted)]

10

Jostled & shouted those war wasted men
And in the midst King Eochas brother stood
He d heard that din on the horizons edge
And ridden out to welcome them & now
Giving his hand to that man & to this
Praised their great victories & gave them joy
Of their return to that ancestral house.

W B Yeats
Jan 8

[NLI 13,586(2) (a), 1]

The Two Kings.
(~~Eocha's pronounced Yohee~~
(Eochaid's pronounced Yohee

'We ride but slowly though so near our home,'
King Eoc~~ha~~ said, and he that bore his shield
Sighing replied: 'What ~~xxxx~~ need have we for haste
Towards the ~~xxxx~~ hour for speaking ~~xxxx xxxx~~ of the dead.
My married sister put into my care
A boy of twenty years - a mound and stone
Between the wood of Duras and Magai
Have been the measure of that care; but Eoc~~hy~~
Having no thought but for his queen Edain
Outrode his troop that after twelve months' war
Toiled with empounded cattle through the mire,
And came into a wood as the sun set
Westward of Tara; ~~xxxx/in~~ and where the middle wood
A clump of beech trees made an empty space
He ~~would~~ thought to have given his horse the spur but saw
Between the pale green light/ of the beech leaves
And the ground ivy's bluer light, a stag
Whiter than curds, its eyes the tint of the sea.
Because it stood upon his path and seemed
More hands in height than any stag in the world
He sat with tightened rein amazed, his horse
Trembling beneath him and then drove the spur
Not doubting to have shouldered it away
But the stag ~~xxxx~~ stooped its heavy branching horn
And ran at him, and passed, and as it passed

[NLI 13,586(2) (a), 1]

The Two Kings.
1 ('Eocha' is pronounced Yo hee
('Eochaid' is pronounced Yo hee
2 **'We ride but slowly though so near our home,'**
3 [?]h/**King Eocka/said, and he that bore his shield** id/
need
4 **Sighing replied: 'What news have we for haste**
hour of
5 **Towards the ~~home~~ for ~~S~~** speaking ~~**lies died.**~~ the dead.
6 **My married sister put into my care**
7 **A boy of twenty years — a mound and stone**
8 **Between the wood of Duras and Magai**
9 **Have been the measure of that care; but Eocka/** h/id/'/
10 **Having no thought but for his queen Edain**
11 **Outrode his troop that after twelve months' war**
12 **Toiled with empounded cattle through the mire,**
13 **And came into a wood as the sun set**
~~and where the~~ Where
14 ⊙ **Westward of Tara/ ~~There~~ /~~in~~ middle wood** ~~Where~~ in the
15 **A clump of beech trees made an empty space**
thought to
16 **He ~~would~~ have given his horse the spur but saw**
the
17 **Between the pale green light/of beech leaves**
18 **And the ground ivy's bluer light, a stag**
19 **Whiter than curds, its eyes the tint of the sea.**
20 **Because it stood upon his path and seemed**
21 **More hands in height than any stag in the world**
22 **He sat with tightened rein amazed, his horse**
23 **Trembling beneath him and then drove the spur**
24 **Not doubting** to have shouldered it away
stooped
25 **But the stag ~~stood~~ its heavy branching horns/** stet
26 **And ran at him, and passed, and as it passed**

2

Ripped through the horse's flank. King Eochaid reeled h/ id/
But drew his sword and thought with levelled point
To stay the stag's next rush. When sword met horn
The horn resounded as though it had been silver.
Horn locked in sword, they tugged and struggled there
As though a stag and unicorn were met
In Africa on mountain of the moon.
Until at last ~~it drove~~ the unlocked horn had torn
Through the entrails of the horse. Dropping his sword
h/id/ Eochaid seized both the horns in his strong hands
And stared into the sea green eyes and so
Hither and thither to and fro they trod
Till all the place was beaten into mire.
The strong thigh and the agile thigh were ~~bent~~ met
The hands that gathered up the might of the world
And hoof and horn that had sucked in k/ their speed
~~Among~~ amid the elaborate wilderness of the air.
Through bush they plunged and over ivied root
And ~~when~~ where the stone struck fire, ~~and~~ while in the leaves
A squirrel whinnied and a bird screamed out;
But when at last he forced those sinewy flanks had
Against a beech bole ~~and~~ threw down the beast he
And knelt above it with drawn knife / on the instant ⊙

[NLI 13,586 (2) (a), 2]

2

Ripped through the horse's flank. King Eocka/reeled h/ id/
But drew his sword and thought with levelled point
To stay the stag's next rush. When sword met horn
The horn resounded as though it had been silver.
Horn locked in sword, they tugged and struggled there
As though a stag and unicorn were met
In Africa on mountain of the moon,
Until at last ~~it drove~~ the unlocked horn/ had torn/
Through the entrails of the horse. Dropping his sword
h/ id/ **Eocka/seized both the horns in his strong hands**
And stared into the sea green eyes and so
Hither and thither to and fro they trod
Till all the place was beaten into mire.
The strong thigh and the agile thigh were ~~bent~~ met
The hands that gathered up the might of the world
And hoof and horn that had suc/ed in their speed k/
Amid
Among the elaborate wilderness of the air.
Through bush they plunged and over ivied root
where while
And when the stone struck fire , and in the leaves
A squirrel whinnied and a bird screamed out ;
~~had [?]~~
[?]
But when at last he/forced those sinewy flanks had/
Against a beech bole ~~and~~ threw down the beast he /
And knelt above it with drawn knife, on the instant ⊙

30/31 A line that is present in the Berg(3) manuscript and that was printed later in *British Review* and *Resp14* is omitted here and in *Poetry:* "A sweet, miraculous, terrifying sound."

3

It vanished like a shadow, and a cry
So mournful that it seemed the cry of one
Who had lost some unimaginable treasure
Wandered between the blue and the green leaf
And climbed into the air crumbling away
Till all had seemed a shadow or a vision
But for the trodden mire, the pool of blood,
The disembowelled horse. King Eochaid gazed,
And then as terror stricken as a child,
Who has seen a garden image or twisted tree
In the half light and runs to its own door
In terror growing wilder at every foot-fall,
He ran towards the house his fathers built
On peopled Tara, nor stood to draw his breath
Until he came before the painted wall,
The posts of polished yew, circled with bronze,
Of the great door, but though the hanging lamps
Showed their faint light through the unshuttered windows
Nor door, nor mouth, nor slipper made a noise
Nor on the ancient beaten paths, that wound
From well side or from plough land, was their noise;
And there had been no sound of living thing
Before him or behind, but that far-off
On the horizon edge bellowed the herds.
Knowing that silence brings no good to kings,
And mocks returning victory, he passed

[NLI 13,586(2) (a), 3]

3

It vanished like a shadow,   and a cry
So mournful that it seemed the cry of one
Who had lost some unimaginable treasure
Wandered between the blue and the green leaf
And climbed into the   air   crumbling   away
Till all had seemed a shadow or a vision
But for the trodden mire, the pool of blood,
The disembowelled horse. King Eocha gazed ,   h/ id/
And then as terror stricken as a child ,
Who has seen a garden image or twisted tree
In the half light , and runs to its own door
Its   growing wilder   ~~grown more~~/
~~In~~ terror ~~grown, wilder~~ at every foot–fall ,   ~~growing~~
He ran towards the house his fathers built
On peopled **Tara, nor stood to draw his breath**
Until he came before the painted wall ,
The posts of polished yew, circled with bronze ,
Of the great door, but through the hanging lamps
Showed their faint light through the unshuttered windows
Nor door, nor mouth, nor slipper **made a noise**
Nor on the ancient\beaten paths, that wound
From well side or from plough land, was their noise { ; .
And there had been no sound of living thing
Before him or behind, but that far–off
On the horizon edge bellowed the herds.
that
Knowing ~~the~~ silence brings no good to kings ,
And mocks returning victory , he passed

50 The extra space between the comma and "and" has an erasure by the typist.

69 The copyediting mark that separates "ancient" from "beaten" was added in a paler ink and with a narrower pen than the other corrections; it perhaps was made by the typist.

[NLI 13,586(2) (a), 4]

4

Between the pillars with a beating heart
And saw where in the midst of the great hall
Pale-faced, alone upon a bench, his wife
Sat upright with a sword before her feet.
A kind mild woman had she been, who poured
Her beauty as the constellations pour
Their richness through the summer and the spring;
But now she had no mild and no kind look:
Her hands on either side had gripped the bench
Her eyes were cold and steady, her lips tight.
Some passion had made her stone. Hearing a foot
She started and then knew whose foot it was;
But/ ~~She~~ when he thought to take her in his arms
she ~~She~~ motioned him afar, and rose and spoke:
'I have sent out into the fields and woods
The fighting men and servants of this house
For I would have your judgment upon one
Who is self accused. If she be innocent
She would not look in any known man's face
Till judgment has been given, and if guilty,
Because that were a guilt against her king,
Will never look again on known man's face.'
And at these words he paled as she had paled
Knowing that he should find upon her lips
The meaning of that monstrous day.

Then she

[NLI 13,586(2) (a), 4]

4

Between the pillars with a beating heart
And saw where in the midst of the great hall
Pale–faced , alone upon a bench , his wife
Sat upright with a sword before her feet.
A kind mild woman had she been, who poured
Her beauty as the constellations pour
Their richness through the summer and the spring{; / .}
But now she had no mild and no kind look{: / .}
Her hands on either side had gripped the bench
Her eyes were cold and steady, her lips tight.
Some passion had made her stone. Hearing a foot
She started and then knew whose foot it was{; / .}
But/ **~~And~~ when he thought to take her in his arms**
stet **~~She~~ motioned him afar , and rose and spoke:**
'I have sent out into the fields and woods
The fighting men and servants of this house
For I would have your judgment upon one
Who is self accused. If she be innocent
She would not look in any known man's face
Till judgment has been given , and if guilty ,
Because that were a guilt against her king ,
Will never look again on known man's face.'
And at these words he paled as she had paled
Knowing that he should find upon her lips
The meaning of that monstrous day.
Then she

5

'You brought me where your brother Ardan sat
Always in his ~~one~~ one seat and bid me care him
Through that strange illness that had fixed him there.
And should he die to heap his burial mound
And raise his pillar stone.', King Eochaid said
Gazing upon her with bewildered eyes ~~King Eochu said~~
'If he be living still the whole world's mine
But if not living, half the world is lost.'
'I bid them make his bed under this roof
And carried him his food with my own hands
And so the weeks ~~winter~~ passed by. But when I said
"What is this trouble?" he would answer nothing
Though always at my words his trouble grew;
And I, that I might find and stub it out,
But asked the more until he spoke these words
Weary of many questions "There are things
That make the heart akin to the dumb stone."
Then I replied: "Although you hide a secret,
Dearer than any that the dumb stone hides,
Speak it, that I may send through the wide world
For medicine.'. Thereon he cried aloud
'Day after day you question me, and I,
Because there is such a storm amid ~~around~~ my thoughts
I shall be carried in the gust, command
Forbid, beseech and waste my breath." Then I
'Although the thing that you have hid ~~had~~ were evil
The speaking of it could be no great wrong,

[NLI 13,586(2) (a), 5]

5

'You brought me where your brother Ardan sat
one
Always in his ~~own~~ seat, and bid me care him
Through that str^ange illness that had fixed him there,
And should he die to heap his burial mound
Eochaid
And raise his pillar stone. '. King ~~Eocha~~ said
eyes
Gazing upon her with **bewildered^ ~~King Eocka said~~**
'If he be living still the whol/d world's mine e/
But if not living, half the world is lost.'
'I bid them make his bed under this roof
And carried him his food with my own hands
weeks
And so the ~~winter~~ passed by. But when I said
{" / **'What is this trouble? " he would answer nothing**
Though always at my words his trouble grew { ; / .
And I , that I might find and stub it out ,
But asked the more until he spoke these words
Weary of many questions { " / **'There are things**
That make the heart akin to the dumb stone. { " / '
Then I replied: { " / **'Although you hide a secret ,**
Dearer than any that the dumb stone hides ,
Speak it , that I may send through the wide world
For medicine.' Thereon he cried aloud
'Day after day you question me , and I ,
amid
Because there is such a storm ~~around~~ my thoughts
I shall be carried in the gust { , / . **C/ommand** lc
Forbid, beseech and waste my breath. { " / **' Then I**
hid
'Although the thing that you have ~~had~~ were evil
The speaking of it could be no great wrong ,

---

127 The comma was added in ink with a narrow pen.

[NLI 13,586(2) (a), 6]

6

And evil must it be, if done 'twere worse
Than mound and stone that keeps all virtue in
And loosens on us dreams that waste our life,
Shadows and shows that can but turn the brain.'
But finding him still silent I stooped down
And whispering that none but he should hear
Said: 'If a woman has put this on you
My men, whether it please her or displease,
And though they have to cross the Loughlan seas
And take her in the middle of armed men,
Shall make her look upon her handiwork
That she may quench the rick she has fired, and though
She may have worn silk clothes, or worn a crown,
she'll
Shall not be proud known within her heart
That our sufficient portion of the world
Is that we give, although it be brief giving
Happiness to children and to men.'
Then he, driven by his thought beyond his thought,
And speaking what he would not though he would,
sighed you
Cried: 'You, even your self could work the cure'.
And at those words I rose and I went out
And for nine days he had food from other hands,
And for nine days my mind went whirling round
The one disastrous zodiac, muttering
That the immedicable mound's beyond

[NLI 13,586(2) (a), 6]

6

And evil must it be , **if done ’twere worse**
Than mound and stone that keep~~s~~ all virtue in 7
And loosen~~s~~ on us dreams that waste our life , 7
Shadows and shows that can but turn the brain.’
But finding him still silent I stooped down
And whispering that none but he should hear
Said: ‘If a woman has put this on you
My men, whether it please her or displease ,
And though they have to cross the Loughlan **seas**
And take her in the middle of armed men ,
Shall make her look upon her handiwork
That she may quench the rick she has fired, and though
She may have worn silk clothes , **or worn a crown** ,
She’ll
~~**Shall**~~ **not be** proud **known**/ **within her heart** ing /
That our sufficient portion of the world
Is that we give, although it be brief giving
Happiness to children and to men.’
Then he, driven by his thought beyond his thought ,
And speaking what he would not though he would,
Sighed you
Cried: ‘You, even your self could work the cure’,
And at these words I rose and I went out
And for nine days he had food from other hands,
And for nine days my mind went whirling round
The one disastrous zodiac, muttering
That the immedicable **mound**’s ~~**and**~~ beyond

147 The closing quotation mark was typed where a period had been erased.

[NLI 13,586(2) (a), 7]

7

Question of ours, beyond our pity even.
But when nine days had gone I stood again
Before his chair and bending down my head
Told him, that when Orion rose, and all
The women of his household were asleep,
To go - for hope would give his limbs the power -
To ~~that~~ an old empty woodman's house that's hidden
Close to a clump of beech trees in the wood
Westward of Tara, there to await a friend
That could, as he had told her, work his cure
And would be no harsh friend.'
When night had deepened
I groped my way through boughs, and over roots,
Till oak and hazel ceased and beech began
And found the house, a sputtering torch within,
And stretched out sleeping on a pile of skins
Ardan, and though I called to him and tried
To shake him out of sleep I could not rouse him.
I waited till the night was on the turn,
Then fearing that some labourer, on his way
To plough or pasture land, might see me there
Went out.
Among the ivy-covered rocks,
As on the blue light of a sword, a man

[NLI 13,586(2) (a), 7]

7

153 **Question of ours , beyond our pity even.**
154 **But when nine days had gone I stood again**
155 **Before his chair and bending down my head**
156 **Told him , that when Orion rose , and all**
157 **The women of his household were asleep ,**
158 **To go — for hope would give his limbs the power —**
an
159 **To ~~that~~ old empty woodman's house that's hidden**
160 **Close to a clump of beech trees in the wood**
161 **Westward of Tara, there to await a friend**
162 **That could, as he had told her, work his cure**
163 **And would be no harsh friend.'**
When night had deepened
164 **I groped my way through boughs , and over roots ,**
165 **Till oak and hazel ceased and beech began**
166 **And found the house, a sputtering torch within ,**
167 **And stretched out sleeping on a pile of skins**
168 **Ardan, and though I called to him and tried**
169 **To shake him out of sleep I could not rouse him.**
170 **I waited till the night was on the turn ,**
171 **Then fearing that some labourer , on his way**
172 **To plough or pasture land , might see me there**
173 **Went out.**
Among the ivy–covered rocks ,
174 **As on the blue light of a sword , a man**

---

158 The dash at the end of the line is in ink.

[NLI 13,586(2) (a), 8]

8

Who had unnatural majesty, and eyes
Like the eyes of some great kite scouring the woods,
Stood on my path. Trembling from hand to foot
I gazed at him like grouse upon a kite,
But with a voice that had unnatural music
"A weary wooing and a long", he said,
'Speaking of love through other lips and looking
Under an alien eyelid ~~as~~ for it was my craft
That put a passion in the sleeper there,
And when I had got my will and drawn you here,
Where I may speak to you alone, my craft
Sucked up the passion out of him again
And left mere sleep. He'll wake when the sun wakes
Push out his vigorous limbs and rub his eyes
And wonder what has ailed him these twelve months.'
I cowered back upon the wall in terror
But that sweet-sounding voice ran on: 'Woman
I was your husband when you rode the air
Danced in the whirling foam and in the dust
In days you have not kept in memory
Being betrayed into a cradle. and I come
That I may claim you as my wife again.'
I was no longer terrified, his voice
Had half awakened some old memory
~~But I replied~~ yet answered him: 'I am King Eochaid's wife
And with him have found every happiness
Women can find.' With a most burning voice

[NLI 13,586(2) (a), 8]

8

Who had unnatural majesty , and eyes
Like the eyes of some great kite scouring the woods ,
Stood on my path. Trembling from hand to foot
I gazed at him like grouse/ **upon a kite ,**
But with a voice that had unnatural music
{" {"
{**'A weary wooing and a long** {**', he said,**
{"
{**'Speaking of love through other lips and looking**
for
Under an alien eyelid ~~**he**~~ **it was my craft**
That put a passion in the sleeper there ,
And when I had got my will and drawn you here ,
Where I speak to you alone, my craft
Sucked up the passion out of him again
And left mere sleep. He'll wake when the sun wakes
Push out his vigorous limbs and rub his eyes
And wonder what has ailed him these twelve months.'
I cowered back upon the wall in terror
But that sweet–sounding voice ran on: 'Woman
I was your husband when you rode the air
Danced in the whirling foam and in the dust
In days you have not kept in memory
Being betrayed into a cradle, and I come
That I may claim you as my wife again.'
I was no longer terrified , **his voice**
Had half awakened some old memory
Yet answered him
~~**But I replied**~~**: 'I am King Eocka's wife** h/ id /
And with him have found every happiness
Women can find.' With a most burning voice

---

197 The comma is in black pencil.

9

That made the body seem as it were a string
Under a bow he cried: ''What happiness
Can lovers have that know their happiness
Must end at the dumb stone, but where we build
Our sudden palaces in the still air
Pleasure itself can bring no weariness,
Nor can time waste the cheek, nor is their foot
That has grown weary of the whirling dance,
Nor an unlaughing mouth, but mine that mourns
Among those mouths that sing their sweethearts' praise
Your empty bed." "How should I love,' I answered
"Were it not that when the dawn has lit my bed
And shown my husband sleeping there I have sighed
'Your strength and nobleness will pass away.'
Or how should love be worth its pains were it not
That when he has fallen asleep within my arms,
Being wearied out, love in man the child.
What can they know of love that do not know
She builds her nest upon a narrow ledge
Above a windy precipice." Then he:
"Seeing that when you come to the death-bed
You must return, whether you would or no,
This human life blotted from memory,
Why must I live some thirty, forty years,
Alone with all this useless happiness.'
Thereon he seized me in his arms, but I

(bow)

[NLI 13,586(2) (a), 9]

9

That made the body seem as it were a string
bow {“
Under a ^ **he cried: {‘What happiness** (bow)
Can lovers have that know their happiness
{d
Must end at the dumb stone, but where we buil {t
Our sudden palaces in the still air
Pleasure itself can bring no weariness ,
there
Nor can time waste the cheek , nor **is ~~their~~ foot**
That has grown weary of the whirling dance ,
Nor an unlaughing mouth , **but mine that mourns**
Among those mouths that sing their sweetheart’s praise
{” {“ should
Your empty bed. {’ {‘How ~~shall~~ I love,’ I answered
{“
{‘Were it not that when the dawn has lit my bed
And shown my husband sleeping there I have sighed
‘} ’}
{“} {”}
{‘Your strength and nobleness will pass away. {’
Or how should love be worth its pains were it not
That when he has fallen asleep within my arms ,
out, I
Being wearied ~~I~~ love in man the child.
What can they know of love that do not know
She builds her nest upon a narrow ledge
{”
Above a windy precipice. {’ Then he :
{“
{‘Seeing that when you come to the death–bed
You must return, whether you would or no,
This human life blotted from memory,
Why must I live some thirty, forty years ,
Alone with all this useless happiness.’
Thereon he seized me in his arms, but I

---

215 The typewritten single quotes had been converted to double quotes by the addition of a penciled single quote at each; then the double quotes were canceled in ink and replaced by a new set of single quotes in ink.

[NLI 13,586(2) (a), 10]

10

Thrust him away with both my hands and cried
"Never will I believe there's any change
Can blot out of my memory this life
Sweetened by death, but if I could believe
That were a double hunger on my lips
For what is doubly brief."

But now the shape,
My hands were pressed to, vanished suddenly.
I staggered, but a beech tree stayed my fall
And clinging to it I could hear the cocks
Crow upon Tara.'

She had fixed her eyes
Upon King Eocha's face, who lowered his face
And touched her forehead with his lips and said
'I thank you for your kindness to my brother,
And for the love that you have shown your king,
For that you promised, and for that refused.'

Thereon the bellowing of the empounded herds
Rose round the walls, and through the bronze ringed door
jostled and shouted those war wasted men,
And in the midst King Eocha's brother stood.
He'd heard that din on the horizon's edge
And ridden out to welcome them, and now,
Giving his hand to that man and to this,
Praised their great victories and gave them joy
Of their return to that ancestral house.

W. B. Yeats.

[NLI 13,586(2) (a), 10]

10

Thrust him away with both my hands and cried
{“
{**‘Never will I believe there’s any change**
Can blot out of my memory this life
Sweetened by death, but if I could believe
That were a double hunger on my lips
{”
For what is doubly brief.{ ’
But now the shape ,
My hands were pressed to , vanished suddenly .
I staggered , but a beech tree stayed my fall
And clinging to it I could hear the cocks
Crow upon Tara.’
She had fixed her eyes
h/id/ **Upon King Eocka’s face, who lowered his face**
And touched her forehead with his lips and said
‘I thank you for you kindness to my brother ,
And for the love that you have shown your king ,
For that she promised , and for that refused.’

Thereon the bellowing of the empounded herds
Rose round the walls , and through the bronze ringed door, 7
Jostled / **and shouted those war wasted men ,**
And in the midst King Eocka’s brother stood . h/
He’d heard that din on the horizon’s edge
And ridden out to welcome them , and now ,
Giving his hand to that man and to this ,
Praised their great victories and gave them joy
Of their return to that ancestral house.
W. B. Yeats.

With the loud host before the sea,
That think sword strokes were better meant
Than lover's music — let that be,
So that the wandering foot's content.

THE TWO KINGS

(Eochaid is pronounced Yo Hee)

"We crawl like snails athough so near our home,"
King Eochaid said, and he that bore his shield
Sighing replied: 'What else but crawl like snails
Towards the hour for speaking of the dead?
My married sister put into my care
A boy of twenty years — a mound and stone
Between the wood of Duras and Magai
Have been the measure of that care,' but Eochaid,
Having no thought but for his queen Edain,
Outrode his troop that after twelve months' war
Toiled with empounded cattle through the mire,
And came into a wood as the sun set
Westward of Tara. Where in the middle wood
A clump of beech trees made an empty space
He thought to have given his horse the spur, but saw
Between the pale green light of the beech leaves
And the ground ivy's bluer light, a stag
Whiter than curds, its eyes the tint of the sea.
Because it stood upon his path and seemed
More hands in height than any stag in the world

6

[Yale, 6]

THE TWO KINGS

(Eochaid is pronounced Yo Hee)
"We crawl like snails athough so near our home,
King Eochaid said, and he that bore his shield
Sighing replied: 'What else but crawl like snails
Towards the hour for speaking of the dead?
My married sister put into my care
A boy of twenty years — a mound and stone
Between the wood of Duras and Magai
Have been the measure of that care,' but Eochaid,
(Having no thought but for his queen Edain,
Outrode his troop that after twelve months' war
Toiled with empounded cattle through the mire,
Eochaid | **And came into a wood as the sun set**
Westward of Tara. / Where in the middle wood
A clump of beech trees made an empty space
He thought to have given his horse the spur, but | saw
Between the pale green light of the beech leaves
And the ground ivy's (blue*)(*r light*)*, a stag

The collations that follow are based on the unrevised printed text (given above in bold face) of the Yale page proofs, pp. 6–15.

1 (Eochaid is pronounced Yo Hee)] Eochaid is pronounced Yohee. [*in bottom margin as a footnote to* "Eochaid" *in l. 3*] *BR, P lacking Resp14*

2–18 *rev to* [in *Yale* and printed thus in *Resp14*:]
King Eochaid came at sundown to a wood
Westward of Tara. Hurrying to his queen
He had out ridden [out-ridden *Resp14*] his war-wasted men
Who with [That with *Resp14*] empounded cattle trod the mire.
Where certain beeches made an empty space *Yale* Where certain beeches mixed a pale green light *Resp14*
And where the pale green boughs *Yale lacking Resp14*
With the ground ivy's blue had mixed their light *Yale* With the ground-ivy's blue, he saw a stag *Resp14* he saw a stag *Yale lacking Resp14*

2 We crawl like snails athough so] We ride but slowly though so *BR, P* home,] home," *BR, P*

4 'What else but crawls like snails] "What need have we for haste *BR, P*

6 Not doubting to have shouldered it away.] *lacking Resp14*

7 years;— *P*

9 care." *P*

12 through the] through th *P*

Sequence of revisions: Pound and Yeats worked on revising the poem in the following sequence: (1) Pound's suggestions in pencil, (2) Yeats in ink, (3) Pound's suggestions in ink using a broad-nibbed pen, (4) Yeats in ink using a narrow-nibbed pen. See pp. 203, 205 below (Yale, 15).

1–18 Canceled in ink.

10–11 Left margin bracket in pencil.

13 "Eochaid" in left margin in Pound's hand, with penciled insertion arrow to after "And".

16 Three words underscored in pencil; vertical line after "but" in pencil.

18 Erased penciled opening parenthesis in front of "blue)(r"; penciled insertion arrow leading from l. 23 penciled revision "er light"; "a stag" underscored in pencil.

With the loud host before the sea,
That think sword strokes were better meant
Than lover's music— let that be,
So that the wandering foot's content.

THE TWO KINGS

~~(Eochaid is pronounced Yo Hee)~~

"We crawl like snails athough so near our home,"
King Eochaid said, and he that bore his shield
Sighing replied: 'What else but crawl like snails
Towards the hour for speaking of the dead?
My married sister put into my care
A boy of twenty years— a mound and stone
Between the wood of Duras and Magai
Have been the measure of that care,' but Eochaid,
Having no thought but for his queen Edain,
Outrode his troop that after twelve months' war
Toiled with empounded cattle through the mire,
And came into a wood as the sun set
Westward of Tara. Where in the middle wood
A clump of beech trees made an empty space
He thought to have given his horse the spur, but saw
~~Between the pale green light of the beech leaves~~
~~And the ground ivy's bluer light, a stag~~
Whiter than curds, its eyes the tint of the sea.
Because it stood upon his path and seemed
More hands in height than any stag in the world

6

King Eochaid came at sundown to a wood
Westward of Tara. Hurrying to his queen
He had out ridden his war-wasted men
Who with empounded cattle trod the mire
Where certain beeches made an empty space

[Yale, 6. continued]

Whiter than curds, its eyes^ the tint of the sea.
had **Because it stood upon his path and seemed**
More hands in height than any stag in the world

he saw
er light

King Eochaid came at sundown to a wood
Westward of Tara. Hurrying to his queen
He had out ridden his war–wasted men
Who with empounded cattle trod the mire.
Where certain beeches made an empty space

And where the pale green boughs had mixed their light
With the ground ivy's blue he saw a stag

19 Caret in pencil.
22 Revision in pencil, in Pound's hand, for l. 16, with penciled insertion arrow.
23 Revision in pencil, in Pound's hand, for l. 18 at "(blue)(r light)."
24–28 Written in ink, in Pound's hand, covering his penciled notes ll. 22–23.
29–30 In Pound's hand.

He sat with tightened rein and loosend mouth
Upon his trembling horse, then drove the spur
~~Not doubting to have shouldered it away.~~
But the stag stooped ~~its heavy branching~~ horns
~~And ran at him, and passed, and as it passed~~
~~Ripped through~~ the horse's flanks. King Eochaid reeled
~~But drew his sword, and thought with levelled point~~
~~To stay the stags next rush.~~ When sword met horn
The horn resounded as though it had been silver.
A sweet, miraculous, terrifying sound.
Horn locked in sword, they tugged and struggled there
(As though a stag and unicorn were met
In Africa on mountain of the moon,)
Until at last the double horns, drawn backward,
Butted below the single and so pierced
The entrails of the horse. Dropping his sword
King Eochaid seized the horns in his strong hands
And stared into the sea-green eyes, and so
Hither and thither to and fro they trod
Till all the place was beaten into mire.
The strong thigh and the agile thigh were met,
The hands that gathered up the might of the world,
And hoof and horn that had sucked in their speed
Amid the elaborate wilderness of the air.
Through bush they plunged and over ivied root,
And where the stone struck fire, while in the leaves
A squirrel whinnied and a bird screamed out;

[Yale, 7]

~~sword~~
~~Then, drew his swored , held out a levelled point~~
[-?-] to hold
Then drew his [-?-] sword, ~~to hold~~ its levelled point
~~holding~~
against the stag — when [?horn] and steel had met

He sat with tightened rein and loosened mouth
Upon his trembling horse, then drove the spur
(~~**Not doubting to have shouldered it away.**~~) And ran at him
But the stag stooped its heavy branching horns and passed
~~**And ran at him, and passed, and as it passed**~~ & ~~and as it passed~~
~~**Ripped through**~~ **the horse's flanks. King Eochaid reeled** & Rending/
Then ~~**But drew his sword**~~ (~~**and thought with levelled point**~~
~~**To stay the stags**~~) ~~**next rush.**~~) ~~**When sword met**~~ **horn** & *the*
The horn resounded as though it had been silver.
were of

---

34 rein and lossened mouth] rein amazed, his horse *P*
35 Upon his trembling horse, then] Trembling beneath him, and then *P*
37–40 *rev to* [in *Yale*, in Pound's hand, and printed thus in *Resp14*:]
But the stag stooped and ran at him [him, *Resp14*] & passed [passed, *Resp14*]
Rending the horse's flanks. [flank. *Resp14*] King Eochaid reeled
Then drew his sword to hold the leveled point [hold its levelled *Resp14*]
37 horns, *P*
39 reeled] reeled, *P* reeled *rev to* reeled, *NLI 30,262*
40 But] Then *Resp14* sword, *BR, P*
41 stags] stag's *BR, P*
41 *rev to* [in *Yale* and printed thus in *Resp14*:]
Against the stag when [stag. When *Resp14*] steel & horn were met. *Yale, Resp14*
42 silver, *BR, Resp14*

31–33 In ink, in Yeats's hand.
31 Canceled in ink.
36–39 Cancels in ink.
37 Words in the right margin are in Yeats's hand, in ink.
38 Words in the right margin are in Yeats's hand, in ink; canceled in ink.
39 Cancel of "s" in ink; "King" is circled in pencil; in right margin "&" is in pencil and "Rending/" is in Yeats's hand, in ink.
40 In left margin, penciled "Then" is in Pound's hand, as a suggested replacement for "But", which is circled in pencil; printed line is canceled in ink.
41 Printed words canceled in ink except that the cancel line continues with an uninked pen nib on "When sword met" after first six printed words and the closing parenthesis; at the penciled closing parenthesis after "rush." are two penciled carets; in the right margin, the penciled "& the" is probably in Pound's hand, and the carets are in pencil.
42 The insertion arrow for the penciled revision "There was" in the bottom left margin ends after "resounded"; underscores of "had been" are in pencil.

He sat with tightened rein and loosend mouth
Upon his trembling horse, then drove the spur
Not doubting to have shouldered it away.
But the stag stooped its heavy branching horns
And ran at him, and passed, and as it passed
Ripped through the horse's flanks. King Eochaid reeled
But drew his sword and thought with levelled point
To stay the stags next rush. When sword met horn
The horn resounded as though it had been silver.
A sweet, miraculous, terrifying sound.
Horn locked in sword, they tugged and struggled there
As though a stag and unicorn were met
In Africa on mountain of the moon,
Until at last the double horns, drawn backward,
Butted below the single and so pierced
The entrails of the horse. Dropping his sword
King Eochaid seized the horns in his strong hands
And stared into the sea-green eyes, and so
Hither and thither to and fro they trod
Till all the place was beaten into mire.
The strong thigh and the agile thigh were met,
The hands that gathered up the might of the world,
And hoof and horn that had sucked in their speed
Amid the elaborate wilderness of the air.
Through bush they plunged and over ivied root,
And where the stone struck fire, while in the leaves
A squirrel whinnied and a bird screamed out;

[Yale, 7, continued]

43 **~~A~~ sweet, miraculous, terrifying sound.**
44 **Horn locked in sword, they tugged and struggled there**
45 *(* **As though a stag and unicorn were met**
46 **In Africa on mountain of the moon,***)*
47 **Until** *(***at last***)* **the double horns***(***, d~~a~~awn backward,***)* r/
48 **Butted below the single and so pierced**
49 **The entrails of the horse. Dropping his sword**
50 **King Eochaid seized the horns** *(***in his strong hands***)*
51 **And stared into the sea–green eye~~s~~,** *(***and so***)*
52 **Hither and thither** *(***to and fro they***)* **trod**
53 **Till all the place was beaten into mire.**
54 *(* **The***)* **strong thigh and** *(***the***)* **agile thigh were met,**
55 **The hands that gathered up the might of the world,**
56 **And hoof and horn that had sucked in their speed**
57 **Amid the elaborate wilderness of the air.**
58 **Through bush they plunged and over ivied root,**
59 **And where the stone struck fire, while in the leaves**
60 **A squirrel whinnied and a bird screamed out;**

61 and ran at him & passed
62 *There was* Re~~n~~ding . . .
63 Then drew his sword to hold the leveled
s [? ? ? ?] point
64 Against the stag ~~[? ?] horn, [?but]~~ when steel & horn
were met.
65 ~~[?Be] [?Against] [?the] stag, [?&] when the horn~~ met
~~steel~~

---

43 A sweet, miraculous, terrifying sound.] *lacking P*
46 Mountain *BR, Resp14* moon] Moon *BR*, Moon, *Resp14* In Africa on Mountain of the Moon, *rev by Yeats to* Among the African Mountains of the Moon, *NLI 30,262*
47 the double horns, drawn backward,] the unlocked horn had torn *P*
48 Butted below the single and so pierced] *lacking P*
49 The entrails] Through the entrails *P*
51 eyes, *BR, P* eye, *Resp14*
54 met— *P*
58 root *P*

---

43 Cancel of "a" in ink.
51 Cancel of "s" in ink.
59 Insertion arrow from "*s*" in bottom margin to the end of "stone" (l. 64/) is in pencil.
61–63 In ink, in Pound's hand.
63/ "s" in pencil, in Pound's hand, with insertion arrow to "stone" (l. 60).
64–65 Yeats wrote the canceled ink revisions, which continue his revisions from the top margin, then Pound used the remaining space for his revisions, which are uncanceled. The cancels are in ink.

Then the
beast

1

One — But when at last he forced those sinewy flanks
Against a beech bole, he threw down the beast
And knelt above it with drawn knife. On the instant
It vanished like a shadow, and a cry— (Then)
So mournful that it seemed the cry of one
Who had lost some unimaginable treasure
Wandered between the blue and the green leaf
amid — And climbed into the air, crumbling away, leaves
un Till all had seemed a shadow or a vision
But for the trodden mire, the pool of blood,
The disembowelled horse. King Eochaid ~~gazed~~, ran
~~And then as terror-stricken as a child,~~
~~Who has seen a garden image or twisted tree~~
~~In the half light, and runs to its own door,~~
~~Its terror growing wilder at every foot-fall,~~
~~He ran towards the house his fathers built~~
Towards ~~On~~ peopled Tara, nor stood to draw his breath
Until he came before the painted wall,
The posts of polished yew, circled with bronze,
Of the great door; but though the hanging lamps
Showed their faint light through the unshuttered windows,
Nor door, nor mouth, nor slipper made a noise,
Nor on the ancient beaten paths, that wound
From well-side or from plough-land, was there noise;
And there had been no sound of living thing
Before him or behind, but that far-off
was — On the horizon edge bellowed the herds.

8

66–67 In top margin, in Pound's hand.

70 Penciled words are in Pound's hand.

71 The dash is in ink.

74 Underscoring in pencil; "leaves" in the right margin is in Pound's hand; the insertion arrow from "leaves" in the right margin to "green" is in pencil.

76 *"un"* in the left margin is in Pound's hand, for revision to "Until".

77 Cancel in ink; "ran" is in Pound's hand.

78–81 Canceled in pencil and then canceled in ink.

83 Canceled in pencil and then canceled in ink.

84 "Towards" is in Pound's hand; cancel of "On" is in ink.

89–92 In left margin, bracket or opening parenthesis in pencil and canceled in pencil.

89–90 "that wound / From well-side or from plough-land", and "there" are circled in pencil

91 "there" cirlced in pencil with a penciled insertion arrow from what probably were several penciled words in the bottom margin that were erased.

92 "had been" circled in pencil with a penciled insertion arrow from "was" in the left margin at l. 98.

94 "Was" is in Pound's hand.

This is the end of gathering "b," which consists of four sheets folded (8 pp.).

[Yale, 8]

Then the
beast
But when at last he forced those sinewy flanks
Against a beech bole, he threw down the beast
Then (**And***)* **knelt** *(***above it***)* **with** *(***drawn***)* **knife.** *(***On the instant***)*
It vanished like a shadow, and a cry — *& then)*
So mournful that it seemed the cry of one
Who had lost some unimaginable treasure
amid **Wandered between the blue** *(***and the***)* **green leaf** *leaves*
And climbed into the air, crumbling away,
un **Till all** *(***had***)* **seemed a shadow or a vision**
But for the trodden mire, the pool of blood,
The disembowelled horse. King Eochaid *(*~~**gazed**~~, ran
And then as terror stricken as a child,
Who has seen a garden image or twisted tree
In the halflight, and runs to its own door,
Its terror growing wilder at every foot–fall,
~~**He) ran towards (the house his fathers built**~~
Towards ~~**On**~~*)* **peopled Tara, nor stood to draw his breath**
Until he came before the painted wall,
The posts of polished yew, circled with bronze,
Of the great door; but though the hanging lamps
Showed their faint light through the unshuttered windows,
Nor door, nor mouth, nor slipper made a noise;
~~**Nor on the ancient**~~ **beaten paths, that wound**
From well–side or from plough–land, was there noise;
And there had been no sound of living thing
Before him or behind, but that far–off
was **On the horizon edge bellowed the herds.**

---

69 beech bole,] beech bole *BR, P* beech bole *rev to* beech-bole *NLI 30,262*
71 cry *BR, Resp14* cry, *P*
73 treasure, *BR, P*
75 away *P*
78 horse. King] horse. / *Remainder of line is set as a deeply indented new line* King *Resp14* gazed,] *rev to* ran, *Yale Resp14*
79–83 *lacking Resp14*
79 then, *P* terror-stricken *BR, P*
81 half light, *BR, P*
82 footfall, *BR*
84 On peopled *rev to* [in *Yale*, in Pound's hand, and printed in *Resp14*] Towards peopled
87 door, *BR*
89 noise, *BR, P, Resp14*
91 wellside *BR* well side *P* plough-land,] ploughland, *BR* plough land *P* there noise;] their noise; *P*

Knowing that silence brings no good to kings,
And mocks returning victory, he passed
Between the pillars with a beating heart
And saw where in the midst of the great hall
Pale-faced, alone upon a bench, ~~his wife~~
Sat upright with a sword before her feet.
~~A kind mild woman had she been, who poured~~
~~Her beauty as the constellations pour~~
~~Their richness through the summer and the spring,~~
~~But now she had no mild and no kind look:~~
Her hands on either side had gripped the bench
Her eyes were cold and steady, her lips tight.
Some passion had made her stone. Hearing a foot
She started and then knew whose foot it was;
But when he thought to take her in his arms
She motioned him afar, and rose and spoke:
'I have sent out into the fields and woods
The fighting men and servants of this house,
For I would have your judgment upon one
Who is self-accused. If she be innocent
She would not look in any known man's face
Till judgment has been given, and if guilty,
~~Because that were a guilt against her king,~~
Will never look again on known man's face.'
And at these words he paled, as she had paled,
Knowing that he should find upon her lips
The meaning of that monstrous day.

9 c

[Yale, 9]

(Knowing that) silence brings no good to kings,
(And mocks returning victory,) he passed
(Between the pillars) with a beating heart
And saw where in the midst of the great hall
{ Edain *Edain*
Pale–faced, alone upon a bench, ~~his wife~~
Sat upright with a sword before her feet.
(A kind mild woman had she been, who poured
Her beauty as the constellations pour
Their richness through the summer and the spring,
But now she had no mild and no kind look:)
Her hands on either side had gripped the bench
Her eyes were cold and steady, her lips tight.
Some passion had made her stone. Hearing a foot
She started and then knew whose foot it was;
But when he thought to take her in his arms
She motioned him afar, and rose and spoke:
'I have sent out (into the fields and woods)
The fighting men and servants of this house,
For I would have your judgment upon one
Who is self–accused. If she be innocent
She would not look in any known man's face
Till judgment has been given, and if guilty,
~~**(Because that were a guilt against her king,)**~~
Will never look again on known man's face.'
And at these words he paled, as she had paled,
Knowing that he should find upon her lips
The meaning of that (monstrous) day.

---

98 hall, *P*
99 bench, his wife *rev to* [in *Yale*, in Pound's hand, and printed thus in *Resp14*] bench, Edain
101–104 *del Yale lacking Resp14*
103 spring; *BR*
105 bench, *BR, P*
113, 115 would] *Yeats rejected a proposed rev to* will *NLI 30,262*
117 *del Yale lacking Resp14*
118 Will never] Would never *rev by Yeats to* Will never *NLI 30,262*
119 paled *BR*

---

99 "his wife" is canceled in pencil and then in ink; Pound wrote the revision "Edain" in pencil and then overwrote it in ink.
101–104 Canceled in ink.
107–112 The bracket in the the right margin is in pencil and canceled in pencil.
107 "Some" is underscored and circled in pencil.
110 "afar" is underscored in pencil and in ink.
117 Cancel in ink.

Then she:
"You brought me where your brother Ardan sat
Always in his one seat, and bid me care him
Through that strange illness that had fixed him there,
And should he die to heap his burial mound
And carve his name in Ogham." Eochaid said,
~~Gazing upon her with bewildered eyes~~:
'If he be living still the whole world's mine
But if not living, half the world is lost.'
'I bid them make his bed under this roof
And carried him his food with my own hands,
And so the weeks passed by. But when I said
'What is this trouble?' he would answer nothing,
Though always at my words his trouble grew;
~~And I, that I might find and stub it out,~~
~~But asked the more, until he spoke these words,~~ said
Weary of many questions: 'There are things
That make the heart akin to the dumb stone.'
Then I replied: 'Although you hide a secret,
Hopeless and dear, or terrible to think on,
Speak it, that I may send through the wide world
For medicine.' Thereon he cried aloud:
'Day after day you question me, and I,
Because there is such a storm amid my thoughts
I shall be carried in the gust, command,
Forbid, beseech and waste my breath.' Then I,
'Although the thing that you have hid were evil,

10

~~but asked the more till he cried out~~
And I but asked the more till he cried out.

128 Cancel in ink.

129–130 In left margin, penciled opening parenthesis canceled in pencil.

130/131 In left margin, in pencil, copyediting *"sp."* with an arrow, for stanza division.

136–137 Canceled in ink.

137 Insertion arrow, in ink, from the start of l. 138 to the bottom margin at an ink revision in Yeats's hand, below which is an ink revision, in Pound's hand, of the Yeats revision; in the right margin, *"said"* is in Pound's hand.

139/140 In left margin, in pencil, copyediting *"sp."* with an arrow, for stanza division.

149 In Yeats's hand, in ink, with insertion arrow to l. 138; cancel in ink.

150 In Pound's hand.

[Yale, 10]

Then she:
“You brought me where your brother Ardan sat
Always in his one seat, and bid me care him
Through that strange illness that had fixed him there,
And should he die to heap his burial mound
And carve his name in Ogham.” Eochaid said,
(~~**Gazing upon her with bewildered eyes:**~~*)*
‘If he believing still the whole world’s mine
But if not living, half the world is lost.’
sp. **‘I bid them make his bed under this roof**
And carried him his food with my own hands,
And so the weeks passed by. But when I said
‘What is this trouble?’ he would answer nothing,
Though always at my words his trouble grew;
~~**And I, (that I might find and stub it out,**~~*)*
~~**But asked the more, until he (spoke these words,**~~*)* *said*
Weary of many questions: ‘There are things
That make the heart akin to the dumb stone.’
sp. **Then I replied: ‘Although you hide a secret,**
Hopeless and dear, or terrible to think on,
Speak it, that I may send through the wide world
For medicine.’ Thereon he cried aloud:
‘Day after day you question me, and I,
Because there is such a storm amid my thoughts
I shall be carried in the gust, command,
Forbid, beseech, and waste my breath.’ Then I,
‘Although the thing that you have hid were evil,

~~B~~
but asked the
more till he cried
out
And I but asked the more
till he cried out

126 burial mound *rev to* burial-mound *NLI 30,262*
127 And carve his name in Ogham.” Eochaid] And raise his pillar stone.” King Eochaid *BR, P*
128 *lacking Resp14*
129 mine, *BR, P*
131 roof, *BR, P*
133 said, *BR, P*
135 grew. *P*
136–137 *rev to* [in *Yale* and printed thus in *Resp14*:] And I but asked the more [more, *Resp14*] till he cried out
137 more *BR, P*
141 Hopeless and dear, or terrible to think on,] Dearer than any that the dumb stone hides, *BR, P*
146 command *P*
147 beseech *BR, P, Resp14* I,] I: *P*
148 evil *P*

The speaking of it could be no great wrong,
And evil must it be, if done 'twere worse
Than mound and stone that keep all virtue in,
And loosen on us dreams that waste our life,
Shadows and shows that can but turn the brain.'
But finding him still silent I stooped down
And whispering that none but he should hear,
Said: "If a woman has put this on you,
My men, whether it please her or displease,
And though they have to cross the Loughlan waters
And take her in the middle of armed men,
Shall make her look upon her handiwork,
That she may quench the rick she has fired; and though
She may have worn silk clothes, or worn a crown,
She'll not be proud, knowing within her heart
That our sufficient portion of the world
Is that we give, although it be brief giving,
Happiness to children and to men.'
Then he, driven by his thought beyond his thought,
And speaking what he would not though he would,
Sighed: 'You, even you yourself, could work the cure!'
And at those words I rose and I went out
And for nine days he had food from other hands,
And for nine days my mind went whirling round
The one disastrous zodiac, muttering
That the immedicable mound's beyond
Our questioning, beyond our pity even.

11

[Yale, 11]

The speaking of it could be no great wrong,
And evil must it be, if done 'twere worse
Than mound and stone that keep all virtue in, *to*
And loosen on us dreams that waste our life, ~~*to*~~
Shadows and shows that can but turn the brain.'
(**But finding him still silent***)* **I stooped down**
And whispering that none but he should hear,
Said, "If a woman has put this on you,
My men, whether it please her or displease,
And though they have to cross the Loughlan waters
And take her in the middle of armed men,
Shall make her look upon her handiwork,
That she may quench the rick she has fired; and though
She may have worn silk clothes, or worn a crown,
She'll be not proud, knowing within her heart
That our sufficient portion of the world
Is that we give, although it be brief giving,
Happiness to children and to men.'
Then he, driven by his thought beyond his thought,
And speaking what he would not though he would,
Sighed: 'You, even you yourself, could work the cure!'
And at these words I rose and I went out
And for nine days he had food from other hands,
And for nine days my mind went whirling round
The one disastrous zodiac, muttering
That the immedicable mound's beyond
Our questioning, beyond our pity even.

---

151 wrong; *P*
153 in *BR, P*
156 down, *P*
157 And, *P*
158 Said: *BR, P, Resp14*   you *P*
160 Loughlan waters] Loughlan seas *BR, P*
162 handiwork *P*
163 fired, *BR, P*
165 proud *BR*
167 giving,] giving *P*
171 yourself *P*   cure.' *BR, P*
172 out, *BR*
177 Our questioning,] Question of ours, *BR, P*   even *P*

---

154 "that" circled in pencil; in right margin, penciled "to" is in Pound's hand and is canceled in ink.

But when nine days had gone I stood again
Before his chair and bending down my head
Told him, that when Orion rose, and all
The women of his household were asleep,
To go—for hope would give his limbs the power—
To an old empty woodman's house that's hidden
Close to a clump of beech trees in the wood
Westward of Tara, there to await a friend
That could, as he had told her, work his cure
And would be no harsh friend.'
When night had deepened,
I groped my way through boughs, and over roots,
Till oak and hazel ceased and beech began
And found the house, a sputtering torch within,
And stretched out sleeping on a pile of skins
Ardan, and though I called to him and tried
To shake him out of sleep, I could not rouse him.
I waited till the night was on the turn,
Then fearing that some labourer, on his way
To plough or pasture-land, might see me there
Went out.
Among the ivy-covered rocks,
As on the blue light of a sword, a man
Who had unnatural majesty, and eyes
Like the eyes of some great kite scouring the woods,
Stood on my path. Trembling from hand to foot
I gazed at him like grouse upon a kite,

12

[Yale, 12]

But when nine days had gone I stood again
Before his chair and bending down my head
Told him, that when Orion rose, and all
(**The women of his household***)* **were asleep,**
To go — for hope would give his limbs the power —
To an old empty woodman's house *(***that's hidden***)*
Close to a clump of beech trees in the wood
Westward of Tara, there to await a friend
That could, as he had told her, work his cure
And would be no harsh friend.'
When night had deepened,
I groped my way through boughs, and over roots,
Till oak and hazel ceased and beech began
And found the house, a sputtering torch within,
And stretched out sleeping on a pile of skins
Ardan, and though I called to him and tried
To shake him out of sleep, I could not rouse him.
I waited till the night was on the turn,
Then fearing that some labourer, on his way
To plough or pasture–land, might see me there
Went out.
Among the ivy–covered rocks,
As on the blue light of a sword, a man
Who had unnatural majesty, and eyes
Like the eyes of some great kite scouring the woods,
Stood on my path. Trembling from hand to foot
I gazed at him like grouse upon a kite,

180–182 Told him, that when Orion rose, and all / The women of his household were asleep, / To go — for hope would give his limbs the power — *rev probably by Yeats to* I bade him go when all his household slept *NLI 30,262*

184–186 Close to a clump of beech trees in the wood / Westward of Tara, there to await a friend / That could, as he had told her, work his cure *rev probably by Yeats to* Westward of Tara, among the hazel-trees — / For hope would give his limbs the power — and await / A friend that could, he had told her, work his cure *NLI 30,262*

186 cure, *P*

187 friend.'] friend. *P* 'When *P* deepened *P*

188–190 way through boughs, and over roots, / Till oak and hazel ceased and beech began, / And found the house, a sputtering torch within, *rev probably by Yeats to* way from beech to hazel wood, / Found that old house, a sputtering torch within, / *question mark in left margin at the uncanceled next printed line:* And found the house, a sputtering torch within *NLI 30,262*

189 began, *P*

191 And, *P* skins, *P*

193 sleep *P*

196 pasture land, *BR*

178–179 In left margin, penciled opening parenthesis canceled in pencil.

180–181 In left margin, penciled opening parenthesis.

But with a voice that had unnatural music
'A weary wooing and a long,' he said,
'Speaking of love through other lips and looking
Under the eyelids of another, for it was my craft
That put a passion in the sleeper there,
And when I had got my will and drawn you here,
Where I may speak to you alone, my craft
Sucked up the passion out of him again
And left mere sleep. He'll wake when the sun wakes
(Push out his vigorous limbs and rub his eyes)
And wonder what has ailed (him these twelve months.)
I cowered back upon the wall in terror
But that sweet-sounding voice ran on: 'Woman
I was your husband when you rode the air,
Danced in the whirling foam and in the dust,
In days you have not kept in memory,
Being betrayed into a cradle, and I come
That I may claim you (as my wife again.')
I was no longer terrified, his voice
Had half awakened some old memory,
Yet answered him: 'I am King Eochaid's wife
And with him have found every happinss
Women can find.' With a most masterful voice,
(That made the body seem as it were a string
Under a bow,) he cried: 'What happiness
Can lovers have that know their happiness
Must end at the dumb stone? but where we build

13

t wonder what he has ailed.

[Yale, 13]

But with a voice that had unnatural music
'A weary wooing and a long,' he said,
'Speaking of love through other lips and looking
Under the eyelids of another, for it was my craft
That put a passion in the sleeper there,
And when I had got my will and drawn you here,
Where I speak to you alone, my craft
Sucked up the passion out of him again
And left mere sleep. He'll wake when the sun wakes
(**Push out his vigorous limbs and rub his eyes***)*
And wonder what ^ **has ailed** *(***him these twelve months.***)* *he)*
I cowered back upon the wall in terror
But that sweet–sounding voice ran on: 'Woman
I was your husband when you rode the air, =
Danced in the whirling foam and in the dust,
In days you have not kept in memory,
Being betrayed into a cradle, and I come
That I may claim you *(***as my wife again.'***)* =
I was no longer terrified, his voice
Had half awakened some old memory, + +
Yet answered him: 'I am King Eochaid's wife
And with him have found every happiness
Women can find.' With a most masterful voice,
(**That made the body seem as it were a string**
Under a bow, *)* **he cried: 'What happiness**
Can lovers have that know their happiness
Must end at the dumb stone? but where we build

\+ wonder what he has ailed .

206 Under the eyelids of another, for] Under an alien eyelid, for *BR* Under an alien eyelid for *P*
211 wakes, *BR, P*
213 months.' *BR, P*
214 terror, *BR*
215 'Woman, *BR, P*
217 dust *BR, P*
219 cradle; *P*
222 half awakened] half wakened *P*
223 wife, *BR, P*
225 voice *BR, P*
229 stone? But] stone, but *P*

211–216 In right margin, penciled opening parenthesis canceled in pencil.
213 Insertion arrow from bottom margin is in pencil; caret in pencil.
216 "husband" is underscored in pencil; in right margin, marking in pencil.
220 "wife" is underscored in pencil; in right margin, marking in pencil.
222 Underscoring in pencil; in right margin, marking in pencil.
225 Underscoring in pencil.

Our sudden palaces in the still air
Pleasure itself can bring no weariness,
Nor can time waste the cheek, nor is there foot
That has grown weary of the whirling dance,
Nor an unlaughing mouth, but mine that mourns,
Among those mouths that sing their sweethearts' praise,
Your empty bed.' 'How should I love,' I answered
'Were it not that when the dawn has lit my bed
And shown my husband sleeping there, I have sighed,
"Your strength and nobleness will pass away."
Or how should love be worth its pains were it not
That when he has fallen asleep within my arms,
Being wearied out, I love in man the child?
What can they know of love that do not know
She builds her nest upon a narrow ledge
Above a windy precipice?' Then he:
'Seeing that when you come to the death-bed
You must return, whether you would or no,
This human life blotted from memory,
Why must I live some thirty, forty years,
Alone with all this useless happiness?'
Thereon he seized me in his arms, but I
Thrust him away with both my hands and cried
'Never will I believe there is any change
Can blot out of my memory this life
Sweetened by death, but if I could believe
That were a double hunger in my lips

14

[Yale, 14]

Our sudden palaces in the still air
Pleasure itself can bring no weariness,
Nor can time waste the cheek, nor is there foot
That has grown weary of the whirling dance,
Nor an unlaughing mouth, but mine that mourns *,*
Among those mouths that sing their sweetheart's praise *,*
Your empty bed.' 'How should I love,' I answered
'Were it not that when the dawn has lit my bed
And shown my husband sleeping there, I have sighed,
"Your strength and nobleness will pass away."
Or how should love be worth its pains were it not
That when he has fallen asleep within my arms,
Being wearied out, *(***I love in man the child?***)*
What can they know of love that do not know
Love
She builds her nest upon a narrow ledge
Above a windy precipice?' Then he:
'Seeing that when you come to the death–bed
You must return, whether you would or no,
((**This human life blotted from memory,** *))*
Why must I live some thirty, forty years,
Alone with all this useless happiness?'
Thereon he seized me in his arms, but I
Thrust him away with both my hands and cried
'Never will I believe there is any change
Can blot out of my memory this life
Sweetened by death, but if I could believe
That were a double hunger in my lips

---

234 whirling] whirling *rev to* wandering *ABY(5)*
236 praise, *P*
237 answered, *BR, P*
239 there *P*
253 cried, *BR* cried: *P*
254 there is] there's *BR, P*
256 believe *rev to* believe, *NLI 30,262*
257 hunger in my] hunger on my *BR, P*

---

235 Comma at end of the line is in pencil.
236 Comma in pencil.
241–243 Circled in pencil.
242 In left margin, marking in pencil.
245 Partial circling of "She" (or insertion arrow with downward facing caret) is in pencil.

~~I cling to a beech tree~~ Till I had the cocks

For what is doubly brief.'
And now the shape,
My hands were pressed to, vanished suddenly.
I staggered, but a beech tree stayed my fall
And clinging to it I could hear the cocks
Crow upon Tara.'
~~She had fixed her eyes~~
~~Upon King Eochaid's face, who lowered his face~~
~~And touched her forehead with his lips and said~~
~~'I thank you for your kindness to my brother,~~
~~And for the love that you have shown your king,~~
For that you promised, and for that refused.'

Thereon the bellowing of the empounded herds
Rose round the walls, and through the bronze-ringed door
Jostled and shouted those war-wasted men,
And in the midst King Eochaid's brother stood.
He'd heard that din on the horizon's edge
~~And ridden out to welcome them, and now~~,
~~Giving his hand to that man and to this,~~
~~Praised their great victories and gave them joy~~
~~Of their return to that ancestral house~~.

And ridden towards it being ignorant.

15

King Eochaid loved his queen
and thanked her for his kindness to his brother
For that she promised & for that refused

[Yale, 15]

~~*I clung to a beech tree*~~
~~*till I heard*~~
~~*the cocks.*~~
For what is doubly brief.'
And now the shape,
My hands were pressed to, vanished suddenly.
I staggered, but a beech tree stayed my fall *))*
And clinging to it I could hear the cocks
Crow upon Tara.'
[**She had fixed her eyes**
Upon King Eochaid's face, who lowered his face
And touched her forehead with his lips and said
'I thank you for your kindness to my brother,
And for the love that you have shown your king,
For that she promised, and for that refused.' *]*

---

261 And now] But now *BR* "But now *P*
263 fall, *BR, P*
265–270 *rev to* King Eochaid bowed his head / And thanked her for his kindness to his brother / For that she promised & for that refused *Yale* King Eochaid bowed his head / And thanked her for her kindness to his brother / For that she promised, and for that refused. *Resp14*
267 said: *BR, P*
270/271 *no stanza break BR*

This page establishes that Pound and Yeats worked on revising the poem in the following sequence: (1) Pound's suggestions in pencil, (2) Yeats's revision in ink, (3) Pound's suggestions in ink using a broad-nibbed pen, (4) Yeats's revision in ink using a narrow-nibbed pen.

That is shown here by the pencil revision canceled in narrow-nibbed pen ink, and then at the bottom margin, the series of three ink passages, one under the other, the first narrow nib and canceled in broad nib, then below that passage Pound wrote a passage in broad nib, and then below both of those Yeats wrote a third passage in narrow nib.

There might be variations in that, but the relatively short length of the poem suggests that Pound could have gone through it in one session.

258–260 In top margin, in Pound's hand, in pencil, and then canceled in ink. Pound proposed this as a revision of l. 264, which is circled in pencil and marked with a double closing parentheses in the right margin. Pound's proposed revision then was canceled in ink by Yeats in the same narrow nib pen that Yeats used in the bottom margin for a revision at ll. 283–285.

263 In right margin, in pencil, doubled closing parentheses enclose ll. 263–264; l. 263 is circled in pencil.
264 "And clinging to it" circled in pencil; "could" circled in pencil.
265 Opening square bracket in pencil.
267 The curved insertion arrow from here to l. 283 is in ink.
268 Underscores in pencil.
270 Closing square bracket in pencil.

~~I clung to a beech tree~~
Till I heard
the cocks

For what is doubly brief.'
And now the shape,
My hands were pressed to, vanished suddenly.
I staggered, but a beech tree stayed my fall
And clinging to it I could hear the cocks
Crow upon Tara.'

~~She had fixed her eyes~~
~~Upon King Eochaid's face, who lowered his face~~
~~And touched her forehead with his lips and said~~
~~'I thank you for your kindness to my brother,~~
~~And for the love that you have shown your king,~~
For that you promised, and for that refused.'

Thereon the bellowing of the empounded herds
Rose round the walls, and through the bronze-ringed door
Jostled and shouted those war-wasted men,
And in the midst King Eochaid's brother stood.
He'd heard that din on the horizon's edge
~~And ridden out to welcome them, and now,~~
~~Giving his hand to that man and to this,~~
~~Praised their great victories and gave them joy~~
~~Of their return to that ancestral house.~~

~~[illegible]~~

And ridden towards it
being ignorant.

15

King Eochaid bowed his head
and thanked her for his kindness to his brother
For that she promised & for that refused

[Yale, 15, continued]

[**Thereon the bellowing of the empounded herds**
Rose round the walls, *]* **and through the bronze–ringed door**
Jostled and shouted those war–wasted men,
And in the midst King Eochaid's brother stood. *)*
He'd heard that din on the horizon's edge
~~**And ridden out to welcome them, and now,**~~
~~**Giving his hand to that man and to this,**~~
~~**Praised their great victories and gave them joy**~~
~~**Of their return to that ancestral house.**~~ *]*

~~And leaped upon a horse to welcome them~~

And ridden towards it
being ignorant.

King Eochaid bowed his head
And thanked her for his kindness to his brother
For that she promised & for that refused

---

274 stood. *rev to* stood *ABY(1)*

274ab *lacking*] And laughed aloud, & named this man & that / And welcomed all & praised their victory *ABY(2)*

275 He'd heard that din on the horizon's edge] *rev to* For he had heard a noise on the horizon *ABY(1) rev to* For he had heard that din on the horizon *ABY(2)*

276–279 *rev to* [*in Yale, in Pound's hand, and printed thus in Resp14*:] And ridden towards it [it, *Resp14*] being ignorant.

281 it, being ignorant. *rev to* it being ignorant *ABY(2)*

284/ *no signature*] W. B. YEATS. *BR*, William Butler Yeats P

---

271 In left margin, opening square bracket (without the bottom horizontal stroke) in pencil.

272 Closing square bracket in pencil.

274 Closing curved half bracket in pencil.

275 In left margin, opening square bracket in pencil.

276–279 Each line is canceled in ink.

279 In right margin, closing square bracket (without the top horizontal stroke) in pencil.

280 In bottom margin, in Yeats's hand, in ink and then canceled in ink by Pound using a broad-nibbed pen.

281–282 In bottom margin, in Pound's hand, in ink using a broad-nibbed pen.

283–285 In bottom margin, in Yeats's hand, in ink using a fine-nib pen; insertion arrow to ll. 265–270.

[NLI 13,586(3) (a), 3r]

You gave but will not give again
Until enough of Paudeen's pence
By Biddy's halfpennies have lain /
To be some sort of "evidence"
Before you'll ~~[illegible]~~ put your guineas down
~~[illegible]~~
That things it were a pride to give
Are what the blind & ignorant town
Imagines best to make it thrive —
Or so you say.

~~[illegible]~~
~~[illegible]~~
~~[illegible]~~
~~[illegible]~~
Duke Ercole bid

The mummers to the market place
Nor cared what the onion sellers did
So that his Plautus set the pace
~~[illegible]~~
~~[illegible]~~
For the Italian comedies,
~~[illegible]~~
And Guidobaldo when he made
That grammar school of courtesies,
~~[illegible]~~
~~[illegible]~~
Where wit & beauty learned their trade
Upon Urbino's windy hill
~~[illegible]~~
~~[illegible]~~
~~[illegible]~~
~~[illegible]~~

TO A WEALTHY MAN WHO PROMISED A SECOND SUBSCRIPTION TO THE DUBLIN MUNICIPAL GALLERY IF IT WERE PROVED THE PEOPLE WANTED PICTURES

[NLI 13,586(3) (a), 3^{r}]

You gave but will not give again
Until enough of Paudeen' pense
~~are~~
By Biddy half penies ~~had~~ lain   have /
To be "some sort of evidence'
ll put your guineas
Before your [?] ~~guineas are laid~~ down
~~Those things~~
That things it were a pride to give
Are what the blind & ignorant town
Imagines best to make it thrive —
Or so you say.
~~They said [?not]~~ so,
~~Duke Erole [?when]~~

---

found in NLI 13,586(3) (a) *transcribed above and below*
Texas(1) *transcribed below*
Texas(2)
TCD(1)
Texas(3)
NLI 13,586(3) (b)
Berg(4)
Berg(5)
NLI 30,262
Foster-Murphy
published in *The Irish Times*, January 11, 1913
Poems Written in Discouragement, 1912–1913
Resp14

December 24, 1912, version, first sheet, recto.

The typescript of the poem designated TCD(1) is an enclosure to Yeats autograph signed letter to Hugh Lane, [?2 *or* 1] Jan 1913, TCD 7001/1728/1:

18, Woburn Buildings, Upper Woburn Place, W.C.

Jan [?2 *or* 1]

My dear Lane: Hear [*sic*, Here] is the poem. If it is not politic tell me so frankly. If you think it is politic I will try & see Hone & see if ~~some~~ fitting publication & comment could be made in the Irish Times. I have tried to meet the argument in Lady Ardilauns letter to somebody, her objection to giving because of Home Rule & Loyd [*sic*, Lloyd] George, & still more to meet the general argument of people like Ardilaun that they should not give unless there is a public demand. I ~~quite I~~ shall quite understand if you think it would be unwise to draw attention to the possible [?slightness] "Paudeen's" (little Patrick) desire for any kind of art. I left Dublin nearly a month ago I have no idea how the fund is or ~~wh~~ what has occured. I kept this poem longer than I intended to make some slight changes.

Yours ever

WB Yeats

The "correspondent" to whom the poem is addressed [?is of] course an imaginary person.

[NLI 13,586(3) (a), 3^r]

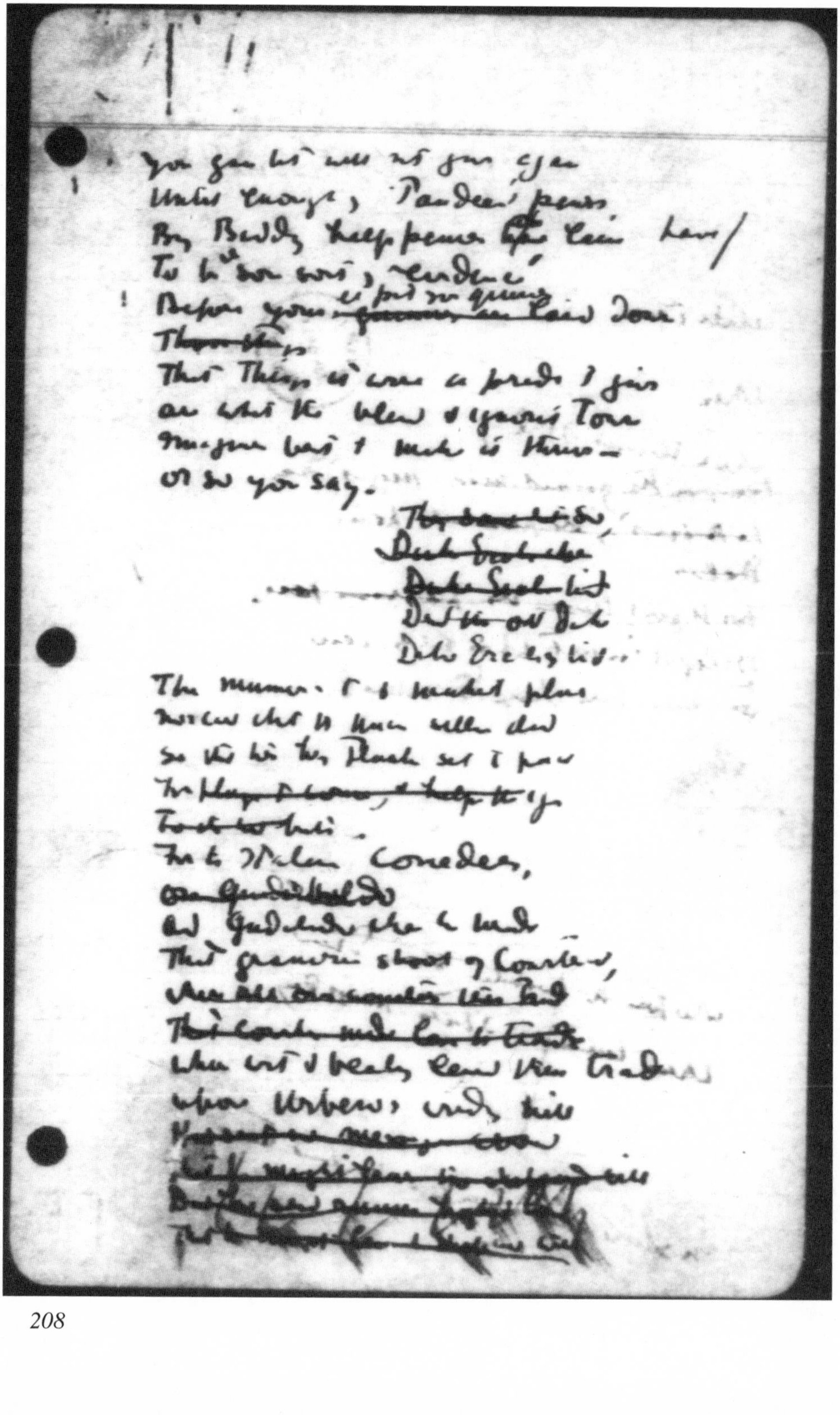

[NLI 13,586(3) (a), 3^r, continued]

~~Duke Erole bid~~
~~Did the old~~ duke
Duke Ercles bid
The mummers to [?the] market place
Nor cared what the union sellers did
So that his [?his] [?Pluates] set the pace
For ~~plays to come, & help the~~ age
~~To its [?new] [?]~~.
For to Italian Comedies,
~~[?On] [?Guidobaldo]~~
And Guidobado when he made
That grammar school of [?Courtesies]
~~Where all [?our] [?courtesies] [?ther] [?Pride]~~
~~That [?courtesy] made [?learn] [?] trade~~
Where [?wit] & beauty learned their trade
Upon Urbenos windy hill
~~Had sent no messenger [?abroad]~~
That he might have the shepherds will
Did he send runners high & low
That he might learn the shepherd will

[NLI 13,586(3) (a), 3v]

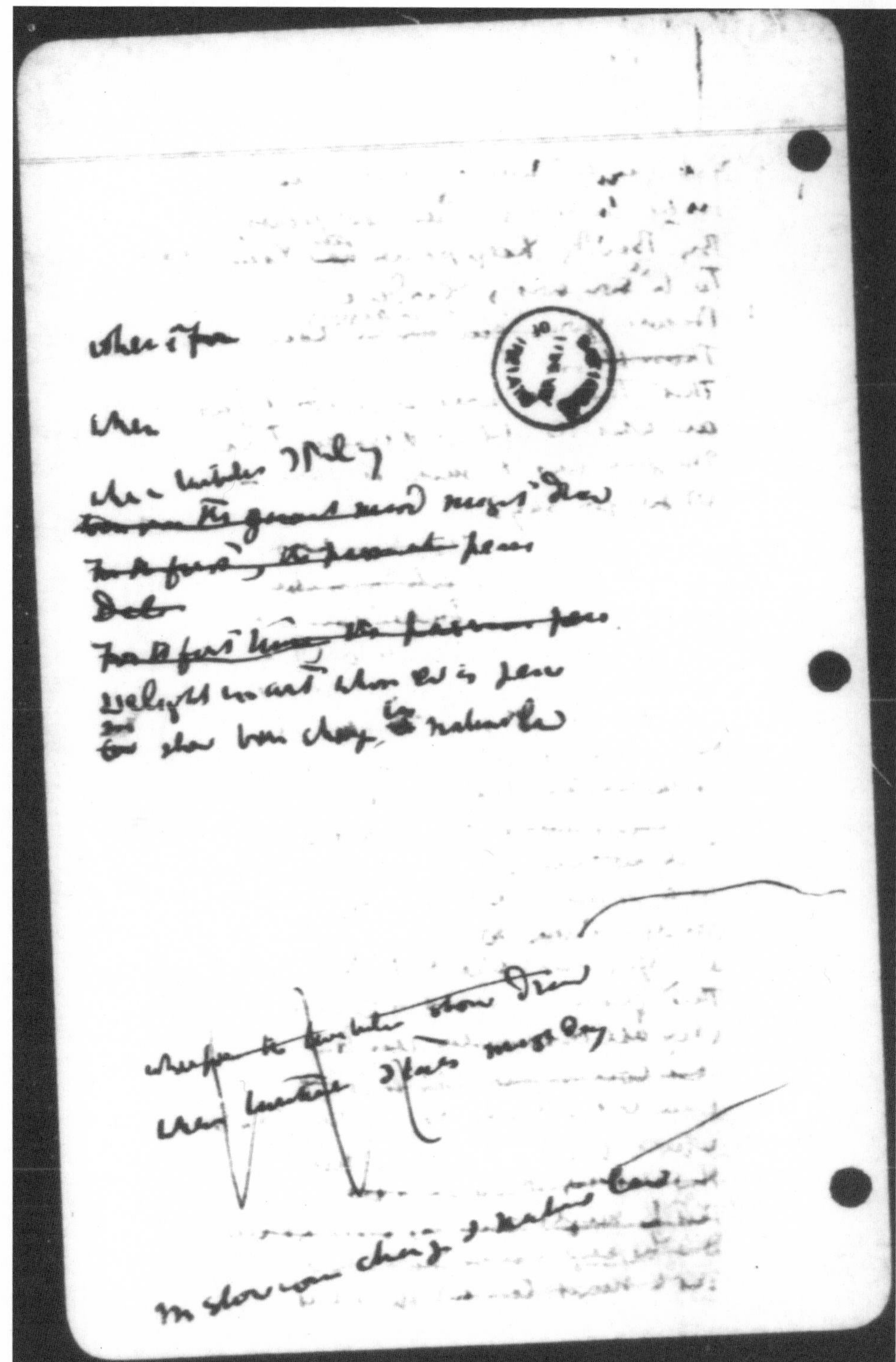

[NLI 13,586(3) (a), 3v]

where ~~for~~

When

[?Whence] [?turbulent] Italy
~~[?] from the general [?mind]~~ might draw
~~For the first, the passionate~~ peace
~~Deli~~
~~For the first time, the [?passions] peace~~
Delight in art whose end is peace
In
~~And~~ slow [?born] change, ~~&~~ natural law

Wherefore the [?turbulent] Italy should [?draw]
[?Whence turbulent] Italy might [?draw]

In slow [?come] change [?&] natural law

December 24, 1912, version, first sheet, verso; insert for 2r.
4 "~~[?mind]~~" or perhaps "~~[?mood]~~".

[NLI 13,586(3) (a), 2r]

[NLI 13,586(3) (a), 2[r]]

~~And what did [?Ducke]~~ Cosimo
~~When trecherous Florence [?drove] him~~ out
Had never [?pleased] a [?huge] & cry
That he might learn the shepherd will
And Cosimo de ~~Medichi~~ Medici
When [?] Florence drove him out

Had ~~he~~ sent runners to & fro
That he might learn the shepherd will;
~~And [?then had broken] Cosimo~~
they
& When ~~Florence~~ drove out Cosimo
It was but the cities way he knew
So much more time & thought ~~had he~~ had he
his For plans [?~~that~~] Michelozzo drew
~~For the~~ S.
For the San Marco library
the
Not knowing [?~~her~~] predestined man
So much more time & thought had he
study To ~~[?] to~~ Michalozzos plan
For that San Marco's library
[? ? ?] [?might]
[?Whence ~~for] [? ?] [?can] all might~~ [?draw]
Delight in arts whose end is peace
[?not]
In Nature [?~~&~~] in [?gradual] law
By sucking at the dugs of Greece

If [?these] men knew the way to live
~~Then [?turn] your [?] hands that way~~
~~And give what fits your pride to give~~
Why copy this & [?live as] they
And give what fits your pride to give —
~~Or what to [?your own] self [?seem] good~~

December 24, 1912, version, second sheet, recto (verso is blank).
9 The cancel begins at "And" as scoring from a dry pen nib.

[NLI 13,586(3) (a), 4^{r}]

You have their open [?handed] way
[?But] if they knew the way to ~~give~~ live
~~Copy that too & [?give] as they~~
Copy this too & [?give] as they,
    [?most]
What [?~~most~~] befits your pride to [?give]
Or what to your heart seems good

When Florence drove out Cosimo
She gave him but the [?time] to pour
Upon [?Mazzucci] [?] plan
~~[?For] the great house that yet [?should store]~~
For that new library to store
[?~~Nicollo~~]
~~Those famous measurements of~~
Nicollo books that men might draw
[?Delight] in Etc

~~Not [?]~~
Not knowing [?his predestined] man
He had but the more time & thought
To [?study Micholas] plan
To house the books the [?scholars] [?brought]

December 24, 1912, version, third sheet, recto.
17 "[?his]" could be "[?her]".

[NLI 13,586(3) (a), 4[v]]

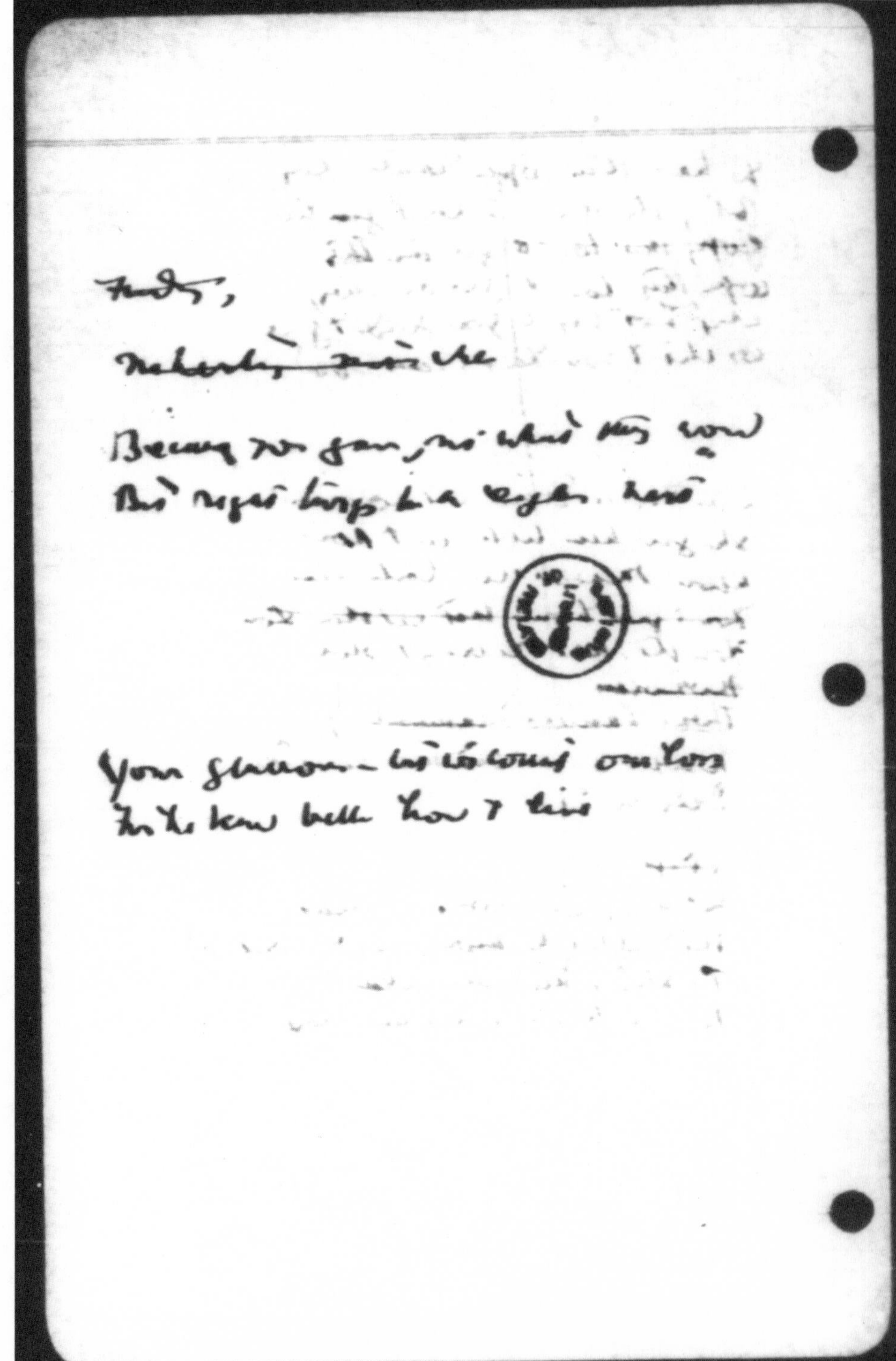

[NLI 13,586(3) (a), 4^{v}]

[~~?Finding~~],

~~[?In] [?] [?not]~~ [?]

Because you gave, not what they would
But right twigs for an eagles nest

Your generous — but [?we] count our loss
For he knew better how to live

December 24, 1912, version, third sheet, verso; revisions for the facing page, 5^{r}.
1 “[?Finding]” could be “[?Friday]”.

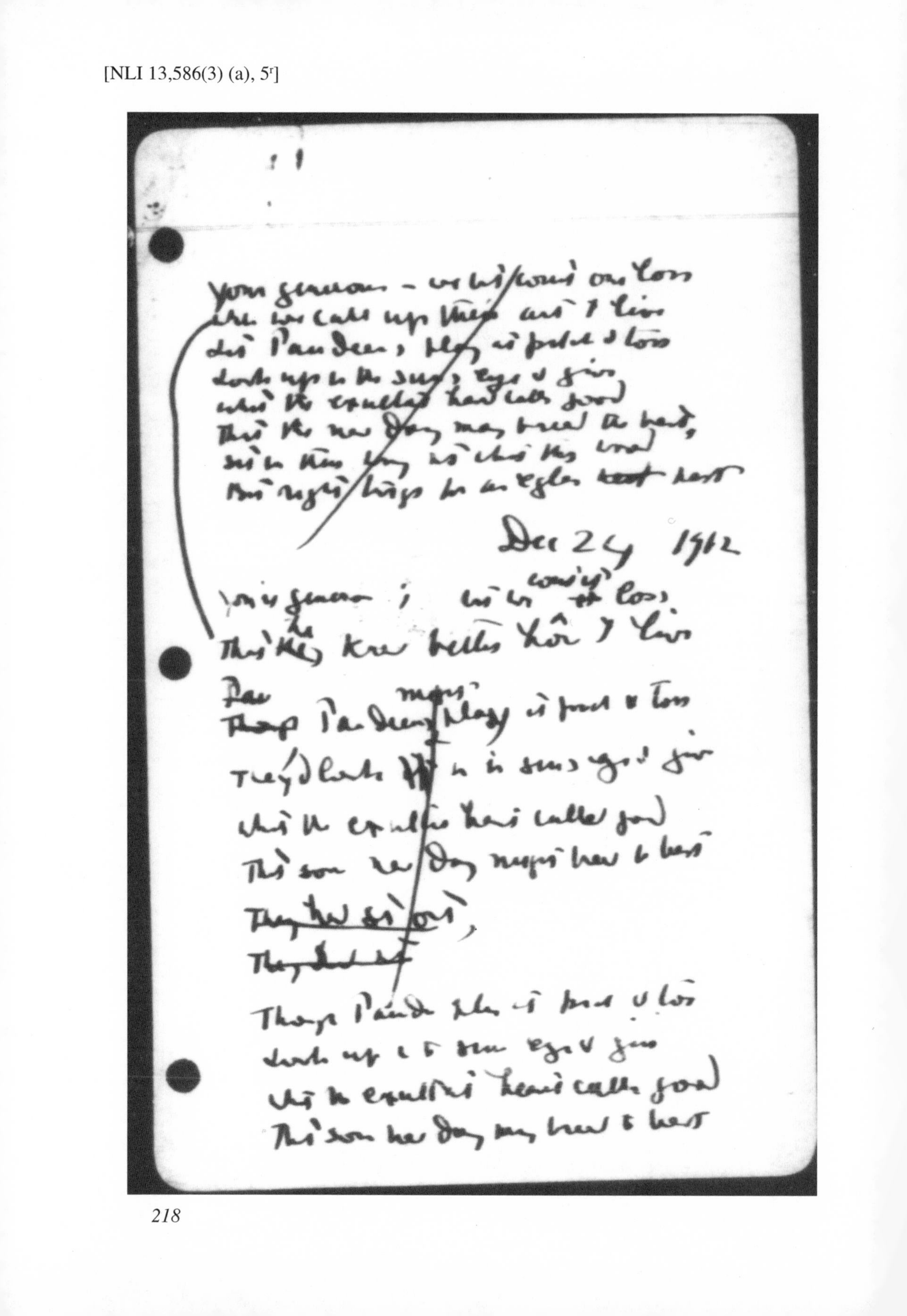

[NLI 13,586(3) (a), 5r]

[NLI 13,586(3) (a), 5r]

Your generous — we but count our loss
When we call up their art to live
Let Paudeen s play at pitch & toss
Look up in the sun s eye & give
What the exultant heart calls good
That the new day may breed the best,
Set in their way not what they wood
But right twigs for an egles ~~nest~~ nest

Dec 24 1912

count it
You're generous; but we ^ [?~~it~~] loss
That ~~they~~ he knew better how to live
~~Pau~~
might
~~Though~~ Paudeens ^ play at [?pitch] & toss
Theyd look ~~at~~ in the suns eye & give
What the exultant heart called good
That some new day might breed the best
~~They had [?set] out~~,
~~They did not~~

Though Paudeen play at [?pitch] & [?tos]
Look up [?in] the suns eye & give
What the exultant heart calls good
That some new day may breed the best

December 24, 1912, version, fourth sheet, recto.

[NLI 13,586(3) (a), 6r, 6v]

[NLI 13,586(3) (a), 6r]

Imagines best to make it thrive

~~Yet~~
~~And when Duke Ercole [?had] brought~~
~~His mummers to the market~~ place
~~And yet~~ Though Duke
~~But Duke~~ Ercole when he ~~brought~~ bid
His mummers to the market place
{o
Cared not what the {union sellers did

[NLI 13,586(3) (a), 6v]

. . . . . make it thrive
Though Duke Ercole when he bid
His mummers to the market place
Cared not what the onion sellers did

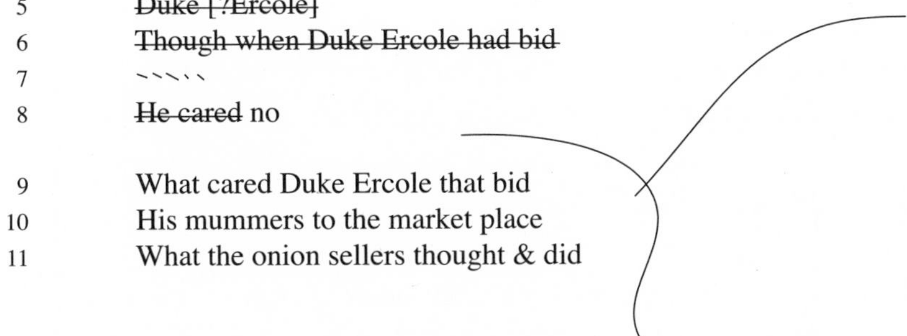

~~Duke [?Ercole]~~
~~Though when Duke Ercole had bid~~
\~\~\~\~\~
~~He cared~~ no

What cared Duke Ercole that bid
His mummers to the market place
What the onion sellers thought & did

6r December 25, 1912, version, first sheet, recto.
6v December 25, 1912, version, first sheet, verso; insert for 1r.

[NLI 13,586(3) (a), 1r]

1]

(1)

To a friend who promises a ~~bigger~~ larger subscription than his first to the Municipal gallery if the amount collected proves that there is large popular demand for such a gallery.

You gave ~~and~~ but will not ~~you~~ give again
Until enough of Paudeen's pence
By Biddy's halfpennies have lain
To be 'some sort of evidence'
Before you'll put your guineas down
That things, it were a pride to give
Are what the blind & ignorant Town
Imagines best to make it thrive—
~~Or so you say.~~
Ercole ~~Duke Ercole~~ that bid
~~His mummers to the market place~~
~~What cared what the onion-sellers thought~~ or did
So that his Plutarch set the pace
For the Italian comedies;
And Guidobaldo when he made
That grammar school of courtesies,
Where wit and beauty learned their trade,
Upon Urbino's windy hill
Had sent no runners to and fro
That he might learn the shepherd's will;
And when they drove out Cosimo
Not knowing their pre-destined man

[NLI 13,586(3) (a), 1^{r}]

To a friend, who promises a ~~better larger~~ bigger
subscription than his first to the Municipal
Gallery, if the amount collected proves
that there is large popular demand for
such a gallery.

but will not
You gave ~~and you will~~ give again
Until enough of P^audeen's pense
By Biddys half pennies have lain
To be 'some sort of evidence'
you've
Before ~~you'll~~ put your guineas down
That things, it were a pride to give
Are what the blind & ignorent town
Imagines best to make it thrive –
~~Or so you say.~~
~~Ercole~~ ~~bid~~
~~Duke Ercles [?] bought~~
? ~~His mummers to the market place~~
~~did~~
~~Nor cared what the onion-sellers thought~~ ^
So that his Plutarch set the pace
For the Italian comedies;
And Guidobaldo when he made
That grammar school of courtesies,
Where wit and beauty learned their trade,
Uppon Urbino's windy hill
Had sent [~~?~~] no runners to and ~~for~~ fro
That he might learn the shepherds will;
And when they drove out Cosimo
Not knowing their pre-destined man

December 25, 1912, version, third sheet, recto.

[NLI 13,586(3) (a), 1v, 7r]

To Michelozzo's latest plan
of his San Marco library
where

not knowing their predestined way
So much more than a thought had they

where turbulent Italy should draw
Delight in art whose end is peace,
In logic & in natural law,
By sucking at the dugs of Greece.

Your open hand but shows our loss
That he knew better how to live.
Let Paudeens play at pitch and toss
Look up in the sun's eye and give
What the exultant heart calls good
That some new day may breed the best
Because you gave not what they would
But the right twigs for an eagle's nest

WB Yeats
Dec 25
1912

[NLI 13,586(3) (a), 1v]

For
~~To~~ Michelozzos latest plan
his
of ~~the~~ ^ San Marco library
Whece

[NLI 13,586(3) (a), 7r]

Not knowing their predestined man
~~gave~~ had
So much more time & thought ~~had~~ he
~~For To study To Michelozzo's plans and his~~
~~For that San Marco Library~~
Whence turbulent Italy should draw
Delight in art whose end is peace,
In logic, & in natural law,
By sucking at the dugs of Greace

Your open hand but shows our loss
That he knew better how to live.
Let Paudeens play at pitch and toss
Look up in the sun s eye, and give
What the exultant heart calls good
That some new day may breed the best
Because you gave, not what they would,
the
But ^ right twigs for an eagles nest

W B Yeats
Dec 25
1912

1v December 25, 1912, version, second sheet, verso; insert for the facing page, 7r.
7r December 25, 1912, version, third sheet, recto.
7r, l. 4 The insertion arrow in the left margin is aligned with an insertion arrow on facing page, 1v.

To a friend who promises a bigger
subscription than his first to the Dublin
municipal gallery if the amount
collected proves that there is a ~~large~~ considerable
'popular demand' for the pictures.

You gave, but will not give again
Until enough of Paudeen's pence
By Biddy's halfpennies have lain
To be 'some sort of evidence',
Before you've put your guineas down,
That things, it were a pride to give,
Are what the blind & ignorant town
Imagines best to make it thrive.

What cared duke Ercole, that bid
His mummers to the market place,
What the onion sellers thought or did
So that his Plautus set the pace
For the Italian comedies?;
And Guidobaldo when he made
That grammar school of courtesies
Where wit & beauty learned their trade,
~~Had sent no runners to and fro~~
Upon Urbino's windy hill,
Had sent no runners to and ~~fr~~ fro
That he might learn the shepherds ~~will~~ will.
And when they drove out Cosimo
Not knowing their predestined man,

[Texas(1), 1]

1

To a friend who promises a bigger
subscription than his first to the Dublin
Municipal Gallery if the amount
collected proves that there is a ~~large~~ considerable
'popular demand' for the pictures.

You gave, but will not give again
Until enough of Paudeen's pense
By Biddy's half pennies have lain
To be 'some sort of evidence,'
Before you've put your guinea's down,
That things, it we're a pride to give,
Are what the blind & ignorant town
Imagines best to make it thrive.

1–5 *title* To a friend who promises a bigger subscription than his first to the Dublin Municipal Gallery and the amount collected proves that there is a [*14 blank spaces in the typescript, with word inserted in pencil, not in Yeats's hand*: Considerable] 'popular demand' for the pictures. *Texas(2)* To a friend who promises a bigger subscription than his first to the Dublin Municipal Gallery if the amount collected proves that there is a considerable 'popular demand' for the pictures. *TCD(1), Texas(3), NLI 13,586(3) (b)* [*no title in typescript; rev in ink in Yeats's hand in top margin*:] ~~A Friend, who had promised a second subscription, if there were "a general public demand" for a gallery the people of Dublin showed that they wanted a gallery. that wanted pictures~~ To a wealthy man, who promised a second subscription if it ~~was~~ were proved the people wanted pictures. *Berg(4)* To ~~a Freind~~ [*sic, rev in pencil to* one] who wont give a subscription to save the Lane collection of pictures for Dublin unless it is proved there is a 'considerable popular demand for them'. *Berg(5)* THE GIFT / [*device*] / BY W. B. YEATS / [To a friend, who promises a bigger subscription than his first to the Dublin Municipal Gallery if the amount collected proves that there is a considerable "popular demand" for the pictures.] *IT* [*square brackets are printed in IT.*]; *so Foster-Murphy but* promised [TO A WEALTHY MAN, WHO PROMISED A SECOND SUBSCRIPTION IF IT WERE PROVED THE PEOPLE WANTED PICTURES *PWD* TO A WEALTHY MAN WHO PROMISED A SECOND SUBSCRIPTION IF IT WERE PROVED THE PEOPLE WANTED PICTURES *Resp14*

6 gave,] gave *Texas(2), Berg(4), Berg(5), Foster-Murphy, PWD, Resp14* gave *rev to* gave, *NLI 30,262*

7 Paudeen's] Pandeen's *Texas(2)* pense] pence *all other texts*

7, 9, 11, 13, 15, 17–18, 20, 23, 25, 27, 29, 32, 34, 36, 38, 40, 42 *indented IT*

8 Biddy's *with* 's *inserted in pencil Texas(2)* half-pennies *TCD(1), Texas(3), NLI 13,586(3) (b), IT* halfpennies *Berg(4), Berg(5), Foster-Murphy, PWD, Resp14*

9 'sort] sort *Texas(2)* evidence,'] evidence *Texas(2)* evidence', *TCD(1), Texas(3), NLI 13,586(3) (b)* evidence' *Berg(4), Berg(5), Foster-Murphy, PWD*

10 you've] you've *rev to* you *TCD(1)* you'll *PWD, Resp14* down *Berg(4), Berg(5), PWD* down *rev to* down, *Foster-Murphy*

11 things *Texas(2), Foster-Murphy, PWD, Resp14* it] is *rev in pencil to* it *Texas(2)* we're] was *added in pencil Texas(2)* were *Texas(3), NLI 13,586(3) (b), Berg(4), Berg(5), IT, Foster-Murphy, PWD, Resp14* give *Berg(4), Berg(5), Foster-Murphy, PWD, Resp14*

13 Imagines] Imagine *Texas(2)* best] best *rev to* best, *Texas(2)*

14 Duke *IT, Foster-Murphy, PWD, Resp14* Ercole *Berg(4), Berg(5), Foster-Murphy, PWD, Resp14*

15 place *Berg(4), Berg(5), Foster-Murphy* place; *PWD*

---

6. 14, 26, 35 In Foster-Murphy, Lady Gregory has added a roman numeral ("I . . . IV") in pencil before each of these lines to mark a new stanza. The typist left an extra line space before ll. 14 and 26 only.

9 The "rt" of "sort" and the rest of the line are added in pencil in Texas(2).

To a friend who promises a bigger
subscription than his first to the Dublin
municipal gallery if the amount
collected proves that there is a ~~large~~ considerable
'popular demand' for the pictures.

You gave, but will not give again
Until enough of Paudeen's pence
By Biddy's halfpennies have lain
To be 'some sort of evidence',
Before you've put your guineas down,
That things, it were a pride to give,
Are what the blind & ignorant town
Imagines best to make it thrive.

What cared duke Ercole, that bid
His mummers to the market place,
What th' onion sellers thought or did
So that his Plautus set the pace
For the Italian comedies?;
And Guidobaldo when he made
That grammar school of courtesies
Where wit & beauty learned their trade,
~~Had sent no runners to and fro~~
Upon Urbino's windy hill,
Had sent no runners to and ~~fr~~ fro
That he might learn the shepherds ~~will~~ will
And when they drove out Cosimo
Not knowing their predestined man.

[Texas(1), 1, continued]

What cared duke Ercole, that bid
His mummers to the market place,
What th' onion sellers thought or did
So that his Plutarch set the pace
For the Italian comedies?;
And Guidobaldo when he made
That grammer school of courtesies
Where wit & beauty learned their trade,
~~Had sent no runners to and fro~~
Upon Urbino's windy hill,
Had sent no runners to and [~~?fr~~] fro
will;. {[~~?will~~]
That he might learn the shepherds [~~?~~] {[~~?~~] ^
And when they drove out Cosimo ~~will~~
Not knowing their predestined man

---

16 th' onion sellers] th'onion sellers *TCD(1), NLI 13,586(3) (b), Berg(4), Berg(5), Foster-Murphy*
17 Plutarch] Plitarch *Berg(4)* Plautus *PWD, Resp14*
18 For the] To the *Berg(4)* comedies?;] comedies? *TCD(1), Texas(3), NLI 13,586(3) (b), IT, Foster-Murphy, PWD, Resp14* comeides? *Berg(4)* comedies *Berg(5)*
19 Guidobaldo] Quidobaldo *rev to* Guidobaldo *TCD(1), NLI 13,586(3) (b)* Guidobaldo, *Resp14*
20 grammer] gramae *Berg(4)* grammar *TCD(1), NLI, Berg(5), IT, PWD, Resp14* courtesies, *PWD*
21 trade *Berg(4), Berg(5), Foster-Murphy, PWD, Resp14*
23 hill *Berg(4), Berg(5), Foster-Murphy*
25 shepherds' *TCD(1), Texas(3), NLI 13,586(3) (b), Berg(4), Berg(5), Foster-Murphy, PWD, Resp14* shepherd's *IT* will *Texas(2), Berg(5)* will *rev to* will; *Berg(4), Foster-Murphy*
26 and *Berg(5)* Cosimo] Cosimo *rev to* Cosimo, *TCD* Cosino *Texas(2)* Cosino, *PWD, Resp14*
27 Not knowing their predestined man] Not knowing their predestined man *rev to* Indifferent how the rancour ran, *TCD(1), Resp14* Not knowing their predestined man *rev to* Indifferent how the rancour ran *Texas(3), NLI 13,586(3) (b)* Indifferent how the rancour ran *Berg(4), Berg(5), IT; so Foster-Murphy but* Indiffurent
Indifferent how the rancour ran. *PWD*

---

27 In Texas(2), "predestined man" was added in pencil.

2

so much more time & thought had he
For Michelozzo's latest plan
Of the San Marco Library
Whence turbulent Italy should draw
Delight in art whose end is peace,
In logic, & in natural law,
By sucking at the dugs of Greece.

Your open hand but shows our loss
That he knew better how to live.
Let Paudeens play at ~~pitch~~ pitch & toss;
Look up in the sun's eye, and give
What the exultant heart calls good,
That some new day may breed the best
Because you gave, not what they would,
But the right ~~for~~ twigs for an eagles nest.

W B Yeats

[Texas(1), 2]

2

So much more time & thought had he
For Michelozzo's latest plan
Of the San Marco Library
Whence turbullent Italy should draw
Delight in Art whose end is peace,
In logic, & in natural law,
By sucking at the dugs of Greece.

Your open hand but shows our loss
That he knew better how to live.
Let Paudeens play at [~~?pitch~~] pitch and toss;
Look up in the sun's eye, and give
What the exultant heart calls good,
That some new day may breed the best
Because you gave, not what they would,
But the right [~~?~~] twigs for an eagles nest.

WB Yeats

---

28 So much more time and thought had he] So much more time and though had he *rev to* He gave the hours they had set free *TCD(1), Texas(3)* So much more time and though had he *rev to* He gave the hours they had set f free *NLI 13,586(3) (b)* He gave the hours they had set free *Berg(4) and all later texts*

29 For] For *rev to* To *TCD(1), Texas(3), NLI 13,586(3) (b)* To *Berg(4) and all later texts*

30 Of] Of *rev to* For *TCD(1), Texas(3), NLI 13,586(3) (b)* For *Berg(4) and all later texts* Library; *Berg(4), PWD* Library, *IT, Resp14* Library *rev to* Library, *Foster-Murphy*

31 turbullent] Turbullent *Texas(2)* turbulent *TCD(1) and all later texts* Italy] [*lacking*] *rev in pencil to* Italy *Texas(2)*

32 Art] art *Texas(2)* rt *Berg(5)* end] snd *Berg(4)* peace *Berg(4), Berg(5), Foster-Murphy, PWD*

33 logic . . . law *Berg(4), Berg(5), Foster-Murphy, PWD, Resp14*

35 loss] loss *rev to* loss, *TCD(1), Texas(3), NLI 13,586(3) (b), Foster-Murphy* 19ss *Berg(4)* loss, *PWD, Resp14*

36 That] That *rev to* For *TCD(1), NLI 13,586(3) (b)* For *Berg(4), Berg(5), IT, Foster-Murphy, PWD, Resp14* live *rev to* live. *Foster-Murphy*

37 Let] Let *rev to* Though *rev to* Let *TCD(1)* Let *rev to* Leave *Texas(3)* Leave *IT* Paudeens] Pandeens *Texas(2)* play at] play at *rev to* to their *Texas(3)* to their *IT* toss, *TCD(1), PWD, Resp14* toss *Berg(4), Berg(5)* toss *rev to* toss; *Foster-Murphy*

38 eye *Berg(4), Berg(5), Foster-Murphy, PWD, Resp14* give] live *rev to* give *Berg(5)*

39 calls good,] thinks good *rev to* calls good *Berg(4), Berg(5)* calls good *Foster-Murphy, PWD, Resp14*

40 best *rev to* best, *Foster-Murphy*

41 gave *Berg(5)* what] wat *Berg(5)* would,] would *Berg(4), Berg(5), Foster-Murphy, PWD, Resp14* would *rev to* would, *NLI 30,262*

42 twigs] twings *Berg(4)* eagles] eagle's *all later texts* nest! *Berg(4), PWD, Resp14*

signature W. B. Yeats. *Texas(2), TCD(1), Texas(3), NLI 13,586(3) (b), IT* ~~W.B.Yeats.1913~~ *Berg(4)* W.B.Y. *Foster-Murphy* *no signature PWD, Resp14*

date January 8th, 1913. *IT; centered at top of p. 1* Jan 15 1913 *Foster-Murphy* December, 1912. *PWD, Resp14*

In Foster-Murphy, Lady Gregory added this note in ink at the foot: "I meant to put this in my letter this morning – it is fine isn't it? It is aimed at L^{d}. Iveagh – but he hates good art!"

[Berg(7), 1^{r}]

August
1913

18, Woburn Buildings,
Upper Woburn Place,
W.C.

What need you, being come to sense
But fumble in a greasy till
And add the halfpence to the pence
And prayer to shivering prayer, until
You've dried the marrow in the bone,
~~Romantic Ireland's dead & gone~~
For man was born to pray & save.
Romantic Ireland's dead & gone;
It's with O'Leary in the grave.

2

Yet they were of a different kind
The names that stilled your childish play:
They've gone about the world like wind;
But little time had they to pray
For whom the hangman's rope was spun.
~~And what—~~God help us—
~~Romantic the~~ could they save.
Romantic Ireland's dead & gone;
It's with O Leary in the grave.

SEPTEMBER 1913

[Berg(7), 1^{r}]

August
1913

1 What need you, being come to sense
2 But fumble in a greasy till
3 And add the half pense to the pense
4 And prayer to shivering prayer, until
5 You've dried the marrow in the bone,
6 ~~Romantic Ireland s dead & g~~
7 For man was born to prey and save.
8 Romantic Ireland s dead & gone;
9 It s with O'Leary in the grave.

2

10 Yet they were of a different kind
11 The names that stilled your childish play:
12 They've gone about the world like wind;
13 But little time had they to prey
14 For whom the hangman s rope was spun.
And what — God help us —
15 ~~Romanatic Ir~~ could they save.
16 Romantic Ireland's dead & gone;
17 It s with O Leary in the grave.

---

found in Berg(7) *transcribed above and below*
Berg(8) (a) *transcribed below*
Berg(8) (b) and (c)
NLI 21,873
Berg(6) (a)
NLI 30,009
NLI 30,262

published in *The Irish Times*, September 8, 1913
Poems Written in Discouragement
Nine Poems
Resp14

3

Was it for this the wild-geese spread
The grey wing upon every tide,
For this that all that blood was shed
For this that Lord & Emmett died
And Lord Fitzgerald & Wolf Tone —
All that delirium of the brave:
Romantic Ireland's dead & gone
It's with O Leary in the grave.

4

Yet could we turn the years again
And call those exiles as they were
In all their loneliness & pain
You'd cry some woman's yellow hair
Has maddened every mothers' son
They weighed so lightly what they gave:
But let them be — they're dead & gone
They're with O Leary in the grave.

I make this poem out of a contemplation
of Mr William Murphy. I have as yet
not changed the line about the Tallow

[Berg(7), 2^{r}]

3

Was it for this the wild–geese spread
The
~~A~~ grey wing upon every tide,
For this that all that blood was shed
For this that Bond & Emmett died
And Lord Fitzgerald & Wolf Tone —
All that delirium of the brave:
Romantic Irelands dead & gone
It s with O Leary in the grave.

4

Yet could we turn the years again
And call those exiles as they were
In all their loneliness & pain
You d cry ~~it~~ "some woman's yellow hair
Has madened every mothers' son
lightly
They weighed so ~~litely~~ what they gave:
But let them be — they re dead & gone
And with O Leary in the grave.

I made this poem out of a contemplation
of Mr William Murphy. I have as you
see changed the line about [?this *or* their *or* the] tabboo

---

20 Oliver Bond (1760?–1798): Irish Republican; charged with treason in 1798 and died in prison.

21 Lord Edward Fitzgerald (1763–1798), fifth son of the 20th Earl of Kildare, repudiated his title in 1792, joined the United Irishmen (1796), died of wounds received while resisting arrest for treason in 1798.

[Berg(8) (a)]

New Ireland
(written after reading certain newspaper correspondence about ~~[illegible]~~ the municipal gallery of modern paintings)

What need you, being come to sense,
But fumble in a greasy till
And add the hapence to the pence,
And prayer to shivering prayer, until
You have dried the marrow from the bone,
For men were born to pray and save:
Romantic Ireland's dead and gone
It's with O'Leary in the grave.

Yet they were of a different kind
The names that stilled your childish play;
They have gone about the world like wind ;
But little time had they to pray
For whom the hangman's rope was spun,
And what, God help us, could they save:
Romantic Ireland's dead and gone
It's with O'Leary in the grave.

[Berg(8) (a)]

New Ireland 2)
(written after reading certain newspaper correspondence
the
about ~~the [? ?] [?in] the proposed~~ Municipal Gallery of
Modern Painting)

do
What need you, being come to sense,
But fumble in a greasy till
And add the hapence to the pence ,
And prayer to shivering prayer, until
You have dried the marrow from the bone ,
For men were born to pray and save :
Romantic Ireland's dead and gone
{O
It's with {**o'Leary in the grave.**

Yet they were of a different kind
The names that stilled your childish play ;
They have gone about the world like wind;
But little time had they to pray
For whom the hangman's rope was spun ,
And what, God help us, could they save :
Romantic Ireland's dead and gone
It's with O'Leary in the grave.

---

title September, 1913 *Berg(8) (b), Berg(6) (a), PWD, Resp14 no title Berg(8) (c)* Romance in Ireland / (On reading much of the correspondence against the Art Gallery.) *IT* Romantic Ireland (September, 1913) *Nine Poems*

1 you do,] you, *Berg(8) (b)and (c), Berg(6) (a), IT, PWD, Nine Poems, Resp14*

3 hapence] ha'pence *IT* halfpence *PWD, Nine Poems, Resp14* pence,] pence *Berg(8) (b), Berg(6) (a), PWD, Nine Poems, Resp14*

4 prayer,] prayer *Berg(8) (b)*

5 bone *Berg(8) (b)* bone; *Berg(8) (c), Berg(6) (a), IT, PWD, Nine Poems, Resp14*

6 save *Berg(8) (b), Berg(6) (a)* save? *IT* save, *PWD, Nine Poems, Resp14*

7 gone, *Berg(6) (a), PWD, Resp14* gone— *IT* gone. *Nine Poems*

9 kind *rev to* kind, *NLI 30,009, NLI 30,262*

10 play *Berg(8) (b), Berg(6) (a), PWD, Nine Poems, Resp14*

11 wind *Berg(8) (b)* wind, *Berg(6) (a), PWD, Nine Poems, Resp14* wind. *IT*

12 pray. *Berg(6) (a)*

13 spun *Berg(8) (b) and (c)* spun; *IT*

14 what *Berg(8) (b) and (c)* us *Berg(8) (b) and (c)* save *Berg(8) (b)and (c)* save *rev to* save? *NLI 30,009*

15 gone, *Berg(6) (a), PWD, Nine Poems, Resp14* gone— *IT*

In the edition of *Responsibilities* published in 1916, and through the final lifetime edition, the title read "September 1913"—without the comma.

[Berg(8) (a)]

New Ireland
(written after reading certain newspaper correspondence about ~~[illegible]~~ the municipal gallery of modern paintings)

What need you, being come to sense,
But fumble in a greasy till
And add the hapence to the pence,
And prayer to shivering prayer, until
You have dried the marrow from the bone,
For men were born to pray and save:
Romantic Ireland's dead and gone
It's with O'Leary in the grave.

Yet they were of a different kind
The names that stilled your childish play;
They have gone about the world like wind;
But little time had they to pray
For whom the hangman's rope was spun,
And what, God help us, could they save:
Romantic Ireland's dead and gone
It's with O'Leary in the grave.

Was it for this the wild geese spread
The Grey wing upon every tide?
For this that all that blood was shed,
For this ~~that Bond and Emmett~~ died, Edward Fitzgerald/
And ~~Lord Fitzgerald~~ and Wolf Tone Robert Emmett/
All that delirium of the brave?
Romantic Ireland's dead and gone
It's with O'Leary in the grave.

Yet could we turn the years again
And call those exiles as they were
In all their loneliness and pain
You'd cry "some woman's yellow hair
Has maddened every mother's son"
They weighed so lightly what they gave;
But let them be, they're dead and gone,
They're with O'Leary in the grave.

WBYeats

[Berg(8) (a), continued]

Was it for this the wild geese spread
The Grey wing upon every tide ?
For this that all that blood was shed ,
For this ~~that Bond and Emmett~~ died , Edward Fitzgerald /
And ~~Lord Fitzgerald~~ and Wolf Tone Robert Emmett /
All that delirium of the brave ?
Romantic Ireland's dead and gone
It's with O Leary in the grave.

Yet could we turn the years again
And call those exiles as they were
In all their loneliness and pain
You'd cry"some woman's yellow hair
Has maddened every mother's son"
They weighed so lightly what they gave ;
But let them be, they're dead and gone ,
They're with O'Leary in the grave.

WBYeats

---

18 grey *Berg(6) (a), PWD, Resp14* gray *Nine Poems* tide *Berg(8) (b)* tide; *Berg(6) (a), PWD, Nine Poems, Resp14*
19 shed *Berg(8) (b)* shed? *Berg(8) (c)*
20 died *Berg(8) (b) and (c)* died? *IT*
21 Tone, *Berg(6) (a), PWD, Nine Poems, Resp14*
22 brave *Berg(8) (b)* brave; *Berg(6) (a), PWD, Nine Poems, Resp14* brave *rev to* brave? *NLI 30,009*
23 gone, *Berg(6) (a), PWD, Nine Poems, Resp14* gone— *IT*
25 again, *Berg(6) (a), PWD, Resp14*
26 were, *Berg(6) (a), IT, PWD, Nine Poems, Resp14*
28 cry— 'Some *IT*
29 son:' *Berg(6) (a), PWD, Nine Poems, Resp14* son'— *IT*
30 gave *Berg(8) (b)* gave, *Berg(6) (a), PWD, Nine Poems, Resp14*
31 be *Berg(8) (b), Berg(6) (a)* gone *Berg(8) (b)* gone: *IT*
32/ *no signature Berg(8) (b), Berg(6) (a), PWD, Nine Poems, Resp14*

Head upon shoulder leans;
"My dear, my dear, O dear
It was an accident"

–

Now all the truth is out
Be secret & take defeat
From any brazen throat
For how can you compete
Being honour bred with one
Who were it proved he lies
Were neither shamed in his own
Nor in his neighbours eyes.
Bred to a harder thing
Than triumph turn away
And like a laughing string
Whereon mad fingers play
Amid a place of stone,
Be secret & exult
Because of all things known
That is most difficult.

TO A FRIEND WHOSE WORK HAS COME TO NOTHING

[NLI 30,358, 29^{r}]

Now all the truth is out
Be secret & take defeat
From any brazen throat
For how can you compeet
Being honour bred with one
Who were it proved he lies
Were neither shamed in his own
Nor in his neighbours eyes.
Bred to a harder thing
Than triumph turn away
And like a laughing string
Where on mad fingers play
Amid a place of stone,
Be secret & exult
Because of all things known
That is most difficult.

---

found in NLI 30,358, 29^{r} (bottom half) *transcribed above*
NYP Berg(9)
Harvard(1)
Emory(1)
published in *Poems Written in Discouragement, 1912–1913*
Poetry (Chicago), May 1914
Resp14

---

title added To a Friend Whose Work has (*rev to* had) Come to Nothing. *Berg(9)* To a Friend Whose Work has Come to Nothing *PWD, Harvard(1), P, Resp14*

1 out, *Berg(9), PWD, Harvard(1), P, Resp14*
3 throat, *Berg(9), PWD, Harvard(1), P, Resp14*
4 compeet] compete, *Berg(9), PWD, Harvard(1), P, Resp14*
5 honour *rev to* honor *Harvard(1)* honor *P* bred, *Berg(9), PWD, Harvard(1), P, Resp14*
6 Who, *Resp14*
6/7 *stanza break Harvard(1)*
8 neighbors' *P* neighbours' *PWD, Harvard(1), P, Resp14* eyes; *Berg(9), PWD, Harvard(1), P, Resp14*
10 triumph] Triumph, *Berg(9), PWD, Harvard(1), P, Resp14*
12 Where on] Whereon *PWD, Harvard(1), P, Resp14*
14 exult, *Berg(9), PWD, Harvard(1), P, Resp14*

In Emory(1) Yeats added, in ink, "This poem was to Lady Gregory though she thought it was for Hugh Lane." He used this information in a note dated 1922 for *Later Poems* (London, 1922), p. 362 (*VP* 819).

Paudeen 

Indignant at the fumbling wits, the obscure spight
Of our old Paudeen in his shop, I stumbled blind
among the stones & thorn trees under morning light
Until a curlew cried out in the luminous wind
A curlew answered & I was startled by the thought
That on the lonely height where all are in God's eye
There cannot be confusion of our sound forgot
A single soul that lacks a sweet crystaline cry

PAUDEEN

[NLI 13,586(4)]

[?~~"~~] Paudeen (6)

g
Indignant at the fumbling wits, the obscure spi{eht
Of our old Paudeen in his shop, I stumbled blind
Among the stones & thorn trees under morning light
Until a curlew cried & in the luminous wind
A curlew answered & I was startled by the thought
That on the lonely height where all are in God's eye
There cannot be confusion of our sound forgot
A single soul that lacks a sweet crystaline cry

~~Sept 16 [?] 1913~~

---

found in NLI 13,586(4) *transcribed above*
NLI 30,358, 27^{v} (bottom half)
published in *PWD*
Poetry (Chicago), May 1914
The New Statesman, May 9, 1914
Resp14

---

title *no title*] Paudeen *PWD, P, NS, Resp14*
1 spight] spite *PWD, P, NS, Resp14*
3 trees, *PWD, P, NS, Resp14* light, *PWD, P, NS, Resp14*
5 answered, *PWD, P, NS, Resp14*
6 Gods *NLI 30,358* eye, *PWD, P, NS, Resp14*
7 be, *all later texts* forgot, *PWD, P, NS, Resp14*
8 crystaline] crystalline *P, NS* cry. *all later texts*
9 ~~Sept 16 [?] 1913~~] Sept 16, 1913 / convert to / And I startled had this thought *NLI 30,358 lacking in all later texts*

---

title The canceled quotation mark might be [?~~Th~~]. The "6" and its enclosing circle are in black ink.
1 The two probably stray marks above "Indignant" are in black ink.

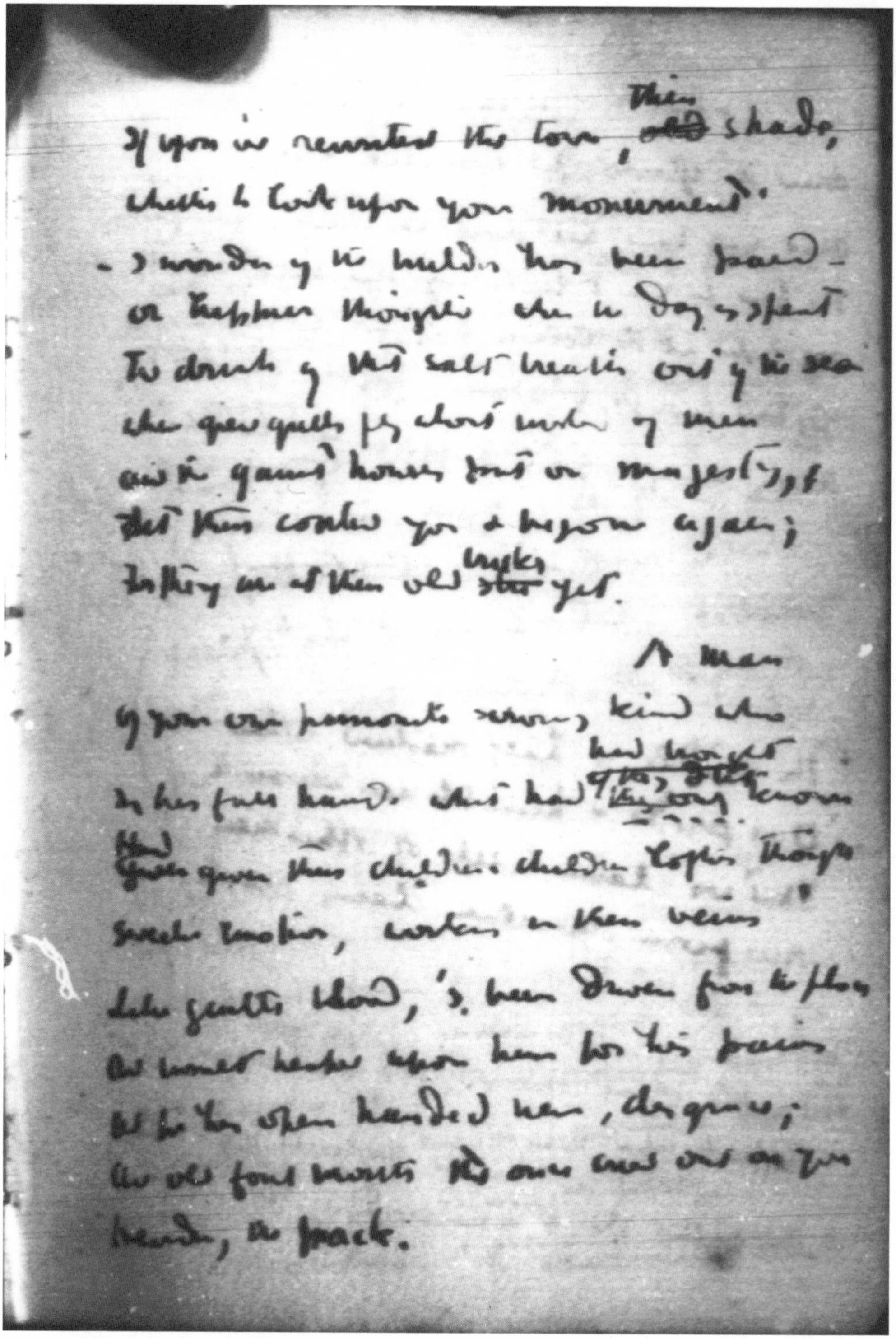

If you have revisited the town, ~~old~~ thin shade,
whether to look upon your monument
– I wonder if the builder has been paid –
or happier thoughted when the day is spent
To drink of that salt breath out of the sea
when grey gulls flit about instead of men
and the gaunt houses put on majesty, &
~~Let~~ then these content you & begone again;
For they are at their old ~~stor~~ tricks yet.

A man
of your own passionate serving kind who
had brought
In his full hands what had ~~they only~~ known
That
~~Had~~ given their children's children loftier thought
Sweeter emotion, working in their veins
Like gentle blood, 's been driven from the place
And insult heaped upon him for his pains
And for his open handed ness, disgrace;
The old foul mouth that once cried out on your
heads, the pack.

TO A SHADE

[NLI 30,358, 31^{r}]

{y thin
If {you've revisited the town, ~~old~~ shade,
Whether to look upon your monument
— I wonder if the builder has been paid —
Or happier thoughted when the day is spent
To drink of that salt breath out of the sea
When grey gulls fly about instead of men
And the gaunt houses put on majesty, [?;]
{L
{Tet these content you & begone again;
tricks
For they are at their old ~~stri~~ yet.
A man
Of your own passionate serving kind who
had brought
~~if they [?I] but~~
In his full hands what had they only known
Had
~~Given~~ given their children s children loftier thought
Sweeter emotion, working in their veins
Like gentle blood, 's been driven from the place
And insult heaped upon him for his pains
And for his open handed ness, disgrace;
An old foul mouth that once cried out on you
[?Herding] the pack.

---

found in NLI 30,358, 31^{r}–31^{v} *transcribed above and below*
TCD(3) *transcribed below*
Emory(2)
AY(3)
AY(6)
NLI 30,009
NLI 30,262
NYPL

published in *PWD*
Poetry (Chicago), May 1914
The New Statesman (London), May 9, 1914
Resp14

---

2 The stray mark at the end is not punctuation, but might be associated with the dash at the start of the next line.

13 The connecting portion of the "s" in "hands" is very lightly inked; dashes underscoring of "they only" to restore the words.

[NLI 30,358, 31v]

unquiet wanderer.

draw the glimmering coverlet anew

What you have [illegible] stopped your ear.

The time for [illegible] of this salt heart

But [illegible] at the corner has not come;

You had brought a sorrow before death

Away away you safer in the tomb

Coole ~~Oct 11~~

Sept 29.

The riddle is half mastered when

Our pride & humble we are such

That we claim little of other men

And from ourselves claim much.

altered

An old foul mouth that clawed you has set

The pack upon him go unquiet wanderer

And gather the glimmering coverlet

[NLI 30,358, 31v]

                                    Unquiet wanderer
draw the Glasnevin coverlet anew
                                                stopped
About your head till dust has ~~stop~~ your ear.
The time for you to taste of that salt breath
And listen at the corners has not come;
You had enough of sorrow before death
Away away your safer in the tomb

                    Coole   ~~Oct 2~~ /
                            Sept 29.

The riddle is half mastered when
Our pride & humbleness are such
That we claim little of other men
And from ourselves claim much.

                    after [?this]
                                    slandered
An old foul mouth that ~~cried on~~ you had set
The pack upon him
                                    Go unquiet wander
And gather the Glasneven coverlet

1 The very faint mark at the end of the line is a stray mark and not punctuation.

8 The slash symbol at the end of the line could be an insertion arrow for the revised date in l. 9.

10–13 The inking of the pen used for this unidentified quatrain is different from that of the poem "Paudeen" but is the same as that used on the next page of the journal for prose comments about the quatrain.

14–18 The inking of the pen used for ll. 14–18 is different from that of the unidentified quatrain (ll. 10–13) but is the same as that used for the revised date at l. 9.

15 The large question mark in the left margin presumably refers to whether to adopt the revision, ll. 14–18.

17 The last two letters of "wander" are written over undecipherable characters.

[TCD(3)]

TO A SHADE

If you've revisited the town, thin shade,
Whether to look upon your monument,
(I wonder if the builder has been paid)
Or happier thoughted, when the day is spent
To drink of that salt breath out of the sea,
When grey gulls fly about instead of men
And the gaunt houses put on majesty;
Let these content you and be gone again;
For they are at their old tricks yet.

A man
Of your own passionate serving kind, who had brought
In his full hands what, had they only known,
Had given their children's children loftier thought
Sweeter emotion, working in their veins
Like gentle blood,'s been driven from the place,
And insult heaped upon him for his pains
And for his openhandedness, disgrace;
An old foul mouth that once cried out on you
Herding the pack.

Unquiet wanderer
Draw the Glasnevin coverlet anew
About your head till dust has stopped your ear.
The time for you to taste of that salt breath
And listen at the corners has not come,
You had enough of sorrow before death,
Away, away! You're safer in the tomb.

W B Yeats
Sept. 1913

---

1 you've] you have *all later texts* Shade, *NYPL and all later texts*
2 monument *NYPL and all later texts*
3 paid) *NYPL and all later texts*
4 happier thoughted,] happier thoughted *NYPL, PWD, P, NS* happier thoughted *rev to* happier-thoughted *NLI 30,009*
5 sea *NYPL and all later texts*
6 fly *rev to* flit *Emory* men, *all later texts*
7 majesty; *NYPL and all later texts*
8 again; *NYPL*
11 kind *NYPL and all later texts*
13 loftire *rev in ink to* loftier *NYPL* thought, *NS, Resp14*

[TCD(3)]

TO A SHADE

If you've revisited the town, thin shade ,
Whether to look upon your monument ,
n
(I wo{mder if the builder has been paid) ,
Or happier thoughted, when the day is spent
To drink of that salt breath out of the sea ,
When grey gulls fly about instead of men
And the gaunt houses put on majesty ;
Let these content you and be gone again;
For they are at their old tricks yet.
A man
r
Of you^own passionate serving kind , who had brought
In his full hands what, had they only known,
Had given their children's children loftier thought
Sweeter emotion , working in their veins
Like gentle blood,'s been driven from the place ,
And insult heaped upon him for his pains
And for his openhandedness, disgrace;
An old foul mouth that once cried out on you
Herding the pack.
Unquiet wanderer
Draw the Glasnevin coverlet anew
About your head till dust has stopped your ear~~s~~ , 7
~~T~~The time for you to taste of that salt breath
And listen at the corners has not come ,
You had enough of sorrow before death ,
Away, away! You're safer in the tomb.

WB Yeats
Sept. 1913

---

15 blood,'s been *so NYPL* blood, has *all later texts* place *NYPL*

16 pains *rev to* pains, *NLI 30,262*

17 open-handedness, *all later texts*

18 An old foul mouth that slandered you had set *rev to* an old foul mouth, has set *rev to* Your enemy that (*rev to* an) old foul mouth, had set *AY(3)* n old foul mouth that slandered you had set *ambiguously rev to* an old foul mouth that had / [?has] set *AY(6)*

21 yhe *strikeover* the *rev in ink to* the *NYPL*

22 till dust has stopped] till the dust stops *NYPL and all later texts* ear *NYPL* ear. *P*

24 come; *NYPL and all later texts*

25 Your *rev in ink to* You *NYPL* death — *NYPL and all later texts*

26 tomb! *NYPL*

signature WB Yeats] *no signature NYPL and all later texts*

date Sept. 1913] September, 29th. 1913. *PWD, Resp14 no date NYPL, P* September 29th, 1913. *NS*

In TCD(3) punctuation in ll. 1–5, 7, 11, 14–15, 22, 24–25 is added in ink.
In NYPL, l. 25, an underscore was typed after "death" and before the dash.

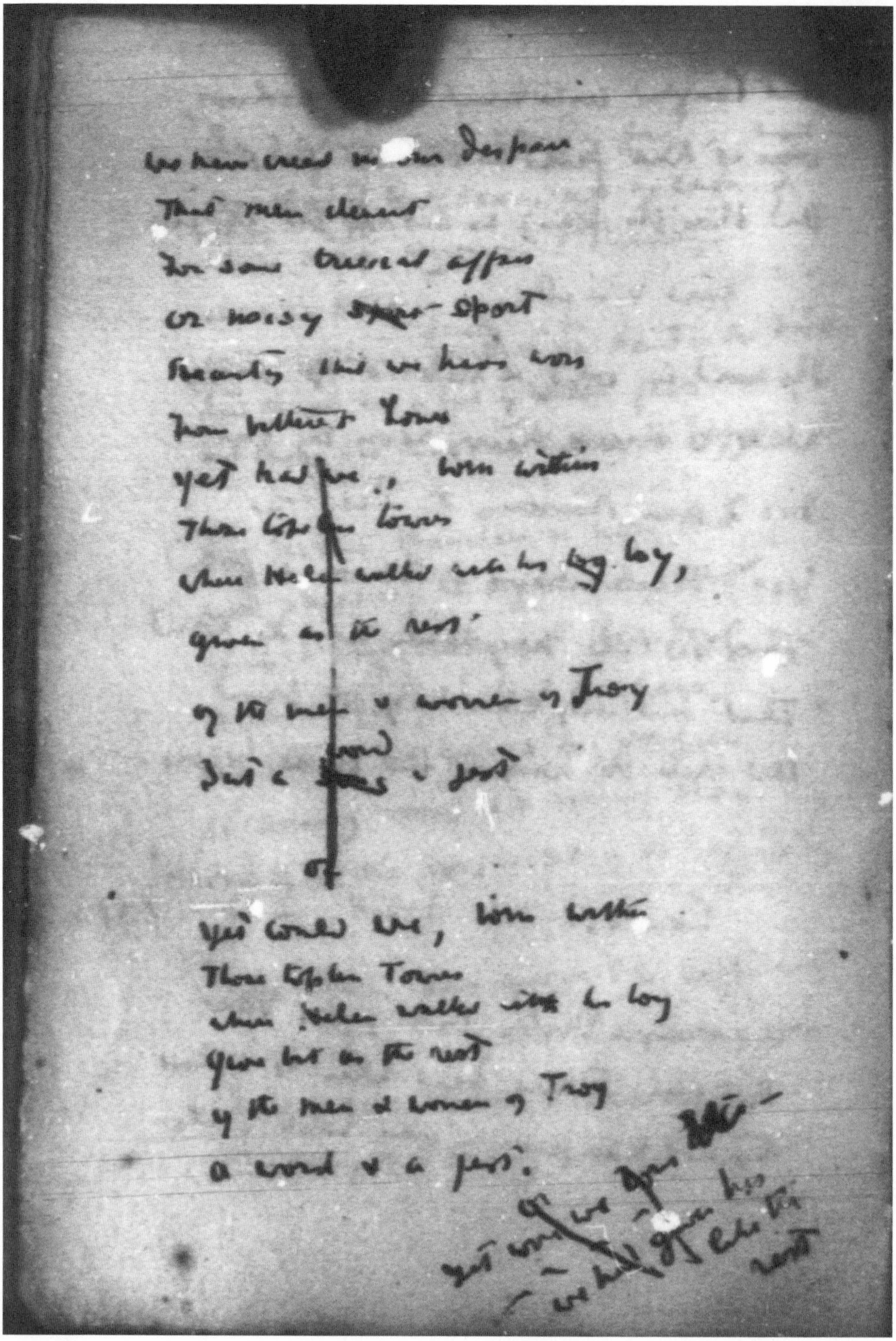

[NLI 30,358, 30v]

WHEN HELEN LIVED

[NLI 30,358, 30^{v}]

We have cried in our despair
That men desert
For some trivial affair
Or noisy ~~sport~~ sport
Beauty that we have won
From bitterest hours
Yet had we, born within
Those tope less towers
Where Helen walked with her ~~boy~~ boy,
Given as the rest
{T
Of the men & women of {troy
word
But a ~~song~~ and jest

or
Yet could we, born within
Those topless Towers
Where Helen walked with her boy
Give but as the rest
Of the men & women of Troy
A word & a jest.

or
Yet were we born [~~?~~] —
— — — —
We had given her
like the
rest

---

found in NLI 30,358, 30^{v} *transcribed above*
NLI 13,586(5) *transcribed below*
Harvard(1), 21
Harvard(1), ts slip *transcribed below*
Berg(6) (b)
NLI 30,262
published in *Poetry* (Chicago), May 1914
Resp14

[NLI 13,586(5)]

When Helen lived

We have cried in our despair
That men desert
For some trivial affair,
Or noisy sport,
Beauty that we have won
From bitterest hours;
Yet would we; lorn within
Those topless towers
Where Helen walked with her boy;
Give, but as the rest
Of the men & women of Troy,
A word and a jest.

[NLI 13,586(5)]

When Helen Lived 

We have cried in our despair
That men desert
For some trivial affair,
Or noisy sport,
Beauty that we have won
From bitterest hours;
Yet could we; born within
Those topless towers
Where Helen walked with her boy;
Give, but as the rest
Of the men & women of Troy,
A word and a jest.

The circled "8" is in ink; this is the eighth poem in *Resp14*, excluding the prefatory "Pardon old fathers."

[Harvard(1), ts slip]

WHEN HELEN LIVED — *sm caps*

35

We have cried in our despair
That men desert ,
For some trivial affair,
Or noisy , insolent sport ,
Beauty that we have won
From bitterest hours ;
Yet *we,* had we walked within
Those topless towers
Where Helen walked with her boy ,
~~We~~ Had given, but/ as the rest
Of the men and women of Troy ,
A word and a jest .

[Harvard(1), ts slip]

WHEN HELEN LIVED —— sm caps

35

We have cried in our despair
That men desert,
For some trivial affair,
Or noisy, insolent sport,
Beauty that we have won
From bitterest hours;
we,
Yet ^ had we walked within
Those topless towers
Where Helen walked with her boy,
H
~~**We**~~ **had given , but as the rest**
Of the men and women of Troy,
A word and a jest.

3 affair *Resp14*
4 insolent, *Resp14* insolent, *rev to* insolent *NLI 30,262*
7 *text and revision identical to Harvard(1), ts slip, and with a fair copy of l. 7 in bottom margin:* Yet we, had we walked within *Berg(6) (b)*
10 Had given,] We had given *rev to* had given *Berg(6) (b)* Had given *Resp14*

[NLI 30,517, 1r (inverted)]

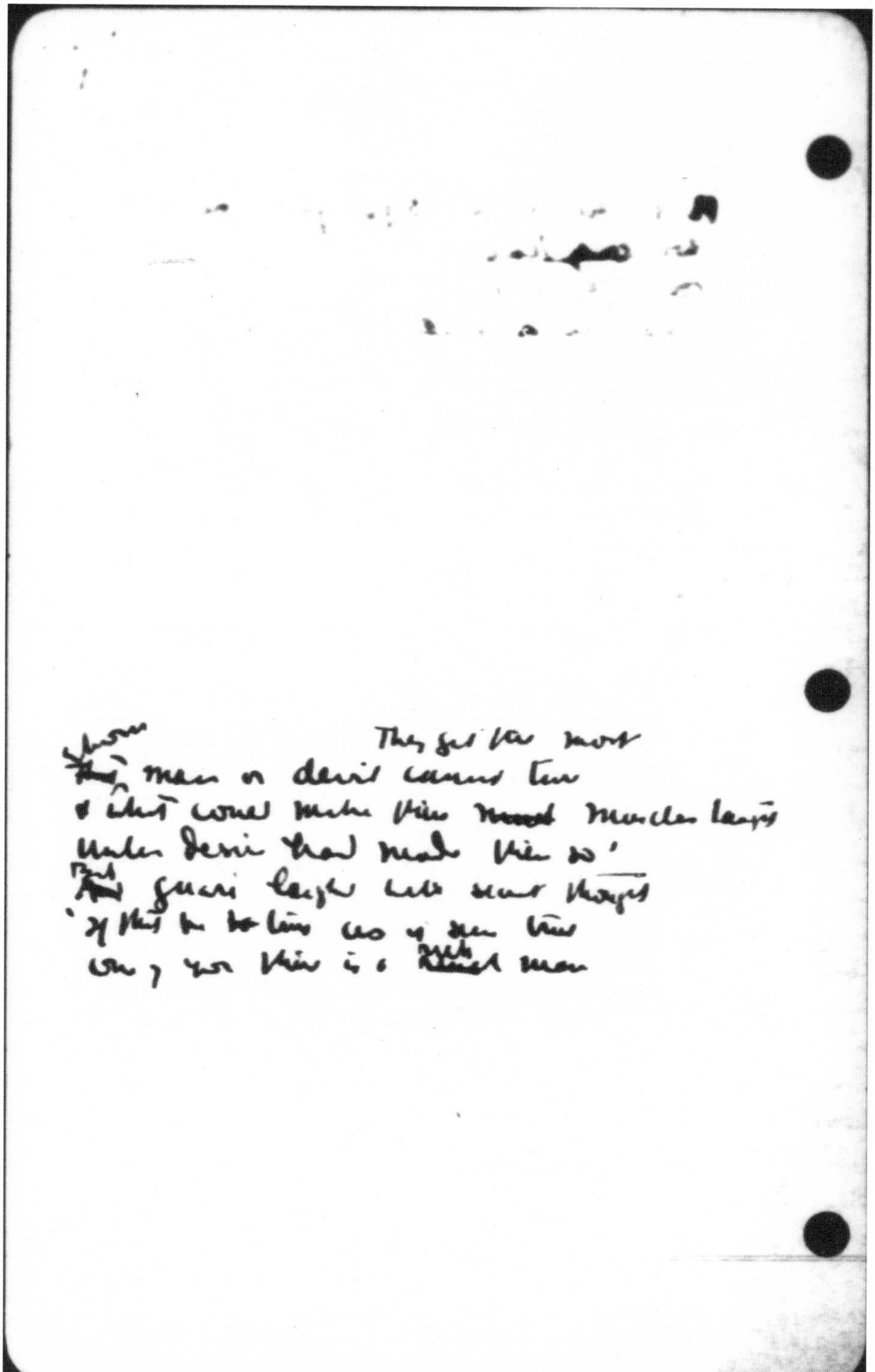

THE THREE BEGGARS

[NLI 30,517, 1[r] (inverted)]

They get the most
Whom
~~That~~ man or devil cannot [?tire]
& w^hat could make these ~~muscel~~ muscles taught
Unless desire had made them so'
But
~~And~~ Guari laughed with secret thought
' If that be [~~?~~] time as it seem true
rich
One of you three is a ~~rich~~ man

---

found in NLI 30,517, 1[r] (inverted) *transcribed above*
NLI 13,586(6) *transcribed below*
Harvard(1) *transcribed below*
ABY(3) *transcribed below*
NLI 13,586(7) *transcribed below*
NLI 30,262
published in *Harper's Weekly* (New York), November 15, 1913
Resp14

The verso (inverted) of this loose sheet has an unidentified fragmentary revision:

But [?where are all the good few gone]
~~For [?only] [?]~~
Only the [? ? ? ?]
[?That ~~in~~ a pale] [? ? ?]

[? ? ? ?] [?and gone]
For only [? ? ? ?]
[?] all [?I]

11

Though to my feathers in the wet
I have stood here from break of day
I have not found a thing to eat
For only rubbish comes my way
Am I ~~[illegible]~~ to live on lebeen-lone?
Muttered the one crane of Gort
For all my pains on lebeen-lone?

King Guari ~~[illegible]~~ walked amid his court
The palace yard & river side
And there to the old beggar said
'You that have wandered far & wide
Can ravel out what's in my head
~~Do men that long the least get most~~
Do men who ~~love~~ least desire get most
Or get the most who most desire?'
The beggar said 'They get the most
Who are so driven they cannot tire,
~~[illegible]~~
~~and what [illegible] hollow hands,~~
~~and [illegible]~~
Desire walks up the stony lands
And holds the handles of the plough'
They held out willing hollow hands
But Guari said 'If this be so
One of you three is a rich man
For ~~[illegible]~~ he shall have a thousand pound
~~For he~~
Who is first asleep, if but he can
Sleep before the third noon sound'

[NLI 13,586(6), 3v (inverted)]

Though to my feathers in the wet
I have stood here from break of day
I have not found a thing to eat
For only rubbish come my way
[-?-] to
Am I ~~And must I~~ live on lebeen-lone?
Muttered th old crane of Gort
For all my pains on lebeen-lone?

walked amid
King Guaire ~~trod among~~ his court
The palace yard & river side
And there to three old beggars said
'You that have wandered far & wide
Can ravel out what s in my head
~~[*o] men that long the least get most~~
do men who ~~have~~ least desire get most
Or get the most who most desire?"
A
~~The~~ beggar said 'They get the most
Who are so driven they cannot tire,
~~[? ? ?] for [? ?] seen all lands~~
~~And The held out [?withered] hollow hands~~
~~And cried~~
Desire breaks up the stony lands
And holds the handles of the plough'
They held out withered hollow hands
But Guari said 'If that be so
One of you three is a rich man
he shall have
For ~~I will give~~ a thousand pounds
~~To [?he]~~
Who is first asleep, if but he can
Sleep before the third noon sounds'

[NLI 13,586(6), 1v (inverted)]

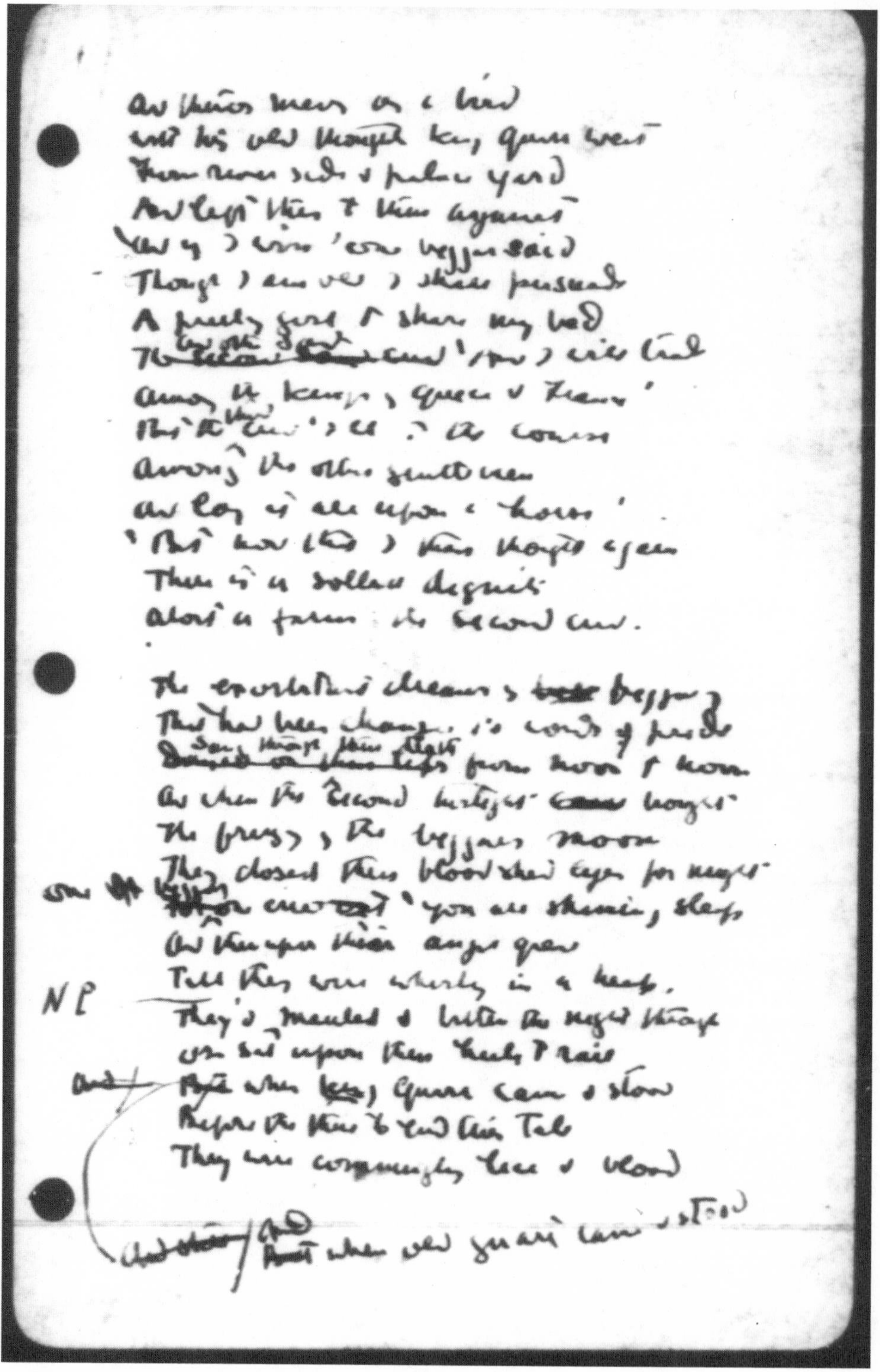

[NLI 13,586(6), 1ᵛ (inverted)]

And thereon merry as a bird
With his old thoughts King Guari went
From river side & palace yard
And left them to their argument
‘ And if I win’ one beggar said
Though I am old I shall persuade
A pretty girl to share my bed
And other said
~~The second said cried~~ ‘And I will trade
Among the Kings & Queens of France’
third
But the ^ cried ‘I ll to the course
Among the other gentlemen
And lay it all upon a horse’
‘ But now that I [?have] thought again
There is a solad dignity
About a farm the second cried.

The exorbitant dreams of [?~~beg~~] beggary
That had been changed [?to] words of pride
Sang through their teeth
~~Danced on their lips~~ from noon to noon
And when the second twilight ~~came~~ brought
The frenzy of the beggars moon
They closed their blood [?shot] eyes for naught
One [~~?~~] beggar
~~For one~~ ^ cried ~~out~~ ‘You are shaming sleep
And thereupon their anger grew
Till they were whirling in a heap.
NP. ——
They’d mauled & bitten the night through
Or sat upon their heels to rail
~~And~~ ~~But~~ when king Guari came & stood
Before the three to end this Tale
They were commingling lice & blood

~~And still~~ / And
~~But~~ when old Guari came & stood

[NLI 13,586(6), 2r]

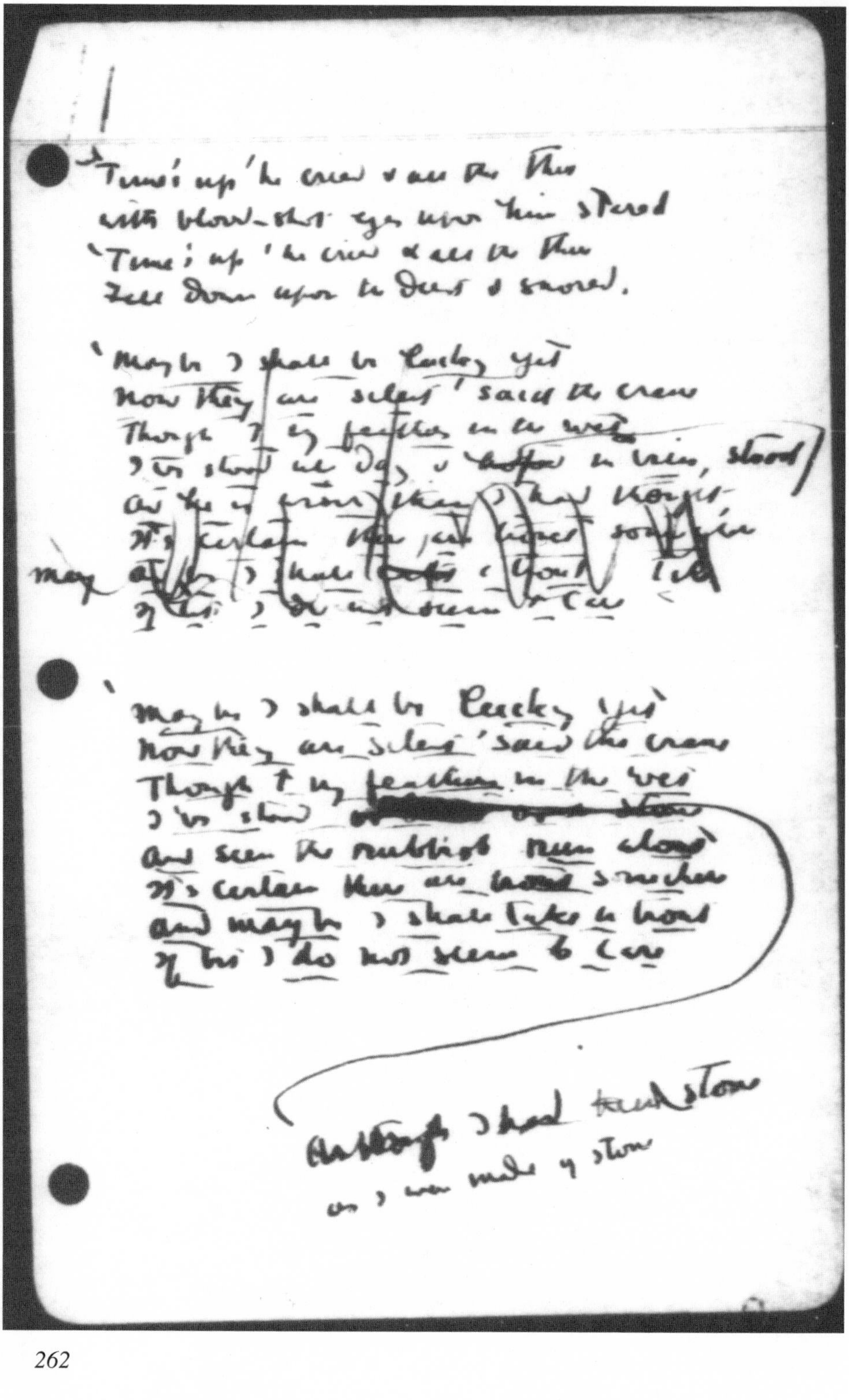
'Time's up' he cried & all the three
With blood-shot eyes upon him stared
'Time's up' he cried & all the three
Fell down upon the dust & snored.

'Maybe I shall be lucky yet
Now they are silent' said the crow
Though all my feathers in the wet
I've stood all day & [illegible] stood
[illegible]

'Maybe I shall be lucky yet
Now they are silent' said the crow
Though all my feathers in the wet
I've stood [illegible] upon stone
And seen the rubbish run along
It's certain there are trout somewhere
And maybe I shall take a trout
If but I do not seem to care

Although I had [illegible] stone
As I were made of stone

[NLI 13,586(6), 2r]

‘ Time’s up’ he cried & all the three
with blood–shot eyes upon him stared
‘ Time’s up’ he cried & all the three
Fell down upon the dust & snored.

‘ Maybe I shall be lucky yet
Now they are silent’ said the crane.
Though to my feathers in the wet
I ve stood all day & ~~hoped~~ in vain,   stood
And he is wiser than I had thought,
It’s certain there are trout some where
~~May~~ And ^be I shall ~~catch~~ a trout   [?take]
If but I do not seem to care

‘ Maybe I shall be lucky yet
Now they are silent’ said the crane
Though to my feathers in the wet
I’ve stood ~~[?as] [?] as a stone~~
And seen the rubbish run about
Its certain there are trout somewhere
And may be I shall take a trout
If but I do not seem to care

~~As though~~ I ~~had been~~ stone
as I were made of stone

THE THREE BEGGARS

'Though to my feathers in the wet,
I have stood here from break of day,
I have not found a thing to eat
For only rubbish comes my way.
Am I to live on Lebeen-lone?'
Muttered the old crane of Gort.
'For all my pains on Lebeen-lone.'

King Guari walked amid his court,
The palace-yard and river-side
And there to three old beggars said:
'You that have wandered far and wide,
Can ravel out what's in my head.
Do men who least desire get most,
Or get the most who most desire?'
A beggar said: 'They get the most
Whom man or devil cannot tire,
And what could make their muscles taut
Unless desire had made them so.'
But Guari laughed with secret thought
'If that be true as it seems true,
One of you three is a rich man
For he shall have a thousand pounds
Who is first asleep, if but he can
Sleep before the third noon sounds.'
And thereon merry as a bird,

22

[Harvard(1), 22]

THE THREE BEGGARS

'Though to my feathers in the wet,
I have stood here from break of day,
I have not found a thing to eat
For only rubbish comes my way.
Am I to live on Lebeen–lone?'
Muttered the old crane of Gort.
'For all my pains on Lebeen–lone.'

King Guari walked amid his court,
The palace–yard and river–side
And there to three old beggars said:
'You that have wandered far and wide,
Can ravel out what's in my head.
Do men who least desire get most,
Or get the most who most desire?'
A beggar said: 'They get the most
Whom man or devil cannot tire,
And what could make their muscles taut
Unless desire had made them so.'
But Guari laughed with secret thought
'If that be true as it seems true,
One of you three is a rich man
For he shall have a thousand pounds
Who is first asleep, if but he can
Sleep before the third noon sounds.'
And thereon merry as a bird,

1–7, 56–63 *set in roman Harper's Weekly*
1 wet *Harper's Weekly*
3 eat *rev to* eat, *NLI 30,262*
5, 7 Lebeen-lone] leeben-lone *Resp14*
7 lebeen-lone.' *rev to* lebeen-lone' *NLI 30,262*
8 Guare *marked with query to rev to* Guaire *NLI 30,262*
9 river-side *Harper's Weekly*
11 'You that have] "You have *Harper's Weekly*
14/15, 24/25, 28/29 *stanza divisions Harper's Weekly*
18 so.' *rev to* so?' *NLI 30,262*
19 Guare *rev to* Guaire *NLI 30,262*
23 can, *Harper's Weekly*
25 thereon merry as a bird, *rev to* thereon, merry as a bird *NLI 30,262*

With his old thoughts King Guari went
From river-side and palace-yard
And left them to their argument.
'And if I win,' one beggar said,
'Though I am old I shall persuade
The second, 'I shall learn a trade
Thereon the third: 'I'll to the course
Among the other gentlemen.
And lay it all upon a horse.'
'But now that I have thought again,
There is a solid dignity
'About a farm,' the second cried.

The exorbitant dreams of beggary
That idleness had borne to pride
Sang through their teeth from noon to noon
And when the second twilight brought
The frenzy of the beggars' moon
They closed their blood-shot eyes for naught.
One beggar cried: 'You're shamming sleep,'
And thereupon their anger grew,
Till they were whirling in a heap.

They'd mauled and bitten the night through
Or sat upon their heels to rail
And when old Guari came and stood
Before the three to end this tale,

23

[Harvard(1), 23]

With his old thoughts King Guari went
From river–side and palace–yard
And left them to their argument.
'And if I win,' one beggar said,
'Though I am old I shall persuade
The second, 'I shall learn a trade
Thereon the third: 'I'll to the course
Among the other gentlemen.
And lay it all upon a horse.'
'But now that I have thought again,
There is a solid dignity
'About a farm,' the second cried.

The exorbitant dreams of beggary
That idleness had borne to pride
Sang through their teeth from noon to noon
And when the second twilight brought
The frenzy of the beggars' moon
They closed their blood–shot eyes for naught.
One beggar cried: 'You're shamming sleep,'
And thereupon their anger grew,
Till they were whirling in a heap.

They'd mauled and bitten the night through
Or sat upon their heels to rail
And when old Guari came and stood
Before the three to end this tale,

---

26 Guare *rev to* Guaire *NLI 30,262*
27 palace-yard, *Harper's Weekly*
30/ *line omitted*] A pretty girl to share my bed. [bed, *Resp14*] *Harper's Weekly, Resp14*
31 The second, 'Ishall learn a trade] Another said: "And I will trade [trade, *Resp14*] *Harpers's Weekly, Resp14*
31/ *line omitted*] Among the Kings of Greece and France." *Harper's Weekly*
32 Thereon the third: 'I'll to] But the third cried: "I'll *Harper's Weekly* The third: 'I'll hurry to *Resp14*
37 'About] About *Harper's Weekly*
38 beggary] beggary, *Resp14*
39 pride] pride, *Resp14*
40 noon] noon; *Resp14*
42 beggars'] beggar's *Harper's Weekly*
47 through, *Harper's Weekly*
48 rail] rail, *Resp14*
49 Guare *rev to* Guaire *NLI 30,262*

[Harvard(1), 24]

They were commingling lice and blood.
'Time's up,' he cried, and all the three
With blood-shot eyes upon him stared.
'Time's up,' he cried, and all the three
Fell down upon the dust and snored.

'*Maybe I shall be lucky yet,*
Now they are silent,' *said the crane.*
'*Though to my feathers in the wet,*
I've stood as I were made of stone
And seen the rubbish run about.
It's certain there are trout somewhere
And maybe I shall take a trout
If but I do not seem to care.'

[Harvard(1), 24]

They were commingling lice and blood.
'Time's up,' he cried, and all the three
With blood–shot eyes upon him stared.
'Time's up,' he cried, and all the three
Fell down upon the dust and snored.

'Maybe I shall be lucky yet,
Now they are silent,' said the crane.
'Though to my feathers in the wet,
I've stood as I were made of stone
And seen the rubbish run about.
It's certain there are trout somewhere
And maybe I shall take a trout
If but I do not seem to care.'

---

60 about.] about, *Resp14*

A farmer has more dignity.'
One to another sighed and cried:
The exorbitant dreams of beggary,
That idleness had borne to pride,
Sang through their teeth from noon
to noon;
And when the second twilight brought
The frenzy of the beggars' moon
They closed their blood-shot eyes for
naught;
One beggar cried: 'You're shamming
sleep;'
And thereupon their anger grew
Till they were whirling in a heap.

They'd mauled and bitten the night
through;
Or sat upon their heels to rail,
And when old Guari came and stood
Before the three to end this tale,
They were commingling lice and blood.
'Time's up,' he cried, and all the
three

[ABY(3)]

A farmer has more dignity.'
On to another sighed and cried:
The exorbitant dreams of beggary,
That idleness had borne to pride,
Sang through their teeth from noon to noon;
And when the second twilight brought
The frenzy of the beggars' moon
None/ **~~They~~ closed ~~their~~ blood–shot eyes ~~for~~** his / but
s/ **~~naught,~~**
To keep his fellows from their sleep
~~One beggar cried: 'You're shamming sleep,'~~
And shouted till
~~And thereupon~~ their anger grew
And/ **~~Till~~ they were whirling in a heap.**

They'~~d~~ mauled and bit~~ten~~ the night through ; whole
They **~~Or~~ sat upon their heels to rail,**
And when old Guari came and stood
Before the three to end this tale,
They were commingling lice and blood.
'Time's up,' he cried, and all the three

They [-?-] ~~&~~ mauled & bit till the day shone;
They mauled & bit through all that day
And till another night had gone,
Or if they made a moments stay

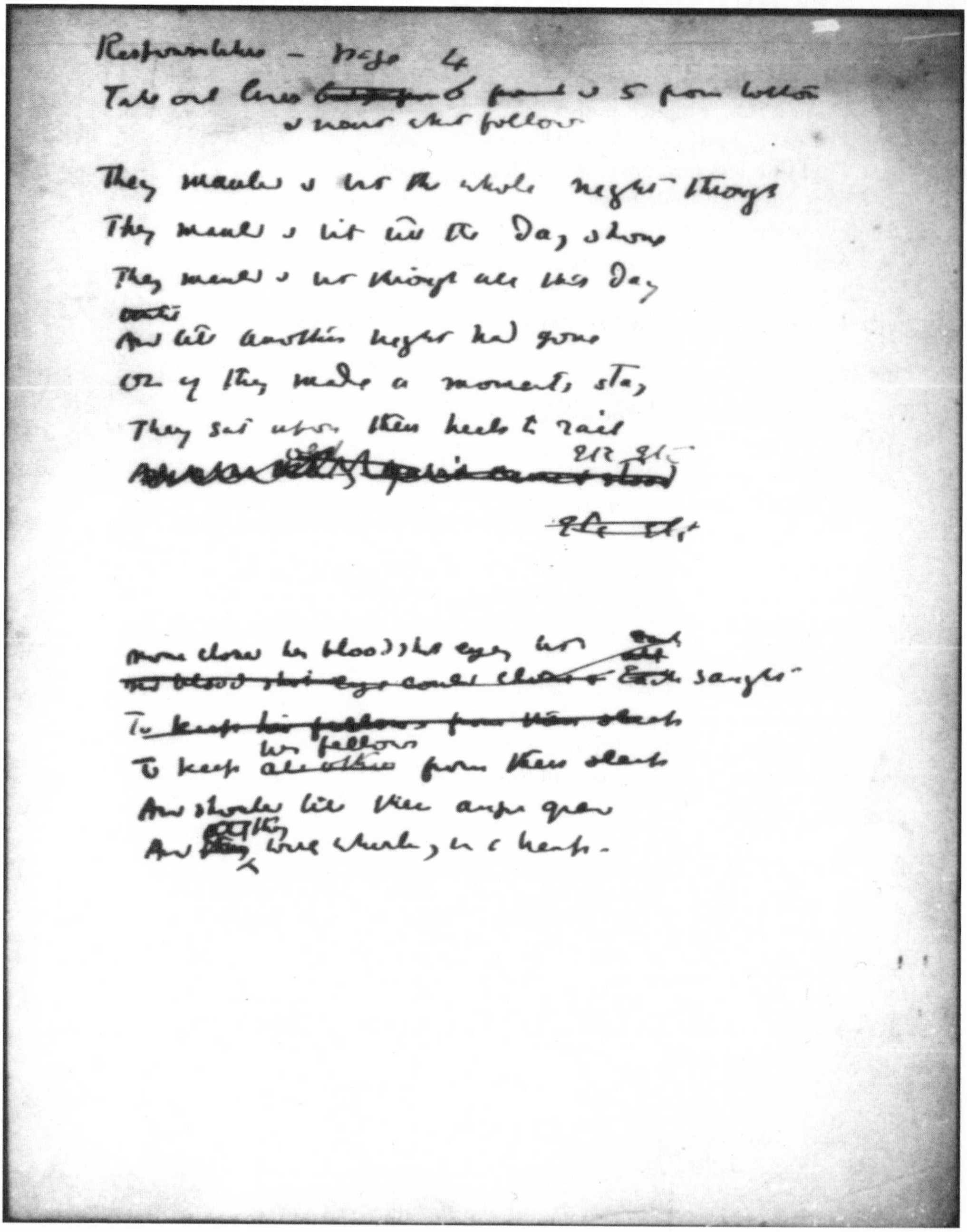
Responsibilities — page 4

[NLI 13,586(7), 4]

Responsibilites – page 4
Take out lines ~~6 & 7 from~~ 6 ~~from t~~ & 5 from bottom
& insert what follows

They mauled & bit the whole night through
The mauled & bit till the day shone
They mauled & bit through all that day
Until
And till another might had gone
Or it they made a moments stay
They sat upon their heels to rail
~~And when King Guari came & stood~~ Etc Etc
~~Etc Etc~~

None closed his blood shot eyes but [?~~Each~~]
~~all~~
~~No blood shot eye could close [?&] Each~~ sought
~~To keep his fellows from their sleep~~
his fellows
To keep ~~all eothers~~ from their sleep
And shouted till their anger grew
~~all~~ they
And ~~they~~ ^ were whirling in a heap.

This revision to the text on p. 43 of *Resp16* (and *Resp17*), was first published in 1922 in *Later Poems*, pp. 204–205.

THE THREE HERMITS

[Berg(10)]

THE HERMITS

———— :: ————

Three old hermits took the air
By a cold and desolate sea;
First, was muttering a prayer,
Second, rumaged for a flea,
On a windy stone, the third,
Giddy with his hundreth year
Sang unnoticed like a bird.

“Though the door of Death is near
And what waits behind the door,
Three times in a single day
I though upright on the shore,
Fall asleep when I should pray.”
So the first, but now the second,
“ We’re but given what we earn
When all thoughts and deeds are reckoned,

---

found in Berg(10) *transcribed above and below*
Princeton(2) *transcribed below*
published in *The Smart Set* (New York), September 1913
Nine Poems
Resp14

[Berg(10), continued]

So it's plain to be discerned
That the shades of holy men,
Who have failed being weak of will
Pass the door of birth again,
And are plagued by crowds, until
They've the passion to escape."
T'other side, "Their shades are cast
Into some most fearful shape."

"Though they're swept up in the blast
They are not changed to anything,
Having loved God once, but maybe
To a poet or a king
Or a witty lovely lady"
While he'd rumaged rags and hair
Caught and cracked his flea; the third,
Giddy with his hundreth year
Sang unnoticed like a bird.

THE SMART SET

THE HERMITS.

By William Butler Yeats

483

Three old hermits took the air
By a cold and desolate sea,
First was muttering a prayer,
Second rumaged for a flea,
On a windy stone, the third
Giddy with his hundreth year
Sang unnoticed like a bird.

space

"Though the door of Death is near
And what waits behind the door,
Three times in a single day
I though upright on the shore,
Fall asleep when I should pray."
So the first but now the second.
" We're but given what we ~~earn~~, have earned/
When all thoughts and deeds are reckoned,
So it's plain to be discerned
That the shades of holy men,
Who have failed being weak of will
Pass the door of birth again,
And are plagued by crowds, until
They've the passion to escape(s)
~~'Thother side, "Their shades are cast~~ moaned the other,' They are thrown
Into some most fearful shape."

blank space

" But the second mocked his moan:
~~"Though they're swept up in the blast~~
"They are not changed to anything,

leave out to make full page

Rush

[Princeton(2), 483]

Three
THE ^ HERMITS .

{eats
By William Butler Y{eats

Three old hermits took the air
By a cold and desolate sea ,
First was muttering a prayer , 483
Second rumaged for a flea .
On a windy stone , the third ,
d
Giddy with his hundreth year
Sang unnoticed like a bird.
------------- ← 9 / Space
"Though the door of Death is near
And what waits behind the door ,
Three times in a single day
I though upright on the shore ,
Fall asleep when I should pray."

So the first but now the second {.
" We're but given what we ~~earn~~ , have earned /
When all thoughts and deeds are reckoned ,
So it's plain to be discerned
That the shades of holy men ,

---

title THE THREE HERMITS *All later texts*
2, 4, 6, 9, 11, 13, 15, 17, 19, 21, 23, 25 *indented SS, Nine Poems*
4 rumaged] rummaged *All later texts* flea; *Resp14*
6 hundredth] hundreth *Resp14* year, *Resp14*
7/8 *no stanza division Resp14*
11 I, *Resp14*
13 second, *Resp14*
14 earned *Resp14*
15 reckoned *Nine Poems*

---

title "Three" in ink in Yeats's hand; caret in ink.
title/ In thick pencil, not Yeats's hand, with overwriting in thick blue pencil.
1, 6, 21 Copyediting in thick pencil.
2–5, 10, 12, 16, 18, 20, 25 All punctuation added in ink.
3 Editorial page number in thick pencil.
7/ Canceled in ink, with delete symbol and slash in ink in right margin; arrow and "space" in right margin in thick pencil; the arrow covers an ink slash in right margin and the last three typewritten dashes.
13 Typewritten period overwritten with an ink period.
14 Cancel and comma in ink; revision in right margin in ink in Yeats's hand.

So it's plain to be discerned
That the shades of holy men,
Who have failed being weak of will
Pass the door of birth again,
And are plagued by crowds, until
They've the passion to escape(s)
'Tother side, "Their shades are cast moaned the other,' They are thrown
Into some most fearful shape."

But the second mocked his moan:
"Though they're swept up in the blast
"They are not changed to anything,

Rush

W B Yeats

Having loved God, once, but maybe
To a poet or a king
Or a witty lovely lady".
While he'd rumaged rags and hair
Caught and cracked his flea; the third,
Giddy with his hundreth year
Sang unnoticed like a bird.

484

Mrs Yeats

Princeton(2), 483:
18 will, *Resp14*

22 Cancels in ink; typewritten cancel of the undeciphered ending; revision in right margin in ink in Yeats's hand.
23 Period added in ink.
23/24 Arrow and notations in right margin in thick pencil.

[Princeton(2), 483, continued]

Who have failed being weak of will
Pass the door of birth again ,
And are plagued by crowds, until
They've the passion to escape".

~~**are cast**~~
' ~~**Thether side, "Their shades**~~ [~~?~~] Moaned the other, 'They are thrown
Into some most fearful shape" . Space
~~blank line~~
But the second mocked his moan:
~~**"Though they're swept up in the blast**~~
" **They are not changed to anything ,**

[Princeton(2), 484]

once ,
Having loved God, but maybe
To a poet or a king
Or a witty lovely lady" .
While he'd rumaged rags and hair 484
Caught and cracked his flea ; the third ,
d
Giddy with his hundreth year
Sang unnoticed like a bird.

WB Yeats

Princeton(2), 484:
24 Cancel in ink; revision in ink in Yeats's hand.
27, 29, 31 *indented SS, Nine Poems*
29 rumaged] rummaged *All later texts* hair, *Resp14*
30 flea, *Resp14*
31 hundredth] hundreth *Resp14*
32/ *no signature All later texts*

26 Caret and comma after "once" in ink; the caret partially obscures the typewritten comma.
28 Period added in ink.
29 Editorial page number in thick pencil.
30 Punctuation added in ink.
31 Revision in ink.

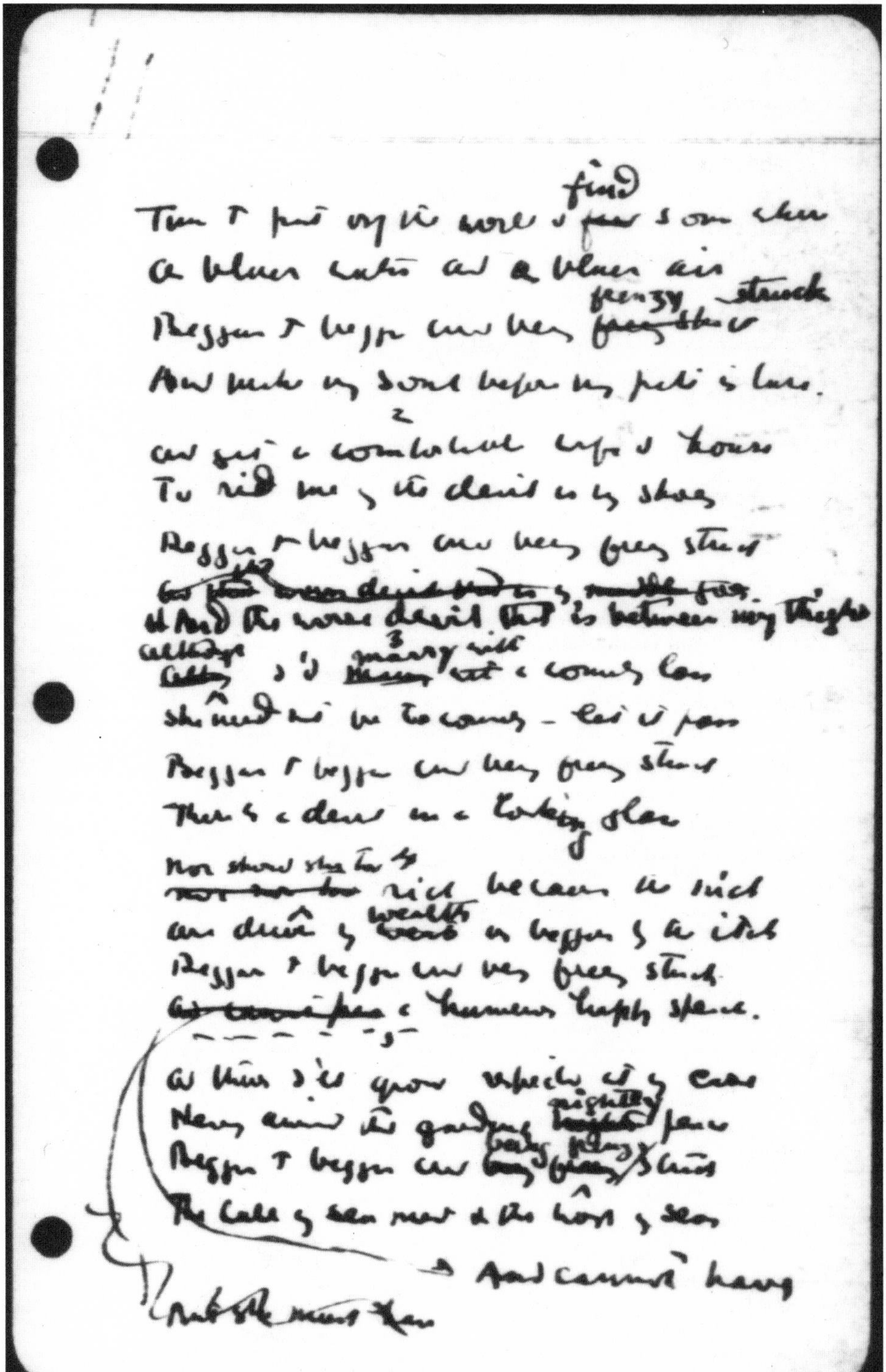
Time to put off the world & ~~fair~~ find some where
A bluer water and a bluer air
Beggar to beggar cried being frenzy struck
And make my soul before my pate is bare.

2
And get a comfortable wife & house
To rid me of the devil in my shoes
Beggar to beggar cried being frenzy struck
~~[illegible]~~
And the worse devil that is between my thighs

3
although I'd marry with a comely lass
She need not be too comely – let it pass
Beggar to beggar cried being frenzy struck
There is a devil in a looking glass

Nor should she be too rich because the rich
Are driven by wealth as beggars by the itch
Beggar to beggar cried being frenzy struck
~~[illegible]~~ a humorous happy speech.

5
And there I'll grow respected at my ease
Hear amid the garden's nightly peace
Beggar to beggar cried being frenzy struck
The [illegible] of [illegible] and the hoot of seas
And cannot hang
But she must [illegible]

BEGGAR TO BEGGAR CRIED

[NLI 13,586(7) (a), 1r]

find
Time to put off the world & [~~?~~] some where
A bluer water and a bluer air
frenzy struck
Beggar to beggar cried being ~~[?frenzy] struc~~
And make my soul before my pate is bare.
2
And get a comfortable wife & house
To rid me of the devil in my shoes
Beggar to beggar cried being [?frenzy] struck
~~the~~
~~And that worse devil that in my middle goes.~~
[~~?~~] And the worse devil that is between my thighs
3
Although marry with
[~~?~~^] I'd ~~marry wit~~ a comely lass
She need not be too comely — let it pass
Beggar to beggar cried being [?frenzy] struck
There is a devil in a looking glass
Nor should she too [?]
~~Nor nor~~^ ~~[?]~~ rich because the rich
wealth
Are driven by ~~weat~~ as beggars by the itch
Beggar to beggar cried being [?frenzy] struck
~~And cannot have~~ a humourous hapy speech.
5
And thus I'll grow respected at my ease
nightly
Hearing amid [?the] gardens ~~nights~~ peace
being frenzy
Beggar to beggar cried ~~being [?frenzy]~~ struck
The call of sea [?mew] & the [?host] of [?seas]
And cannot have
~~But she must have~~

---

found in NLI 13,586(7) (a) *transcribed above and below*
NLI 13,586(7) (b) *transcribed below*
Harvard(1) *transcribed below*
published in *Poetry* (Chicago), May 1914
Resp14

[NLI 13,586(7) (a), 2[r]]

[NLI 13,586(7) (a), 2^{r}]

1 ~~We [?]~~
the edge of the sea
2 We, shall have a garden by ~~the sea side~~
3 ~~Full of cheeries [?] & apples~~

4 ~~Sa~~
[?pear]
5 And, [?an] [?quiet] garden full of ^ apples

6 And beggar to beggar being [?frenzy] struck

7 ~~A~~
8 Where, the world [?trouble] shal [?forget] [?our] feet

[NLI 13,586(7) (a), 2^{v}]

[NLI 13,586(7) (a), 2^{v}]

Somday Ill get a wife & build a hous
To rid me of the devil in my shoes
Beggar to beggar cried [?being] frenzy struck
~~And that worse one that in my middle~~ goes
~~And of the devil that in my my middle~~
And the worse devil that in [?my] middle goes.

Nor Nor Yet rich
~~Not a rich wife~~, for if one rightly [?weights]
There too much hurry in rich womens days
Beggar to beggar cried being [?frenzy] struck
But full of humerous & happy ways.

Paper clip marks at the top left show this leaf was filed with the verso facing up.

[NLI 13,586(7) (b), 1r]

Time to put off the world & go somewhere
And get my health again in the sea air
Beggar to beggar cried being frenzy struck
And make my soul before my pate is bare

And get a comfortable wife & house
To rid me of the Devil in my shoes
Beggar to beggar cried being frenzy struck
And the worse devil that is between my thighs

And though I'd marry with a comely lass
She need not be too comely — let it pass
Beggar to beggar cried being frenzy struck
But there's a devil in a looking glass

And there I'll grow respected at my ease
And hear amid the gardens nightly peace
Beggar to beggar cried being frenzy struck
The wind blown clamour of the barnacle geese.

Nor should she be too rich, because the rich
Are driven by wealth, as beggars by the itch
Beggar to beggar cried being frenzy struck
And cannot have a humorous happy speech

[NLI 13,586(7) (b), 1^{r}]

Time to put off the world & go some where
And get my health again in the sea air
Beggar to beggar cried being frenzy struck
And make my soul before my pate is bare

And get ~~myself~~ a comfortable wife & house
~~Nor [?shoe]~~
To rid me of the devil in my shoes
Beggar to beggar cried being frenzy struck
And the worse devil that is between my thighs

And though I'd marry with a comely lass
She need not be too comely — let it pass
Beggar beggar
~~Devil~~ to ~~devil~~ cried being frenzy struck
But there's a devil in a looking glass

And there I ll grow respected at my ease
And hear amid the gardens nightly peace
Beggar to beggar cried being frenzy struck
The wind blown clamour of the barnicle geese.

Nor should she be too rich, because the rich
Are driven by wealth, as beggars by the itch
Beggar to beggar cried being frenzy struck
And cannot have a humerous happy speech

[Harvard(1), 25, 26]

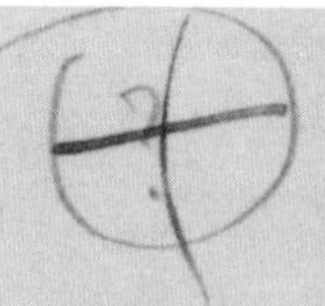

BEGGAR TO BEGGAR CRIED

"Time to put off the world and go somewhere
And find my health again in the sea air,"
Beggar to beggar cried, being frenzy-struck,
"And make my soul before my pate is bare."

25

"And get a comfortable wife and house
To rid me of the devil in my shoes,"
Beggar to beggar cried, being frenzy-struck,
"And the worse devil that is between my thighs."

"And though I'd marry with a comely lass,
She need not be too comely— let it pass,"
Beggar to beggar cried, being frenzy-struck,
"But there's a devil in a looking-glass."

"Nor should she be too rich, because the rich
Are driven by wealth as beggars by the itch,"
Beggar to beggar cried, being frenzy-struck,
"And cannot have a humourous happy speech."

"And there I'll grow respected at my ease,
And hear amid the garden's nightly peace,"
Beggar to beggar cried, being frenzy-struck,
"The wind-blown clamour of the barnacle-geese."

THE REALISTS

Hope that you may understand !
What can books of men that wive
In a dragon-guarded land/
Paintings of the dolphin-drawn
Sea-nymphs in their pearly waggons

26

[Harvard(1), 25]

BEGGAR TO BEGGAR CRIED

“Time to put off the world and go somewhere
And find my health again in the sea air,”
Beggar to beggar cried, being frenzy–struck,
“And make my soul before my pate is bare.”

[Harvard(1), 26]

“And get a comfortable wife and house
To rid me of the devil in my shoes,”
Beggar to beggar cried, being frenzy–struck,
“And the worse devil that is between my thighs.”

“And though I’d marry with a comely lass,
She need not be too comely — let it pass,”
Beggar to beggar cried, being frenzy–struck,
“But there’s a devil in a looking–glass.”

“Nor should she be too rich, because the rich
Are driven by wealth as beggars by the itch,”
Beggar to beggar cried, being frenzy–struck,
“And cannot have a humourous happy speech.”

“And there I’ll grow respected at my ease,
And hear amid the garden’s nightly peace,”
Beggar to beggar cried, being frenzy–struck,
“The wind–blown clamour of the barnacle–geese.”

---

page 25: 4 bare *rev to* bare.”] bare; *P*

---

title At the right of the title, penciled question mark in a penciled circle was converted to a target symbol by adding the “+” in ink.

1, 2, 4 Double quotation marks written in ink over penciled double quotation marks.

---

page 26: 8 thighs. *rev to* thighs.”] thighs. *P*

12 looking-glass. *rev to* looking-glass.”] looking-glass. *P*

16 humourous *rev to* humorous] humourous *Resp14* speech. *rev to* speech.”] speech. *P*

20 clamour *rev to* clamor] clamour *Resp14*

5–6, 8–10, 12–14, 16–18, 20 Double quotation marks added in ink.

7 Double quotation mark added in ink and then canceled in pencil.

16, 20 Penciled cancel of “u”.

[NLI 8773(2)]

THE WELL AND THE TREE

[NLI 8773(2), (*near the end of the folder*)]

1 [?He] has made a [?heap] of leaves
2 He l

3 The man that I praise
4 Cried out the empty well
~~Lives out the [?whole of]~~
5 ~~Will live out~~ his ~~days~~ Has lived all his day
Where the clang of a bell
6 ~~Where gather the crows~~ Can [?gather] the cows
[?To]
7 [?~~At~~] the door of his ancient house
who but
8 For ~~only~~ a jay [?only] would praise
9 The dry stones [?of] a well.

---

found in NLI 8773 *transcribed above and below*
ABY(3)
WashStU
published in *Resp16* and *Resp17*

8, 23 jay: A stupid or silly person; a simpleton. *OED*

18 The line perhaps reads: "Where none [*or* "nor"] hear & sea".

The only printings as a poem separate from the play *At the Hawk's Well* were in *Resp16* and, without any changes, *Resp17;* that text is given below. It is marked in two copies of *Resp17,* ABY(3), where the entire poem is canceled in pencil (p. 49), and in WashStU, where it is replaced in the table of contents (ink revision on p. v) by "To a Friend" [later titled "The New Faces"] and where its text (p. 49) has been covered with a pasted-in, ink holograph of "To a Friend." The text of "The Well and the Tree" in *Resp16* and *Resp 17* reads:

THE WELL AND THE TREE

'The Man that I praise,'
Cries out the empty well,
'Lives all his days
Where a hand on the bell
Can call the milch-cows
To the comfortable door of his house.
Who but an idiot would praise
Dry stones in a well?'

[*stanza break*]

'The Man that I praise,'
Cries out the leafless tree,
'Has married and stays
By an old hearth, and he
On naught has set store
But children and dogs on the floor.
Who but an idiot would praise
A withered tree?'

[NLI 8773(2)]

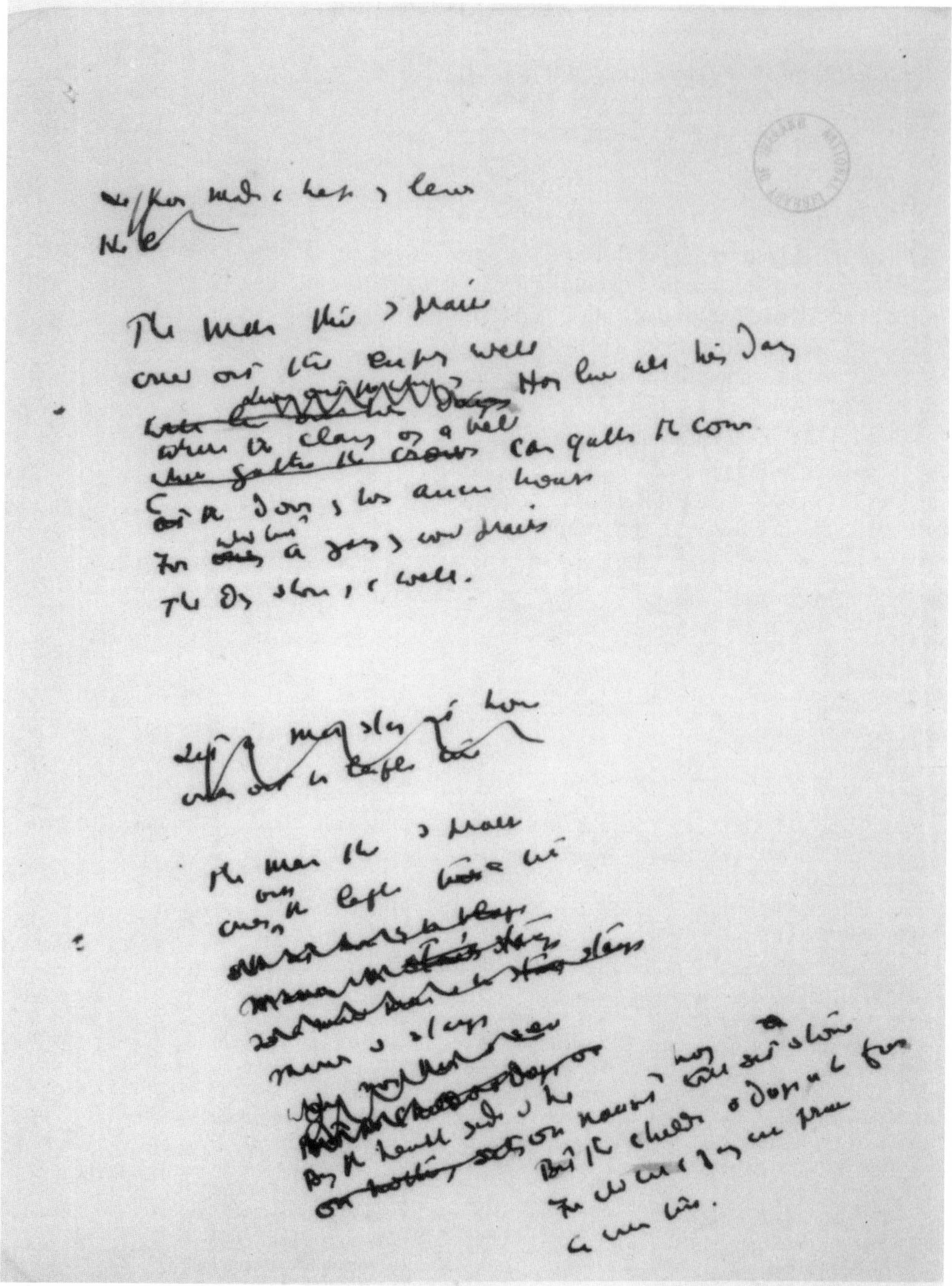

[NLI 8773(2), continued]

Let a man stay at home
Cries out [?the] leafless tree

The man that I praise
[?out]
Cries ^ the leafless ~~trees~~ [?& tree]
~~Sits at home by the blaze~~
~~Maries & [?stae's] stays~~
~~Is a mild man & he [?staes] stays~~
[?Marries] & stays
Where [?none] [? ?] sea
~~But the [?children] & dogs on~~
By the hearth side & he
has [?]
~~On nothing sets~~ On naught ~~will~~ set store
But the children & dogs on the floor
For who but a jay [?will] praise
A [?withered] tree.

As I came over windy gap
They threw a half penny into my cap
For I am
While I am running to Paradise
And all that I need do is to wish
puts
And some body stoops his hand in the dish
To
And throw me a bit of salted fish
And there the king is but as the beggar

My brother Mourteen is worn out
With skelping his big brawling lout
While I am running to Paradise
A poor life do what he can
And though he keep a dog & a gun
A serving maid & a serving man
And there the king is but as the beggar

Poor men have grown to be rich men
And rich men grown to be poor again
While I am running to Paradise
And many a darling wit grown dull

RUNNING TO PARADISE

[NLI 30,358, 29v]

As I came over Windy Gap
They threw a half penny into my cap
          am
For   was
~~While~~ I ~~am~~ running to Paradize
               [?]
And all that I need do is to wish
                         puts
And somebody ~~'ll put~~ his hand in the dish
To
~~And~~ throw me a bit of salted fish
                              [?]
And there the king is but as the beggar

My brother Maurteen is worn out
With skelping his big brawling lout
While I am running to Paradize
A poor life do what he can
And though he keep a dog & a gun
A serving maid & a serving man
And there the king is but as the beggar

Poor men have grown to be rich men
And rich men grown to be poor again
While I am running to Paradize
And many a darling wit grown dull

---

found in NLI 30,358 *transcribed above and below*
Harvard(1) *transcribed below*
NLI 30,009
published in *Poetry* (Chicago), May 1914
Resp14

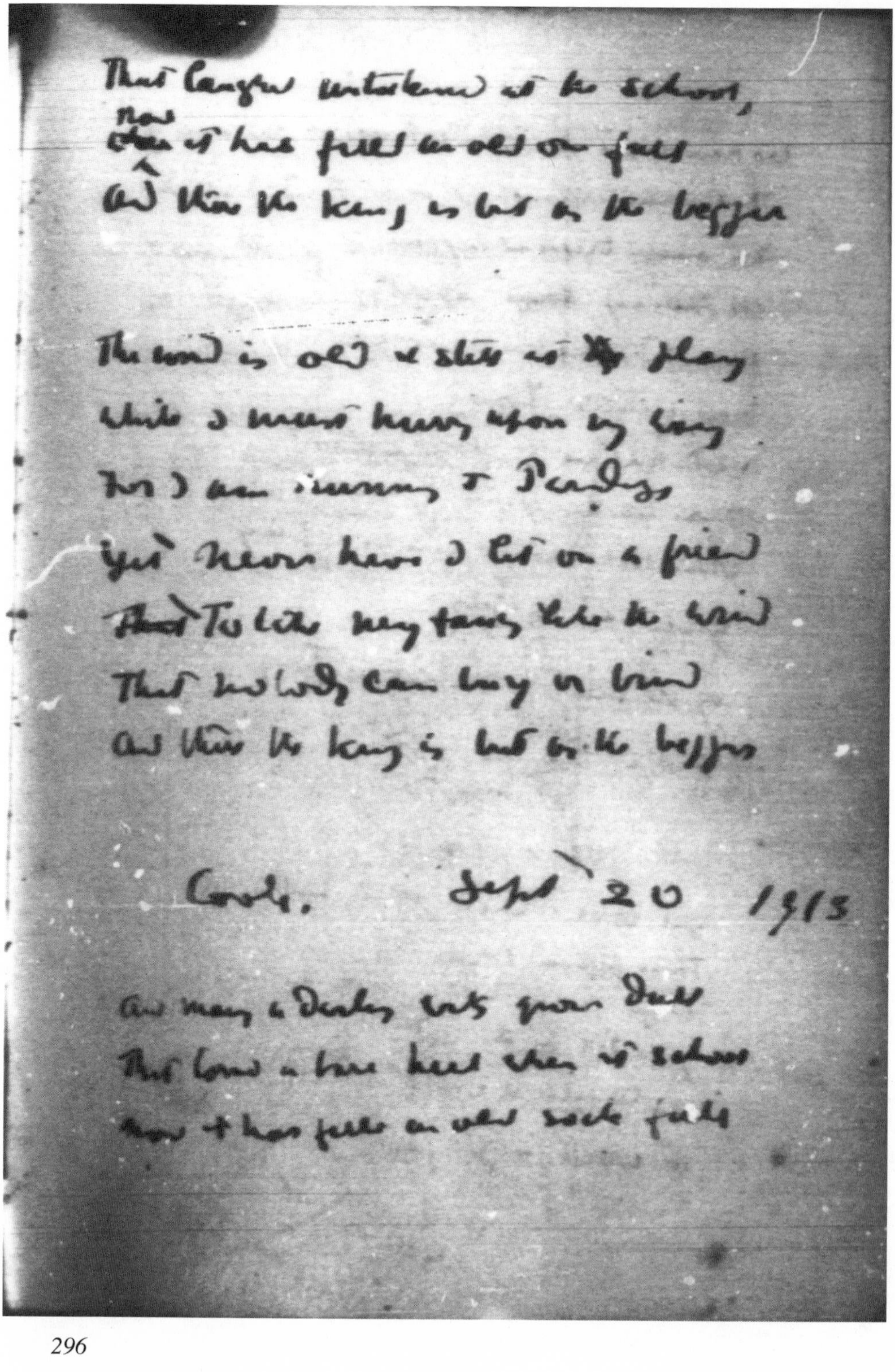

NLI 30,358, 30r]

That laughed [?untutored] at the school,
  Now
~~When~~ it has filled an old one full
And there the king is but as the beggar

The wind is old & still at ~~the~~ play
While I must hurry upon my way
For I am running to Paradize
Yet never have I lit on a friend
~~That~~ To take my fancy like the wind
That nobody can buy or bind
And there the king is but as the beggar

Coole. Sept 20 1913

And many a darling wits grown dull
That tossed a bare heel when at school
Now it has filled an old sock full

[Harvard(1), 28, 29]

[Harvard(1), 28]

⊕ **RUNNING TO PARADISE**

As I came over Windy Gap
They threw a halfpenny into my cap
For I am running to Paradise.
And all that I need do is to wish ,
And somebody puts his hand in the dish
To throw me a bit of salted fish
And there the king is but as the beggar.

My brother Mourteen is worn out
With skelping his big brawling lout,

---

2 cap, *P*
4 wish *rev to* wish,] wish *Resp14*
6 fish, *P*

---

title Copyediting in left margin is all in pencil.
4 Comma added in pencil.

[Harvard(1), 29]

38

While I am running to Paradise.
A poor life do what he can.
And though ~~we~~ keep a dog and a gun, he/
A serving maid and a serving man,
And there the king is but as the beggar . . .

Poor men have grown to be rich men, Gal 4.
And rich men grown to be poor again,
While I am running to Paradise.

And many a darling wits grow dull '/ n/ wit's
That tossed a bare heel when at school,
Now it has filled an old sock full,
And there the king is but as the beggar.

The wind is old and still at play
While I must hurry upon my way
For I am running to Paradise.
Yet never have I let on a friend i/
To take my fancy like the wind
That nobody can buy or bind —
And there the king is but as the beggar.

---

11 life] life, *P* life *Resp14* life *rev to* life, *NLI 30,009* can, *P, Resp14*
12 though we *rev to* though he] though he *P* though we *Resp14*
14 beggar . . .] beggar. *P, Resp14*
19 school; *P*
27 bind *rev to* bind —] bind — *P* bind *Resp14*

/10 Number in the top right corner is in faint, but thick blue pencil.
12 Cancel in ink; revision in right margin is in ink, not Yeats's hand; the insertion arrow from "he /" to the canceled "we" is in pencil.
15 The last word of the line is circled, with a penciled faint (erased?) compositor's notation in the right margin.
18–19, 25 Copyediting in ink, not Yeats's hand.
27 Dash added in pencil.

[NLI 13,586(8) (a), 1ᵛ inverted]

found in NLI 13,586(8) (a) *transcribed opposite and below*
NLI 13,586(8) (b) *transcribed below*
Harvard(1)
Emory(2)
ABY(7)
ABY(3)
Berg(11)
ABY(4)
NLI 30,009
published in Resp14

THE HOUR BEFORE DAWN

[NLI 13,586(8) (a), 1^{v} inverted]

~~Before dawn~~ (1
The Hour before dawn.
A one legged, one armed, one eyed man
A bundle of rags upon a cruch
Stumbled on windy Cruccaun
Cursing the wind — It was as much
As the one ~~stud~~ sturdy leg could do
To keep him upright while he cursed
And counted where long years ago
Queen Maeves nine Maines had been nursed
A pair of lapwing, one old sheep
And not a house to the plains edge;
When/~~But~~ close to his right hand a heap
Of grey stones & a rocky ledge.
Reminded him that he could make
If he but shifted a few stones
A shelter till the day light broke
But
~~And~~ while he fumbled with the stones
They toppled over. 'Were it not
I have a lucky wooden shin
~~They might have hurt my leg~~
I had been hurt' the old beggar thought
saw
thereon ~~theron say~~
And ~~thereupon~~, where stones had been,
A dark deep hole in the rocks face
~~should~~
Trembled & gasped & [?~~would~~] have run should
~~would~~

This collation excludes ABY(4) and NLI 30,009, which are given in a supplementary collation on pp. 313, 315, 317 below.

Title THE HOUR BEFORE DAWN *Resp14,*
1 one-legged, one-armed, one-eyed *Resp14*
2 cruch] crutch *Resp14*
3 Cruccaun] Cruachan *Resp14*
4 wind — It] wind. It *Resp14*
6 cursed. *Resp14*
7 And counted] He counted, *Resp14*
8 Maeve's *Resp14* nursed] nursed. *rev to* nursed, *Harvard(1)* nursed. *Resp14*
9 lapwing,] lapwings, *Resp14*
10 plains edge;] plain's edge, *rev to* plain's edge; *Harvard(1)* plain's edge, *Resp14*
12 ledge *Resp14*
13 make, *Resp14*
14 stones, *Resp14*
15 day light broke] daylight broke, *Resp14*
17 over; *Resp14*
20 hurt,' *Resp14*
21 been,] been *Resp14*
22 rocks face] rock's face, *Resp14*

[NLI 13,586(8) (a), 2ᵛ inverted]

37 The period after "light" is changed in ink to a comma; the closing single quotation mark after "light" is canceled in pencil.

44 Underscores are in ink; "~~[?a]~~" could be "~~[?the]~~".

[NLI 13,586(8) (a), 2ᵛ inverted]

2

24 Being certain it was no right place
25 But the hell mouth at Cruachan
26 And stuffed with all that s old and bad,
27 ~~Yet shtood~~ And yet stood still because inside
28 He d seen a red haired jolly lad
29 In some outlandish coat, beside
30 A ladle & a tub of beer
31 Plainly no phantom by his look
32 So with a laugh at his own fear
33 He crawled into that pleasant nook
Young red head
34 ~~The young man~~ stretched himself to yawn
35 And murmured 'May God curse the night
36 That's grown uneasy near the dawn
{ ,
37 So that it seems even I sleep light{ :
38 And who are you that wakens me?
{ o
39 Has one of Maeves nine brawling s{ ans
40 Grown tired of his own company
41 But let him keep his grave for once
~~Ive to make up the sleep I ve lost~~
42 I ~~ll~~ drink & drop asleep & then
~~I have to~~
43 ~~For anger I made him wide awake~~
44 ~~'I took you for [?a] [?buried] man~~
45 ~~' say that you~~
have
46 I have to find the sleep I lost'

---

25 Hell Mouth *Resp14*
26 that's *Resp14* bad; *Resp14*
27 still, *Resp14*
28 He d] He had *Resp14* red-haired *Resp14*
29 coat *Resp14*
30 beer, *Resp14*
31 look] look *rev to* lok; *Harvard(1)* look; *Resp14*
32/33 *stanza division ABY(7)*
33 nook. *Resp14*
34 Red-head *Resp14*
37 light; *Resp14*
39 Maeve's *Resp14*
40 company? *Resp14*
46 lost.' *Resp14*

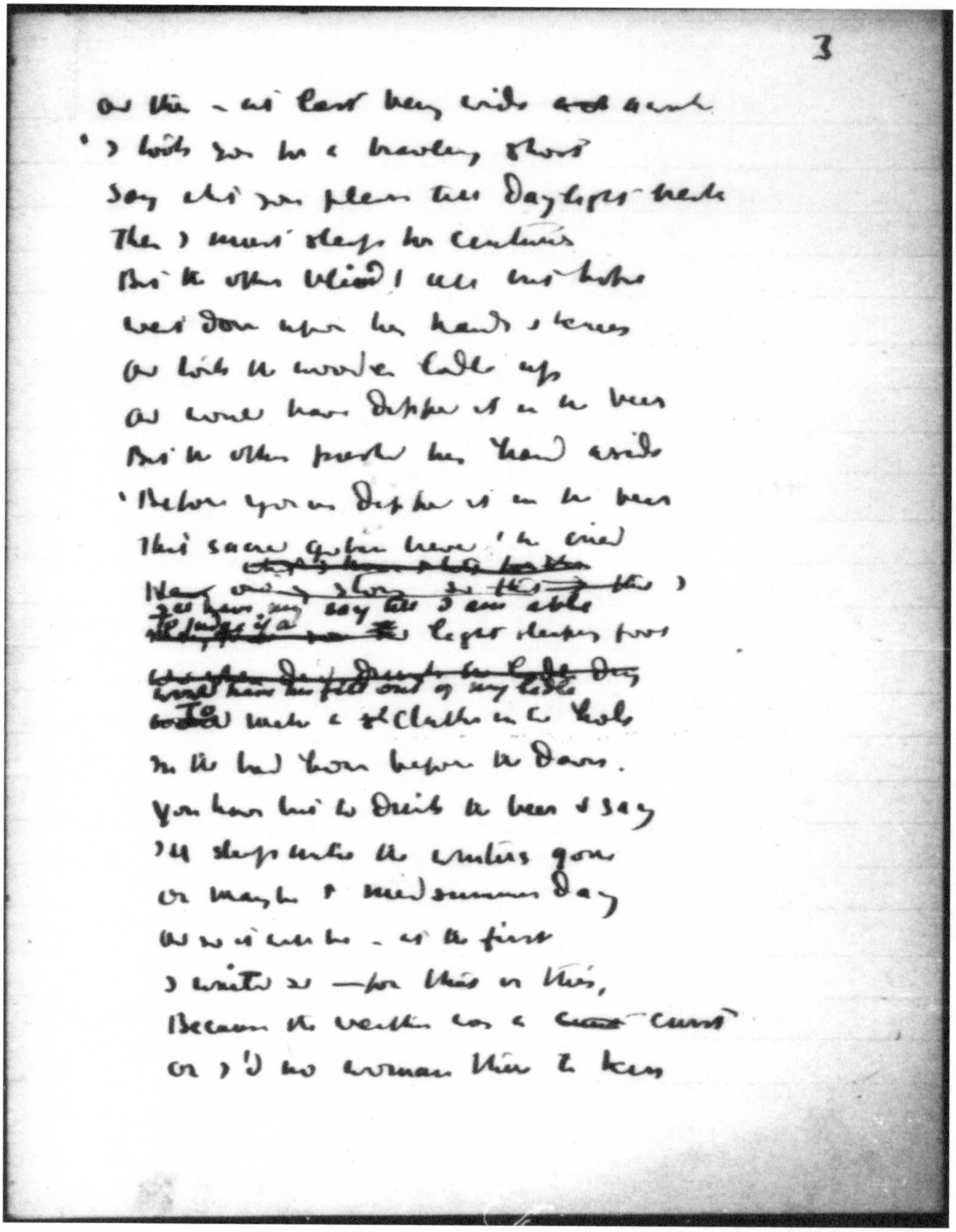
3

And then – we have been wide awake
'I would give you for a travelling show'
Say what you please till daylight break
Then I must sleep for centuries
But the other cried! all [illegible]
Went down upon her hands & knees
And took the wooden ladle up
And would have dipped it in the beer
But the other pushed her hand aside
'Before you can dip it in the beer
That sacred golden beer' he cried
~~[illegible]~~
~~[illegible]~~ that I
~~[illegible]~~ say till I am able
~~[illegible]~~ light sleepers [illegible]
~~[illegible]~~ day
~~would have [illegible] fell out of my table~~
To make a [illegible]
[illegible] before the Dawn.
You have but to drink the beer & say
I'll sleep until the winter's gone
Or maybe to midsummer day
And so it will be – as the first
I wrote it – for this or this,
Because the weather was a ~~[illegible]~~ curse
Or I'd no woman there to kiss

[NLI 13,586(8) (a), 3v inverted]

3

47 And then — at last being wide ~~a [?]~~ awake
48 ‘ I took you for a brawling ghost
49 Say what you please till daylight break
50 Then I must sleep for centuries
51 But the other blind, to all but hope
52 Went down upon his hands & knees
53 And took the wooden ladle up
54 And would have dipped it in the beer
55 But the other pushed his hand aside
56 ‘ Before you ve dipped it in the beer
57 That sacred Goban brewed’ he cried
~~What I have to tell for the~~
58 ~~Hear our my story so that I that~~ I
I ll have my say till I am able
To judge if a ~~a~~
59 ~~May [?give] you no~~ light sleeping fool
60 ~~Who when did drink the ladle dry~~
Would have his fill out of my ladle
To
61 [~~? ?~~] make a [~~?~~] clatter in the hole
62 In the bad hour before the dawn.
63 You have but to drink the beer & say
64 I ll sleep until the winters gone
65 Or maybe to Midsummer day
66 And so it will be — at the first
67 I waited so — for that or this,
68 Because the weather was a ~~curst~~ curst
69 Or I’d no woman there to kiss

---

47 then at *Resp14*
48 ghost, *Resp14*
49 please till daylight break] please, but from day-break *Resp14*
50 Then I must sleep for centuries] I’ll sleep another century.’ *Resp14*
51 But the other blind, to] The beggar deaf to *Resp14*
52 upon his hands & knees] upon a hand and knee *Resp14*
55 aside, *Resp14*
55/56 *stanza division ABY(7)*
56 you ve] you have *Resp14*
57 brewed,’ *Resp14*
58/ I’ll *Resp14* say, *Resp14*
63 You have] You’ve *Resp14*
63/64 *stanza division ABY(7)*
64 I’ll *Resp14* winter’s gone, *Resp14*
65 maybe, *Resp14* Day *Resp14*
66 be — at the] be. / At the *rev to* be. At the *Harvard(1)* be. At the *Resp14*
66/67 *stanza division ABY(7)*
67 I] At the first I *rev to* I *Harvard(1)* so — for that or this,] so for that or this — *Resp14*
68 a curst] a-cursed *Resp14*
69 kiss, *Resp14*

---

51 The comma after “blind” is very lightly inked.

[NLI 13,586(8) (a), 4v inverted]

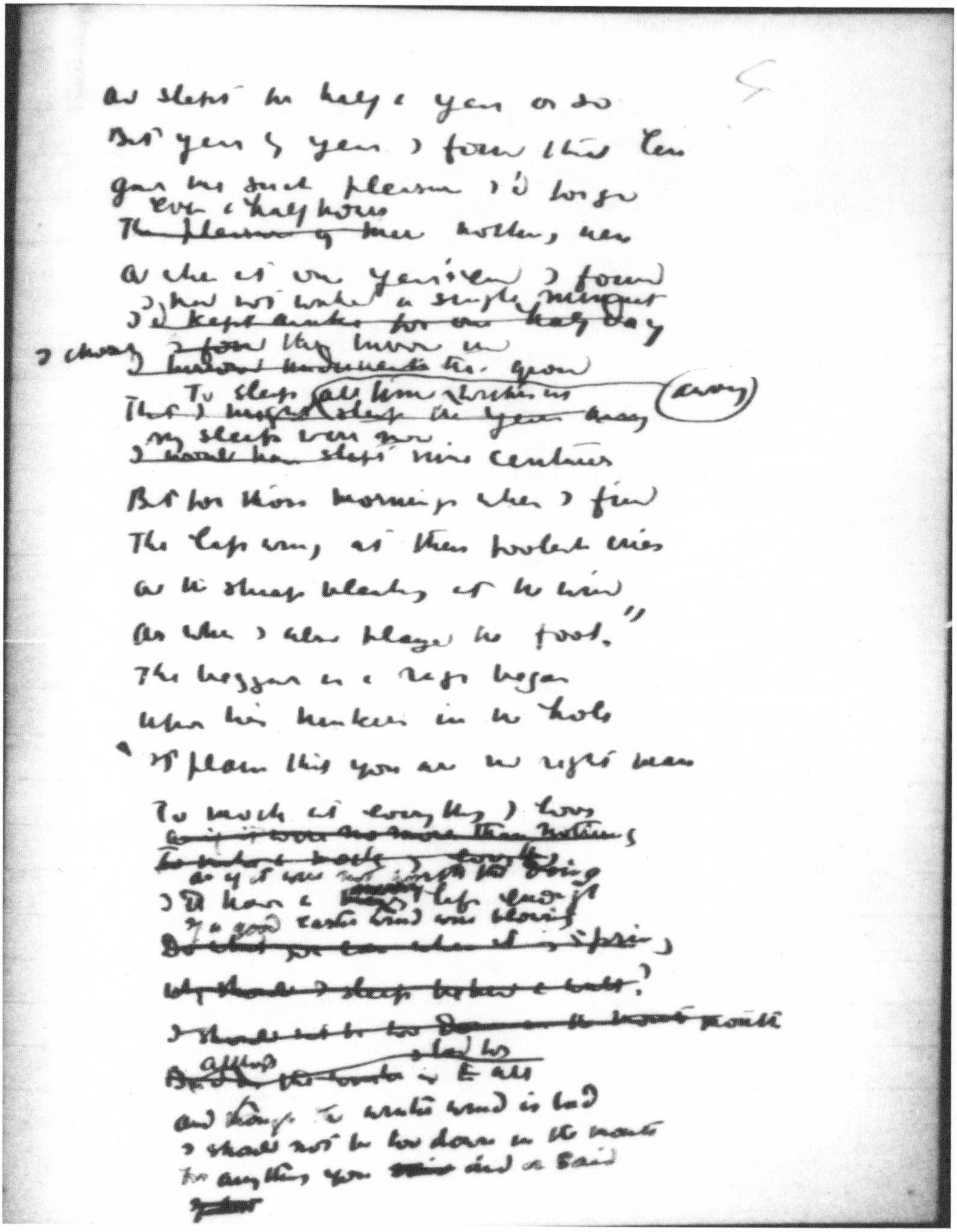

87/ doing. *Resp14*
88 I'd *Resp14*
89 blowing, *Resp14*

76 There is a stray mark between "the" and "ground".

[NLI 13,586(8) (a), 4v inverted]

4

70 And slept for half a year or so
71 But year by year I found that less
72 Gave me such pleasure I'd forgo
Even a half hours
73 ~~The pleasure of [?mere]~~ nothing ness
74 And when at one year's end I found
I had not waked a single minuet
75 I ~~d kept awake for one half day~~
I chose ~~I found~~ this burrow [?und]
76 ~~I burrowed underneath~~ the ground
To sleep all time within [?] away
77 ~~That I might sleep the years away~~
My sleep were now
78 ~~I would have slept~~ nine centuries
79 But for those mornings when I find
80 The lap wing at their foolish cries
81 And the sheep bleating at the wind
82 As when I also played the fool."
83 The beggar in a rage began
84 Upon his hunkers in the hole
85 "Its plain that you are no right man
86 To mock at every thing I love
~~As if it were no more than nothing~~
87 ~~To make a mock of every thing~~
As if it were not worth the doing
{d merry
88 I {ll have a [?~~merry~~] ^ life enough
If a good Easter wind were blowing
89 ~~Do what you can when it is Spring~~
90 ~~Why should I sleep behind a wall?~~
91 ~~I should not be too down in the mouth mouth~~
~~Although [?s] bad [?for]~~
92 ~~Bad as the winter is to all~~
93 And though the winter wind is bad
94 I should not be too down in the mouth
95 For anything you ~~said~~ did or said
96 ~~If [?but]~~

---

70 so; *Resp14*
72 forgo] forego *Resp14*
73 hour's nothingness, *Resp14*
75 minuet] minute *Resp14*
76 [?und]] under *Resp14*
77 To sleep] And sleep *Resp14* time within [?] Time within it, *Resp14*
80 lapwing *Resp14*
85 It's *Resp14*
86 everything *Resp14*

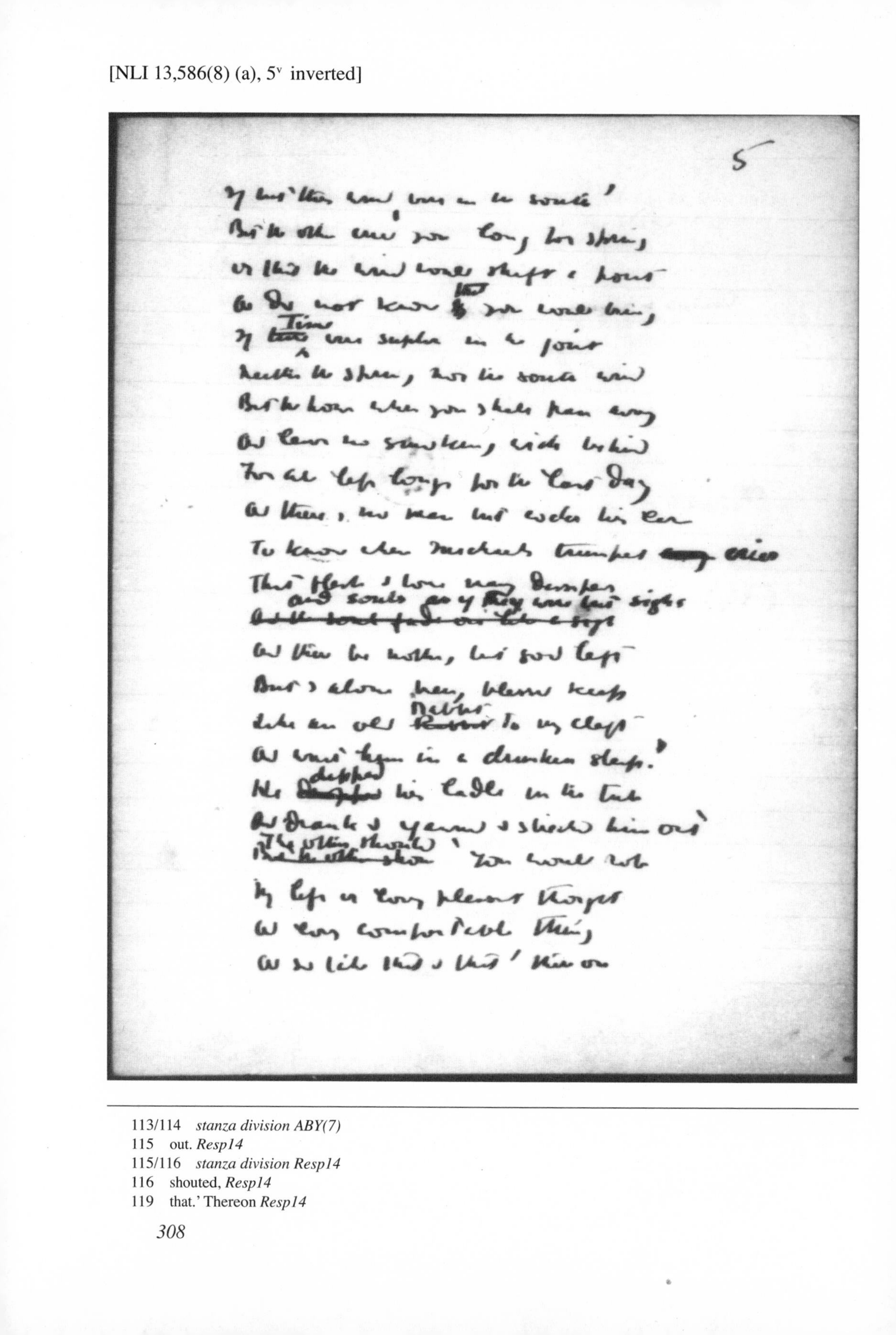

[NLI 13,586(8) (a), 5ᵛ inverted]

113/114 *stanza division ABY(7)*
115 out. *Resp14*
115/116 *stanza division Resp14*
116 shouted, *Resp14*
119 that.' Thereon *Resp14*

[NLI 13,586(8) (a), 5[v] inverted]

5

97 If but this wind were in the south'
98 But the other cried 'You long for Spring
99 Or that the wind would shift a point
that
100 And do not know ~~if~~ you would bring
Time
101 If ~~time~~ ^ were supler in the joint
102 Neither the Spring nor the south wind
103 But the hour when you shall pass away
104 And leave no smoking wick behind
105 For all life longs for the last day
106 And there s no man but cocks his ear
107 To know when Michaels trumpet ~~cry~~ cries
108 That flesh & bone may dissapear
And souls as if they were but sighs
109 ~~And the soul fade out like a sigh~~
110 And there be nothing but god left
111 But I alone being blessed keep
rabbit
112 Like some old ~~Rabbit~~ to my cleft
113 And wait him in a drunken sleep.{' ”
dipped
114 He ~~dropped~~ his ladle in the tub
115 And drank & yawned & stretched him out
The other shouted
116 ~~But the other shou~~ 'You would rob
117 My life of every pleasant thought
118 And every comfortable thing
119 And so take that & that' There on

97/98 *stanza division ABY(7)*
98 cried, *Resp14* spring *Resp14*
100 bring, *Resp14*
101 supler] suppler *Resp14* joint, *Resp14*
102 spring *Resp14*
104 behind, *Resp14*
105 Last Day *Resp14*
106 there's *Resp14*
107 Michaels trumpet] Michael's trumpets *rev to* Michael's trumpet *Harvard(1)* Michael's trumpets *Resp14* Michael's trumpets *rev to* Michael's trumpet *Emory(1)*
108 dissapear] disappear, *Resp14*
109 sighs, *Resp14*
110 God left; *Resp14*
112 cleft] cleft, *rev to* cleft; *Harvard(1)*
113 Him *Resp14*

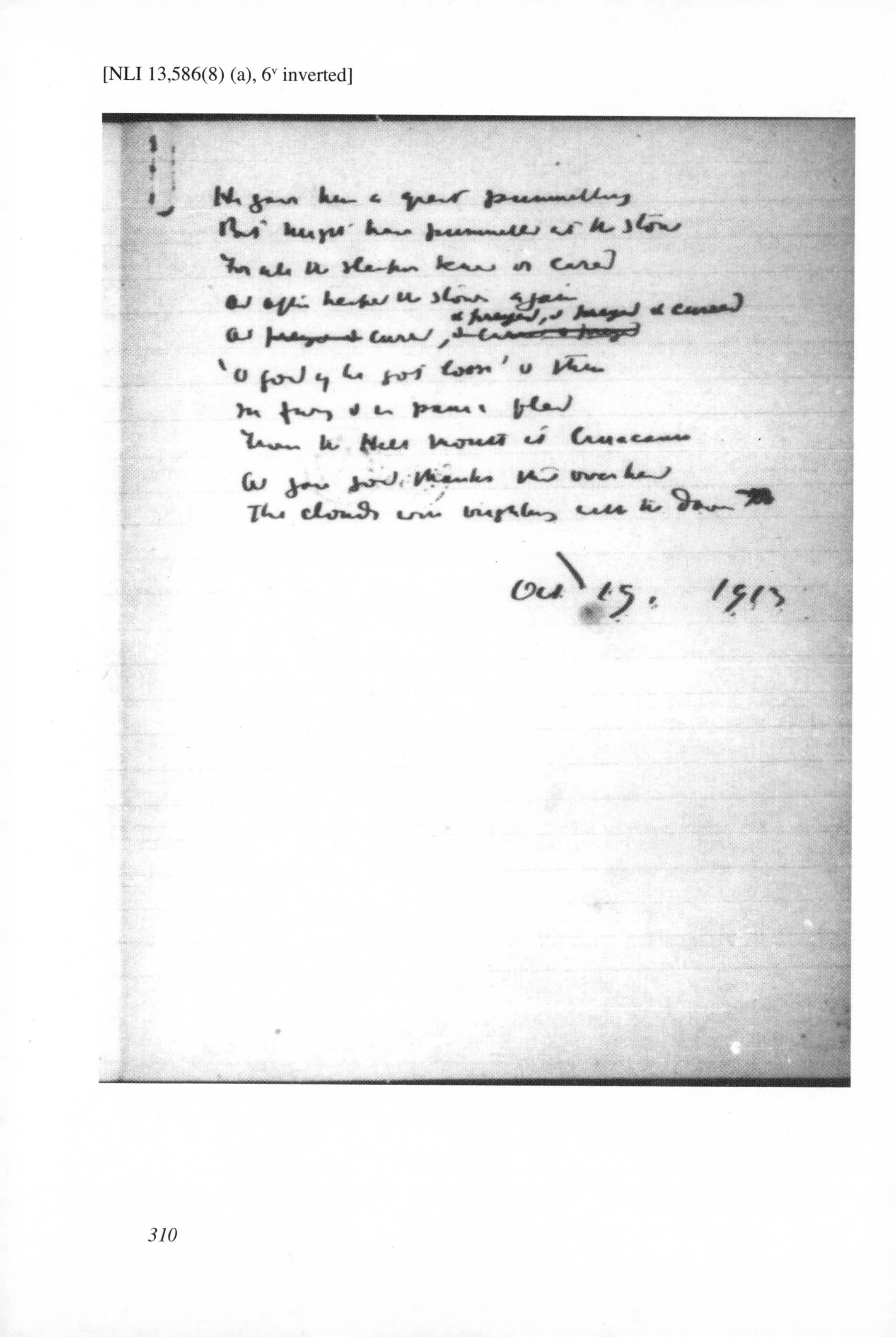

[NLI 13,586(8) (a), 6^{v} inverted]

[NLI 13,586(8) (a), 6^v inverted]

He gave him a great pummelling
But might have pummelled at the stone
For all the sleeper knew or cared
And after heaped the stones again
& preyed, & preyed & cursed
And ~~preyed &~~ cursed, ~~& cursed & preyed~~
‘ O God if he got loose’ & then
In fury & in panic fled
From the Hell Mouth at Cruacaun
And gave God thanks that overhead
The clouds were brightening with the dawn

Oct 19, 1913

---

120 pummelling, *Resp14*

122 cared; *Resp14*

123 And after heaped the stones again] And heaped upon [*rev (in thick green pencil ABY[4]) to* up] stone on stone again, *ABY(4), Berg(11)*

124 cursed and prayed, and prayed *Resp14*

125 O] Oh *Resp14* loose’ &] loose! And *Resp14*

127 Cruacaun] Cruachan *Resp14*

129 dawn. *Resp14*

[NLI 13,586(8) (b), 1]

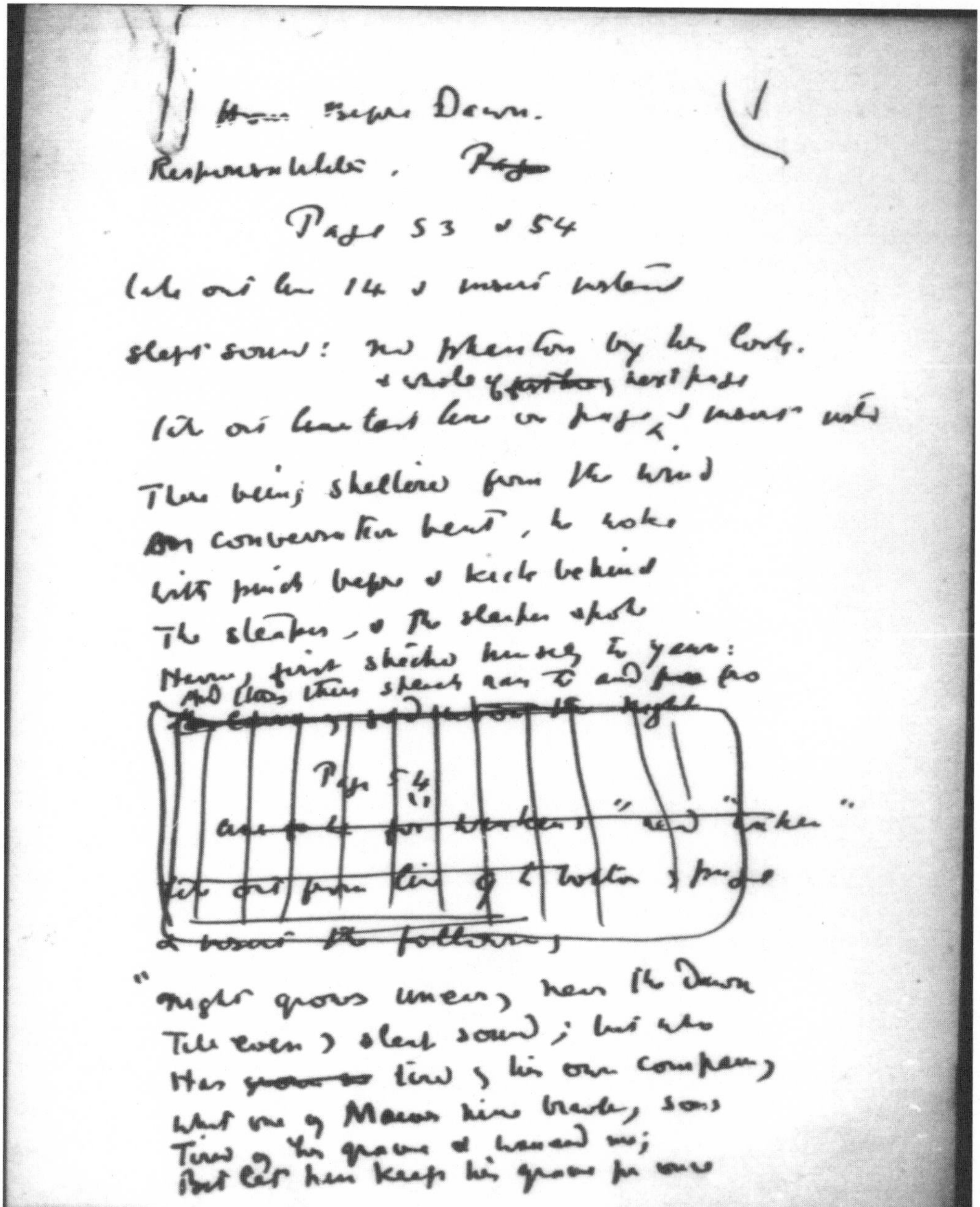

[NLI 13,586(8) (b), 1]

Hour Before Dawn. 1
Responsibilities. ~~Page~~
Page 53 & 54
take out line 14 & insert instead

1 slept sound: no phamtom by his look.
& whole of ~~first lines~~ next page
take out ~~lines~~ tast line on page ^ & insert instead

2 There being sheltered from the wind
3 On conversation bent, he woke
4 With pinch before & kick behind
5 The sleaper, & the sleeper spoke
6 Having first streched himself to yawn:
7 And thus their speech ran to and [?~~fro~~] fro
8 The curse of god upon the night

Page 54
line ~~fo~~ 4 for "wakens" read "waken"
take out from line 9 to bottom of page
& insert the following

9 "Night grows uneasy near the dawn
10 Till even I sleep sound; but who
11 Has ~~grown so~~ tired of his own company
12 What one of Maeves nine brawling sons
13 Tired of his grave & [?wakened] me;
14 But let him keep his grave for once

The following is a supplementary collation of NLI 13,586(8) (b) with the closely related ink revisions, in Yeats's hand, written in *ABY(3)* and with an ink revision on NLI 30,009, a later page proof; it is in addition to the collation on pp. 301, 303, 305, 307, 309, 311 above.

1/2 *lacking*] *horizontal rule above the ink-canceled last line of p. 53, with notation in right margin for a stanza division:* N.P *ABY(3)*

2–8/ *lacking in ABY(3)*

10 sound;] light *ABY(3)*

11 company? *ABY(3)*

12 Maeve's *ABY(3)*

13 [?wakened]] wakened *ABY(3)*

These revisions are keyed to the printed text of *Responsibilites and Other Poems* (London and New York: Macmillan, 1916) (Wade 115, 116); they were adopted in *Later Poems* (London: Macmillan, 1922) (Wade 134).

3 "On" is partially obscured by a blot and is not canceled.

[NLI 13,586(8) (b), 2]

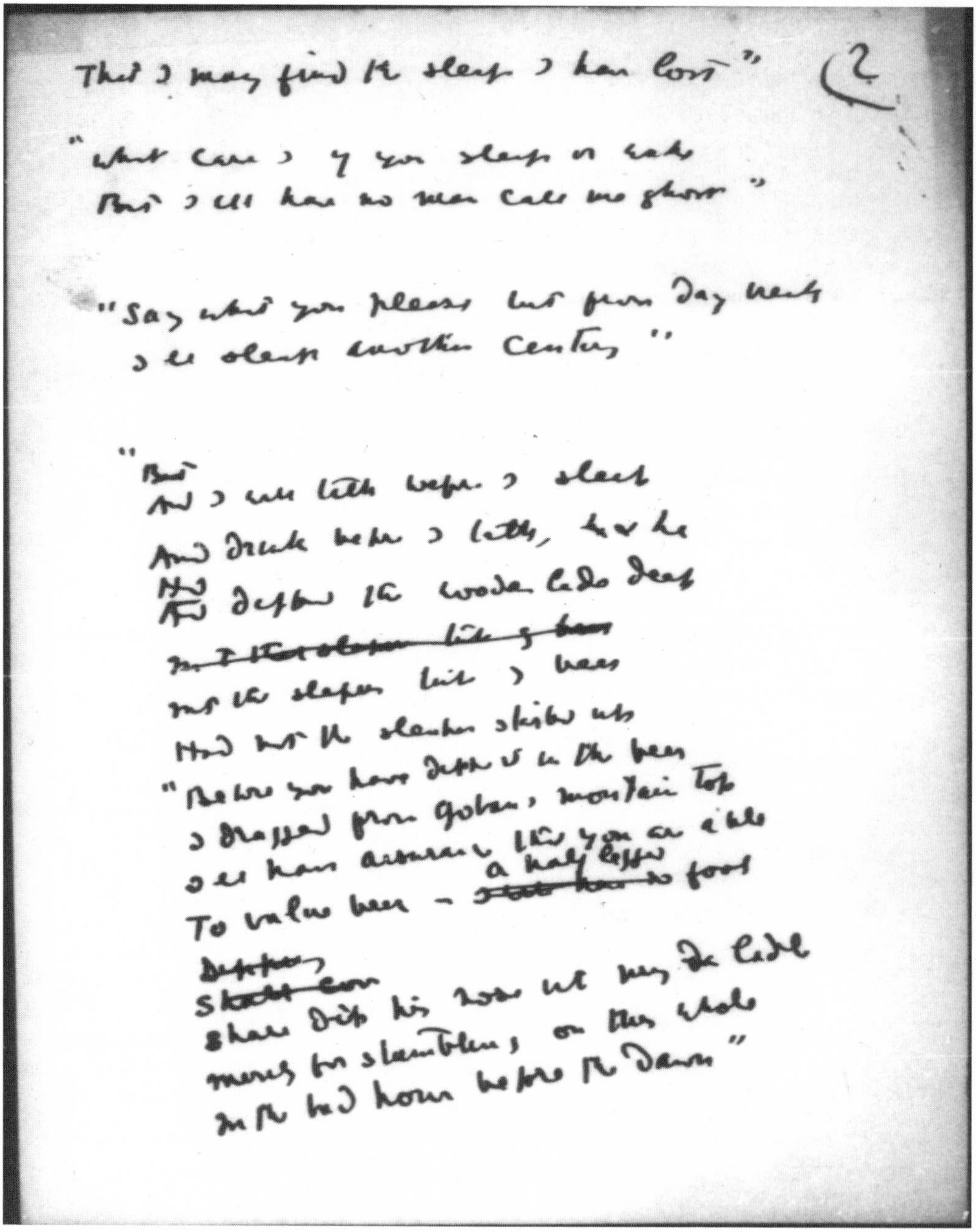

[NLI 13,586(8) (b), 2]

15 That I may find the sleep I have lost" 2

16 "What care I if you sleep or wake
17 But I ll have no man call me ghost"

18 "Say what you please but from day break
19 I ll sleep another century"

"~~But~~
20 And I will talk before I sleep
21 And drink before I talk, ~~he~~ & he
Had
22 ~~And~~ dipped the wooden lade deep
~~In to that slepers tub of beer~~
23 Into the slepers tub of beer
24 Had not the sleeper started up
25 "Before you have dipped it in the beer
26 I dragged from Gobans montain top
27 I ll have assurance that you are able
a half legged
28 To value beer — ~~I will have no~~ fool
~~Dipping~~
~~Shall [?]~~
29 Shall dip his nose into my [~~?~~] ladle
30 Merely for stumbling on this whole
31 In the bad hour before the dawn"

---

15 lost.' *ABY(3)*
15/16 *blank line*] *horizontal rule at left ABY(3)*
16 wake *rev to* wake? *NLI 30,009*
17 I'll *ABY(3)*
17/18 *blank line*] *horizontal rule at left ABY(3)*
18 "Say] 'Stay day break] day-break *ABY(3)*
19 century"] century *ABY(3)*
19/20 *blank line*] *horizontal rule at left ABY(3)*
21 talk, & he] talk' / [*deeply indented*] And he *ABY(3)*
22 lade] ladle *ABY(3)*
23 slepers] sleepers *ABY(3)*
24 up. *ABY(3)*
24/25 *no stanza division*] *horizontal rule at left ABY(3)*
28 beer — a half] beer [?] no half *ABY(3)*

[NLI 13,586(8) (b), 3]

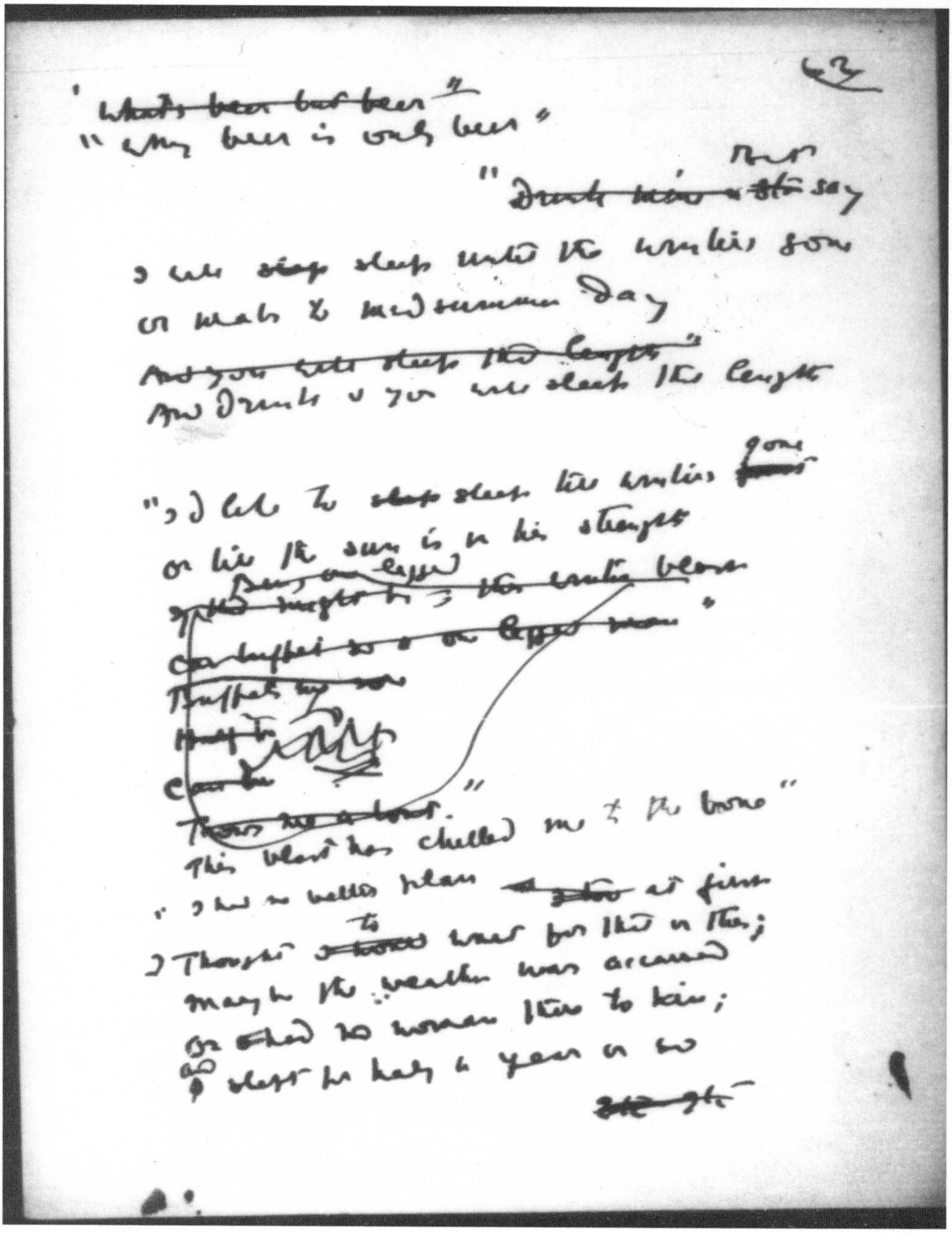
"Why beer is only beer"

say

I will sleep sleep until the winter's gone

Or walk to Midsummer Day

And drunk or you will sleep the length

", I will to sleep sleep till the winter's gone

Or till the sun is in his strength

This blast has chilled me to the bone"

I had no better plan at first

I thought to wait for this or that;

Maybe the weather was accursed

Or I had no woman there to kiss;

So slept for half a year or so

[NLI 13,586(8) (b), 3]

‘ ~~Whats beer but beer”~~ 3

32 “ Why beer is only beer”

[?But]

“~~Drink mine & [?]~~ say

33 I will ~~slep~~ sleep until the winters gone

34 Or may be to midsummer day

~~And you will sleep that length”~~

35 And drink & you will sleep that length

gone

36 “ Id like to ~~slep~~ sleep till winters ~~past~~

37 Or till the sun is in his strength

Being one legged

38 If that might be —, this winter blasts

39 Can buffet so a one legged man”

40 Buffets me sore

41 Half [?]

42 Can be —

43 Trows me a bout.”

44 This blast has chilled me to the bone”

45 “ I had no better plan

to ~~“I too~~ at first

46 I Thought ~~I would~~ wait for that or this;

47 Maybe the weather was accursed

48 Or I had no woman there to kiss;

And

49 ~~I~~ slept for half a year or so

~~Etc Etc~~

---

33 gone] gone, *ABY(3)*
35 length] length’ *ABY(3)*
44 bone”] bone. *ABY(3)*
44/45 *probable stanza division*] *horizontal rule at left ABY(3)*
46 this;] this, *ABY(3)*
47 accursed] *the printed text (*“a-cursed”*) is left unrevised ABY(3)*
48 kiss;] *the printed text (*“kiss,”*) is left unrevised ABY(3)*
49 so] the printed text (“so;”*) is left unrevised ABY(3)*

The following ink revisions, in Yeats’s hand, written in ABY(3), p. 56, are not extant in NLI 13,586(8) (b):

ll. 1/2 NP *horizontal rule*
ll. 12/13 NP *horizontal rule*
l. 13 But the other cried, ‘You long for spring *rev to* ‘You cry aloud O would I’ [*or perhaps* it] were spring

---

49 “I” is partially obscured by a blot and is not canceled.

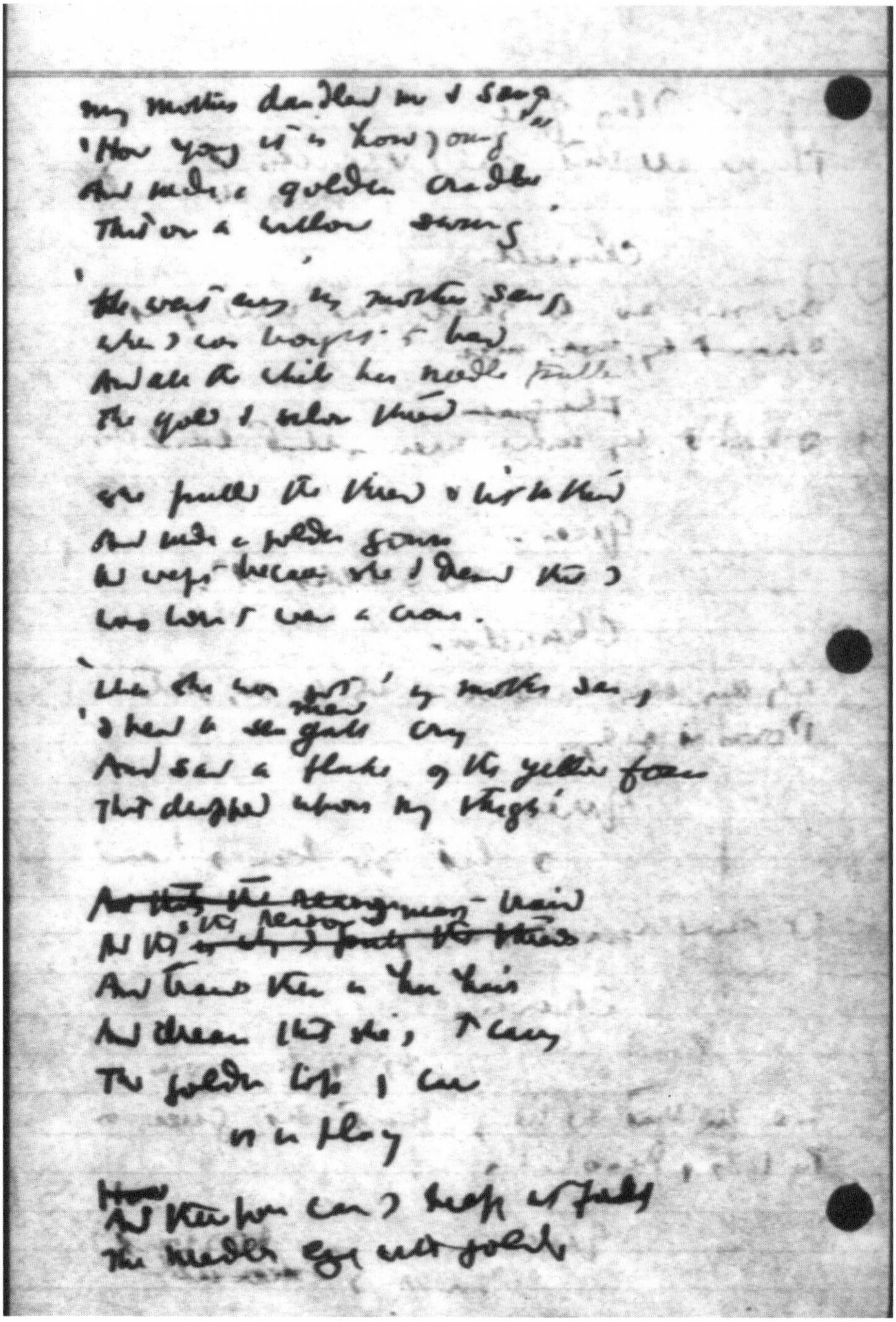

[NLI 8764(5), 27v]

The recto of the next leaf in the manuscript does not continue the song, but a note on the verso of that next leaf suggests the the song was written during a revision of the rectos of this manuscript. The note, which is the only writing on that verso, reads: “The line about fortunes hair should be put in rhyme & sung”.

THE PLAYER QUEEN (SONG FROM AN UNFINISHED PLAY)
[A SONG FROM 'THE PLAYER QUEEN']

[NLI 8764(5), 27v]

My mother dandled me & sang
'How young it is how young'"
And made a golden cradle
That on a willow swung'

' He went away my mother sang
When I was brought to bed
And all the while her needle pulled
The gold & silver thread

She pulled the thread & bit [?the] thread
And made a golden gown
And wept because she d dreamed that I
Was born to wear a crown.

' When she was got' my mother san g
mew
' I heard a sea gull cry
And saw a flake of the yellow foam
That dropped upon my thigh'

~~And thats the reason~~
I
s the reason { I must braid
And that ~~is why I pull the threads~~
And [?braids] them in her hair
And dream that she s to carry
The golden top of care
[?or in] play

[~~?~~]
And therefore can I [?keep at full]
The needles eye with gold,

---

found in NLI 8764(5) *transcribed above*
NLI 8764(5), 11
NLI 8764(6), 11–12
NLI 8764(7), 20–21
NLI 8764(7), 21
NLI 8764(8), 8, 10
NLI 8764(11)
NLI 8764(7), 9–10
NLI 8764(10), 19–20
Bradford, *Writing of* The Player Queen
NLI 30,286, 31
NLI 13,586(9) (a), (b) *transcribed below*
Harvard(1)

published in *Poetry* (Chicago), May 1914
Resp14

[NLI 13,586(9) (a)[r]]

1.

My mother dandled me & sang
'How young it is how young
And made a golden cradle
That on a willow swung.

2

My mother said, he went away
When I was brought to bed
But all the while her needle pulled
The gold & silver thread

3

She pulled the thread & bit the thread
And made a golden gown
But wept because she had dreamt that I
Was born to wear a crown.

[NLI 13,586(9) (a)[r]]

1.

My mother dandled me & sang
  'How young it is how young
And made a golden cradle
  That on a willow swung.

2

My mother sang he went away
  When I was brought to bed
But all the while her needle pulled
  The gold & silver thread

3

{S
The pulled the thread & bit the thread
  And made a golden gown
But cried because she had dreamt that I
  Was born to wear a crown.

No stanza numbering in any other texts

Even-numbered lines not indented in any other texts

Title *untitled*] THE PLAYER QUEEN / *Song from an Unfinished Play. P* THE PLAYER QUEEN / (Song from an Unfinished Play) *Resp14*

1–4 *lacking in NLI 8764(6), NLI 8764(7) (a, b), NLI 8764(11), NLI 8764(7) (c), NLI 8764(10)*

1–4 *Decima (putting on dress, sings). /* My mother dandled me and sang / How young it is, how young / And made a golden cradle / That on a willow swung. *Bradford pp. 378–379* [*similar to NLI 8764(8) (b)*]

1 dandled] dangled *NLI 8764(10)* sang, *P, Resp14*

2 'How] How *NLI 8764(8), NLI 8764(10)* is, *NLI 8764(10), P, Resp14* young, *NLI 8764(10)* young!' *P, Resp14*

3 And made] That made *NLI 8764(8)*

5 My mother sang he went away] He ['He *NLI 8764(7) (a), NLI 8764(11), P, Resp14*] went away [away, *NLI 8764(8), NLI 8764(7) (c)* away" *NLI 8764(11)* away," *P* away,' *Resp14*] my mother sang [sang, *P, Resp14*] *NLI 8764(6), NLI 8764(7) (a, b), NLI 8764(8), NLI 8764(11), NLI 8764(7) (c), NLI 764(10)*

6 When] "When *P* 'When *Resp14* bed] bed" *NLI 8764(7) (b)* bed;" *P* bed,' *Rsep14*

7 But] And *NLI 8764(6), NLI 8764(7) (b), NLI 8764(11), NLI 8764(7) (c), P, Resp14*

8 gold] golden *NLI 8764(7) (a)* thread] thread. *NLI 8764(7) (a), NLI 8764(7) (c), NLI 8764(10), P, Resp14* thread." *NLI 8764(11)*

8/9 *stanza division NLI 8764(7) (c), NLI 8764(10)*

9–10 *Decima (singing). /* She pulled the thread, and bit the thread / And made a golden gown. *Bradford, p. 392*

10 gown. *NLI 8746(10)* gown, *P, Resp14*

11 But cried] She wept *NLI 8764(6), NLI 8764(7) (a, b), NLI 8764(11), NLI 8764(7) (c), NLI 8764(10), NLI 30286* She dreamed *NLI 8764(8)* had dreamt] had dreamed *NLI 8764(6), NLI 8764(8), NLI 8764(7) (c)* 'She wept because she dreamed that I *NLI 8764, fol.10)* And wept because she'd dreamt that I *P, Resp14*

11–12 *Decima (singing). /* She wept because she dreamt that I / Was born to wear a crown. *Bradford p. 393*

12 crown.' *NLI 8764(8, fol. 10)*

[NLI 13,586(9) (b)[r]]

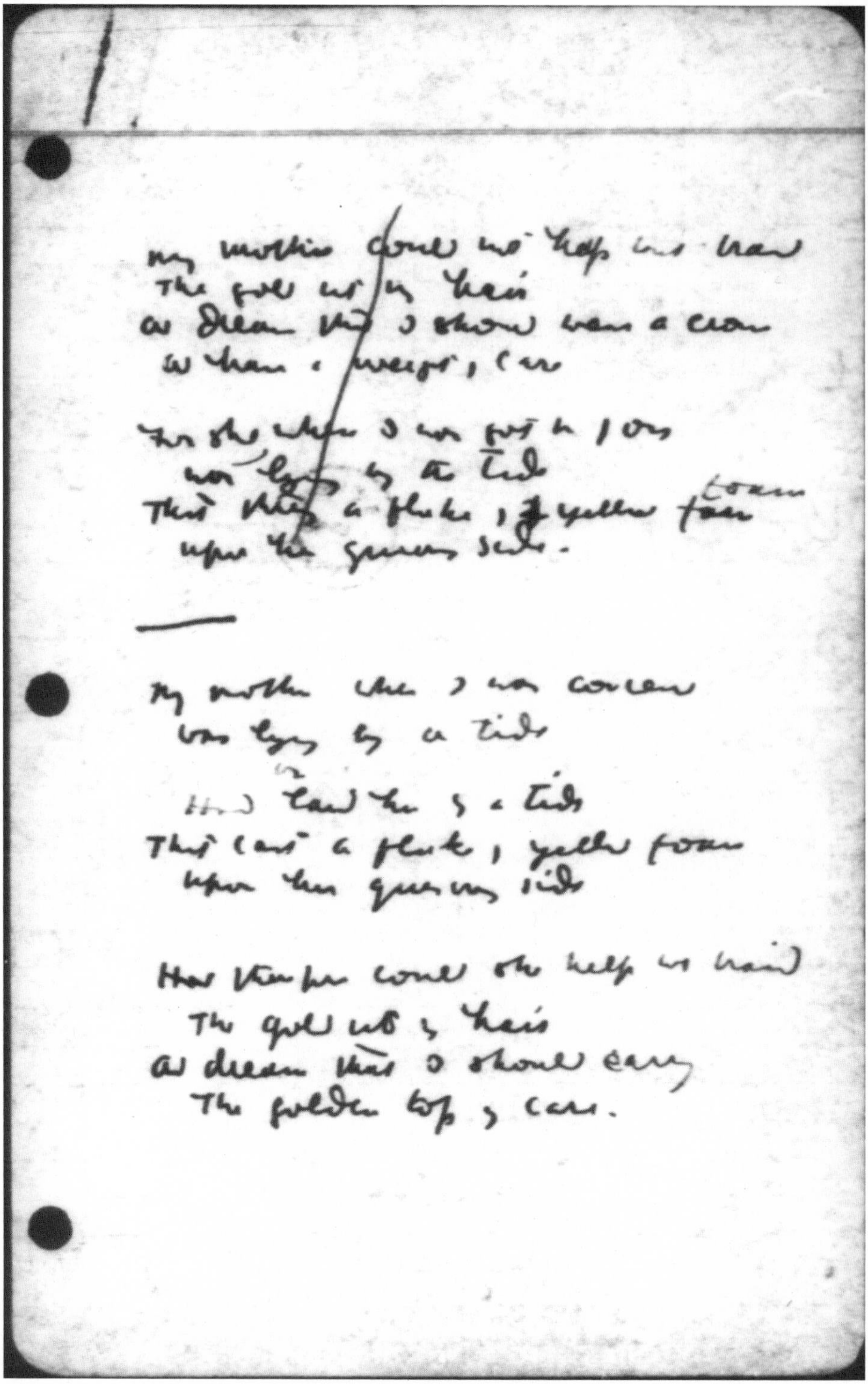

[NLI 13,586(9) (b)[r]]

My mother could not help but braid
   The gold into my hair
And dream that I should wear a crown
   And have a weight of care

For she, when I was got [?in] joy
   was lying by the tide
                                        foam
That [?threw] a flake of ~~f~~ yellow [?~~fom~~]
   Upon her [?quivering] side.

———

13 My mother when I was conceived
14   Was lying by a tide
         or
   Had laid her by a tide
15 That cast a flake of yellow foam
16   Upon her [?quivering] side

17 How therefore could she help [?but] braid
18   The gold into my hair
19 And dream that I should carry
20   The golden top of care.

---

13 My mother when I was conceived] [It is *rev to* is *NLI 8764(5) in the left margin with no indication of how to be used*] 'When [When *NLI 8764(7) (a, c)* When *rev in ink to* 'When *Harvard(1)*] she was got' [got, *NLI 8764(7) (a)* got *NLI 8764(7) (c), rev in ink to* got' *Harvard(1)* got," *P*] my mother sang [sang, *P, Resp14*] *NLI 8764(6), NLI 8764(7) (a), NLI 8764(8), NLI 8764(11), NLI 8764(7) (c), NLI 8764(10), Harvard(1), P, Resp14*

14 Was lying by a tide / or / Had laid her by a tide] Had laid her by the tide *NLI 8764(5), [11]* 'I [I *NLI 8764(7) (a, b, c)*] heard a sea mew [sea [?mew] *NLI8764(7) (a) (added, in pencil probably in Yeats's hand, where the typist left two blank spaces)* seamew *NLI8764(7) (b)* sea-mew *NLI 8764(7) (c), P, Resp14*] cry [cry. *NLI 8764(6)* cry, *P, Resp14*] *NLI 8764(6), NLI 8764(7) (a, b, c), NLI 8764(11), NLI 8764(10), P, Resp14*

15 That cast a flake of yellow foam] And saw [I saw *NLI 8764(8), NLI 8764(11), NLI 8764(7) (c), NLI 8764(10)*] a flake of yellow foam [form *NLI 8764(7) (a)*] *NLI 8764(6), NLI 8764(7) (a, b), NLI 8764(8), NLI 8764(11), NLI 8764(7) (c), NLI 8764(10), P, Resp14*

16 Upon her [?quivering] side] Upon her [?groaning] side. *NLI 8764(5, fol. 11)* [*Bradford, p. 264, has "Upon her quivering side."*] That dropped [dripped *NLI 8764(7) (c)*] upon my [thigh *NLI 8764(6), NLI 8764(11)*] thigh.' *NLI 8764(10)*] *NLI 8764(6), NLI 8764(7)[a], NLI 8764(8), NLI 8764(11), NLI 8764(7) (c), NLI 8764(10), Resp14* thigh." *P*

17 [?but]] but *NLI 8764(5, fol. 11), NLI 8764(6), NLI 8764(7) (a, b) NLI 8764(8), NLI 8764(11), NLI 8764(7) (c), NLI 8764(10), P, Resp14* braid] fill *NLI 8764(5) [11]* pray *NLI 8764(7)[a]*

18 into] upon *NLI 8764(8), NLI 8764(11), NLI 8764(7) (c), NLI 8764(10)* hair, *P, Resp14* [*NLI 8764(5, fol. 11) reads:* Her needle's eye with gold]

20 care" *NLI 8764(11)* care? *P, Resp14*

The two canceled stanzas at the top of the page are, respectively, drafts of ll. 17–20 and 13–16 here.

[NLI 13,586(10) (a), 2r (inverted)]

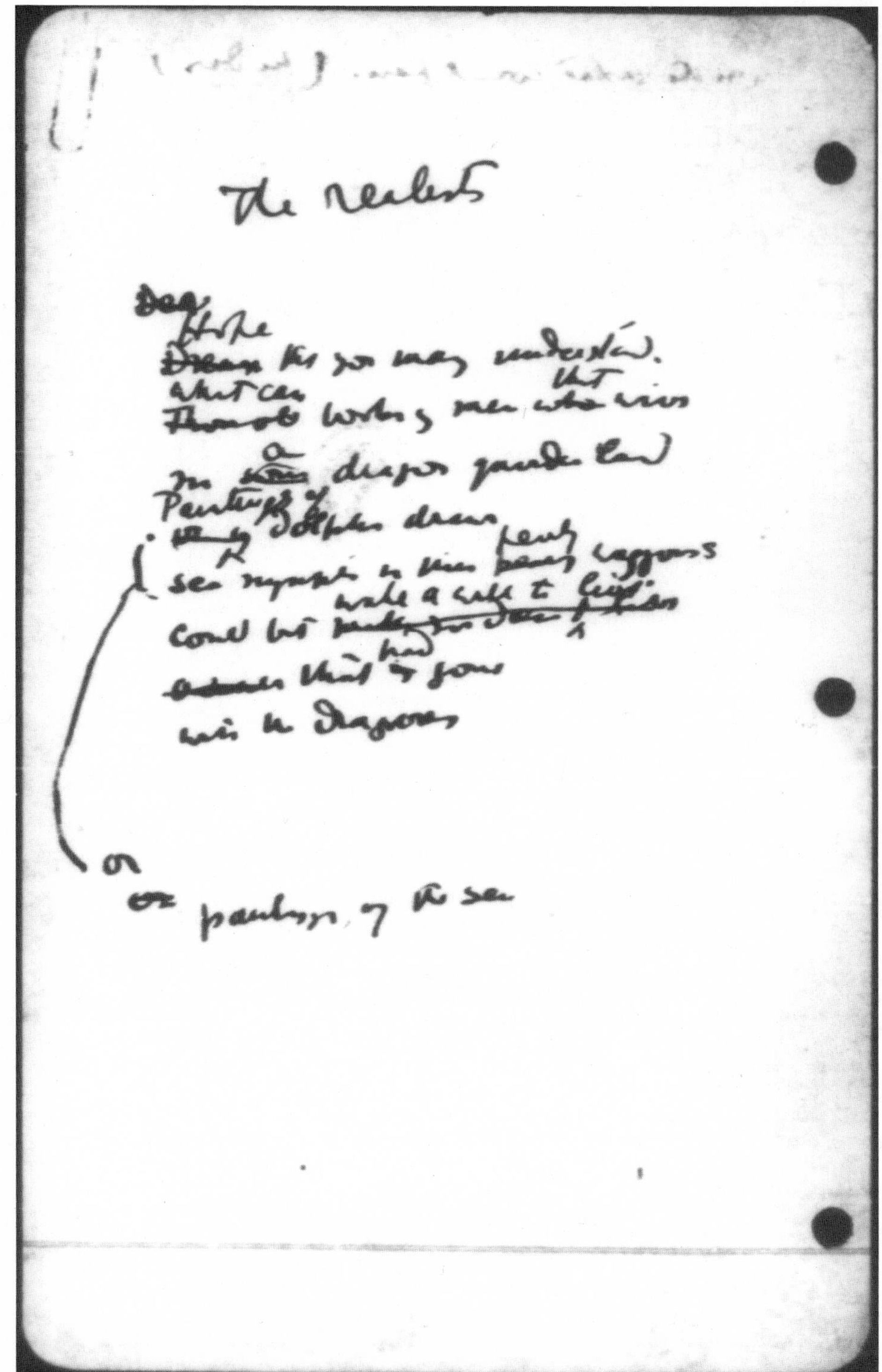

THE REALISTS

[NLI 13,586(10) (a), 2r (inverted)]

The realists

{[?] { [?]
{~~De~~ { ~~[?]~~

Hope
1 ~~Dream~~ that you may understand.
What can that
2 ~~Those old~~ books of men ~~who~~ wive
a
3 In ~~some~~ dragon guarded land
Paintings of
4 ~~Or of~~ ^ dolphin drawn
pearly
5 Sea nymphs in their ~~peary~~ waggons
wake a will to live
6 Could but ~~make you [?dare] [?to] live~~ ^
had
7 ~~And all~~ that ~~is~~ gone
8 With the dragons

9 or
10 ~~or~~
11 [?paintings], of the sea

---

found in NLI 13,586(10) (a), 2r (inverted) *transcribed above*
NLI 13,586(10) (a), 1v (inverted) *transcribed below*
Chicago(2), 3 *transcribed below*
Harvard(1)
published in *Poetry* (Chicago), December 1912
Resp14

---

11 The comma is very lightly inked but does not seem to be a stray mark.

The verso (inverted) of this sheet has a note that could be related to the note on the verso (inverted) of NLI 13,586(10) (a), [1]v (inverted) and/or to this poem: "On the [?instant come to pass]. (he [?dies])".

[NLI 13,586(10) (a), 1ᵛ (inverted)]

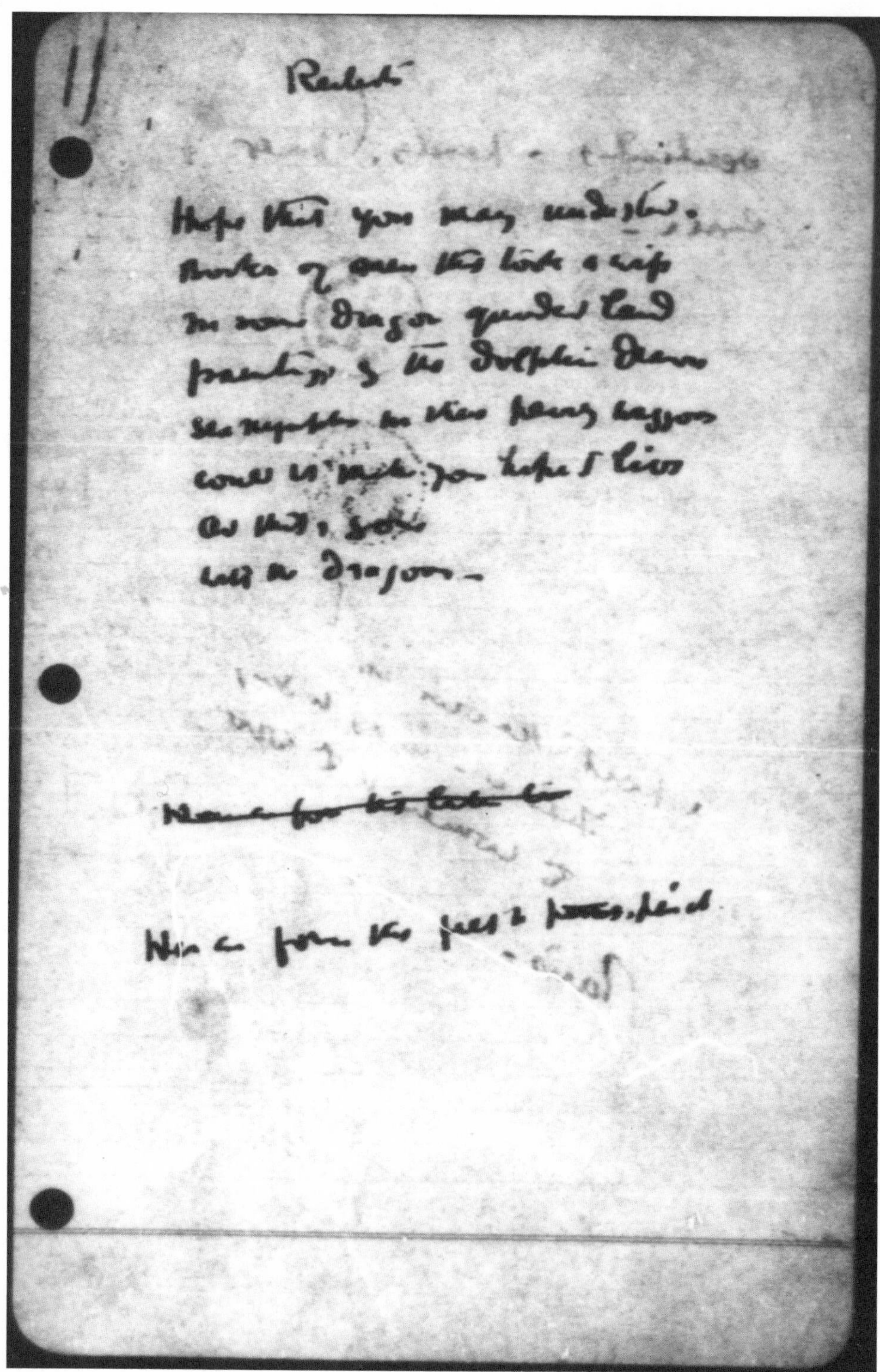

[NLI 13,586(10) (a), 1^{v} (inverted)]

Realists

Hope that you may understand.
Books of men that took a wife
In some dragon guarded land
Paintings of the dolphin drawn
Sea nymphs in their pearly waggons
Could not make you hope to live
And that s gone
With the dragons —

~~[?Here a form that later] [?]~~

[?Has an] form that [?felt the] [~~?~~], [?pinch]

The recto (inverted) of this sheet has a note that could be related to the note on the verso (inverted) of NLI 13,586(10) (a), $[2]^{r}$ (inverted) and/or to this poem: "[?ecentricity] — [?painters], [?poets] / lyric — / a poet [?known] in / France — used to be sung / to women & [?to] wine / Paris — ".

(3

I sat as silent as a stone
And knew, though she'd not said a word,
That even the best of love must die,
And had been savagely undone
Were it not that love, upon the cry
Of a most ridiculous little bird,
Threw up in the his marvellous moon.

up in

THE REALISTS

Hope that you may understand.
What can books, of men that wive
In a dragon-guarded land,
Paintings of the dolphin drawn;
Sea nymphs, in their pearly waggons,
Do but wake the hope to live
That had gone
With the dragons.

I have had to correct the punctuation in a great hurry to catch the first post. I would be very obliged if you would revise the punctuation.

W B Yeats

[Chicago(2), 3]

{I
THE REAL (STS

Hope that you may understand .
What can books , of men that wive
{n
In a dragon–guarded land ,;
{n
Paintings of the dolphim drawn ;
Sea nymphs , in their pearly waggons ,
Do but wake the hope to live
That had gone
With the dragons .

---

1 understand! *R14*
2 books *R14*
3 land; *P*; land, *rev. in ink to* land *and then restored to* land, *Harvard(1)*; land, *R14*
4 dolphin-drawn *R14*
5 Sea-nymphs *R14* waggons *R14*
6 Do but wake the hope] Do, but awake a hope *R14*
8 dragons? *R14*
8/ *no signature*] William Butler Yeats *P*

---

title, 1, 3–5 Corrected letters and all punctuation are added in ink.

Bottom margin, in ink, in Yeats's hand: "I have had to correct & punctuate in a great hurry / to catch the first post. I would be much obliged if / you would revise the punctuation / W B Yeats".

[NLI 13,586(11), 1r]

THE WITCH

[NLI 13,586(11), 1r]

{W
~~He~~ {~~who [?toils] toils to~~ grow rich
~~Shall all the night~~ lie
~~Shall lie~~
~~[?With a foul~~ witch
~~And after [?]~~
Who toils to grow rich
All night shall lie
With a foul witch
And after be brought
Worn out & drained [?~~driy~~] dri
To a lady fair
Long loved & saught
With despair.

Toil & grow rich
No that is to lie — What that but to lie
With a foul witch
~~That I may be brought.~~
~~And after be~~
And then be brought — And after be brought
Weary & drained dry — ~~weary~~
To a lady fair
Long loved & long saught — Long loved & saught
With despair.

---

found in NLI 13,586(11), 1r *transcribed above*
NLI 13,586(11), 1v (inverted) *transcribed below*
NLI 30,358, 33r–33v *transcribed below*
Boston College *transcribed below*
Harvard(1) *transcribed below*
published in *Poetry* (Chicago), May 1914
Resp14

[NLI 13,586(11), 1v (inverted)]

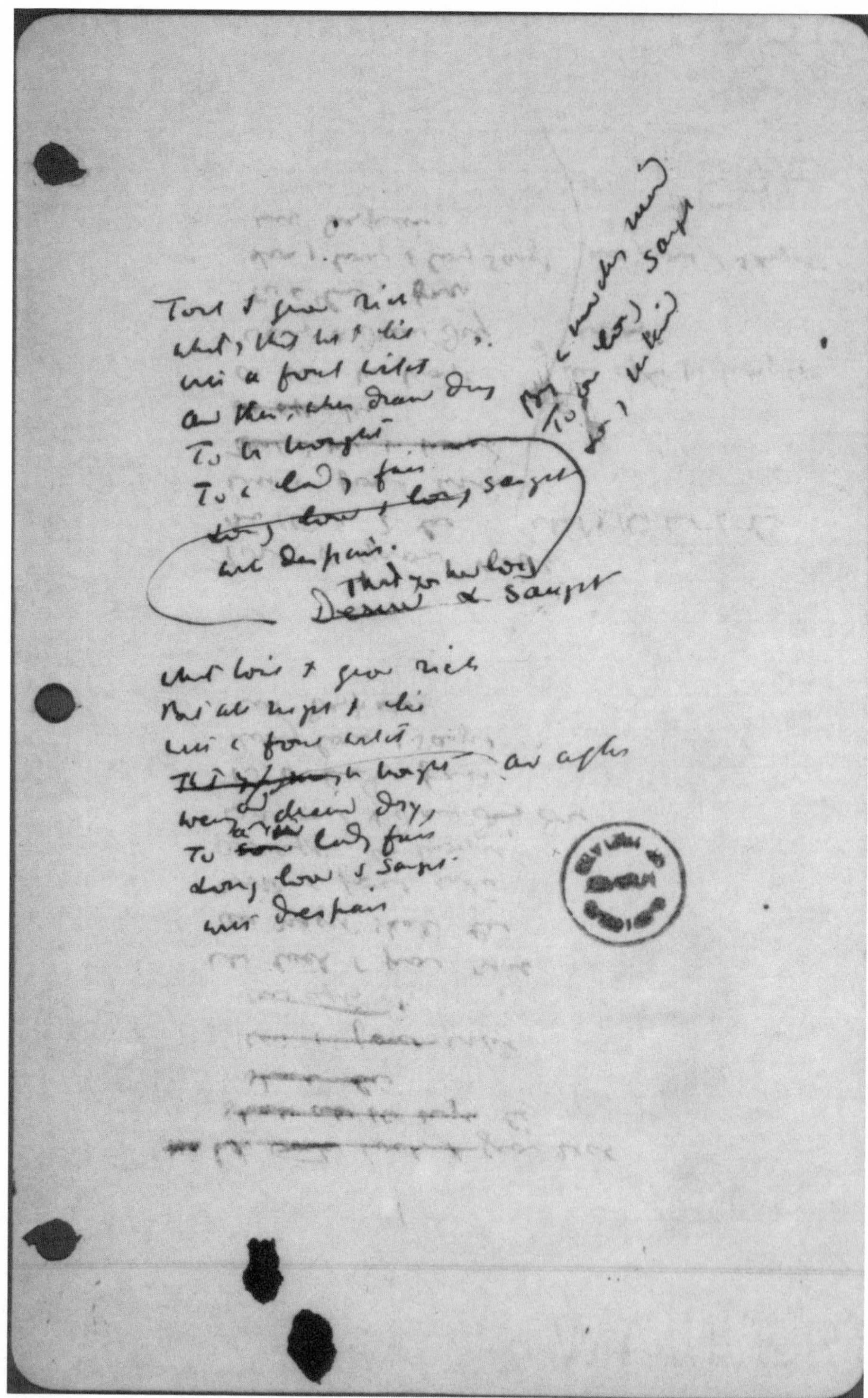

[NLI 13,586(11), 1v (inverted)]

Toil & grow rich
Whats that but to lie
With a foul witch
And then, when drained dry
To be brought
To a lady fair
~~Long loved & long~~ saught
With despair.
That you had long
~~Desired &~~ saught

By a [?]ing maid
To one long saugh
Long unkind

What toil to grow rich
But all night to lie
With a foul witch
~~That you may~~ be brought And after
and
Weary ^ drained dry,
a ~~the~~
To ~~some~~ lady fair
Long loved & saught
With despair

4 The unintelligible word "[?]ing" has a total of about seven letters; it is not "raunchy," "randy," "chamber," "mincing," or "modest."

[NLI 30,358, 33[r]]

[NLI 30,358, 33^{r}]

Toil & grow rich
Whats that but to lie
        ~~a [?]~~ some stale bitch   ~~or~~
With a ~~foul [?witch] witch~~
    then when
And ~~after~~ drained dry (and after drained dry)
To be brought
To the chamber where
Lies one long saught
With despair.

The spacing suggests that 33^{v} could perhaps be a second stanza of the poem.

[NLI 30,358, 33^{v}; Boston College, 88^{r}]

[NLI 30,358, 33^{v}]

9 She has us by the throat
10 She'll make an end of us
11 Unless God grant a [?vote]
12 Or grant an incubus
Nov [?~~18~~] 16.

[Boston College, 88^{r}]

1 To Toil and grow rich
2 Is all night to lie
3 With a ~~Fowl~~ foul [?witch]
4 And after be brought
5 [?Weary] [?&] drained dry
6 To a lady fair
7 Long loved & saught
8 With despair.

Toil & grow rich
What's that but to lie
With a foul with
And then when drayned dry
To be brought
To a lady fair
Long loved & long saght
With despair.

[Harvard(1), 27, no photograph]

37

~~I~~

THE WITCH

1 **Toil and grow rich,**
2 **What's that but to lie**
3 **With a foul witch**
4 **And after, drained dry,**
5 **To be brought**
6 **To the chamber where**
7 **Lies one long sought**
8 **With despair.**

[Boston College, 88^{r}]
2 The apostrophe in "what's" is very faint.
The verso of this page has an entry dated "Oct 1912".

[Harvard(1), 27]
title I / THE WITCH *Resp14*

I have been so busy with 'Theatre of Beauty' that I have not worked for some days on your notes though I have been reading for them. I wrote a little song, I wrote it the day before yesterday,

What's riches to him
who has made a great Peacock
with the Pride of his Eye.
The wind-beaten, stone gray,
And desolate Three-Rock
Would nourish his whim.
Live he or die
amid wet rocks & heather
His ghost would be gay
adding feather to feather
For the Pride of his Eye.

I dont know why I put capitals to 'Pride of the Eye' — it is an error

THE PEACOCK

[Berg(12), 2^r]

What s richness to him
Who has made a great Pea cock
{E
With the Pride of his {eye.
beaten
The wind–[?~~beating~~], stone gray
And desolate Three–Rock
Would nourish his whim.
Live he or die
amid wet rocks & heather
His ghost would be gay
Adding feather to feather
For the Pride of his Eye.

[Harvard(1), 27, no photograph]

37

~~II~~

THE PEACOCK

What's riches to him
That has made a great peacock
With the pride of his eye?
The wind–beaten, stone–grey,
And desolate Three–rock
Would nourish his whim, ;/
Live he or die
Between rock and wet heather,
His ghost will be gay
Adding feather to feather
For the pride of his eye.

---

found in Berg(12) *transcribed above*
Harvard(1) *transcribed above*
Berg(6) (b)
published in *Poetry* (Chicago), May 1914
Resp14

---

title THE PEACOCK *P* II / THE PEACOCK *Resp14*
6 whim;] whim, *rev to* whim. *Berg(6) (b)* whim. *Resp14*
8 Amid *P, Resp14*

In Berg(12), 2^r, Yeats commented above the poem, "I wrote a little scrap of verse the day before yesterday"; immediately below the poem, he wrote, "I dont know why I put capitals [?P] 'Pride of [?~~the~~] his Eye' — it is an error" (see ll. 3, 11).

[NLI 13,586(12) (b), 1r]

Pour wine & dance if manhood still have pride
Bring roses if the rose be yet in bloom;
The cataract smokes on the mountain side
Our Father Rosecross is in his Tomb

Pull down the blinds, bring fiddle and clarionett
That there be no foot silent in the room
Nor mouth with kissing, or the wine unwet
Our Father Rosecross is in his Tomb.

In vain, in vain: the cataract still cries
The everlasting taper lights the gloom;
All wisdom shut into his onyx eyes
Our Father ~~F~~ Rosecross sleeps in his tomb.

Collocutio.

If you that have grown old were the first dead
Neither catalpa tree nor scented lime
Should hear my living feet, nor would I tread
Where we wrought that shall break the teeth of time
Let the new faces play what tricks they will
In the old rooms; for all they do or say
Our shades ~~rove~~ walk the garden gravel still
The living ~~seem~~ seem more shadowy than they.

Dec, 1912.

THE MOUNTAIN TOMB

[NLI 13,586(12) (b), 1^{r}]

Pour wine & dance if Manhood still have pride
Bring roses if the rose be yet in bloom.
The cataract smokes on the mountain side
Our Father Rosicross is in his Tomb

Pull down the blinds: bring fiddle and clarionet [~~?~~]
That there be no foot silent in the room
Nor mouth with kissing or the wine unwet
Our Father Rosicross is in his Tomb.

In vain, in vain: the cattaract still cries
The everlasting taper lights the gloom;
All wisdom shut into his onyx eyes
Our Father ~~Fos~~ Rosicross sleeps in his tomb.

Collevile.

---

found in NLI 13,586(12) (b) *transcribed above*
Chicago(2) *transcribed below*
Chicago(3)
NLI 30,009
published in *Poetry* (Chicago), December 1912
The Quest (London), April 1913
A Selection from the Poetry of W. B. Yeats (Leipzig: Tauchnitz, 1913)
Resp14

The bottom one-third of the page contains an untitled draft of the poem "New Faces," in Yeats's hand, dated "Dec. 1912." It was first published in *Seven Poems and a Fragment* (1922) and then in *The Tower* (1928).

[Chicago(2)]

(1

THE MOUNTAIN TOMB.

Pour wine and dance if manhood still have pride,
Bring roses if the rose be yet in bloom;
The cataract smokes on the mountain side.
Our Father Rosicross is in his tomb.

stet

Pull down the blinds, bring fiddle and clarionet,
Let there be no foot silent in the room,
Nor mouth with kissing nor with wine unwet.
Our Father Rosicross is in his tomb.

In vain, in vain; the cataract still cries,
The everlasting taper lights the gloom,
All wisdom shut into its onyx eyes
Our Father Rosicross sleeps in his tomb.

TO A CHILD DANCING UPON THE SHORE

Dance there upon the shore;
What need have you to care
For wind or water's roar?
And tumble out your hair
That the salt drops have wet;
Being young you have not known
The fool's triumph, nor yet
Love lost as soon as won,
Nor him, the best labourer, dead
And all the sheaves to bind.
What need that you should dread
The monstrous crying of wind?

Poems
by.
W. B. Yeats.

[Chicago(2)]

THE MOUNTAIN TOMB. 1

Pour wine and dance, if manhood still have pride ,
Bring roses, if the rose be yet in bloom ;

The cataract smokes on the mountain side ;

Our Father Rosicross is in his Tomb ; space

Pull down the blinds , bring fiddle and clarionet ,
Let there be no foot silent in the room ,
nor with
Nor mouth with kissing ~~or the~~ wine unwet .
Our Father Rosicross is in his tomb.

In vain , in vain ; the cataract still cries ,
The everlasting taper lights the gloom ,
All wisdom shut into its onyx ~~sides~~ eyes
Our Father Rosicross sleeps in his tomb.

---

title THE MOUNTAIN TOMB *P*

1 dance *rev to* dance, *rev to* dance] dance, *P, Quest* dance *Tauchnitz, Resp14* Manhood *Tauchnitz, Resp14* pride *rev to* pride,] pride, *P, Quest, Tauchnitz* pride. *Resp14* [*The period in Resp14 is very lightly printed and might be a comma, as it is in Harvard(2), Resp14 (NewYork), Resp16 and all later printings.*]

2 roses if *rev to* roses, if *rev to* roses if] roses, if *P, Quest* roses if *Tauchnitz, Resp14* bloom *rev to* bloom;] bloom; *in all later texts*

2, 4, 6, 8, 10, 12 *unindented*] *indented two spaces Quest*

3 side, *rev to* side.] side. *P, Quest* side, *Tauchnitz, Resp14*

5 *indented one space*] *unindented in all printings* clarionet *rev to* clarionet: *rev to* clarionet,] clarionet, *P, Quest* clarionet *Tauchnitz, Resp14*

6 room *rev to* room,] room, *P, Quest* room *Tauchnitz, Resp14*

7 or the wine *rev to* nor with wine] nor the wine *Chicago(3), P, Quest* nor from wine *Tauchnitz, Resp14* unwet *rev to* unwet.] unwet. *P, Quest* unwet; *Tauchnitz, Resp14*

9 vain the *rev to* vain; the] vain; the *P, Quest, Resp14* vain: the *Tauchnitz* cries *rev to* cries,] cries *Tauchnitz, Resp14* cries *rev to* cries, *NLI 30,009*

10 gloom *rev to* gloom,] gloom. *Quest* gloom; *Tauchnitz, Resp14*

11 eyes] eyes. *P* eyes, *Quest*

unsigned] William Butler Yeats. *P, Quest*

1, 2 The comma after “dance” (l. 1) and the comma after “roses” (l. 2) were added in ink, probably by Yeats, then were deleted with copyediting marks by Ezra Pound; and then they were marked out in thick red pencil or crayon of compositor/printer. Even so, the commas were printed in *P*.

[NLI 30,515^{r}]

TO A CHILD DANCING IN THE WIND [and TWO YEARS LATER]

TO A CHILD DANCING IN THE WIND I.

[NLI 30,515^{r}]

We broke up the dance on the shore
We [?have] heard you call & we come
And yet our hearts are sore
—
[?Sound] has made me dumb

What [?her] Etc
— — — —

Take sides [?with] her.

[?Have] [?] — She still
[?a child]
You are not [?her life Mans days flee]

---

found in NLI 30,515^{r} *transcribed above*
NLI 8763(2) *transcribed below*
NLI 13,586(13)^{r} *transcribed below*
NLI 13,586(12) (b)^{v} *transcribed below*
Chicago(2)
Chicago(3)
Chicago(4)
Emory(3) *transcribed below*
NLI 30,528
ABY(8)
NLI 30,009
published in *Poetry* (Chicago), December 1912
A Selection from the Poetry of W. B. Yeats (Leipzig: Tauchnitz, 1913)
Resp14

[NLI 8763(2)]

[NLI 8763(2)]

~~Dance~~
You are [?young]   what need you care
~~[?what matter] [?]~~
~~For waters roar~~
~~The [?] roar~~ or the winds cry or the waters roar
~~Dancing [?]~~ [?]
~~[?Let]~~
~~Let the wind shake [?out] your [?hair]~~
~~[?Dance]~~
~~Dance on the level shore~~
The wind ~~[?has]~~ shaken out your hair
~~And [?] [?feet]~~ the
~~You~~ While dance [?upon the level]

Let the wind [?loose] your hair
The water & the wind cry
[?Why] you dance

[?You] [?] [?what] need you care
[?That] waters roar [?&] wind cry [?while] ~~you dance~~
~~[?While] you dance~~
~~You [?dance]~~ &
~~[?Dance] [?] [?and] shake [?out] your~~ hair
~~[?It] shakes [?out] hair~~
~~For~~ The wind shakes your hair
While you dance on the level shore
You [?have lost] no lover [?]

10 The cancel extends to the "d" of "And".

[NLI 13,586(13)^{r} (top)]

[NLI 13,586(13)[r] (top)]

Dance there upon the shore
What need is there to care
For wind or waters roar?
And tumble out your hair
            salt
That the ~~foam~~ drops have wet,
Being young you have not known
    fools'   ~~of fools~~
The ~~fool~~ triumph nor yet
Love ^lost as soon^ as won
Nor he the best labourer dead
And all the sheafs to bind
What need that you should dread
The monstrous crying of wind?

Colleville

The bottom half of the page is "Fallen Majesty"; see p. 365 below.

[NLI 13,586(12) (b)v]

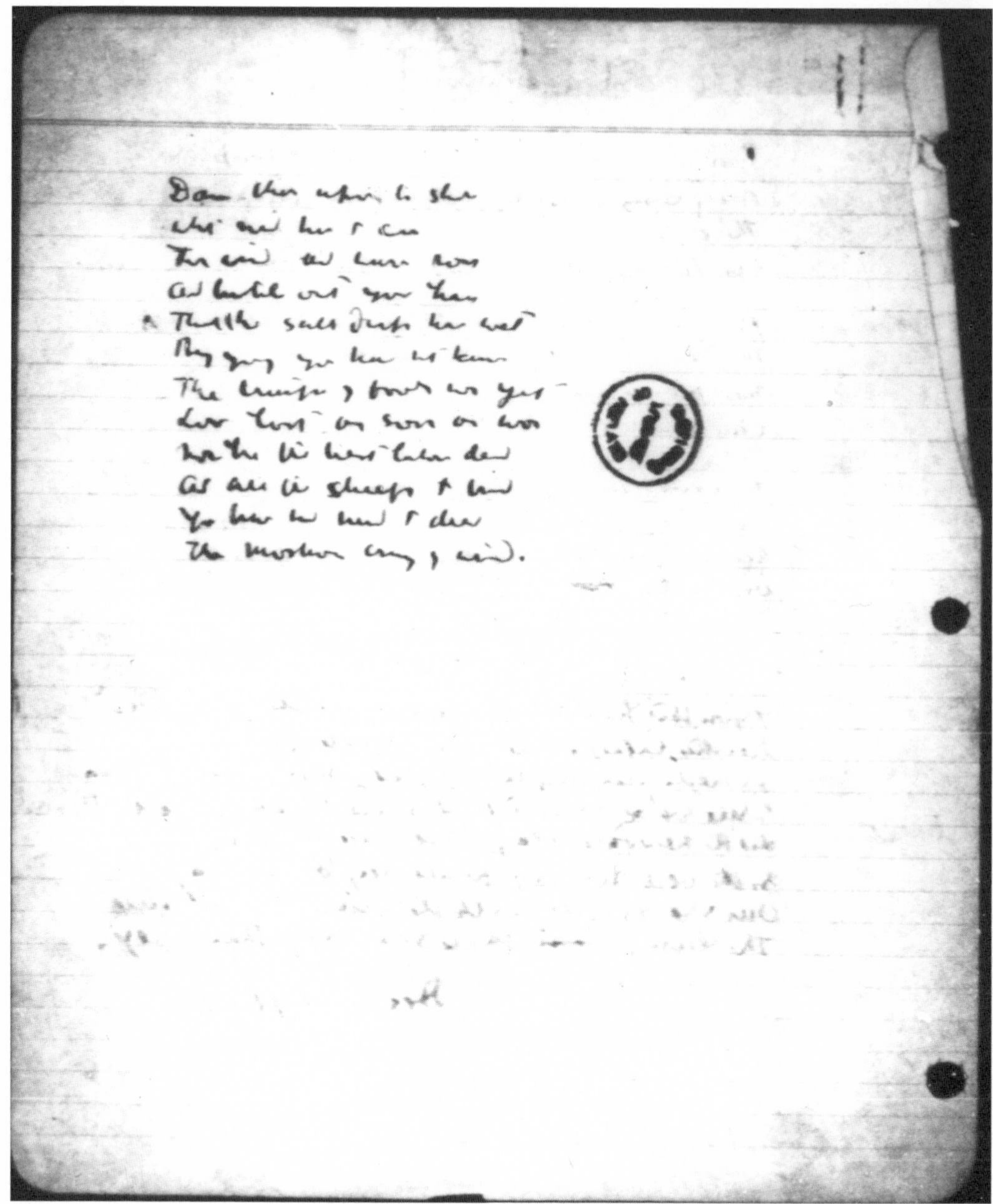

[NLI 13,586(12) (b)[v]]

Dance there upon the shore
What need [?her] to [?care]
For wind or [?waves] roar
And tumble out your hair
That the salt [?drops have] wet
Being young you have not known
The triumph of fools nor yet
Love lost as soon as won
Nor he the best labourer dead
And all the sheefs to bind
You have no need to [?dread]
The monstrous crying of wind.

[Emory(3)]

To a child dancing on the shore

Dance there upon the shore;
What need have you to care
For wind or waters roar?
And tumble out your hair
That the salt drops have wet;
Being young you have not known
The fools triumph, nor yet

---

title TO A CHILD DANCING UPON THE SHORE, *Chicago(2), P* TO A CHILD DANCING IN THE WIND. *Tauchnitz* TO A CHILD DANCING IN THE WIND / I *Resp14* Pages 66 & 67 / Treat part ~~two~~ two of "To a child dancing in the wind" as a seperate poem, & bring title to top of page 6. Put 'I' & 'II' above the titles and in the same type as in the case of "The Witch' and "The Peacock' pages 62 & 63 *NLI 30,528* TO A CHILD DANCING IN / THE WIND / I *rev in ink to* I / TO A CHILD DANCING IN / THE WIND *ABY(8)*

1 shore;] shore *rev in ink to* shore; *Chicago(2)*

3 water's *Chicago(2), P, Resp14* roar?] roar *rev in ink to* roar, *rev in ink to* roar? *Chicago(2)*

5 wet;] wet *rev in ink to* wet; *Chicago(2)*

6 *not indented*] *indented one space Chicago(2)*

7 fool's *Chicago(2), P, Tauchnitz, Resp14* triumph,] triumph *rev in ink to* triumph, *Chicago(2)*

[Emory(3), continued]

Love lost as soon as won,
N
[?]or the best labourer dead
A
Tnd all the sheaves to bind.
What need have you to dread
The monstrous crying of wind?
W B Yeats.

---

8 won,] won *rev in ink to* won, *Chicago(2)* won. *Chicago(4), P* won (full stop) *Chicago(4)*

9 Nor the] Nor he the *rev in ink to* him, the *Chicago(2)* And he, the *Chicago(3), Chicago(4), P* labourer] labourer *rev in ink to* labourer, *Chicago(2)* labourer, *Chicago(4)* warrior, *P*

10 sheaves] sheafs *Chicago(4)* bind.] bind *rev in ink to* bind. *Chicago(2)* bind! *Chicago(4), P*

11 need have you to dread] need that you should dread [dred *Chicago(4)*] *Chicago(2), Chicago(4), P*

12 wind?] wind. *rev in ink to* wind? *Chicago(2)*

unsigned Chicago(2), Tauchnitz, Resp14; William Butler Yeats *P*

[NLI 30,385, 47v]

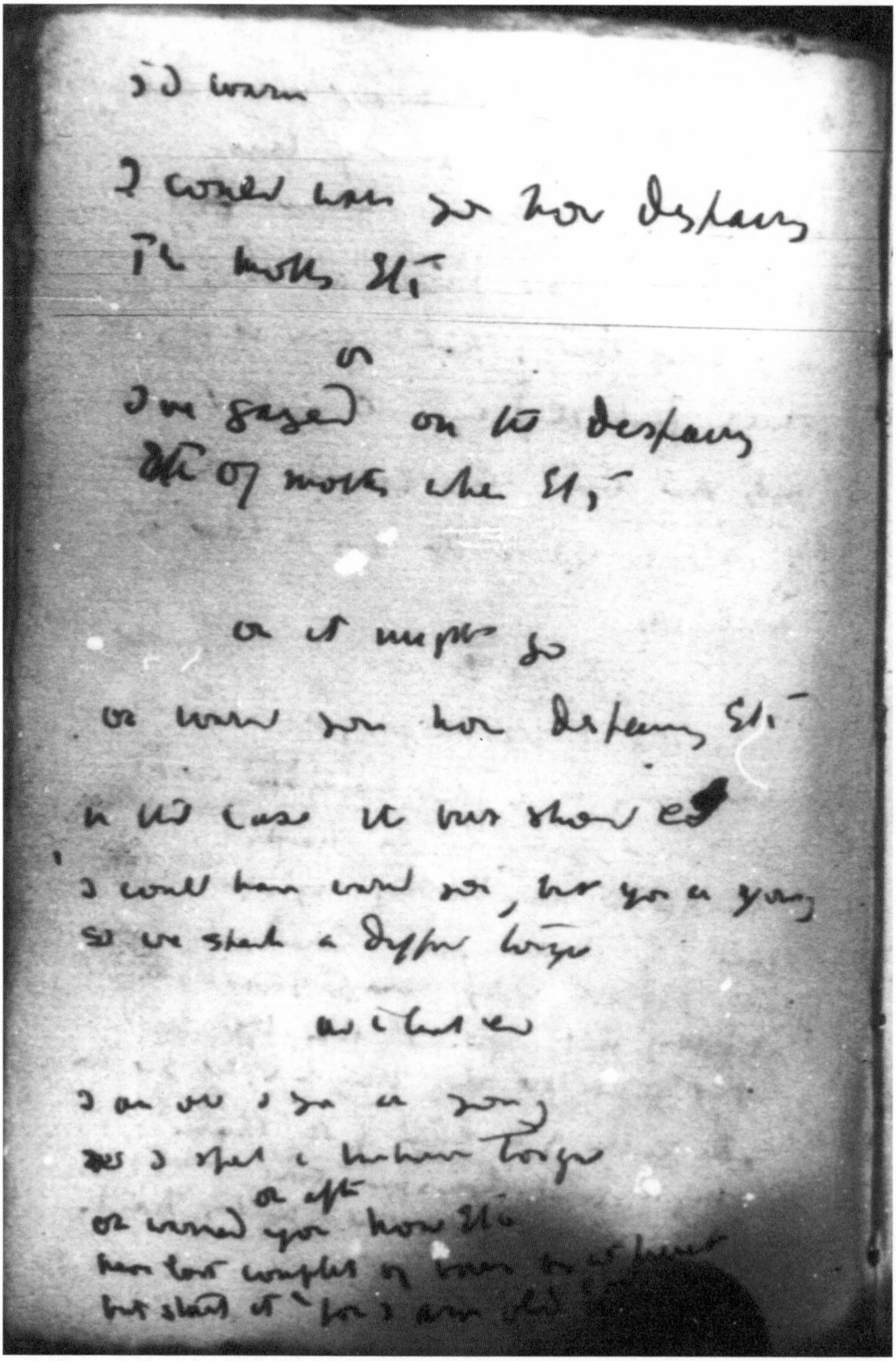

TO A CHILD DANCING IN THE WIND II. [TWO YEARS LATER]

[NLI 30,385, 47^{v}]

I'd warn

I could warn you how despairing
The moths Etc

or
I ve gazed on that despairing
Etc of moths when Etc

or it might go

or warned you how despairing Etc

in that case the verse should end
'I could have warned you, but you are young
So we speak a different tongue

and the last end

I am old & you are young
{And
{so I speak a barbarous tongue
or after
Or warned you how Etc
have last couplet of verse as at present
but start it 'for I am old Etc

---

found in NLI 30,385, 47^{v} *transcribed above*
NLI 13,586(14) *transcribed below*
Berg(6) (b)
Harvard(1)
NLI 30,528
ABY(8)
NLI 30,009
published in *Resp14*
Poetry (Chicago), May 1914

---

9 The blot is not a cancel.

Though you may be young & daring
There is something to be learned;
I could tell you how despairing
The moth feels when it's burned,
But I'm old & you are young
So we speak a different tongue.

You will take whatever's offered,
Take the enemy for friend,
Suffer as your mother suffered,
Be as broken in the end.
I would warn you, but you are young
And I speak a barbarous tongue

WBY
Dec 3

[NLI 13,586(14)]

Though you may be young & daring
There is something to be learned;
I could tell you how despairing
The moth feels when it's burned,
But I'm old & you are young
So we speak a different tongue.

You will take what ever's offered,
Take the enemy for friend,
Suffer as your mother suffered,
Be as broken in the end.
I could [~~?~~] warn you, but you are young
And I speak a barberous tongue

WBY
Dec 3

---

title II *rev in pencil and then canceled in pencil [printed numeral] and ink [penciled title] to* ~~II To a young girl~~ *Harvard(1)* Pages 66 & 67 / Treat part ~~two~~ two of "To a child dancing in the wind" as a seperate poem, & bring title to top of page 6. Put 'I' & 'II' above the titles and in the same type as in the case of "The Witch' and "The Peacock' pages 62 & 63 *NLI 30,528* II *rev in ink to* II / TWO YEARS LATER. *ABY(8)* TO A CHILD DANCING IN THE WIND *P* TO A CHILD DANCING IN THE WIND II *Resp14*

1 Though you may be young & daring] Has no one said those daring *P, Resp14*

2 There is something to be learned;] Kind eyes should be more lear n d? [learnd? *Harvard(1)*] *rev in pencil to* Kind eyes should be more learned? *Berg(6)[b], Harvard(1)*; Kind eyes should be more learn'd? [learned? *P*] *P, Resp14*

3 I could tell you how] I have found out how *P*

4 moth feels when it's burned,] moths are when they are burned. [burned, *rev in ink to* burned? *NLI 30,009*] *P, Resp14, NLI 30,009*

5 But I'm old & you] But I am old and *Harvard(1), P* I could have warned you, *rev in ink to* I could have warned you; *NLI 30,009*   young] young *rev in pencil to* young, *Harvard(1)* young, *P* young, *rev in ink to* young *NLI 30,009*

7 You] O you *rev in pencil to* Oh you *Harvard(1)*; Oh you *P*; O you *Resp14*   what ever's offered,] whatever's offered *P, Resp14*

8 Take the enemy for friend,] And dream that all the world's a friend, *P, Resp14*

10 end.] end. *rev in ink to* end; *NLI 30,009*

11 could warn you, but] could have warned you — but *P, Resp14*   young] young, *P, Resp14*

12 barberous *rev in pencil to* barbarous *Harvard(1)*; barbarous *P, Resp14*   tongue] tongue. *P, Resp14*

unsigned P

undated P

[NLI 13,586(15)[r]]

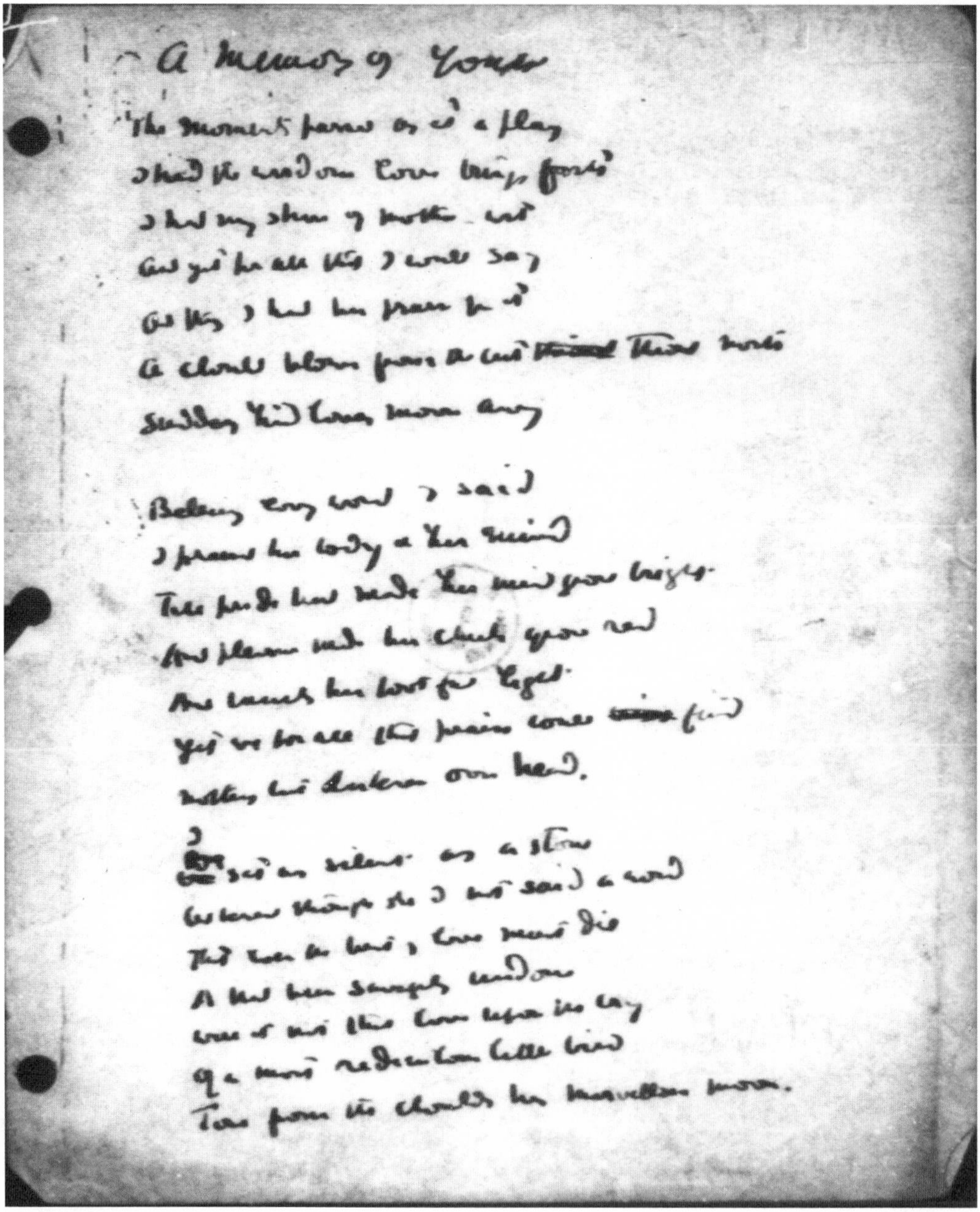

---

found in NLI 13,586(15) *transcribed below*
NLI 13,586(13)[v] *transcribed below* [*in note*]
Chicago(2) *transcribed below*
Harvard(1)

published in *Poetry* (Chicago), Dec. 1912
Resp14

A MEMORY OF YOUTH

[NLI 13,586(15)^{r}]

A Memory of Youth

The moments passed as at a play
I had the wisdom love brings forth
I had my share of mother-wit
And yet for all that I could say
And thoug I had her praise for it
A clould blown from the cut ~~through~~ throat north
Suddenly hid loves moon away

Believing every word I said
I praised her body & her mind
Till pride had made her mind grow bright
And pleasure made her cheeks grow red
And vanity her foot fall light
Yet we for all that praise could [?~~bring~~] find
Nothing but darkness over head

I
~~We~~
[?~~We~~] sat as silent as a stone
And knew though she d not said a word
That even the best of love must die
[?And] had been savagely undone
Were it not that love upon the cry
Of a most ridiculous little bird
Tore from the cloulds his marvellous moon.

10–11 A canceled draft of these two lines is found on NLI 13,586(13)^{v}, together with an unidentified two-line verse fragment; the recto of the sheet has a lightly revised, untitled draft of ["To a Child Dancing in the Wind"] and a fair copy of "Fallen Majesty." The canceled draft of lines 10–11, written on an upward slant at the center of the page, reads:

[?made]
Till pleasure ~~made~~ her foot fall light
pride [?had made] [? ?] red
And ~~[?] her [?cheeks turn]~~ red

The unidentified two-line verse fragment, which is written vertically on the lower half of the page, reads:

I ~~[?see why many all]~~
In the [?depth of my thought]

[Chicago(2), 2 (bottom)]

(2

FALLEN MAJESTY.

~~Although~~

Although crowds gathered once if she but showed her face
and Even old men's eyes grew dim, this hand alone,
Like some last courtier at a gipsy camping place
Babbling of fallen majesty, records what's gone.
The lineaments, the heart that laughter has made sweet,
These, these remain, but I record what's gone. A crowd
Will gather and not know that through its very street
Once walked a thing that seemed, ~~as it were~~, a burning cloud.

Love & the ~~moon~~ bird

~~THE ROBIN~~

Love and
The bird

The ~~moments~~ moments passed as at a play,
I ~~have~~ had the wisdom love can bring,
I had my share of mother wit;
And yet for all that I could say,
And though I had her praise for it,
And she seemed happy as a king,
Love's moon was withering away.

Believing every word I said
I praised her body and her mind,
Till pride had made her eyes grow bright,
And pleasure made her cheeks grow red,
And vanity her footfall light;
Yet we for all that praise, could find
Nothing but darkness overhead.

[Chicago(2), 2 (bottom)]

Love & the ~~Moon~~ bird
~~THE ROBIN~~ Love and

{ts
The ~~monets~~ momen{s passed as at a play, The bird
had
I ~~have~~ the wisdom love can bring ,
I had my share of mother wit ;
And yet for all that I could say ,
And though I had her praise for it ,
And she seemed happy as a king ,
Love's moon was withering away.

Believing every word I said
{ai
I pr{iased her body and her mind ,
Till pride had made her eyes grow bright ,
And pl easure made her cheeks grow red ,
and vanity her footfall light ;
Yet we , for all that praise , could find
Nothing but darkness overhead.

---

title LOVE AND THE BIRD *P* A MEMORY OF YOUTH *Resp14*
2 love can bring] love brings forth; *Resp14*
3 wit *Resp14*
6–7 And she seemed happy as a king, / Love's moon was withering away] A cloud blown from the cut-throat north / Suddenly hid love's moon away. *Resp14*
9 priased *rev in ink to* praised] pressed *rev in pencil to* praised *and then canceled in ink* mind,] mind, *Resp14*
12 light, *Resp14*

---

title The the ink revision is in Yeats's hand; the repeated title in the right margin is in an unidentified hand, perhaps Ezra Pound's.
1–6, 9–13 All punctuation is added in ink.
11 Copyediting close-up symbol is added in ink.
12 Copyediting underscore of "a" for uppercase is added in ink.

(3

I sat as silent as a stone

And knew, though she'd not said a word,

That even the best of love must die,

And had been savagely undone

Were it not that love, upon the cry

Of a most ridiculous little bird,

Threw up in the air his marvellous moon.

up in

THE REALISTS

Hope that you may understand.

What can books, of men that wive

In a dragon-guarded land,

Paintings of the dolphin drawn;

Sea nymphs, in their pearly waggons,

Do but wake the hope to live

That had gone

With the dragons.

I have had to correct a punctuation in a great hurry to catch the first post. I would be much obliged if you would revise the punctuation.

WBYeats

[Chicago(2), 3 (top)]

\3

I sat as silent as a stone
And knew , though she'd not said a word ,
That even the best of love must die ,
And had been savagely undone
were it not that love, upon the cry
Of a most ridiculous little bird ,
{i air
Threw up { **on the** ^ **his marvellous moon.** up in
~~upon~~

---

15 I sat] We sat *Resp14* stone, *Resp14*
16 And knew] We knew *Resp14*
19 love *Resp14*
20 bird *Resp14*
21 Threw up in the air his] Tore from the clouds his *Resp14*
21/ *unsigned*] William Butler Yeats *P*

---

18 The typescript has a blank space in which "o" is added in ink.
19 Copyediting underscore of "w" for uppercase is added in ink.
21 The repetition in the right margin is in ink in an unidentified hand.

[NLI 13,586(13)r (bottom)]

FALLEN MAJESTY

[NLI 13,586(13)^{r} (bottom)]

{F
{Mallen Majesty

Although crowds gathered once if she but showed her face
And even old men s eyes grew dim, this hand alone,
Like some last courtier at a gypsy camping place
Babbling of fallen majesty, records what s gone.
The lineaments, a heart that laughter has made sweet
These, these remain but I record what s gone. A crowd
Will gather & not know that through its very street
Once waked a thing that seemed, as it were, a burning
cloud.

[?Colleville]

---

found in NLI 13,586(13)^{r} (bottom) *transcribed above*
Chicago(2) (top) *transcribed below*
Chicago(3)
published in *Poetry* (Chicago), Dec. 1912
A Selection from the Poetry of W. B. Yeats (Leipzig: Tauchnitz, 1913)
Resp14

The top half of the page is "To a Child Dancing in the Wind"; see p. 349 above.

[Chicago(2), 2 (top)]

(2

FALLEN MAJESTY.

~~Although~~

Although crowds gathered once if she but showed her face
And even old men's eyes grew dim, this hand alone,
Like some last courtier at a gipsy camping place
Babbling of fallen majesty, records what's gone.
The lineaments, the heart that laughter has made sweet,
These, these remain, but I record what's gone. A crowd
Will gather and not know that through its very street
Once walked a thing that seemed, ~~as it were~~, a burning cloud.

Love & the moon bird

~~THE ROBIN~~

Love and The bird

The ~~months~~ moments passed as at a play,
I had the wisdom love can bring,
I had my share of mother wit;
And yet for all that I could say,
And though I had her praise for it,
And she seemed happy as a king,
Love's moon was withering away.

Believing every word I said
I praised her body and her mind,
Till pride had made her eyes grow bright,
And pleasure made her cheeks grow red,
And vanity her footfall light;
Yet we for all that praise, could find
Nothing but darkness overhead.

[Chicago(2), 2 (top)]

2

FALLEN MAJESTY.

~~fo~~
~~Althh~~{~~gugh~~
Although crowds gathered once if she but showed her face
and
^ **Even old men's eyes grew dim , this hand alone ,**
Like some last courtier at a gipsy camping place
Babbling of fallen majesty , records what's gone .
The lineaments , the heart that laughter has made sweet ,
{A
These , these remain, but I record what's gone . {**a crowd**
Will gather and not know that through its very street
Once walked a thing that seemed , ~~as it were~~ , a burning cloud.

---

title FALLEN MAJESTY *P, Tauchnitz, Resp14*

2 And *P, Tauchnitz, Resp14*

3 place, *Tauchnitz, Resp14*

4 Majesty, *Tauchnitz*

4/5 *no stanza division*] *stanza division Tauchnitz (page break between ll. 4 and 5, without clear indication of whether it has a stanza division), Resp14*

5 the heart] a heart *Tauchnitz, Resp14*

7 gather, *P, Tauchnitz, Resp14* know that through its very] know it walks the very *Tauchnitz, Resp14*

8 Once walked a thing that seemed, ~~as it were~~, a] Once walked a thing that seemed, as it were, a] *Chicago(3), P*; Whereon a thing once walked that seemed a *Tauchnitz, Resp14*

8/ *unsigned*] William Butler Yeats *P*

---

1 The mark for removing the indentation is in ink.

2–8 All punctuation except "what's" (l. 4) is added in ink.

On the appointment of Count Plunkett to Curatorship of Dublin Museum & T. W. Russell & Birrell, Hugh Lane being a candidate –

Being out of heart with government
I ~~took up a small stone~~ found a broken root to fling
Where the proud wayward squirrel went,
Taking delight that he could spring;
And he with that low whinnying sound
That is like laughter ~~ran~~ sprang again
And so to the other tree ~~with~~ at a bound,
~~For~~ Nor timid ~~...~~ will nor the tame brain
Nor ~~solemn~~ heavy knitting of the brow
Bred that fierce tooth & cleanly limb
Nor threw him up to laugh on the ~~bow~~ bough
No government appointed him.

August ~~24~~ 25
1907.

AN APPOINTMENT

[Emory(4)]

Being out of heart at government
found a broken root
I ~~took up a small stone~~ to fling
^
Where the proud wayward squirrel went,
Taking delight that he could spring;
And he with that low whinnying sound
sprang
That is like laughter ~~ran~~ again
at
And so to the other tree ^~~with~~ a bound.
Nor will
[?~~Nor~~] timid ~~heart~~ nor the tame brain
heavy
Nor [?~~solemn~~] knitting of the brow
^
Bred that fierce tooth & cleanly limb
bough
Nor threw him up to laugh on the [?~~bow~~]
No government appointed him.

August [~~?~~] 25
1907.

---

found in Emory(4) *transcribed above*
NLI 21,855
Berg(6) (b)
ABY(7)

published in *The English Review* (London), Feb. 1909
Resp14

Title Three Poems I. ON A RECENT GOVERNMENT APPOINTMENT IN IRELAND *English Review* ON A RECENT GOVERNMENT APPOINTMENT *rev in ink to* AN APPOINTMENT *Berg(6) (b)* AN APPOINTMENT *Resp14*

1 at government] with Government *NLI 21,855* with government *Resp14*

2 took up a small stone *rev to* found a broken root] took up a small stone *rev to* took a broken root *NLI 21,855* took a broken root *Resp14*

3 proud, *Resp14* went *NLI 21,855* was *rev in ink to* went *Berg(6) (b)*

5 he, *Resp14*

6 laughter, *NLI 21,855, Resp14* ran *rev to* sprang] ran *rev to* can *rev to* sprang *NLI 21,855* sprang *Resp14*

7 tree with *rev to* tree at] tree with *NLI 21,855*

8 Nor timid heart will nor the tame brain *rev to* Nor timid will nor the tame brain] Nor the tame will, nor timid brain, *Resp14*

9 [?solemn] *rev to* heavy] solemn *rev to* heavy *NLI 21,855* *entire line missing Resp14* *entire line missing rev to* Nor heavy knitting of the brow, *ABY(7)*

11 Nor threw *rev to* And threw *NLI 21,855* And threw *Resp14* bough; *NLI 21,855, Resp14*

12 government *rev to* Government *NLI 21,855*

12/ 25 / 1907.] 27, '07 *rev to* 25, '07 *NLI 21,855* *undated Resp14*

Above the poem, Lady Gregory added in ink: "On the appointment of Count Plunkett to Curatorship of Dublin Museum & Geo. Russell & Birrell, Hugh Lane being a candidate —".

[NLI 30,358, 28^{v} (top)]

THE MAGI

[NLI 30,358, 28^{v} (top)]

I

Now as at all times I can see in the minds eye
In their stiff painted clothes, the pale unsatisfied ones
Appear or disappear in the blue depth of the sky
With all their ancient faces like rain beaten stones
And all their helms of silver hovering side by side
And all their eyes still fixed hoping to find once more
Being by Calvarys turbullence unsatisfied
The uncontrollable mystery upon the bestial floor.

---

found in NLI 30,358, 28^{v} (top) *transcribed above*
Harvard(1)
published in *Poetry* (Chicago), May 1914
NS, May 9, 1914
Resp14

---

title THE MAGII *rev. in ink to* THE MAGI *Harvard(1)* THE MAGI *P, NS, Resp14*
1 mind's *P, NS, Resp14* eye, *P*
2 stiff, *P, NS, Resp14* clothes *NS, Resp14*
3 or] and *P, NS, Resp14*
4 rain beaten stones] rain—beaten stones, *P, NS, Resp14*
5 by side, *P, NS, Resp14*
6 fixed, *P, NS, Resp14* more, *P, NS, Resp14*
7 Calvarys turbullence unsatisfied] Calvary's turbulence unsatisfied, *P, NS, Resp14*
8 upon] on *P, NS, Resp14*

[NLI 30,358, 28^{v} (bottom), 29^{r} (top)]

See also "Notes to Poems" below.

THE DOLLS

[NLI 30,358, 28v (bottom)]

II

A doll in the doll makers house
Looks at the cradle & ~~balls~~ bawls
"That is an insult to us"
But the oldest of all the dolls
Who had seen, being kept for show,
Generations of his sort,
Out screams the whole shelf with "although
There s not a man can report
Evil of this place
The man & the woman bring
Hither to our disgrace
A noisy & filthy thing"
Hearing him groan & stretch
The do{l / cl} maker's wife is [?~~aware~~] ^aware
Her husband has heard the wretch;
And crouched by the arm of his chair
She murmurs into his ear,

[NLI 30,358, 29r (top)]

Head upon shoulder leant;
"My dear, my dear, O dear
It was an accident"

---

found in NLI 30,358, 28v–29r *transcribed above*
Harvard(1)
ABY(7)
published in *Resp14*

---

entire poem canceled Harvard(1)
title II / THE DOLLS *Resp14*
1 dollmaker's *Resp14*
2 ~~balls~~ bawls] balls: *Resp14* balls: *rev in ink to* bawls: *ABY(7)*
3 'That *rev. in pencil to* "That *Harvard(1)* us;' *rev in pencil to* us;" Harvard(1) us.' *Resp14*
7 Out-screams *Resp14* shelf with "although] shelf: 'Although *Resp14*
8 There's *Resp14*
9 place, *Resp14*
12 thing.' *Resp14*
14 doll-maker's *Resp14*
15 wretch, *Resp14*
16 chair, *Resp14*
19 O dear] oh dear, *Resp14*
20 accident.' *Resp14*

[NLI 30,514 (a)[r]]

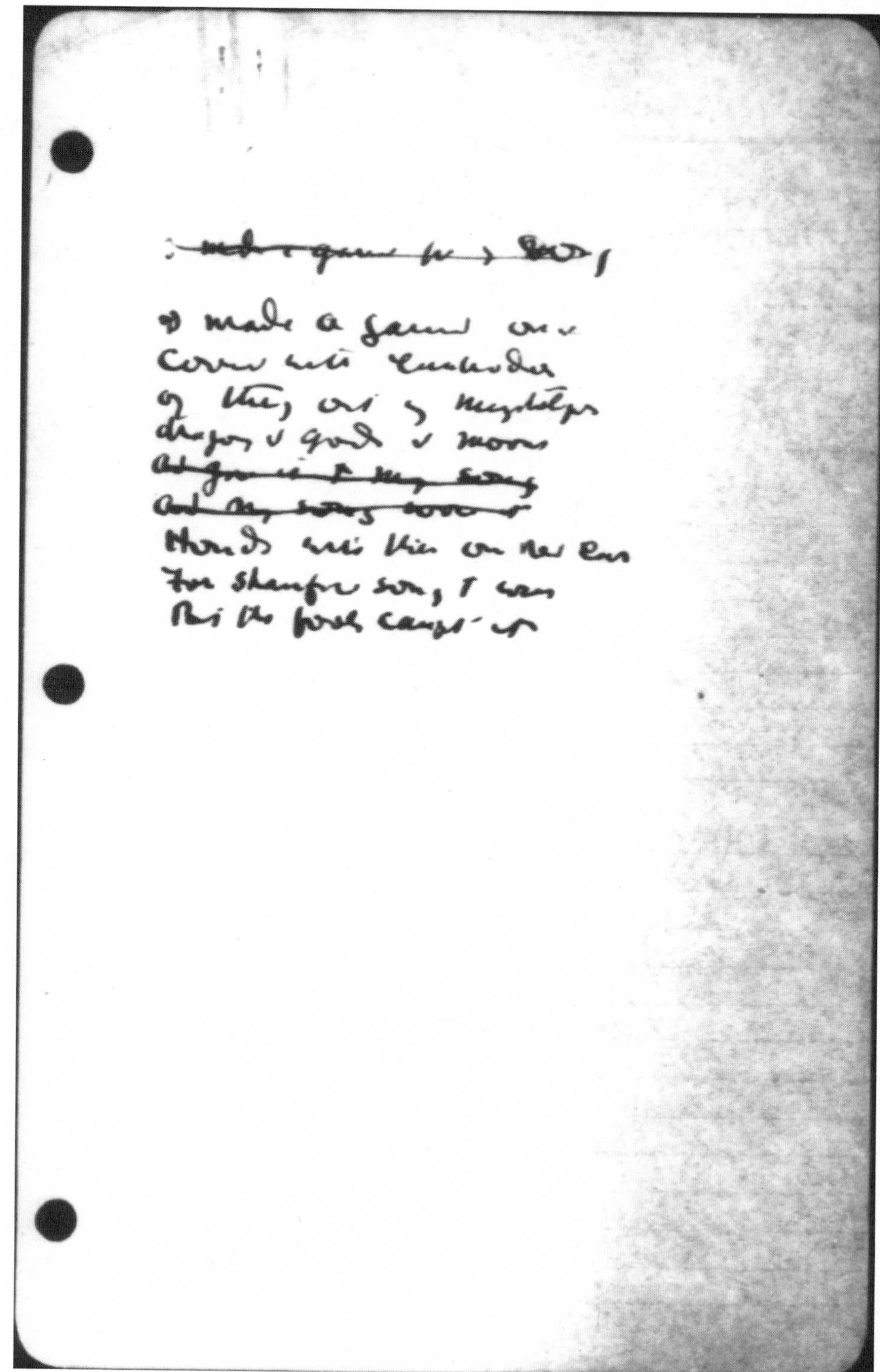

A COAT

[NLI 30,514 (a)^{r}]

S
~~I made a [?garment] for my Mong~~

I made a [?garment] once
Covered with embroideries
Of thing out of mythologies
dragons & gods & moons
~~And gave it to my song~~
~~And my song wore it~~
Hounds with [?their] one red ear
For shamfull song to wear
But the fools caught it

found in NLI 30,514 (a) *transcribed above*
NLI 30,514 (b) *transcribed below*
Berg(13)
ABY(7)
Stanford
published in *Poetry* (Chicago), May 1914
Resp14

1 A much less likely reading for [?garment] is [?gown].

[NLI 30,514 (b)r]

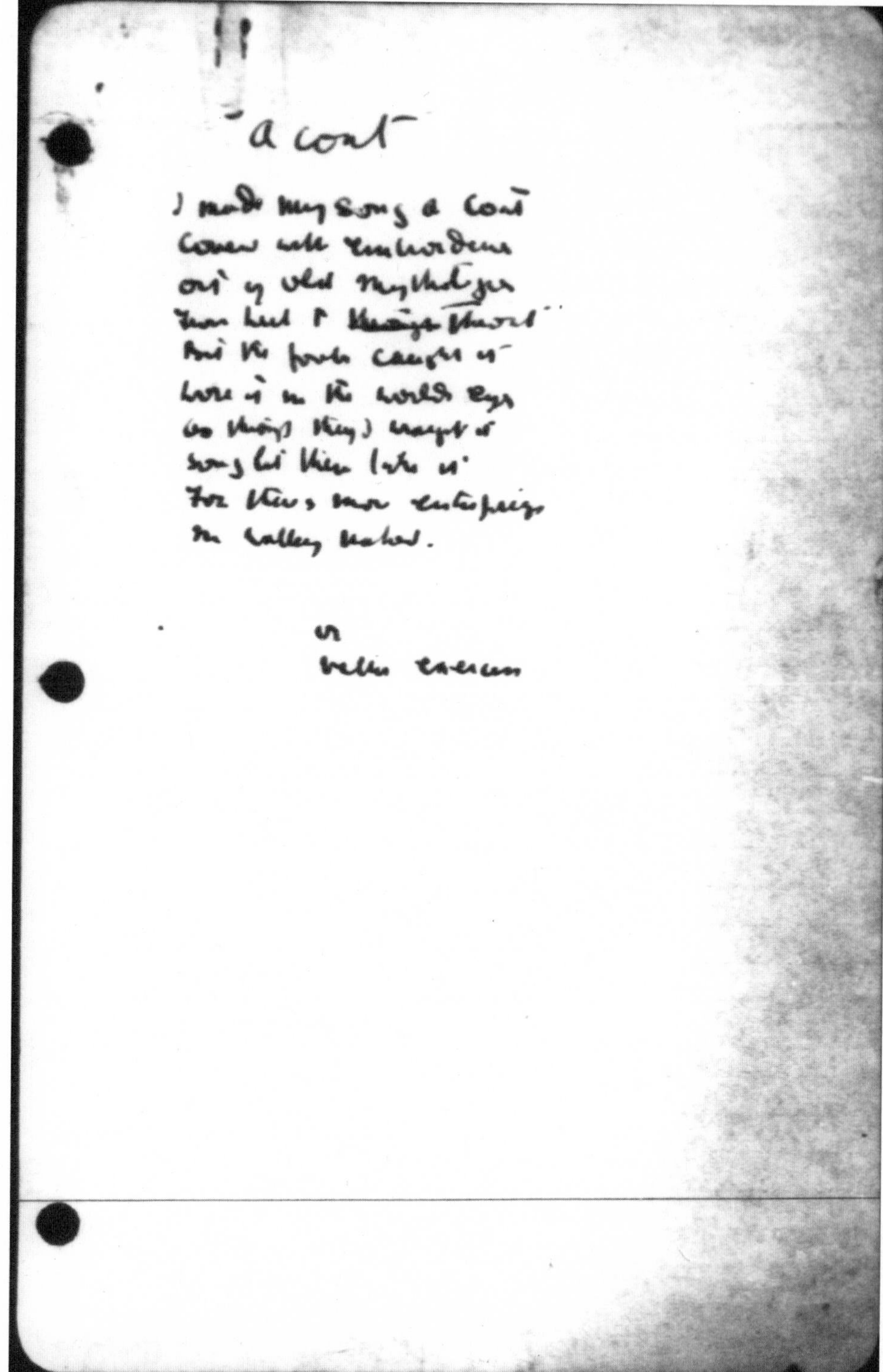

A Coat

I made my song a coat
Covered with embroideries
Out of old mythologies
From heel to throat
And the fools caught it
Wore it in the world's eyes
As though they'd wrought it
Song let them take it
For there's more enterprise
In walking naked.

or

[NLI 30,514 (b)^{r}]

A Coat

I made my song a coat
Covered with embroideries
Out of old mythologies
From heel to ~~[?througt]~~ throat
But the fools caught it
Wore it in the worlds eyes
As though they d wrought it
Song let them take it
For there s more enterprize
In walking naked.

or
[?] exercise

---

2 with embroideries] with old embroideries *rev in ink to* with embroideries *Berg(13)*
4 throat] throat; *P, Resp14, Stanford*
5 it] it, *P, Resp14, Stanford*
6 worlds eyes] world's eye *P, Resp14* world's eye *rev to* world's eyes *ABY(7)* world s eye *Stanford*
7 they'd *P, Resp14, Stanford* it. *P, Resp14, Stanford*
8 Song, *P, Resp14*
9 there's *P, Resp14* enterprise *P, Resp14*
10 naked.] nakid. *Stanford*
12/ *unsigned*] William Butler Yeats. *P*

---

12 The unintelligble word probably is not "velum". If, however, that word is "velum", then there might be an additional draft of this poem in a velum notebook that I have not located, or perhaps Yeats was considering replacing this poem with an entirely different poem from a velum notebook.

[Emory(5), 1^{r}]

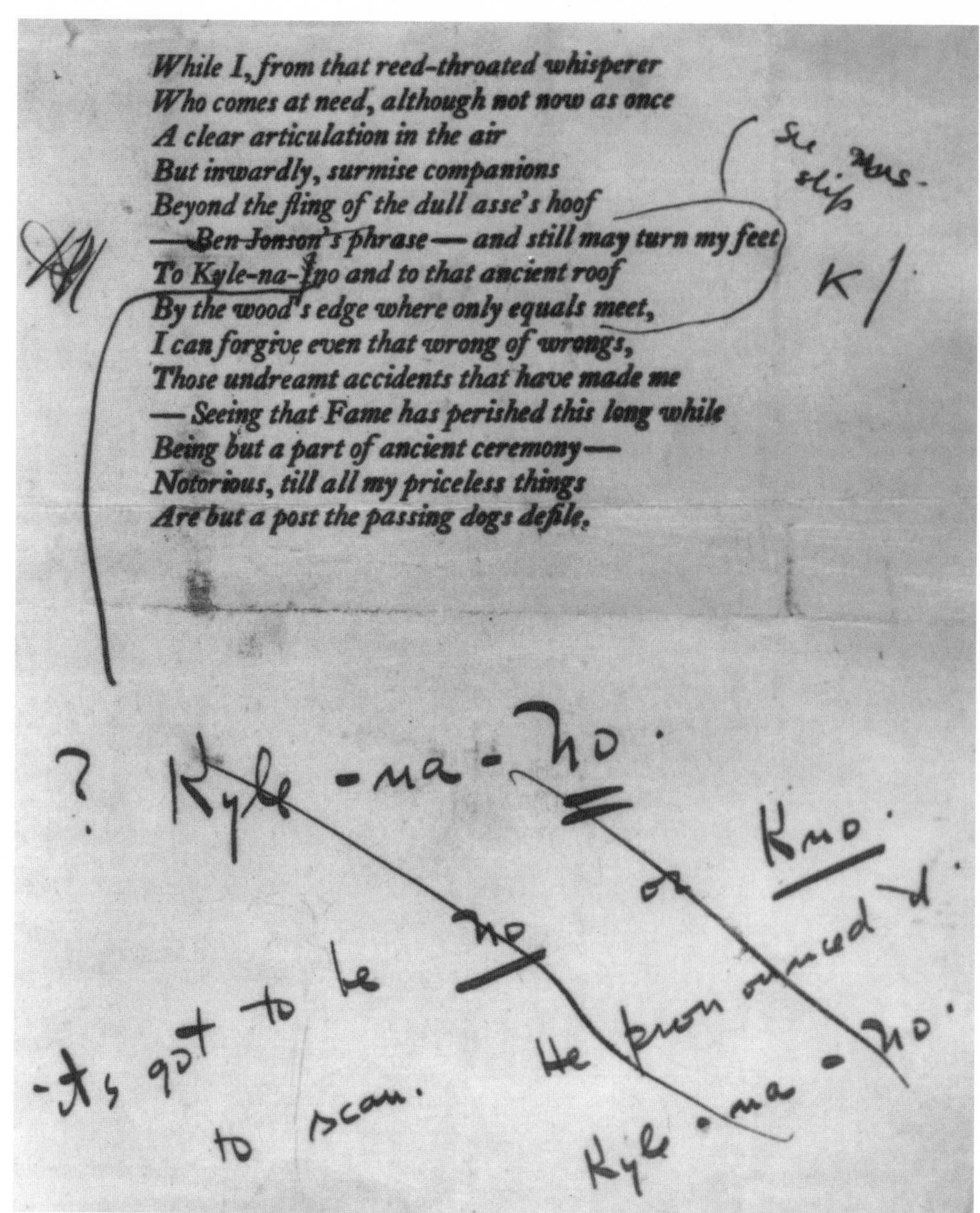

While I, from that reed-throated whisperer
Who comes at need, although not now as once
A clear articulation in the air
But inwardly, surmise companions
Beyond the fling of the dull asse's hoof
—~~Ben Jonson's phrase~~—and still may turn my feet
To Kyle-na-~~I~~no and to that ancient roof
By the wood's edge where only equals meet,
I can forgive even that wrong of wrongs,
Those undreamt accidents that have made me
—Seeing that Fame has perished this long while
Being but a part of ancient ceremony—
Notorious, till all my priceless things
Are but a post the passing dogs defile.

See Mss. slip

K/

? Kyle-na-no.

Kno.

or

it's got to be

to scan.

He pronounced it

Kyle-na-no.

All of the printed text is in boldface italic.

6 The cancel and its deletion are by Yeats, in ink, as are the markings and instructions in the right margin.

7 "I" was first canceled by EP in ink and with a delete symbol at left margin and a line running from the "I" of "Ino" down to EP's comment at the bottom of the page: "?"; then EP's comment and the delete symbol were deleted in Yeats's ink. The instruction in right margin to insert "K" is by Yeats, in ink.

15–18 EP hand and ink comment.

[WHILE I, FROM THAT REED–THROATED WHISPERER]

[Emory(5), 1r]

While I, from that reed–throated whisperer
Who comes at need, although not now as once
A clear articulation in the air See { M / [?]s — slip
But inwardly, surmise companions
Beyond the fling of the dull asse's hoof
— ~~Ben Jonson's ph~~rase — and still may turn my feet
To Kyle–na–Ino and to that ancient roof K/
By the wood's edge where only equals meet,
I can forgive even that wrong of wrongs,
Those undreamt accidents that have made me
— Seeing that Fame has perished this long while
Being but a part of ancient ceremony —
Notorious, till all my priceless things
Are but a post the passing dogs defile.

? Kyle–na–No.
it s got to be No or Kno.
to scan. He pronounced it.
Kyle–na–No.

---

found in Emory(5) *transcribed above*
Chicago(5)
Harvard(2)
Berg(6) (d)
Emory(1)
Emory(2)
published in *The New Statesman*, February 7, 1914
Resp14

---

proof printed in italic type, black ink] *printed in italic type, red ink Resp14*
title Notoriety / (Suggested by a recent magazine article.) *Harvard(2), NS*
2 need *Chicago(5)*
3 air, *Chicago(5), NS* air, *rev in ink to* air *Berg(6) (d)*
4 inwardly *Chicago(5)* inwardly *rev in ink to* inwardly, *Berg(6) (d)* companions *rev in ink to* companions, *Berg(6) (d)*
5 asses *Harvard(2)* asse's *rev in pencil and ink to* ass's *Berg(6) (d)* ass's *Resp14* hoof — *NS*
6 — Ben] Ben *NS, Resp14* Jonson's] Johnson's *rev in pencil* [*in ink Berg(6) (d)*] *to* Jonson's *Chicago(5), Berg(6) (d)* and still may turn my feet] and find when June is come *Resp14*
7 To] At *Resp14* Kyle-na-Ino *rev in ink to* Kyle-na-Kno] Kyle-na-kno *Chicago(5)* Kyle-na-Ino *Harvard(2), NS* Kyle-na-kno *rev in ink to* Kyle-na-no *Berg(6) (d)* Kyle-na-no *Resp14* and to that] under that *Resp14*
8 By the wood's edge where only equals meet,] A sterner conscience and a friendlier home *Resp14*
9 wrongs. *Resp14*
10 me, *Chicago(5)* me — *NS*
11 — Seeing] Seeing *NS* fame *Chicago(5)* while, *NS*
13 my] of *rev in pencil to* my *Emory(1), Emory(2)*
unsigned] W. B. Yeats [*added in pencil, not in Yeats's hand*] *Chicago(5)* W B Yeats. [*added in ink, in Yeats's hand*] *Harvard(2)* W. B. Yeats. *NS*

Beyond the fling of the dull asse's hoof,
And still can find when only equals come,
At Kyle-na-Kno under that ancient roof,
A sterner conscience and a second home,
I can forgive Etc

(insert at marked place
in proof)

[Emory(5), 2r]

Beyond the fling of the Dull asse's hoof,
And still can find where only equals come,
At Kyle-na-Kno under that ancient roof,
A sterner conscience and a second home,
I can forgive Etc

(insert at marked place
in proof)

Appendix

Yeats's Notes to *Responsibilities: Poems and a Play* (1914)

["Poems beginning with that 'To a Wealthy Man' and ending with that 'To a Shade'"][1]

[NLI 30,314, 1[r]]

Poems written in Despondency

I did write these poems, because I thought to reply to the argument that Dublin where there is such poverty could not afford, to build a house for Sir Hugh Lane gift of pictures should not be weighed, Nor because I thought the temper, & but because, the temper of those that used it seemed to me was exceedingly base.

During the ~~twenty or~~ thirty years or so during which I ~~I observed Irish events~~ I have been reading Irish newspapers there have been three events which stirred my imagination profoundly. public controversies, which ~~have~~ stirred my imagination. ~~profoundly.~~ One was the fall of Parnell. ~~& [?]~~ There were sound reasons ~~why a man might like either side~~ to justify upon one side or upon the other a man in joining either party, but there were none to justify ~~the base passion, the violent~~ lying accusations forgetful of passed [*sic*, past] service, ~~the~~ a frenzy of detraction. And another was the dispute over the ~~play~~ Play Boy. ~~& there again there were sound reasons for one or other side~~

[NLI 30,314, 2[r]]

~~But none~~ There were ~~natural reasons~~ sound reasons for opposing, as for supporting, that violent laughing thing but none ~~the untruthful~~ for the lies, & the unscrupulous rhetoric / ~~of~~ spread against it, in Ireland and ~~in~~ from Ireland to America. The third has been the Corporation[']s refusal of the ~~grant~~ building to for Sir Hugh Lane'[s] ~~for his~~ famous collection of pictures. ~~Much could be said~~ for One could respect the argument that Dublin with its poverty & its slums, could not afford the twenty three thousand pounds ~~the bu buil Mr Lel Lutchens~~ the building would have cost the city, ~~but here again the ignoble thing was the not the argument,~~ but not the minds that made use of it. ~~One saw the public mind in decomposition., & wondered if it could ever again be a living thing no [?]~~ One frezied man ~~even~~ compared ~~the Corots & Manets & Degas~~ the pictures to Troy Horse, which destroyed a city & innumerable correspondents described Sir Hugh Lane, & those who [?had] subscribed many thousands of pounds to give Dublin many Corots, Manets, Degas, & Renoirs as 'self seekers' 'self advertizers' 'picture dealers, log-rollers cranks, & faddists', ~~&~~ [. A] clerical paper told ~~Sir Hugh~~ 'Picture Dealer Lane' to take himself & his pictures out of that. A member of the Corporation said that there

[1]See *VP* 818–819.

[NLI 30,314, 3r]

were Irish artists who could paint as good ~~pictures as they [?wanted]~~ to, if they had a mind to, & another said that a half hour in the gallery was the most dismal of his life. ~~Another~~ some one else asked to be given instead of these eccentric pictures[,] pictures ~~to be given pictures~~ 'like those beautiful productions displayed in the windows of our city picture shops' Another thought that ~~it would be much more patriotic to devote~~ we would all be more patriotic if we devoted our energy to fighting the insurance act. Another ~~who was very persistent a voluminous person voluble~~ described ~~the our liking for~~ 'The vogue' of the French Impressionist painting ~~as a~~ as having go [*sic*, gone] ~~for far~~ such ~~as extent~~ a length among 'log rolling enthusiasts' ~~that [?]~~ they even admired 'works that were reflected [*sic*, rejected] from the Salon forty years ago by the finest critics in the world'. The first serious opposition began in the 'Irish Catholic' ~~the~~ [?] the chief Dublin clerical paper & Mr William Murphy, ~~[?] organizer of the recent Dublin~~ the the organizer of the recent lock out[,] a man of great influence, ~~throu the influence of a group of papers which he controls~~ brought to its support a few days later ~~a few weeks days later,~~ he brought the ~~[?] three whole incluence of~~ his newspapers 'The Irish Independent' & the 'The Evening Herald,' [?] ~~against against to its support.~~ the most popular paper in Ireland. He replied to ~~my~~ the poem on page — of this book from what he described as 'Paudeens point of view['], & Paudeens point of view it was. The enthusiasm for 'Sir Hugh Lane[']s [~~?~~] Corots' — one [~~?~~] paper spelt [~~?~~] [~~?refer~~] the name repeatedly 'Crot' – ~~was would he said vanish~~ being but 'an exotic fashion' [that] waited 'some satirist like Gilbert' ~~to~~ [~~?~~] who 'killed the aesthetic craze', & as for the rest 'there were no greater humbugs in the world than art critics &

[NLI 30,314, 4r]

and so called experts' The [~~?~~] first avowed ~~object~~ reason for opposition, the necessities of the poor, got but a few lines ~~from any body,~~ ~~& &~~ not so many certainly as the objection of various ~~speakers & writers~~ persons to supply ~~/~~Sir Hugh Lane with 'a monument at the cities expense,' & as the gallery was supported by Mr James Larkin, the chief labor leader, & by many slum workers, I ~~think I am right that the opposition~~ assume ~~that supporter s~~ then the purpose ~~was~~ of ~~not exclusively charitable~~ the opposition was not exclusively charitable. These controversies, political, literary, & artistic have alike showed that neither religion nor politics can of themselves ~~create~~ make minds, ~~generous enough, [?receptive] enough [?to] all fine sh sufficiently just, sufficiently receptive, with proud & humble enough, sufficiently just receptive with~~ with enough [?receptivity] to become wise, or just & generous enough to make a nation. Other cities have been as stupid, Samuel Butler mocks shocked Montreal for hiding the Discobolus in a cellar, but Dublin is the capital of a nation the ~~[?chief] center of education, for [?an] race~~ & an ancient race has no where else to look to for its education[.] Geothe in Wilheim Meister describes a saintly woman

[NLI 30,314, 5r]

who getting into ~~a debate as to the [?] legality~~ of ~~religious pictures or objects, [?decorative power]~~ a quarrel ~~about~~ over some [~~?~~] trumpery matter of religious ~~religious pictures or objects, [?decorative power]~~ observance grows, ~~& [?as] all~~ she & all her little religious community, angry & indictive. In Ireland I constantly remember that fable. Religious Ireland — & the pious protestants of my childhood were ~~note~~ signal examples — think of ~~ideal~~ divine things as ~~part of~~ a round of duties separate from life, & not as an element to be discovered in all ~~emotions & circumstance~~ circumstance & emotion, while Political Ireland sees the good citizen ~~not as the~~ man of good will but as a man who holds to certain opinions & not as a man of good will. ~~It may be that Ireland will have to become irreligious, & unpolitical even, before she can change her habits, but till she does, every~~ sort of [?excitement], can but Against these habits & [?this] result ~~we who aim to educate Ireland are trying~~ we have a few educated men, & the remnants of an old traditional culture among the poor. Both were stronger forty years ~~ago~~ before the rise, of ~~a middle class~~ our new middle class, ~~who first~~ which showed at [?these] first public events how ~~ignoble~~ base, at moments of excitment, are minds without culture, ~~in~~ during the nine years of the Parnellite split.

["The Dolls"][2]

[NLI 13,586(17)]

~~The Magi &~~ The Dolls[3]

The fable for this poem came into my head while I was giving some lectures in Dublin. I [~~?~~] noticed once again, how all thought among us is frozen into 'something other than human life' to quote Blake. ~~All thought & emotion is expected to go in some pre-ordained way to [?journey in] to follow to take the old shape~~ After I had made, it,[4] I looked up one day into the blue of the sky, & saw suddenly in the minds eye, as if lost in the blue, stiff figures going as if on procession. I remembered, that they were the habitual image suggested [~~? ?~~] by blue sky [?&] on looking for a fable ~~for them~~ called them the Magi complimentary forms to those enraged dolls.

---

[2]See *VP* 820.

[3]In the top margin, the editorial labeling "Notes to Poems" appears in black pencil, probably not in Yeats's hand.

[4]The comma before "it" was left uncanceled, but the comma after "it" is very heavily inked, perhaps to indicate its precedence.